Alice & Zoroku

9

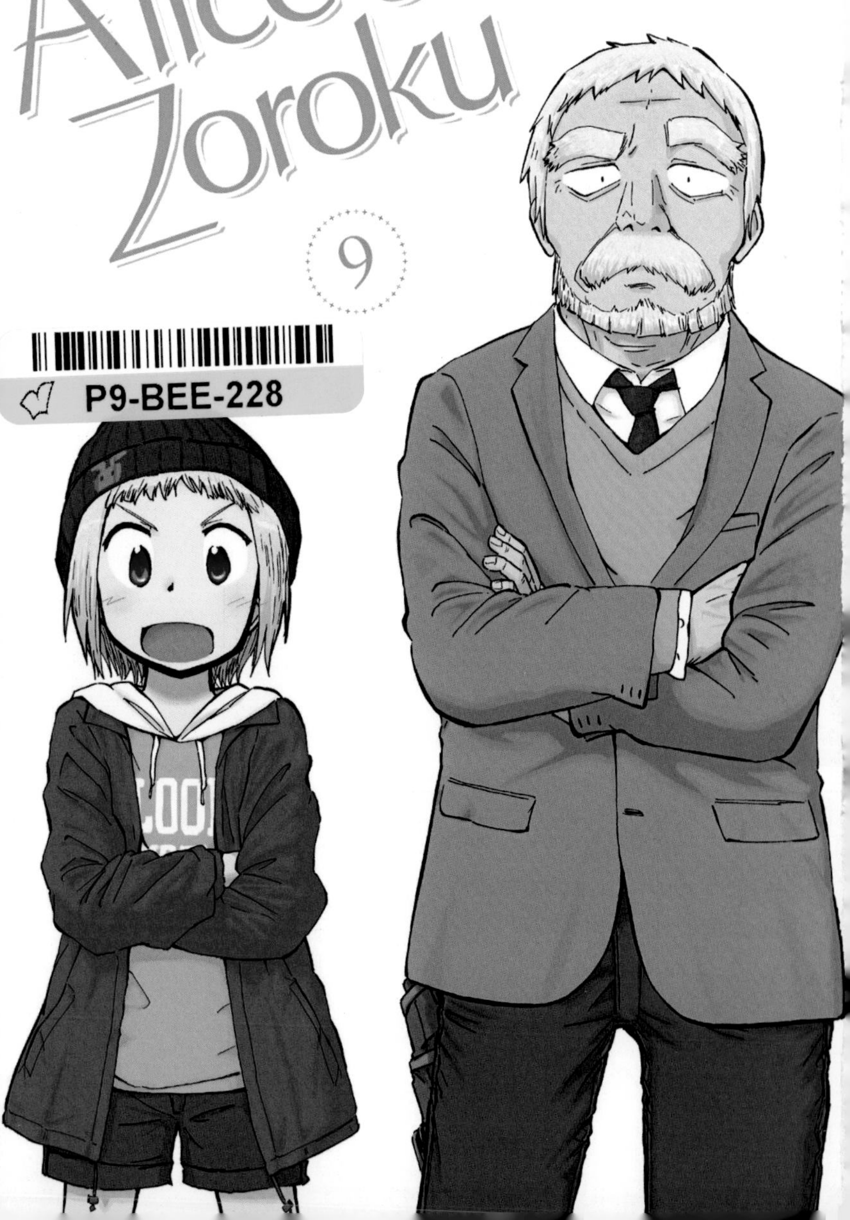

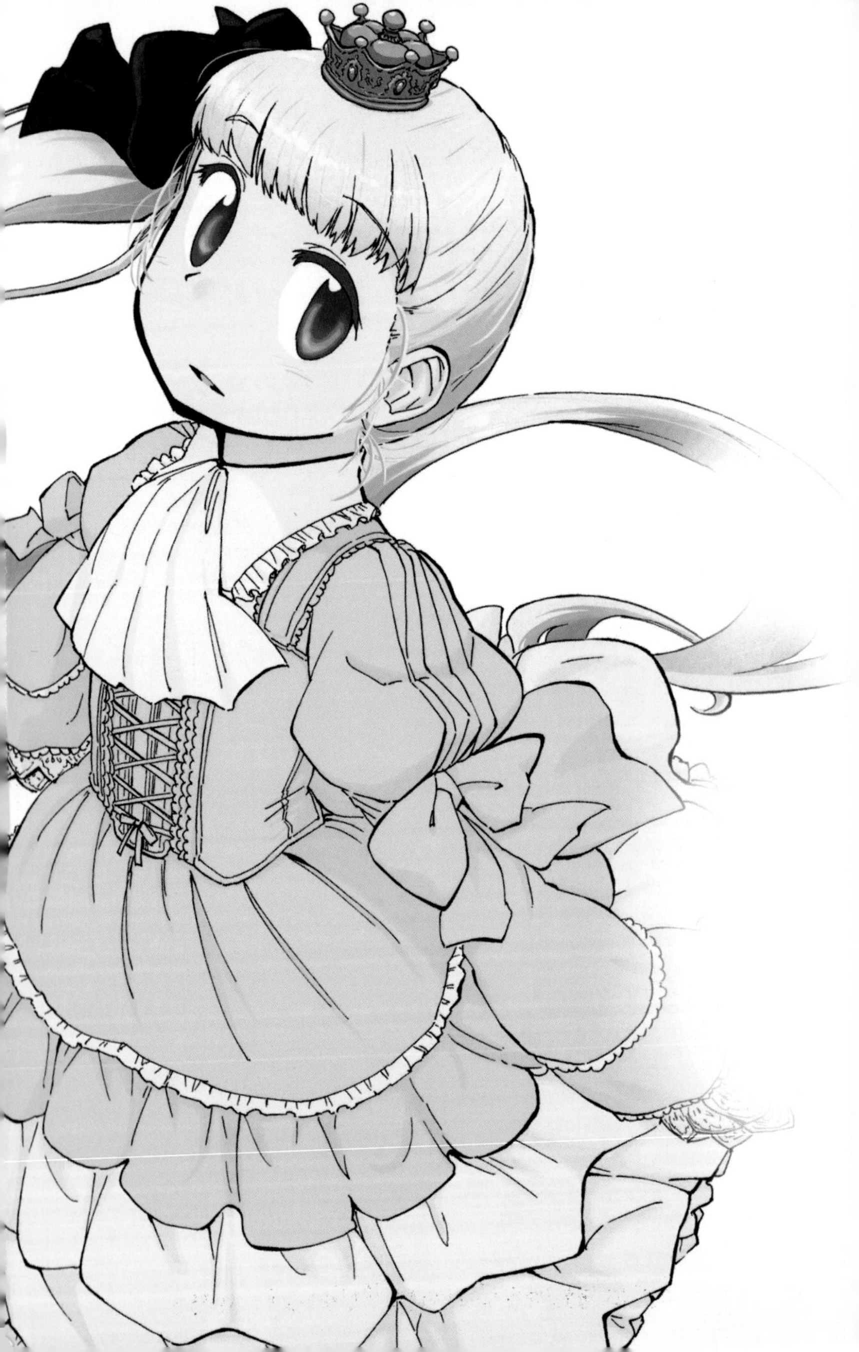

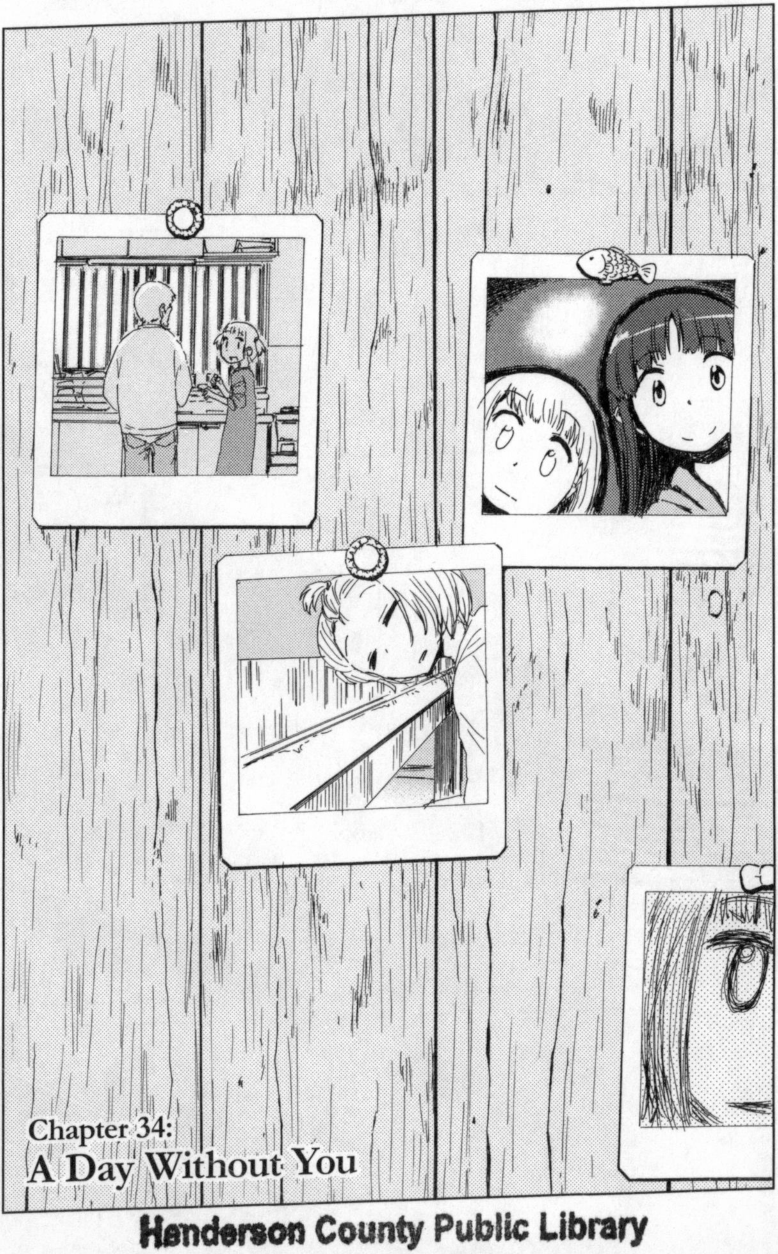
Chapter 34:
A Day Without You

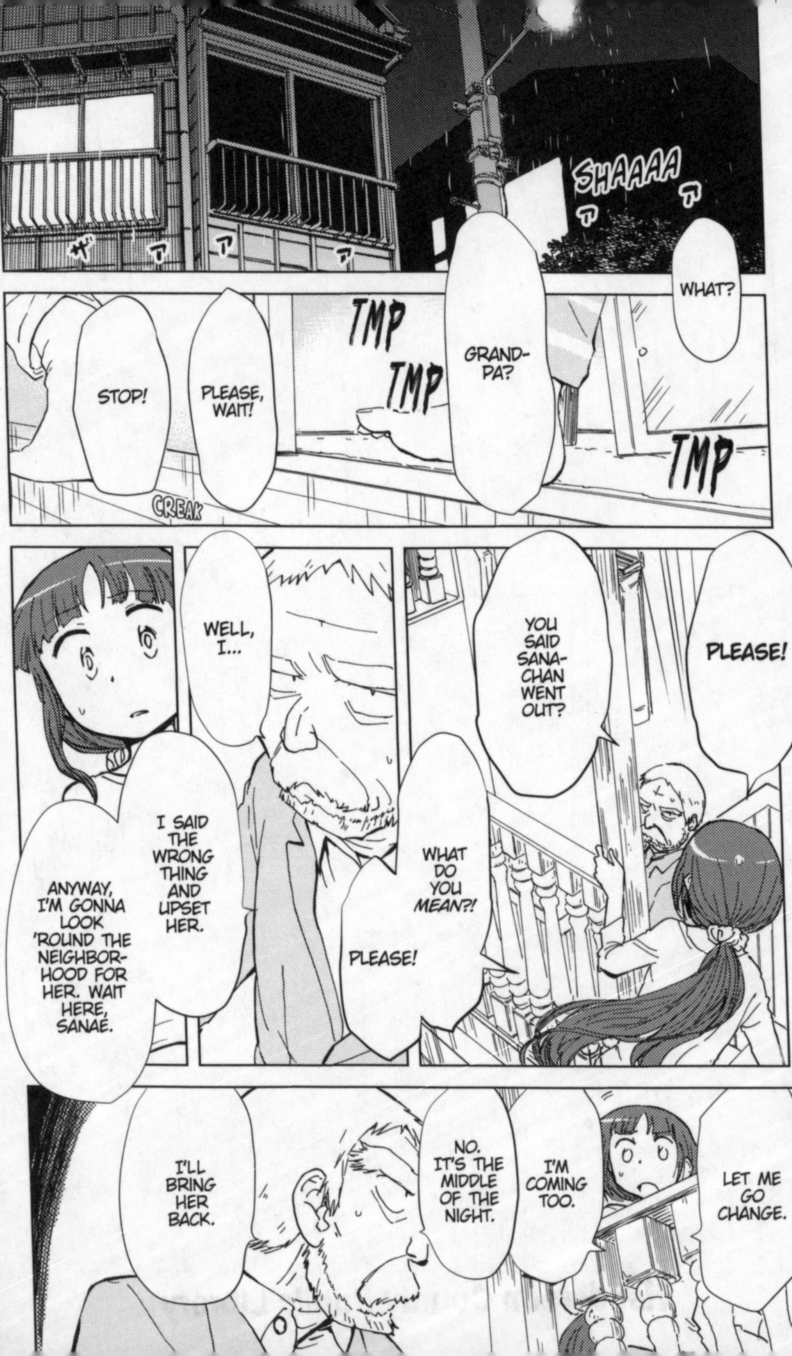
SHAAAA
WHAT?
TMP
GRAND-PA?
TMP TMP
PLEASE, WAIT!
STOP!
CREAK
PLEASE!
YOU SAID SANA-CHAN WENT OUT?
WHAT DO YOU MEAN?!
PLEASE!
WELL, I...
I SAID THE WRONG THING AND UPSET HER.
ANYWAY, I'M GONNA LOOK 'ROUND THE NEIGHBOR-HOOD FOR HER. WAIT HERE, SANAE.
LET ME GO CHANGE.
I'M COMING TOO.
NO. IT'S THE MIDDLE OF THE NIGHT.
I'LL BRING HER BACK.

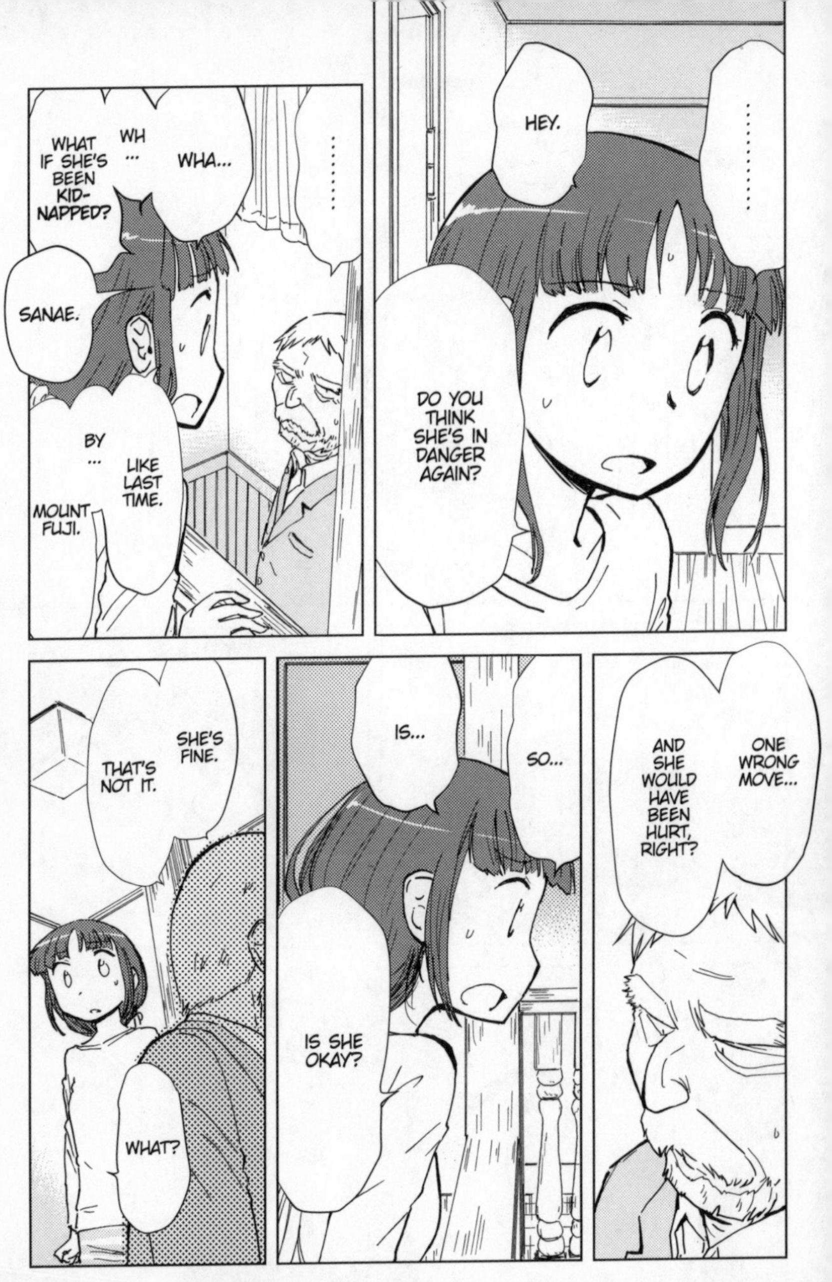
......
HEY.
DO YOU THINK SHE'S IN DANGER AGAIN?
......
WHA...
WH ...
WHAT IF SHE'S BEEN KID-NAPPED?
SANAE.
LIKE LAST TIME.
BY ... MOUNT FUJI.
ONE WRONG MOVE...
AND SHE WOULD HAVE BEEN HURT, RIGHT?
SO...
IS...
IS SHE OKAY?
SHE'S FINE.
THAT'S NOT IT.
WHAT?

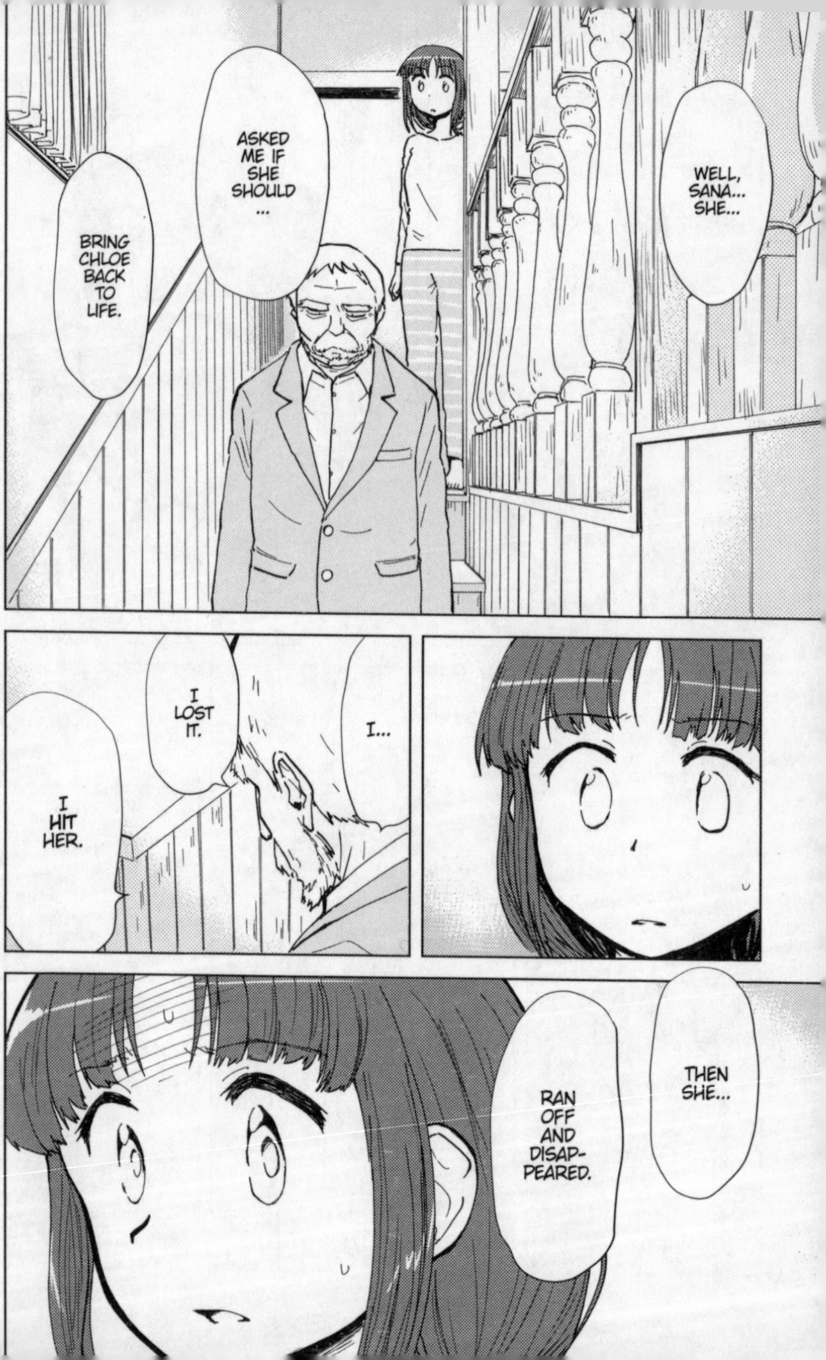
WELL, SANA... SHE...
ASKED ME IF SHE SHOULD ...
BRING CHLOE BACK TO LIFE.
I...
I LOST IT.
I HIT HER.
THEN SHE...
RAN OFF AND DISAPPEARED.

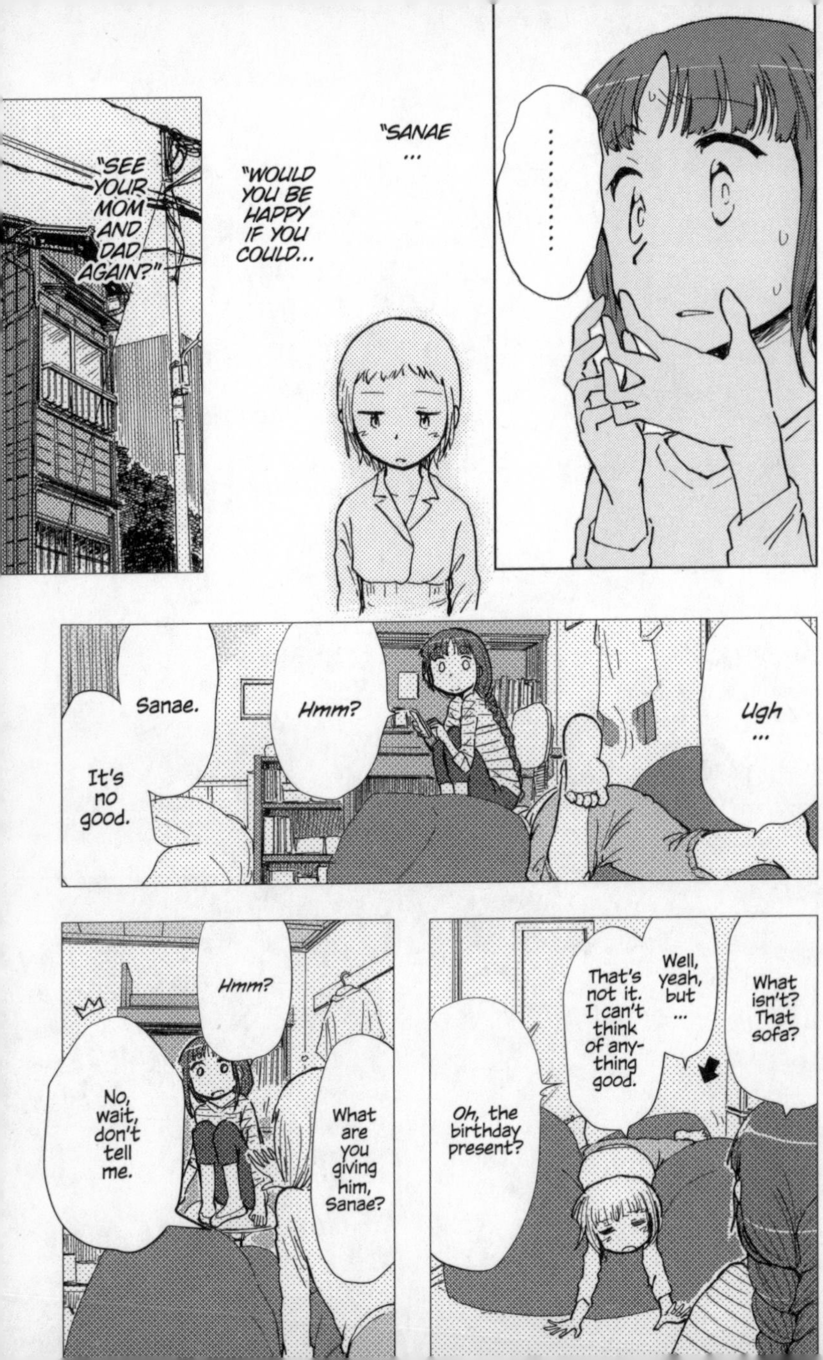
......
"SANAE ...
"WOULD YOU BE HAPPY IF YOU COULD...
"SEE YOUR MOM AND DAD AGAIN?"
Ugh ...
Hmm?
Sanae.
It's no good.
What isn't? That sofa?
Well, yeah, but ...
That's not it. I can't think of any-thing good.
Oh, the birthday present?
What are you giving him, Sanae?
Hmm?
No, wait, don't tell me.

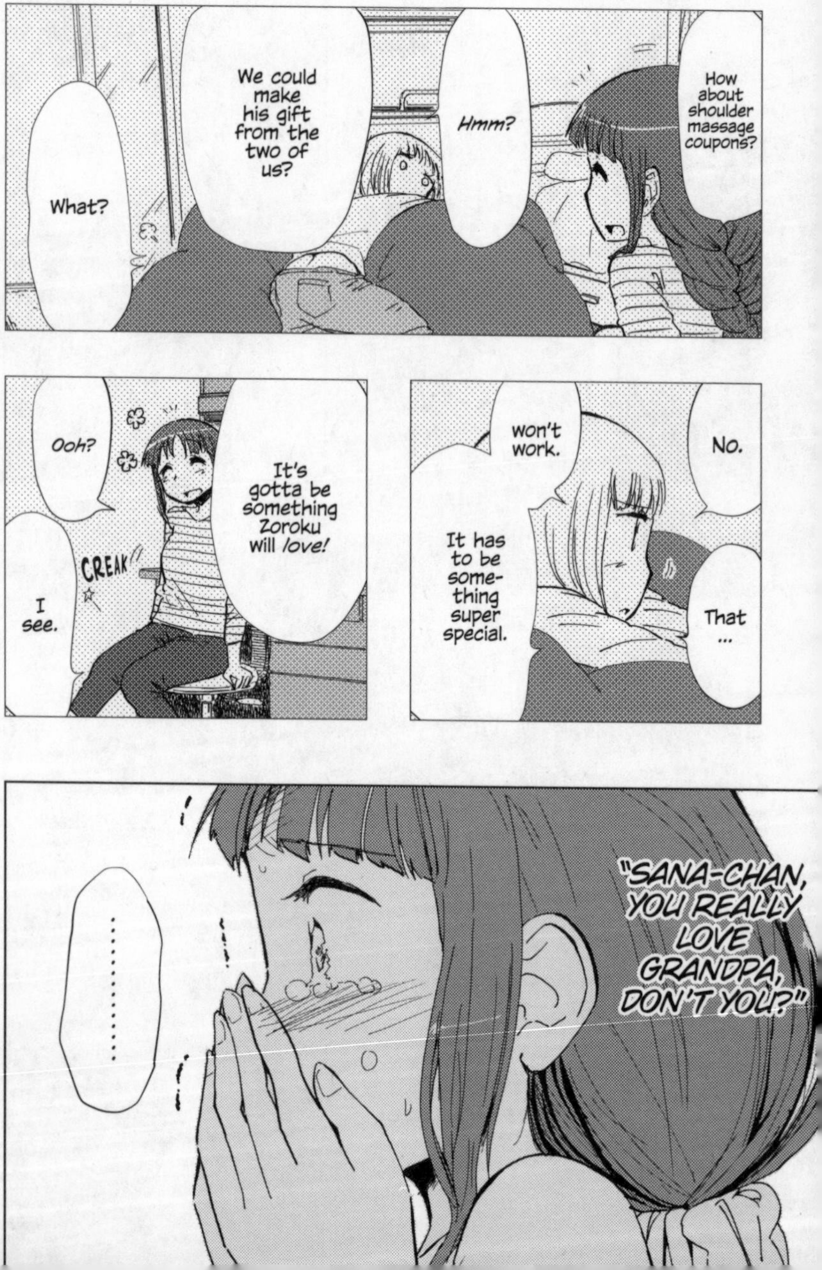
How about shoulder massage coupons?
Hmm?
We could make his gift from the two of us?
What?
No.
That ...
won't work.
It has to be something super special.
Ooh?
It's gotta be something Zoroku will *love!*
CREAK
I see.
"SANA-CHAN, YOU REALLY LOVE GRANDPA, DON'T YOU?"
......

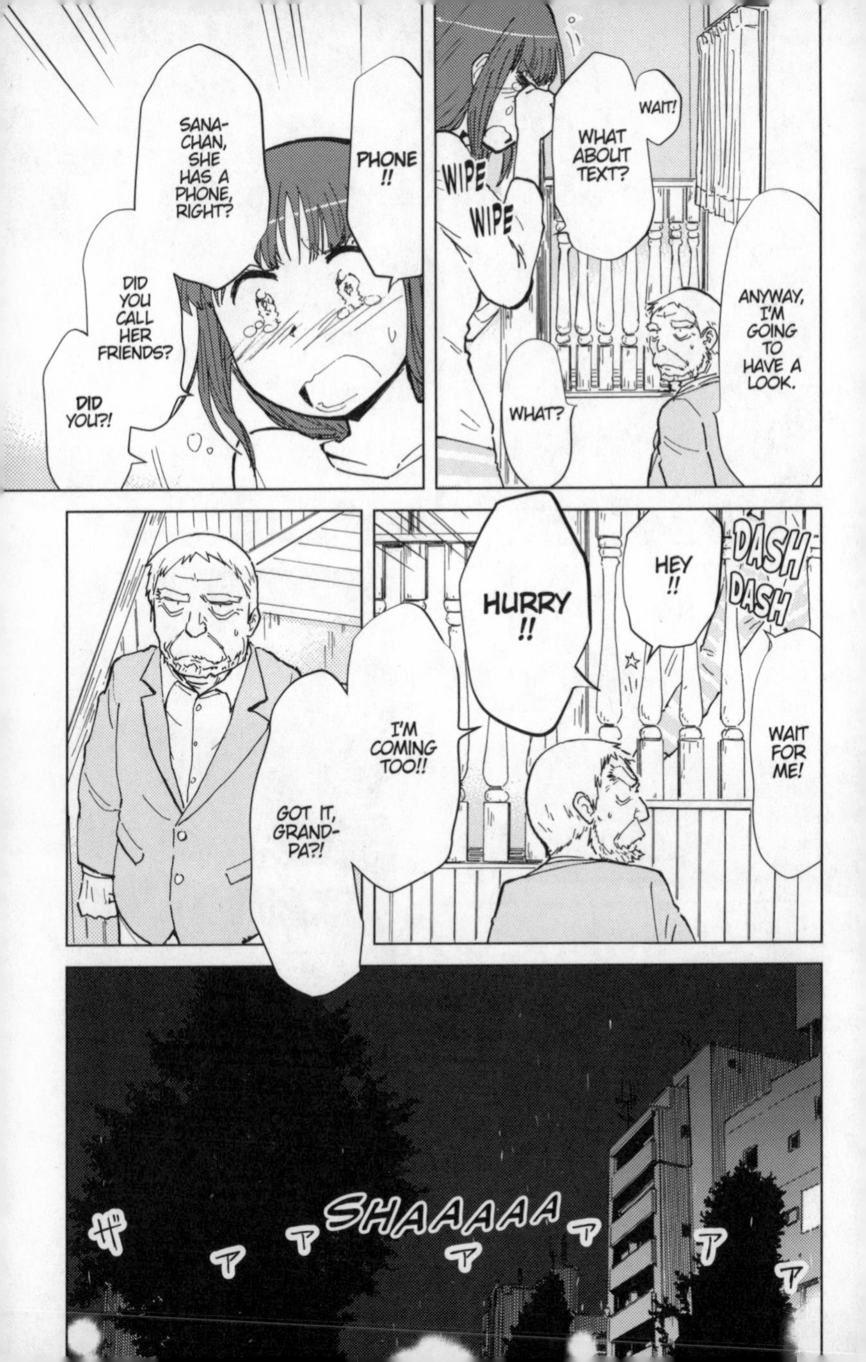
WAIT!
WHAT ABOUT TEXT?
WIPE WIPE
ANYWAY, I'M GOING TO HAVE A LOOK.
WHAT?
PHONE!!
SANA-CHAN, SHE HAS A PHONE, RIGHT?
DID YOU CALL HER FRIENDS?
DID YOU?!
DASH DASH
HEY!!
WAIT FOR ME!
HURRY!!
I'M COMING TOO!!
GOT IT, GRANDPA?!
SHAAAAA
ザァァァァァァ

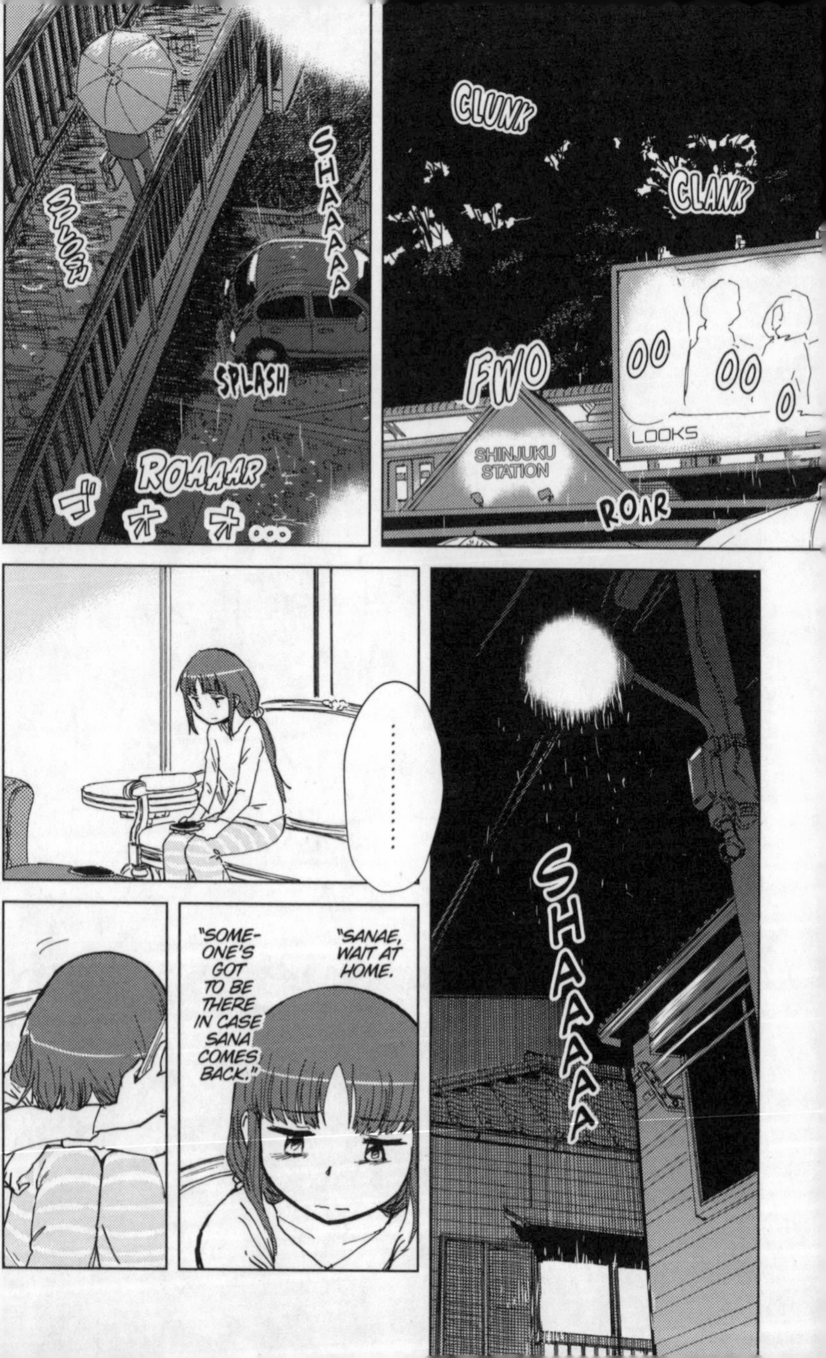
CLUNK
CLANK
FWO
OO
OO
O
LOOKS
SHINJUKU STATION
ROAR
SHAAAAA
SPLOSH
SPLASH
ROAAAR
ゴオオ...
SHAAAAA
......
"SANAE, WAIT AT HOME.
"SOME-ONE'S GOT TO BE THERE IN CASE SANA COMES BACK."

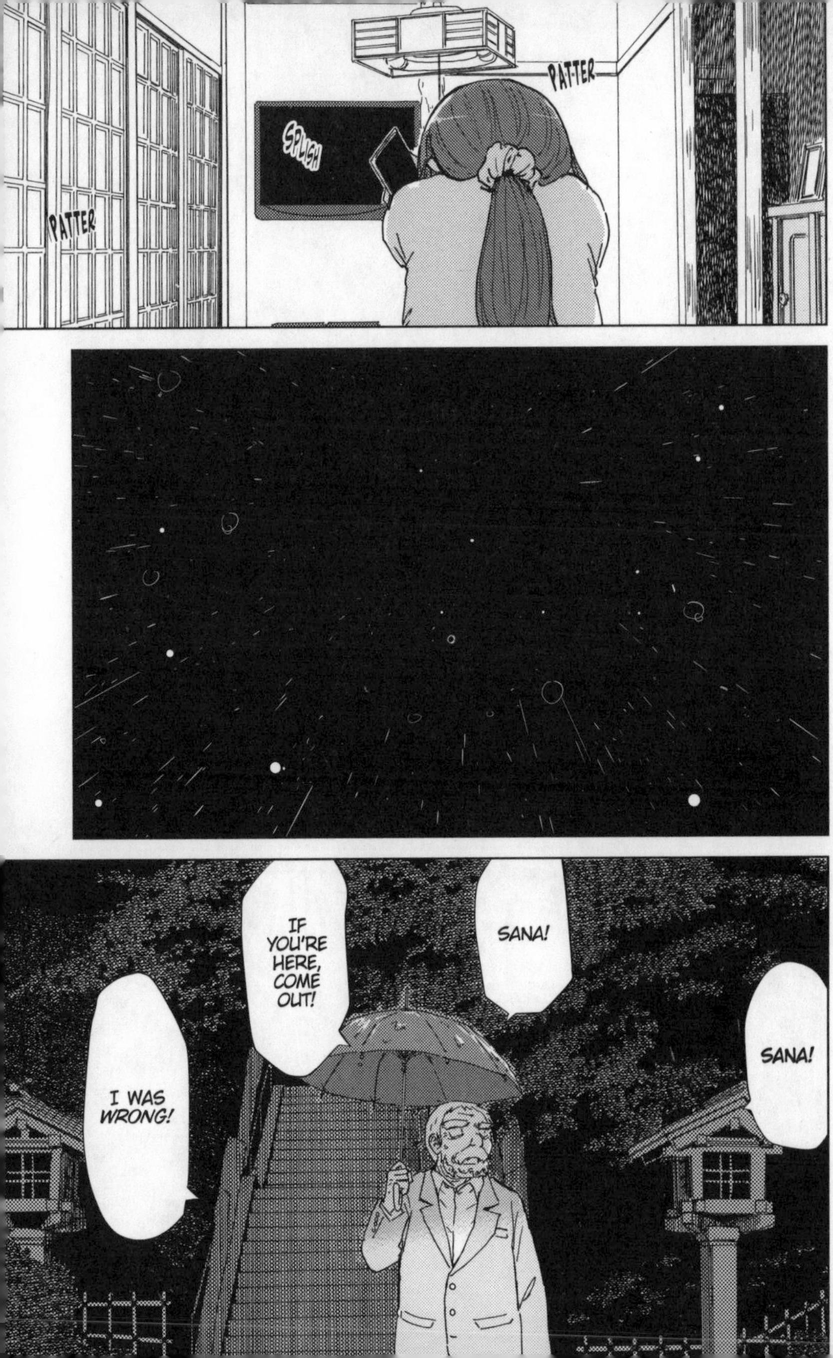
PATTER
SPLISH
PATTER
SANA!
SANA!
IF YOU'RE HERE, COME OUT!
I WAS WRONG!

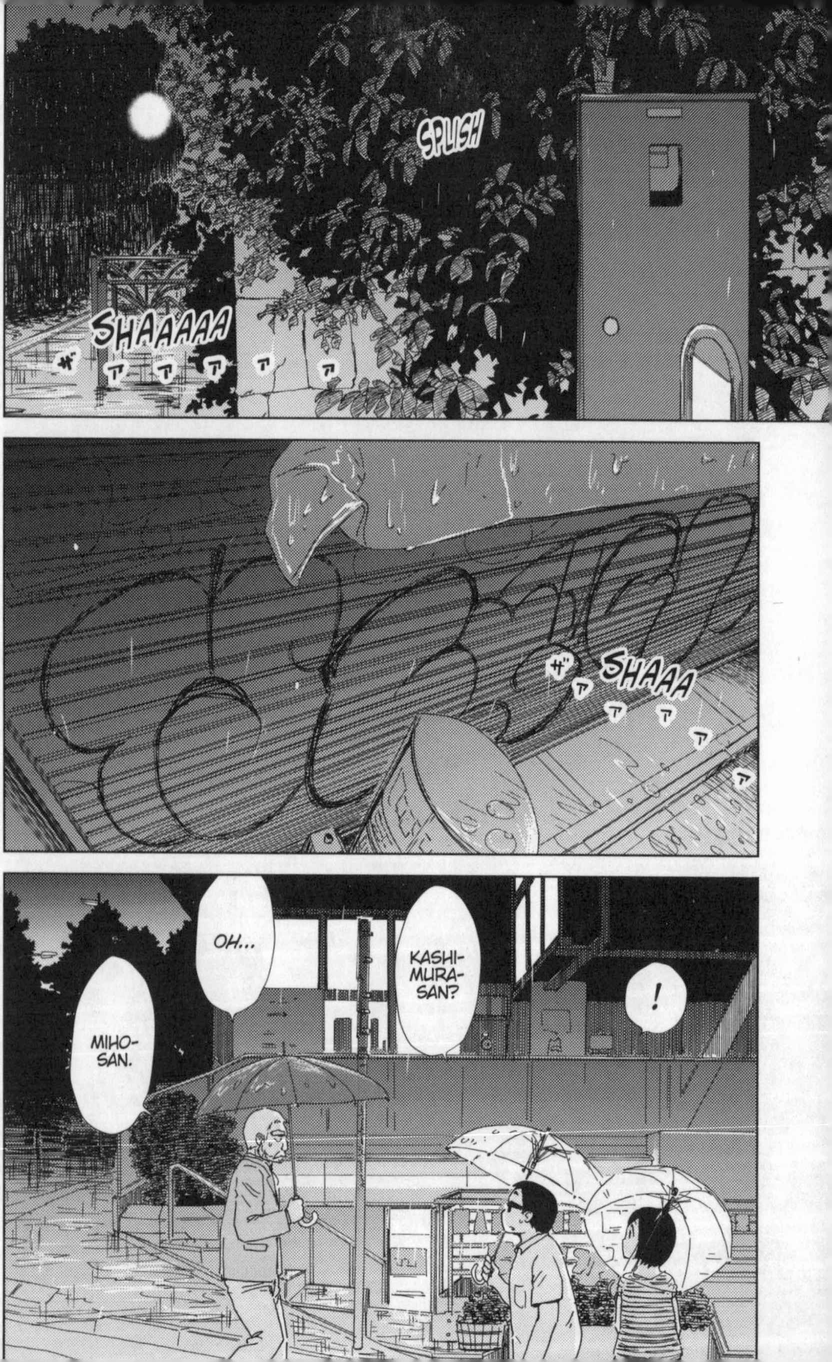
SPLISH
SHAAAAA
ザァァァァァ
SHAAA
ザァァァァァ
!
KASHIMURA-SAN?
OH...
MIHO-SAN.

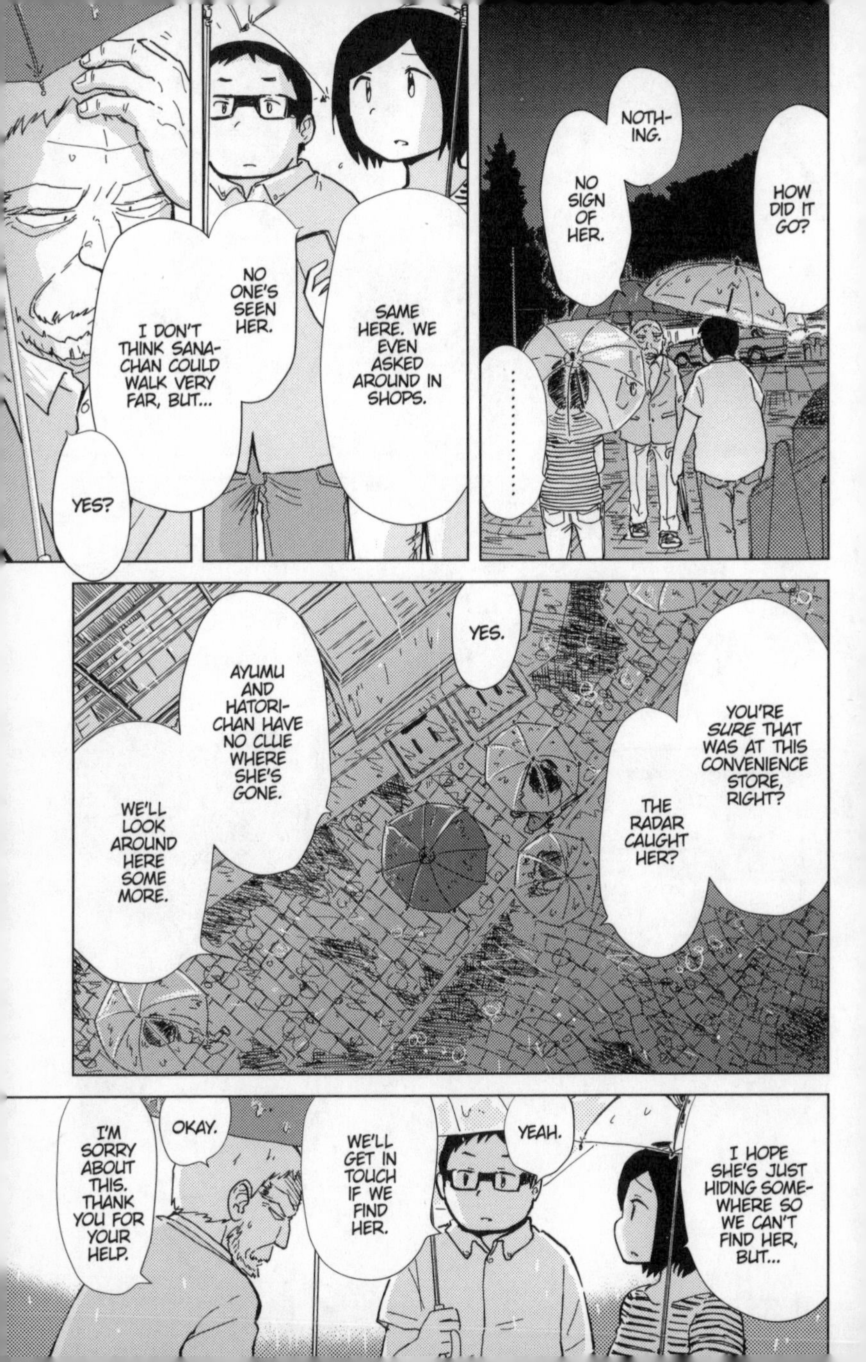
HOW DID IT GO?
NOTHING.
NO SIGN OF HER.
......
SAME HERE. WE EVEN ASKED AROUND IN SHOPS.
NO ONE'S SEEN HER.
I DON'T THINK SANA-CHAN COULD WALK VERY FAR, BUT...
YES?
YOU'RE *SURE* THAT WAS AT THIS CONVENIENCE STORE, RIGHT?
THE RADAR CAUGHT HER?
YES.
AYUMU AND HATORI-CHAN HAVE NO CLUE WHERE SHE'S GONE.
WE'LL LOOK AROUND HERE SOME MORE.
I HOPE SHE'S JUST HIDING SOMEWHERE SO WE CAN'T FIND HER, BUT...
YEAH.
WE'LL GET IN TOUCH IF WE FIND HER.
OKAY.
I'M SORRY ABOUT THIS. THANK YOU FOR YOUR HELP.

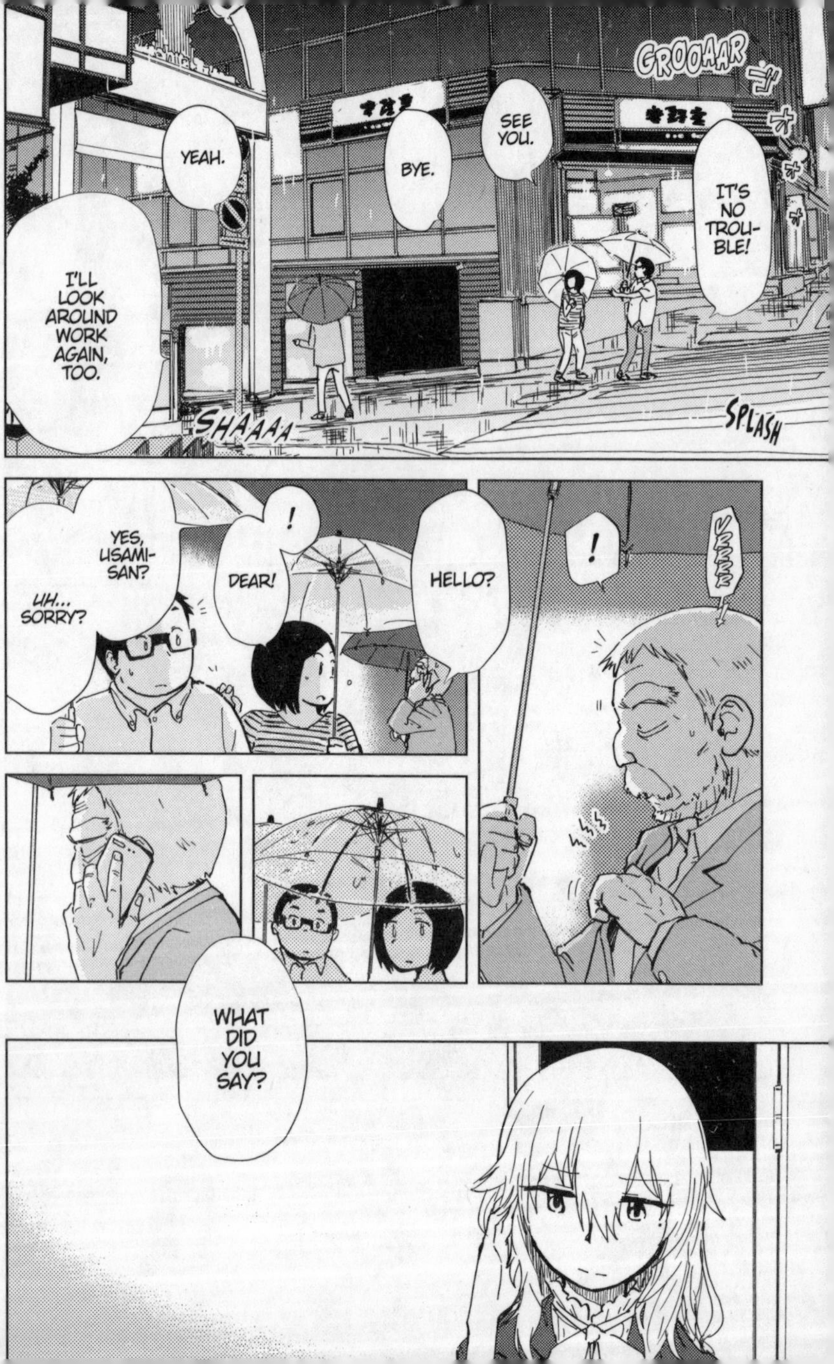
GROOAAR
IT'S NO TROUBLE!
SEE YOU.
BYE.
YEAH.
I'LL LOOK AROUND WORK AGAIN, TOO.
SPLASH
SHAAAA
VRRRR
!
!
HELLO?
DEAR!
YES, USAMI-SAN?
UH... SORRY?
WHAT DID YOU SAY?

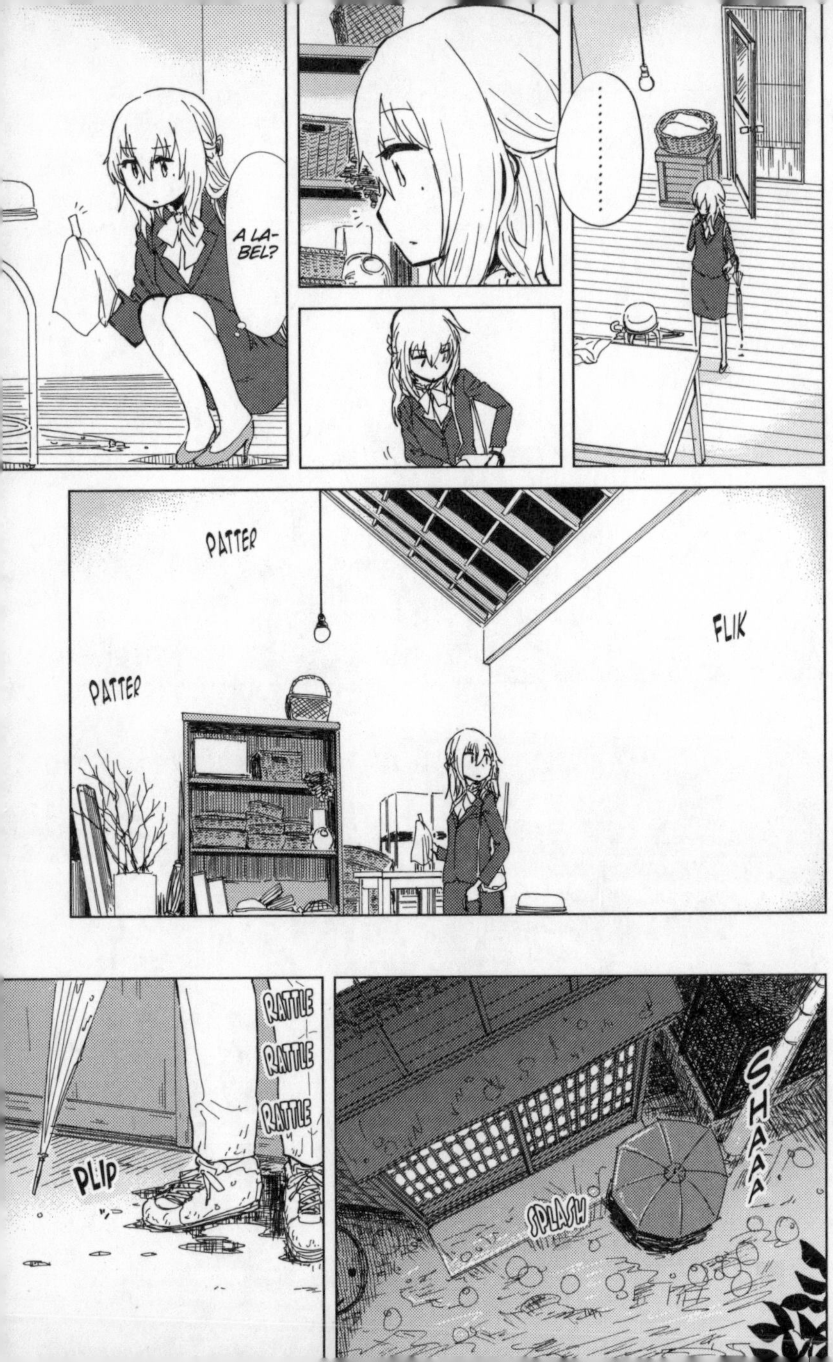
......
A LA-BEL?
FLIK
PATTER
PATTER
SHAAA
SPLASH
RATTLE
RATTLE
RATTLE
PLIP

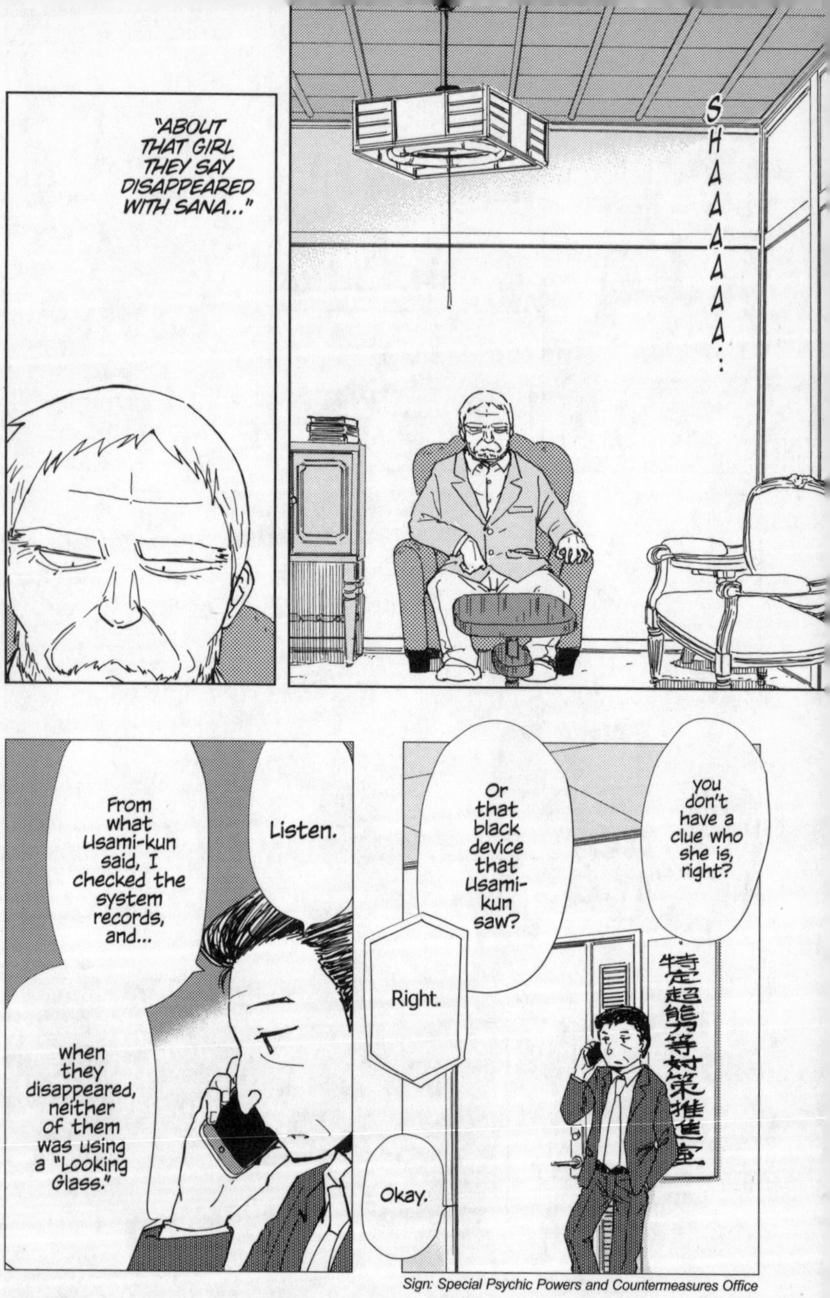
SHAAAAA...
"ABOUT THAT GIRL THEY SAY DISAPPEARED WITH SANA..."
you don't have a clue who she is, right?
Or that black device that Usami-kun saw?
特定超能等対策推進室
Right.
Okay.
Listen.
From what Usami-kun said, I checked the system records, and...
when they disappeared, neither of them was using a "Looking Glass."

Sign: Special Psychic Powers and Countermeasures Office

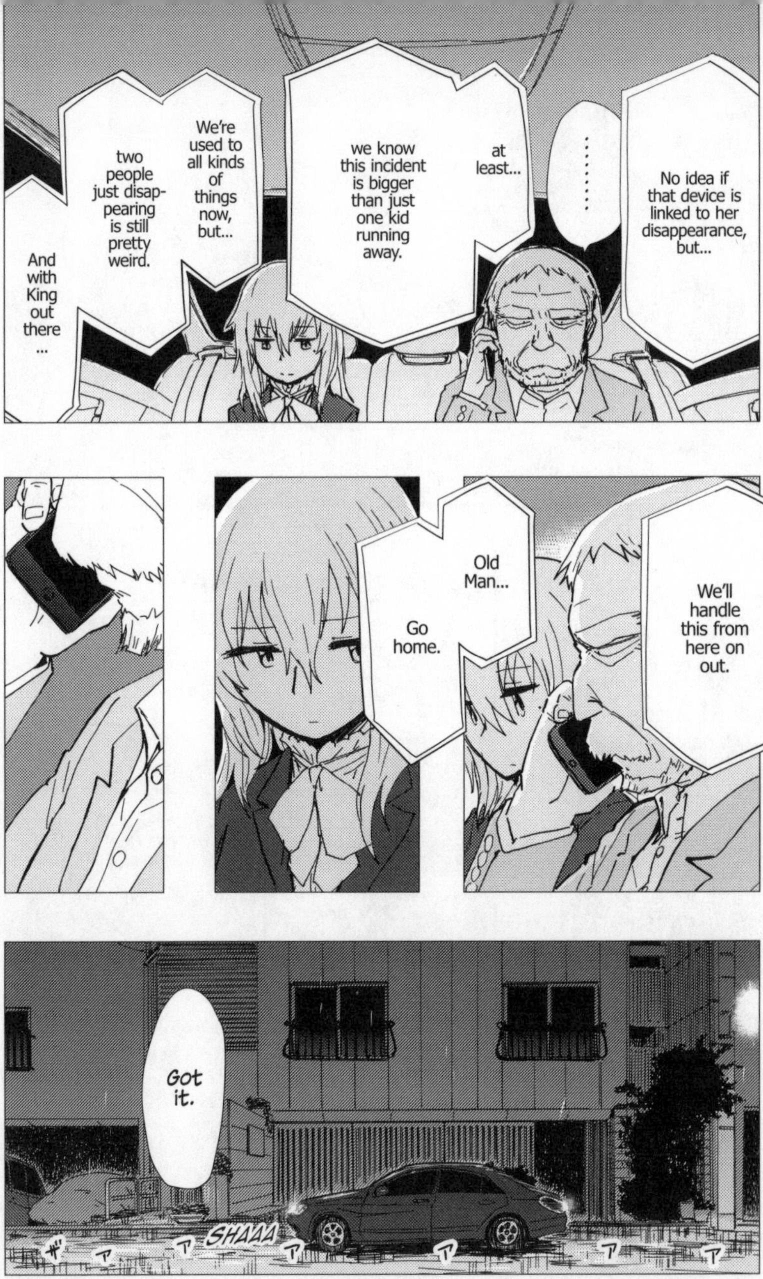
No idea if that device is linked to her disappearance, but...
....
at least...
we know this incident is bigger than just one kid running away.
We're used to all kinds of things now, but...
two people just disappearing is still pretty weird.
And with King out there ...
We'll handle this from here on out.
Old Man...
Go home.
Got it.
SHAAA
ザァァァァァァァ

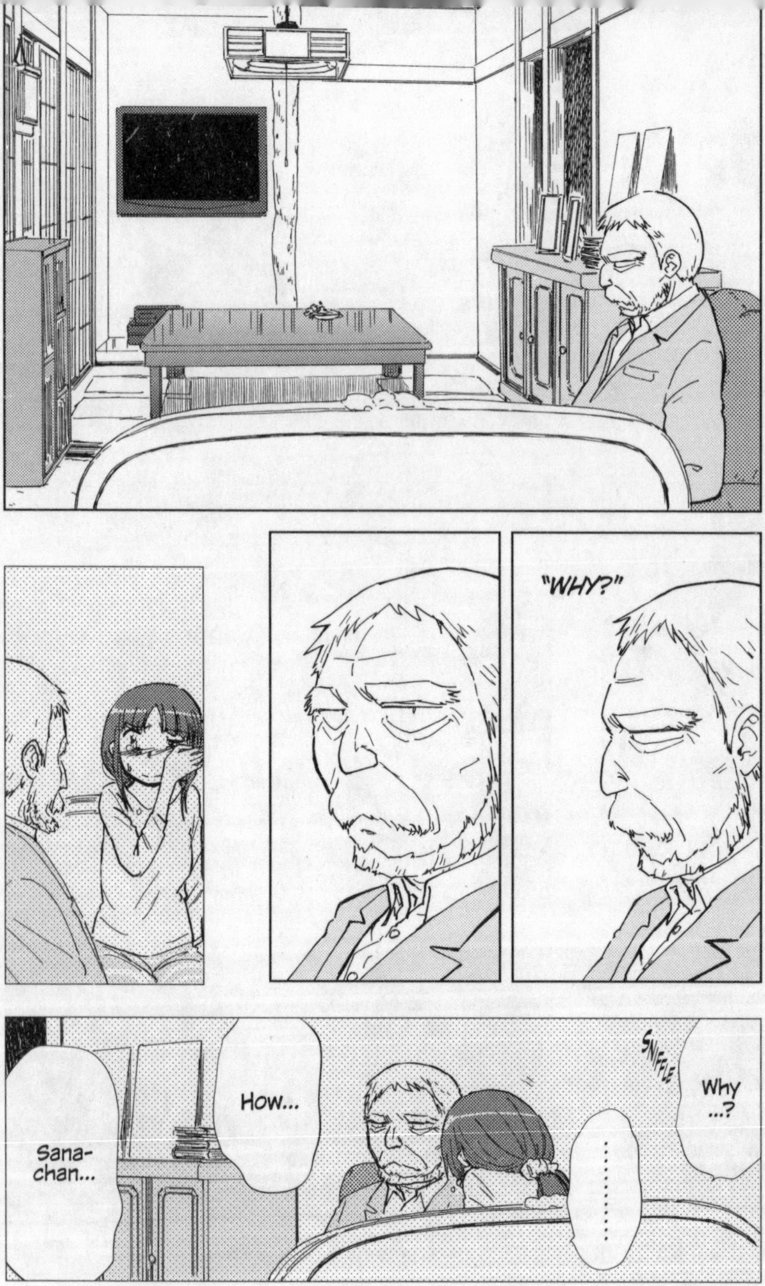
"WHY?"
SNIFFLE
Why ...?
......
How...
Sana-chan...

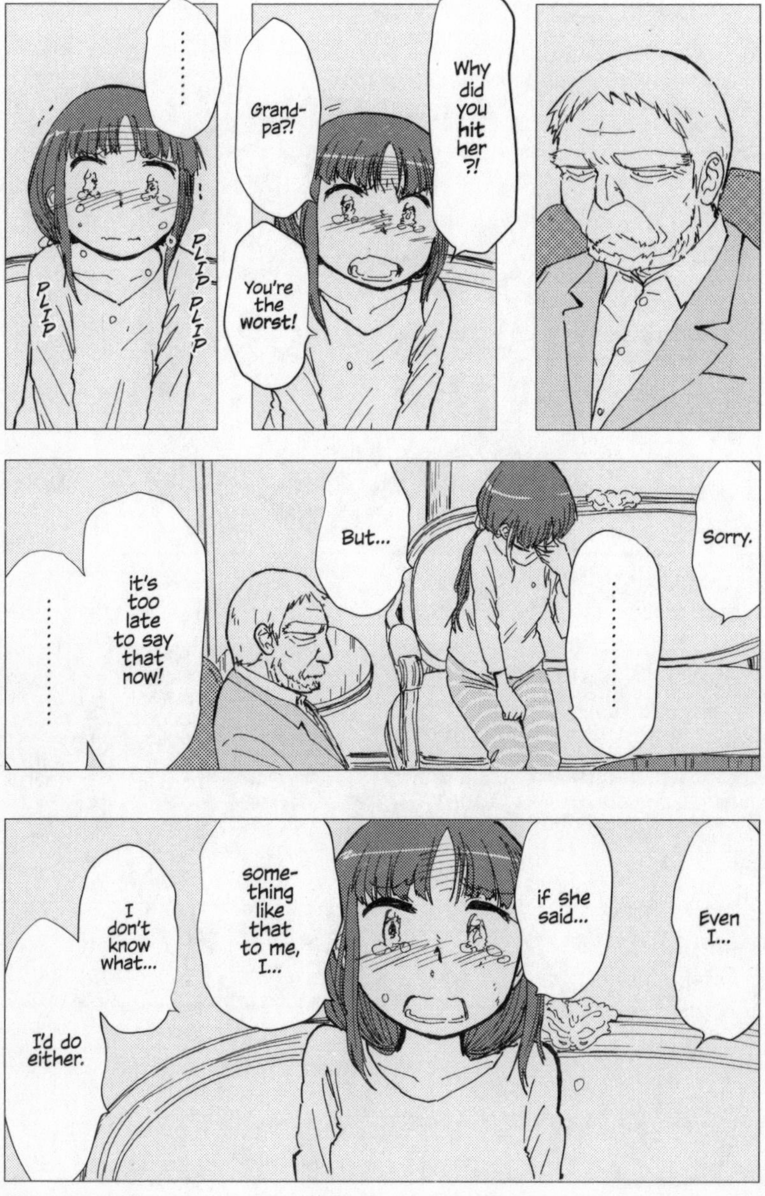
Why did you hit her?!
Grandpa?!
You're the worst!
......
PLIP PLIP
PLIP
Sorry.
......
But...
it's too late to say that now!
......
Even I...
if she said...
something like that to me, I...
I don't know what...
I'd do either.

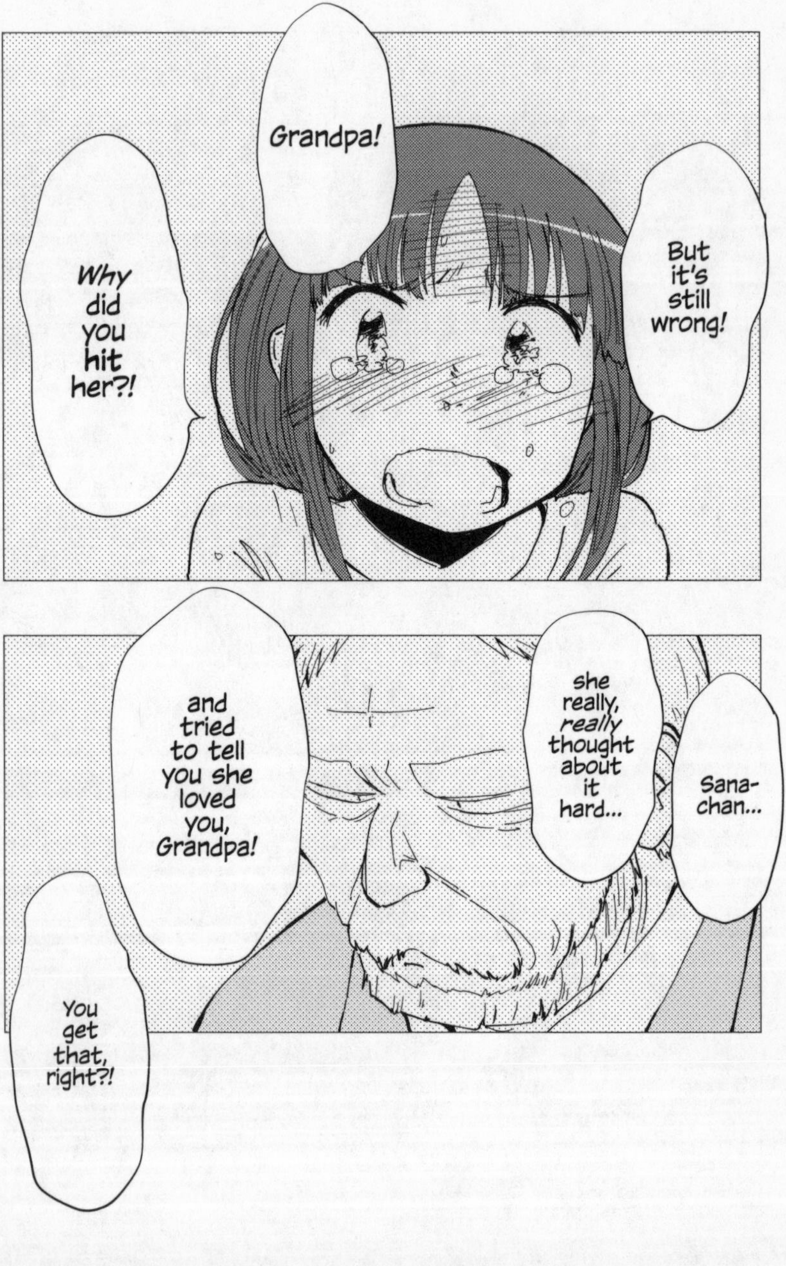
Grandpa!
But it's still wrong!
Why did you hit her?!
Sana-chan...
she really, *really* thought about it hard...
and tried to tell you she loved you, Grandpa!
You get that, right?!

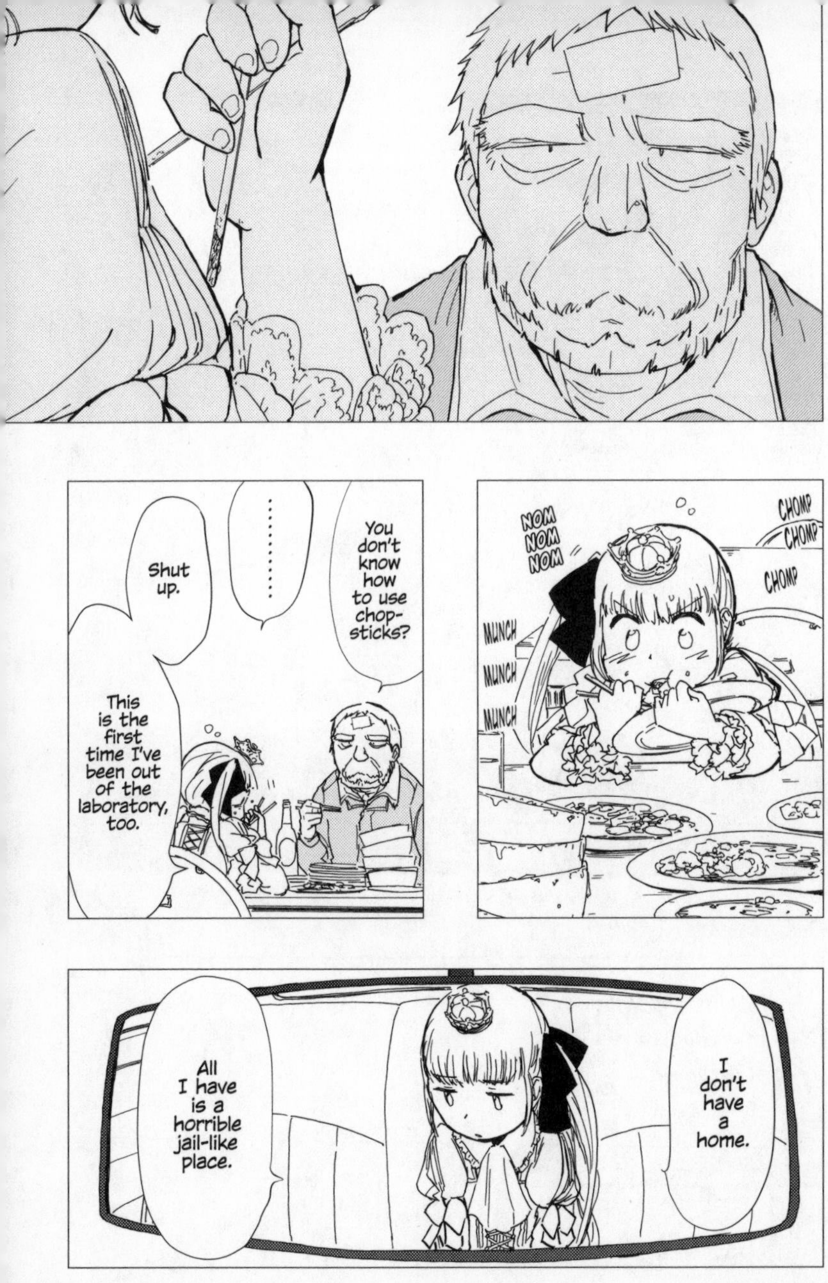
CHOMP CHOMP
CHOMP
NOM NOM NOM
MUNCH MUNCH MUNCH
You don't know how to use chop-sticks?
......
Shut up.
This is the first time I've been out of the laboratory, too.
I don't have a home.
All I have is a horrible jail-like place.

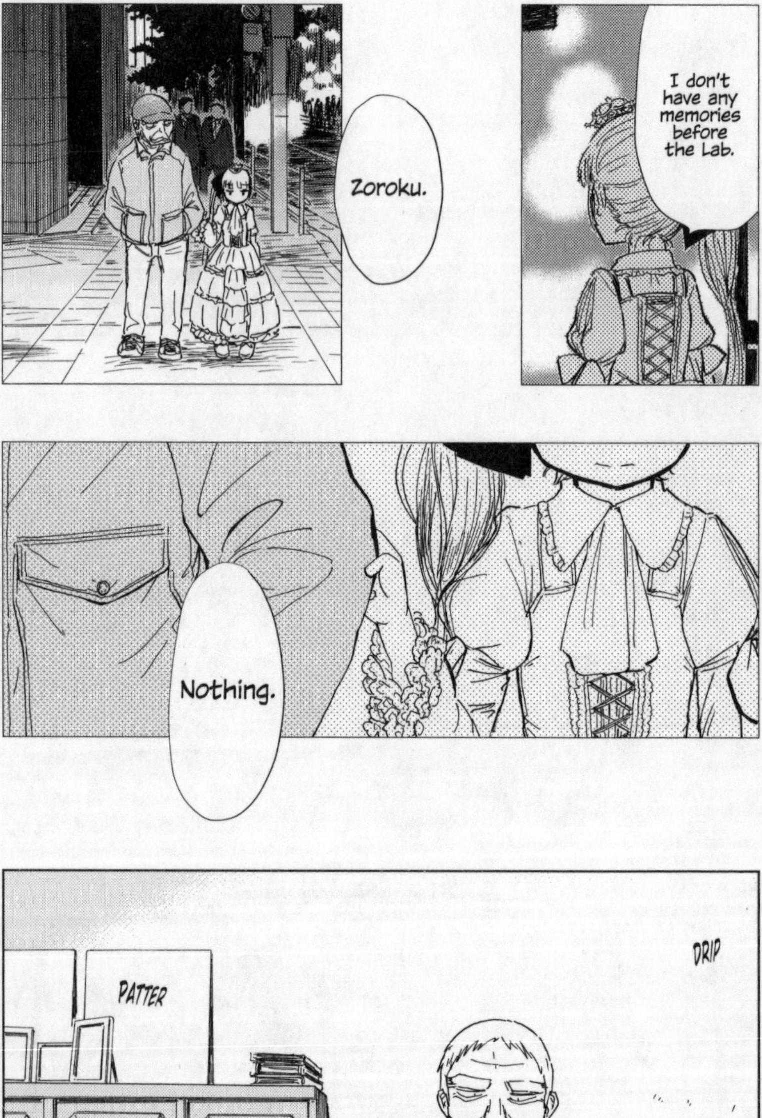
I don't have any memories before the Lab.
Zoroku.
Nothing.
DRIP
PATTER

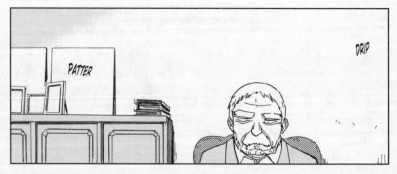

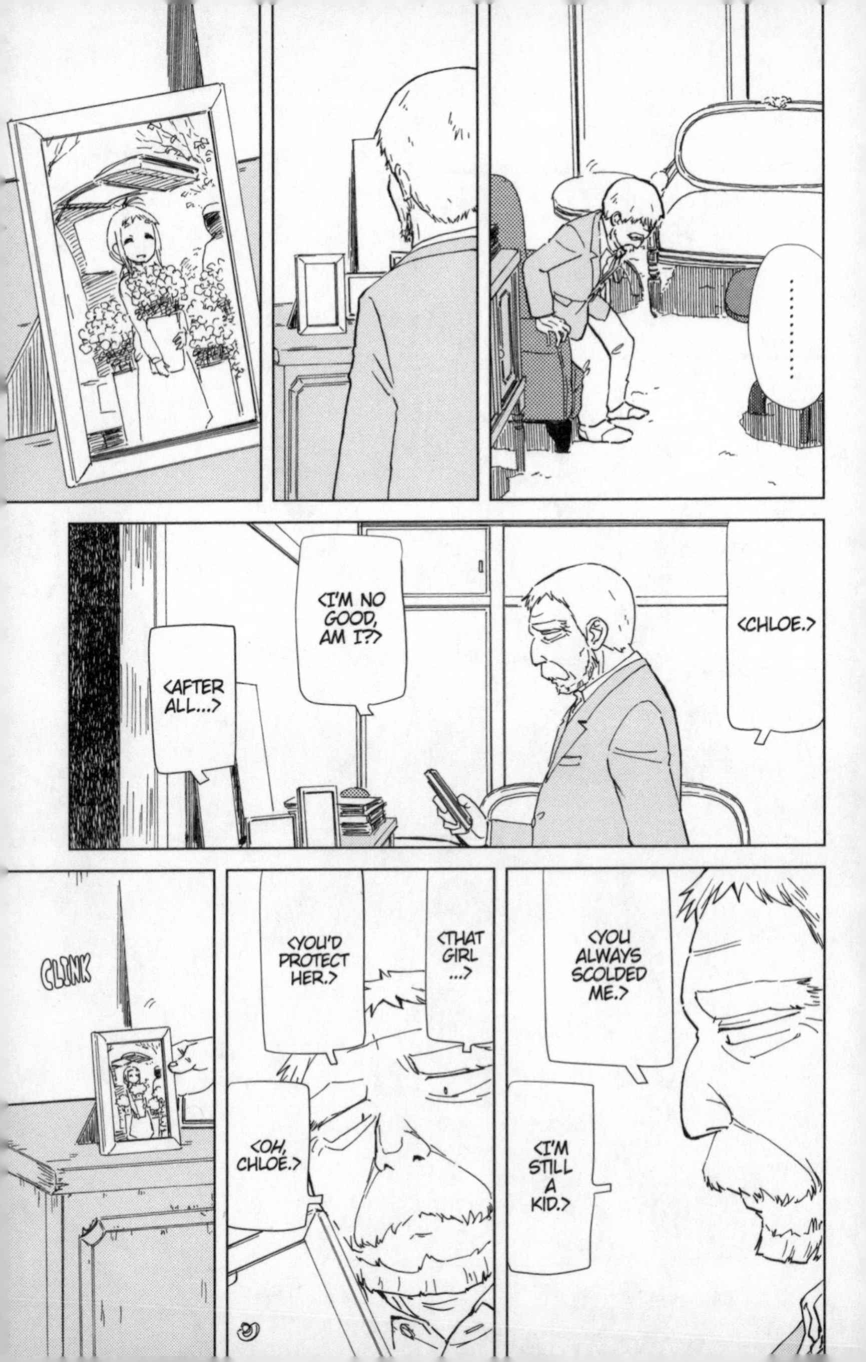
<......>
<CHLOE.>
<I'M NO GOOD, AM I?>
<AFTER ALL...>
<YOU ALWAYS SCOLDED ME.>
<I'M STILL A KID.>
<THAT GIRL ...>
<YOU'D PROTECT HER.>
<OH, CHLOE.>
CLINK

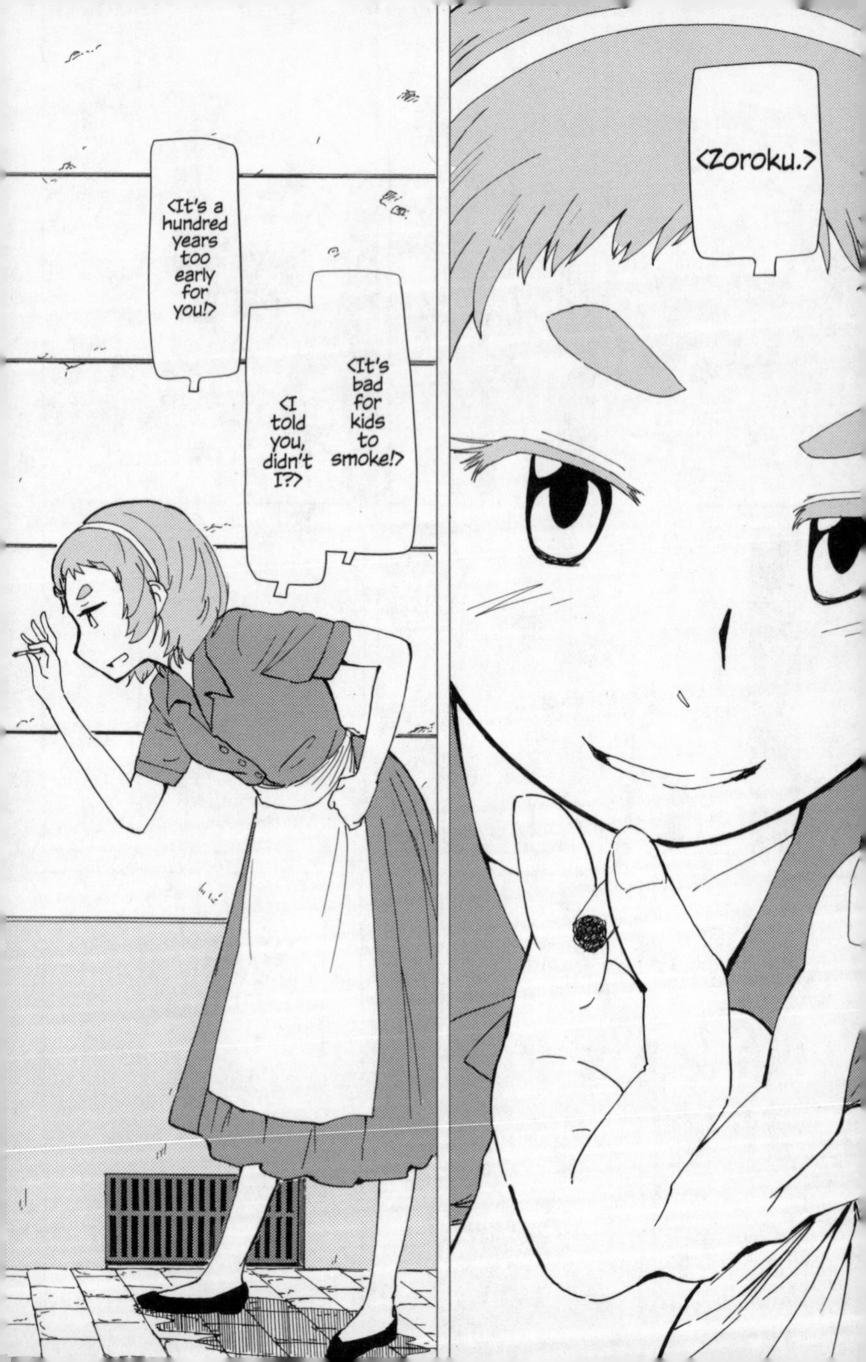
<Zoroku.>
<It's bad for kids to smoke!> <I told you, didn't I?>
<It's a hundred years too early for you!>

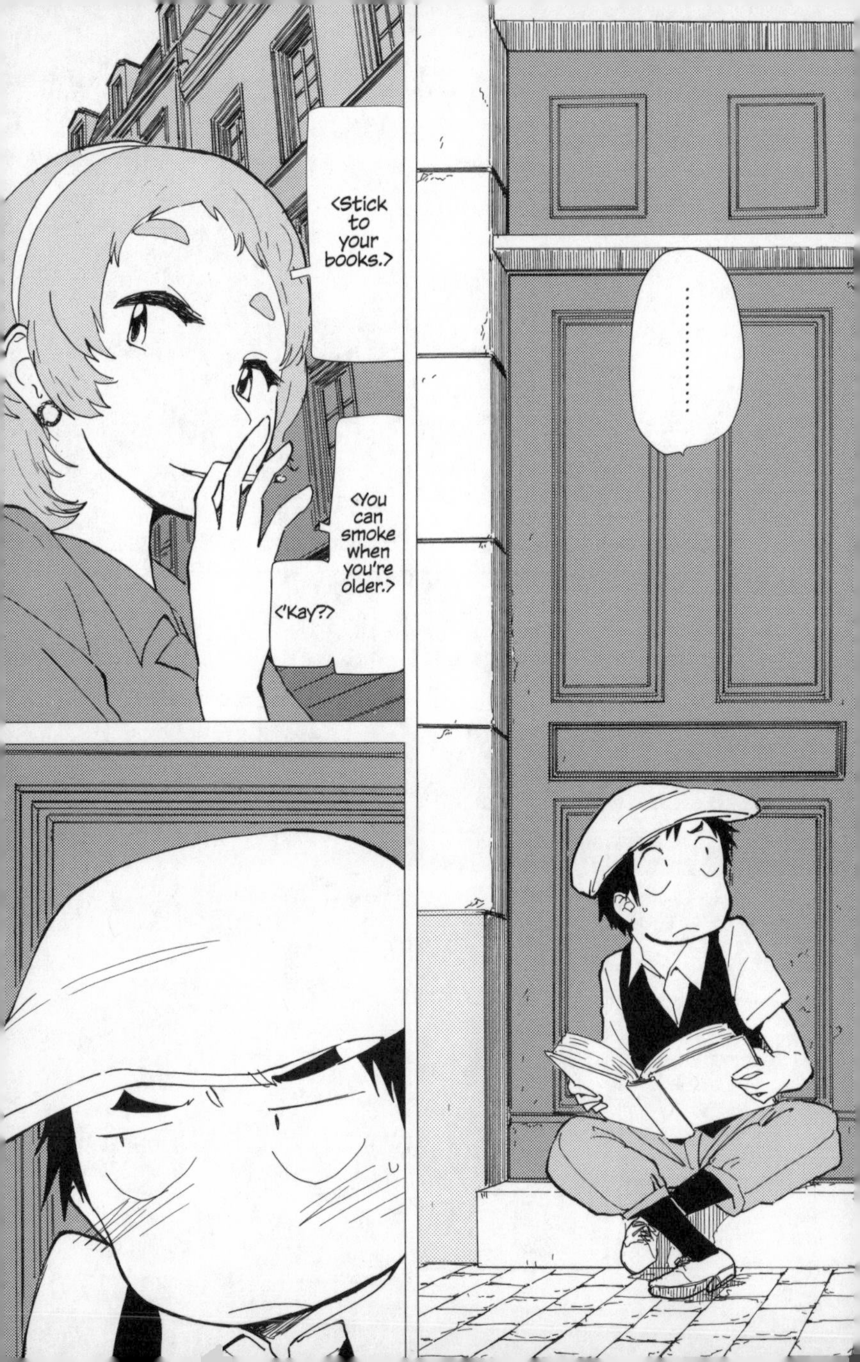
......
<Stick to your books.>
<You can smoke when you're older.>
<'Kay?>

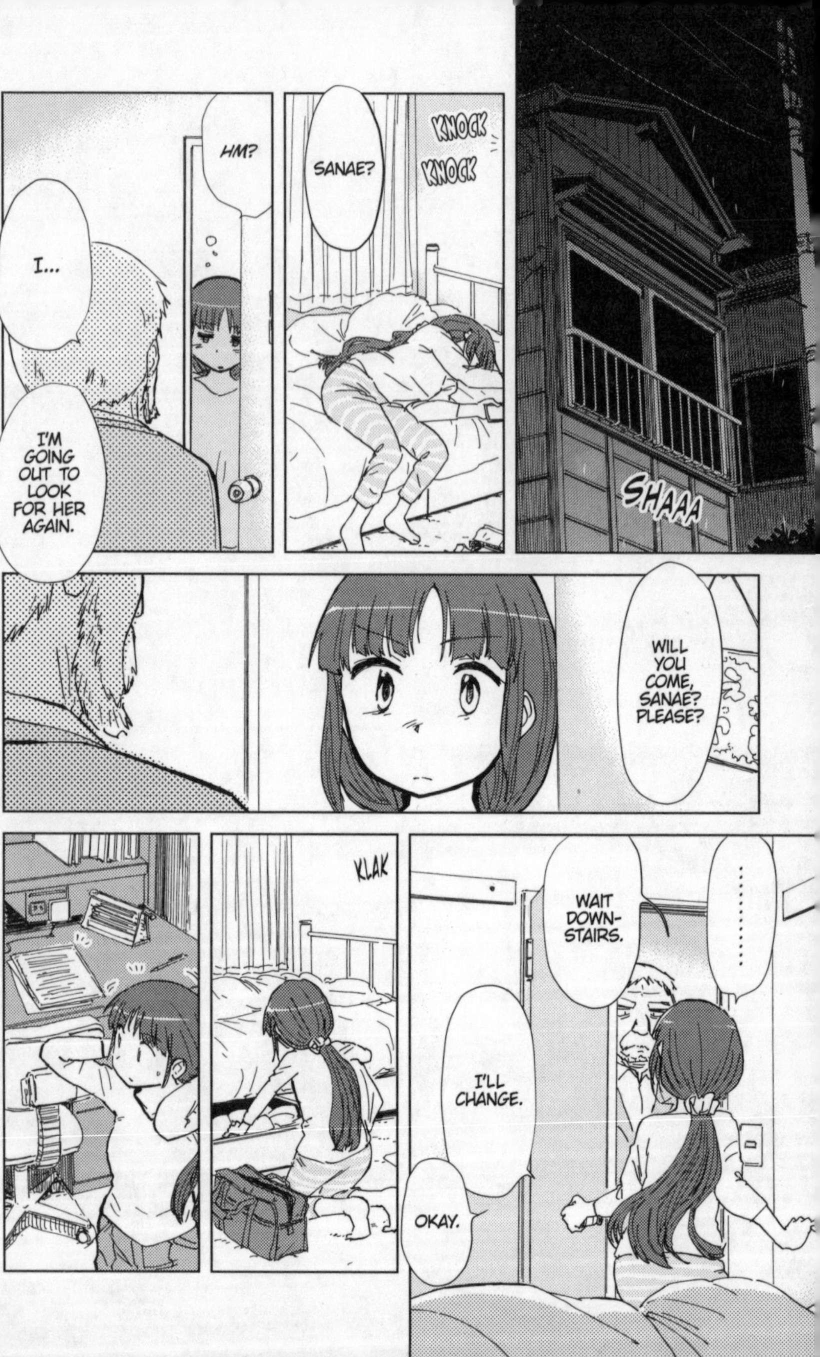
SHAAA
KNOCK
KNOCK
SANAE?
HM?
I...
I'M GOING OUT TO LOOK FOR HER AGAIN.
WILL YOU COME, SANAE? PLEASE?
......
WAIT DOWN-STAIRS.
I'LL CHANGE.
OKAY.
KLAK

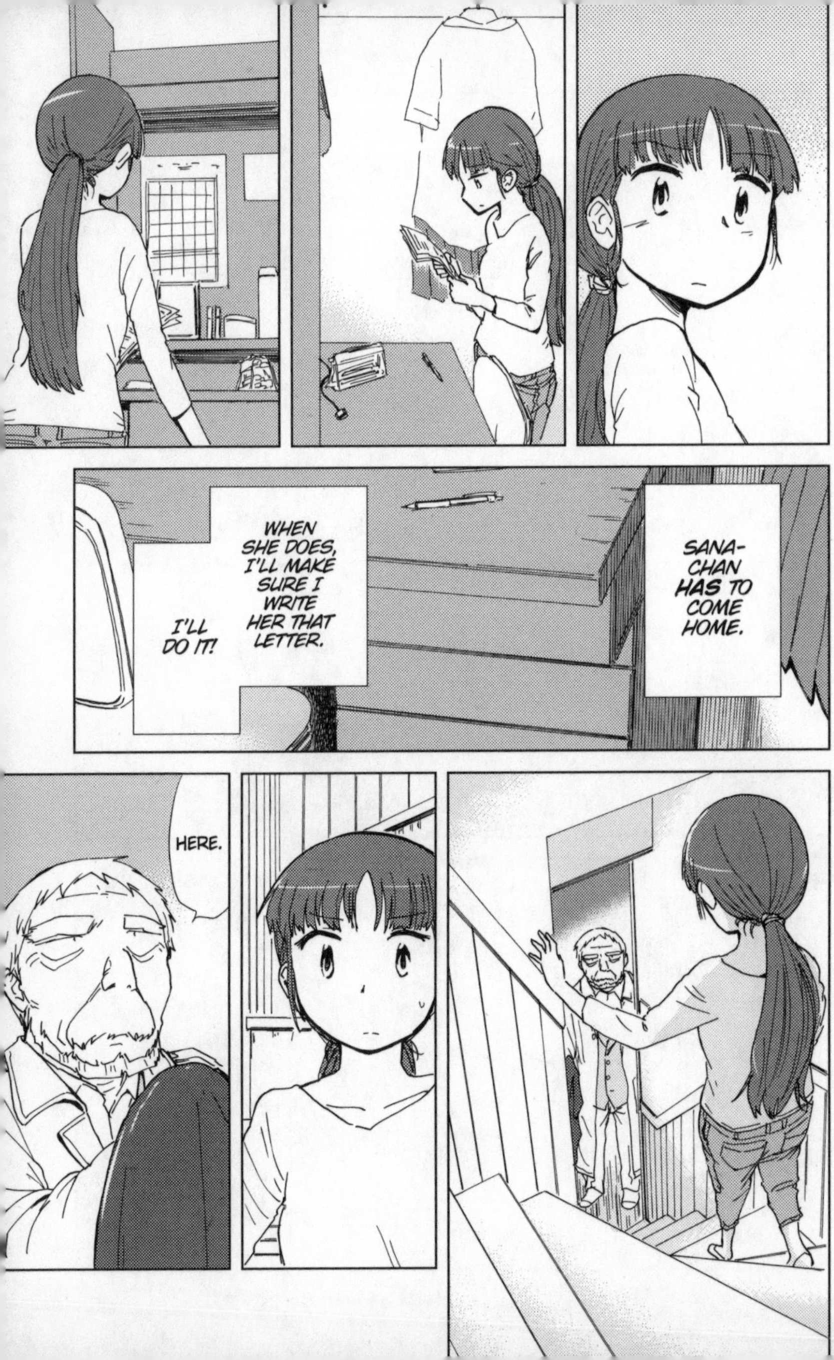
SANA-CHAN HAS TO COME HOME.
WHEN SHE DOES, I'LL MAKE SURE I WRITE HER THAT LETTER.
I'LL DO IT!
HERE.

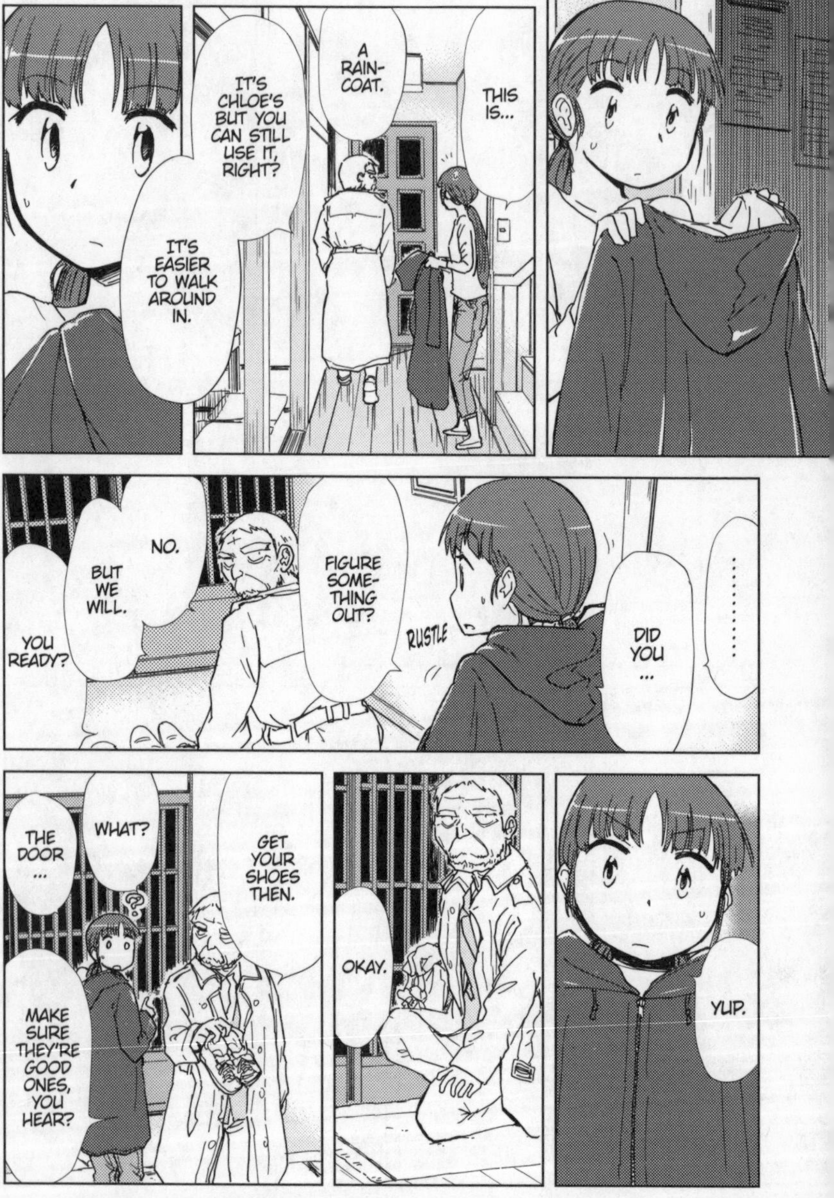
THIS IS...
A RAIN-COAT.
IT'S CHLOE'S BUT YOU CAN STILL USE IT, RIGHT?
IT'S EASIER TO WALK AROUND IN.
......
DID YOU ...
RUSTLE
FIGURE SOMETHING OUT?
NO.
BUT WE WILL.
YOU READY?
YUP.
OKAY.
GET YOUR SHOES THEN.
WHAT?
THE DOOR ...
MAKE SURE THEY"RE GOOD ONES, YOU HEAR?

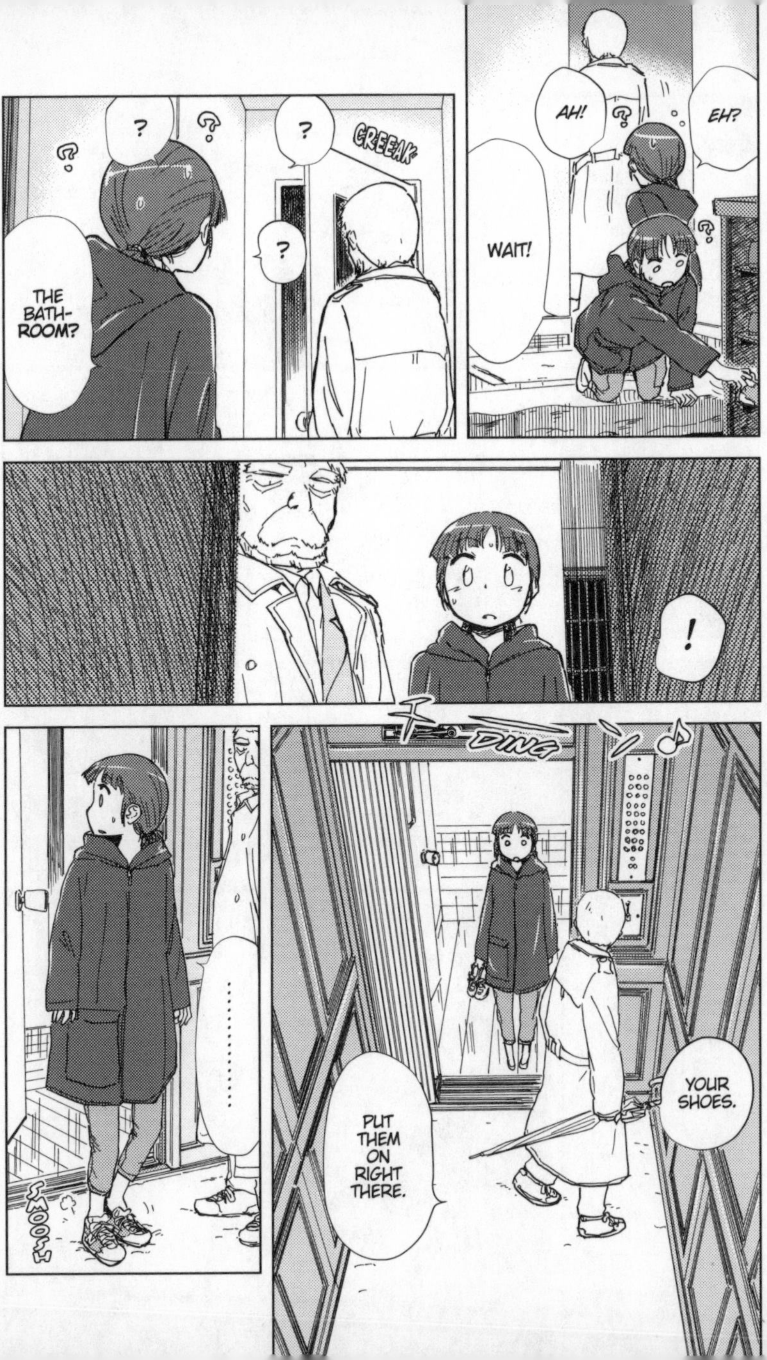
EH?
AH!
WAIT!
CREEAK
?
?
?
THE BATH-ROOM?
!
DING
YOUR SHOES.
PUT THEM ON RIGHT THERE.
......
SMOOSH

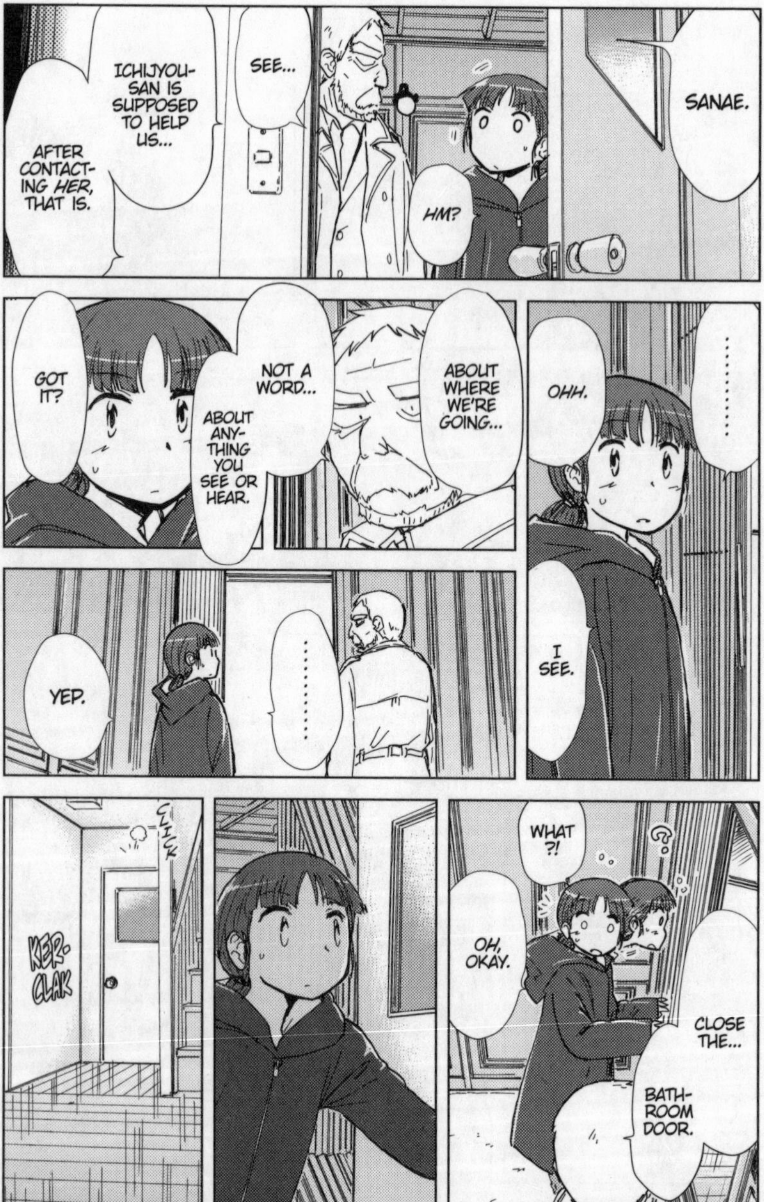
SANAE.
HM?
SEE...
ICHIJYOU-SAN IS SUPPOSED TO HELP US...
AFTER CONTACTING HER, THAT IS.
......
OHH.
I SEE.
ABOUT WHERE WE'RE GOING...
NOT A WORD...
ABOUT ANYTHING YOU SEE OR HEAR.
GOT IT?
......
YEP.
CLOSE THE...
BATHROOM DOOR.
WHAT?!
OH, OKAY.
CLICK
KER-CLAK

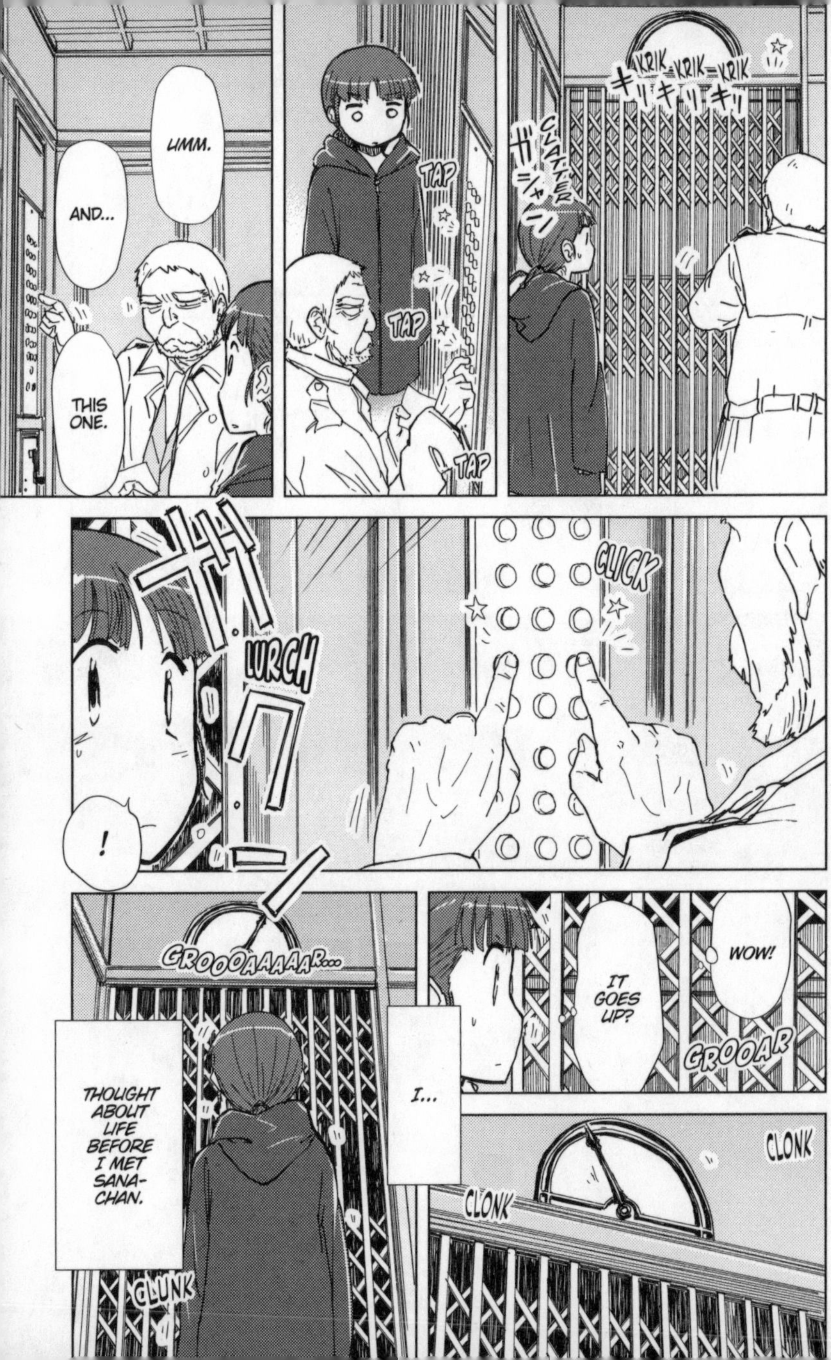

KRIK KRIK KRIK
キリキリキリ
CLATTER
ガシャン
TAP
TAP
TAP
UMM.
AND...
THIS ONE.
CLICK
LURCH
!
WOW!
IT GOES UP?
GROOAR
CLONK
CLONK
GROOOAAAAAR...
I...
THOUGHT ABOUT LIFE BEFORE I MET SANA-CHAN.
CLUNK

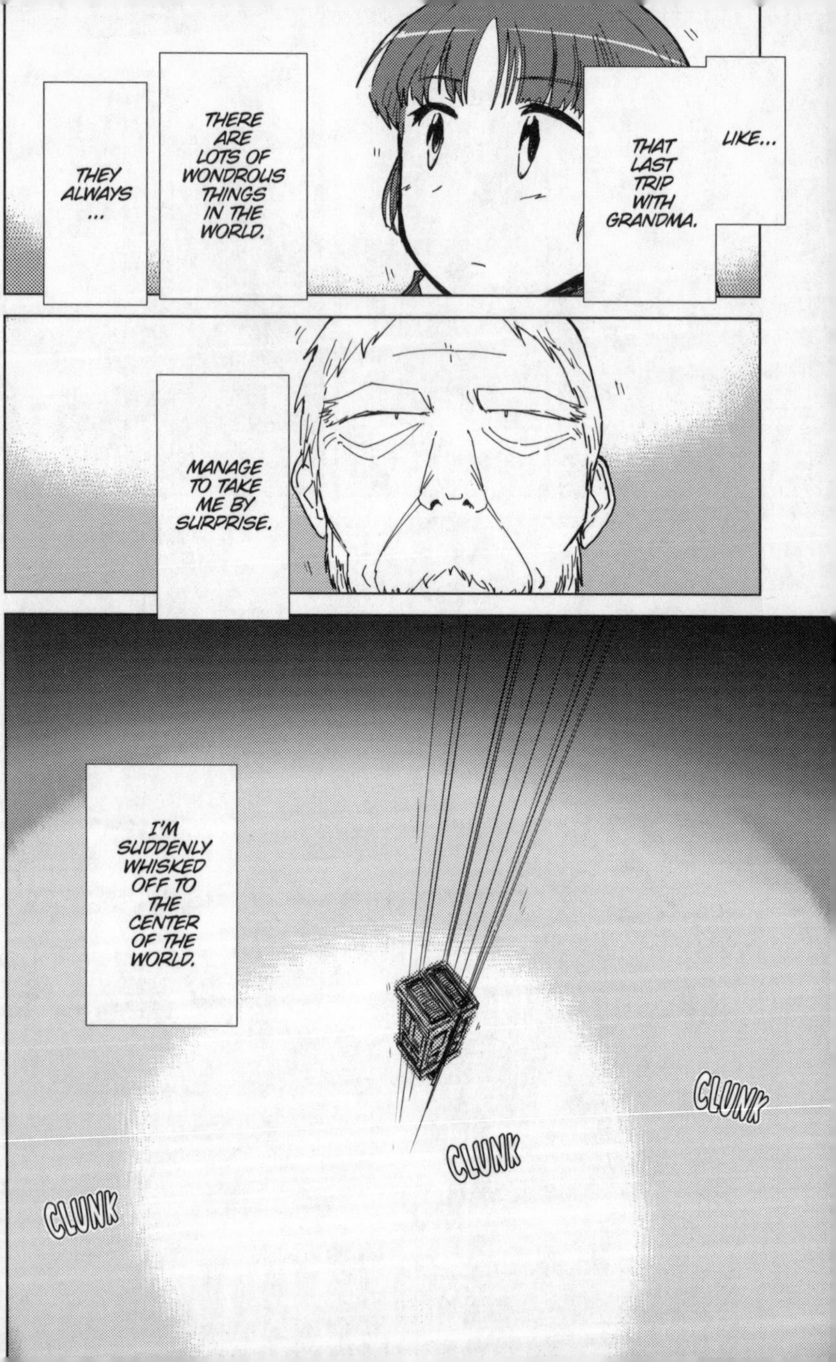
LIKE...
THAT LAST TRIP WITH GRANDMA.
THERE ARE LOTS OF WONDROUS THINGS IN THE WORLD.
THEY ALWAYS ...
MANAGE TO TAKE ME BY SURPRISE.
CLUNK
CLUNK
I'M SUDDENLY WHISKED OFF TO THE CENTER OF THE WORLD.
CLUNK

Alice & Zoroku

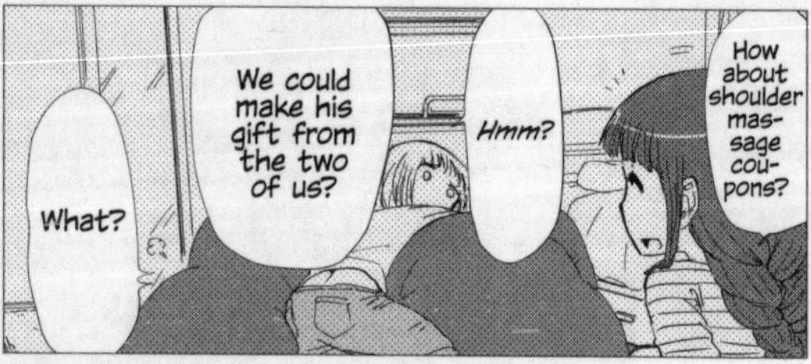
How about shoulder mas-sage cou-pons?
Hmm?
We could make his gift from the two of us?
What?

Chapter 35:
Pursuit, Down the Rabbit Hole

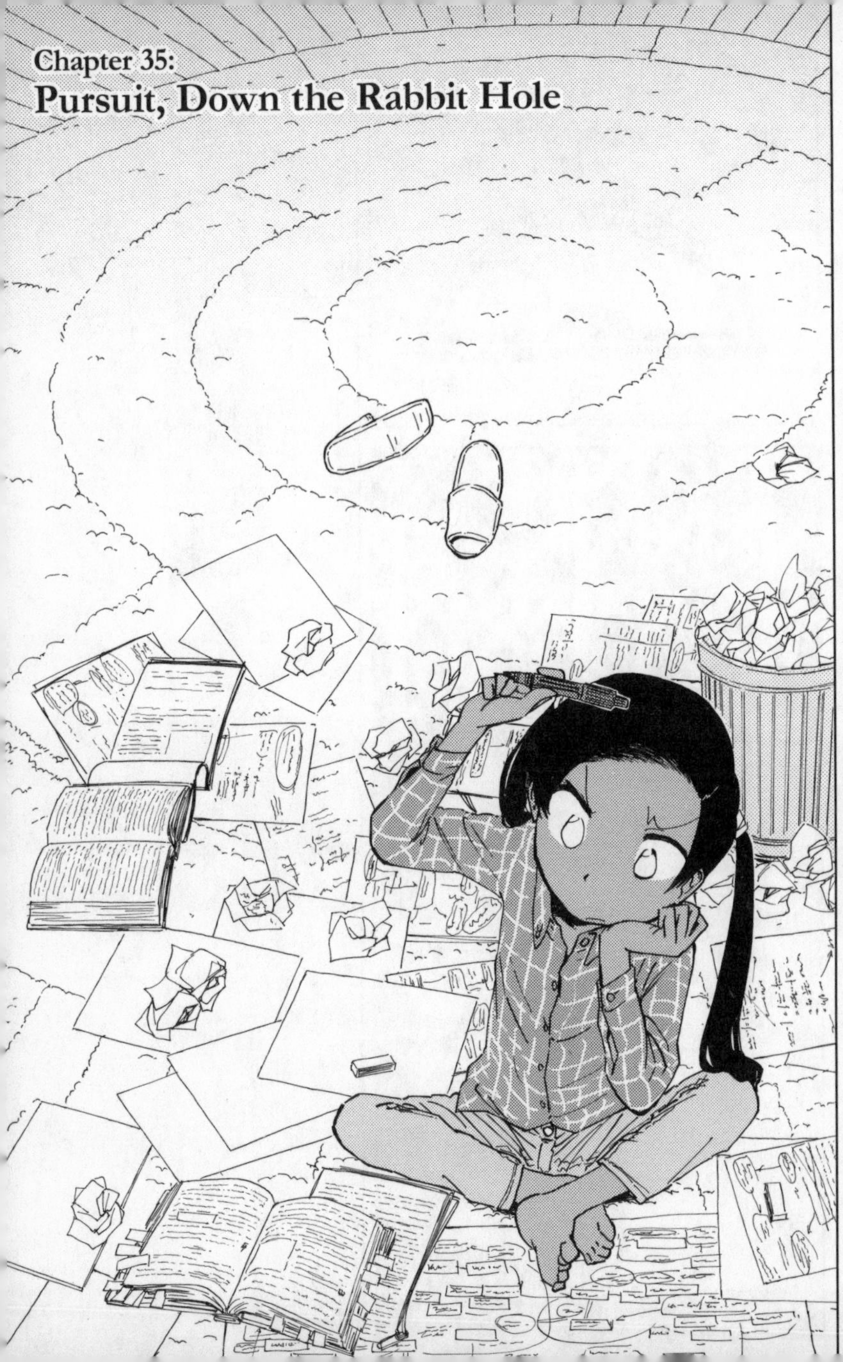

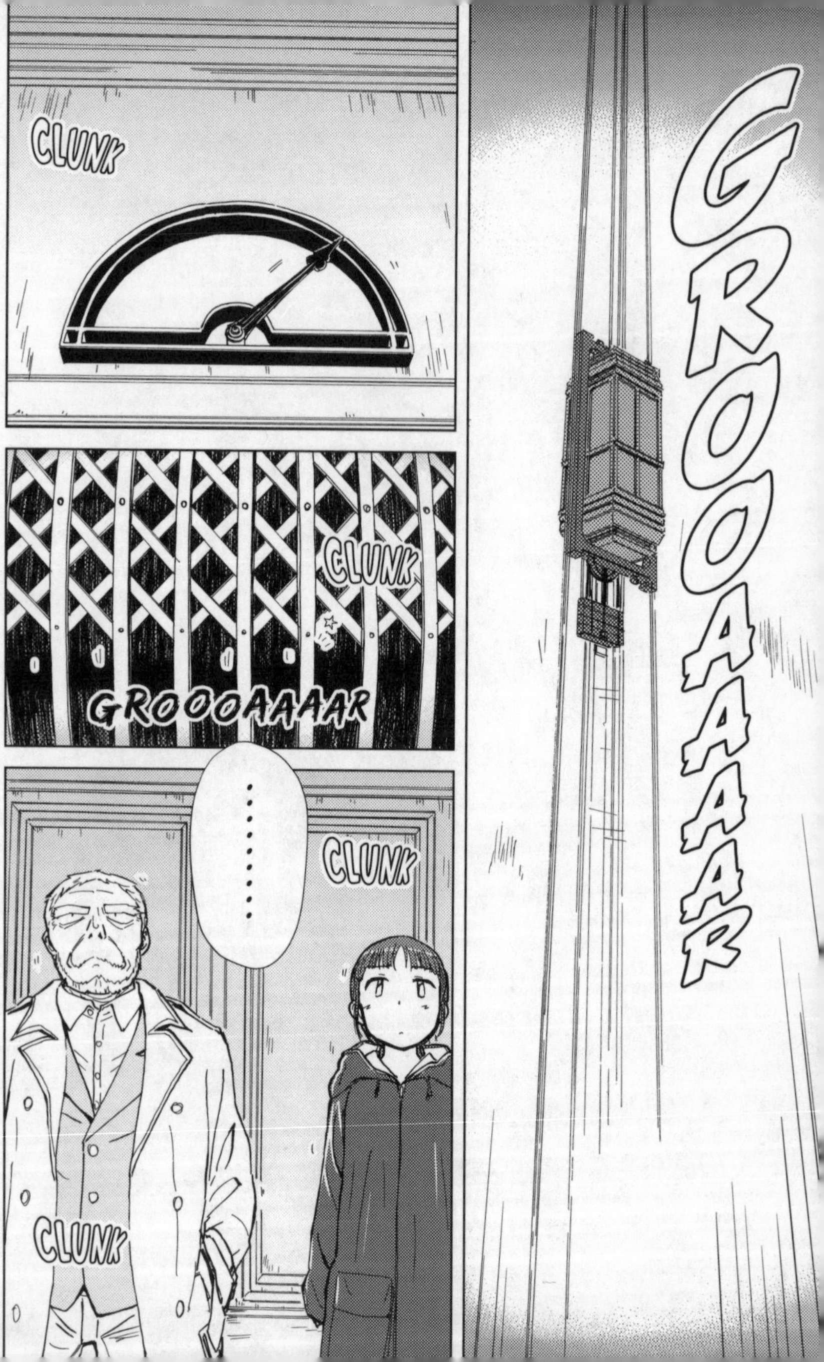
GROOOAAAAR
CLUNK
CLUNK
GROOOAAAAR
......
CLUNK
CLUNK

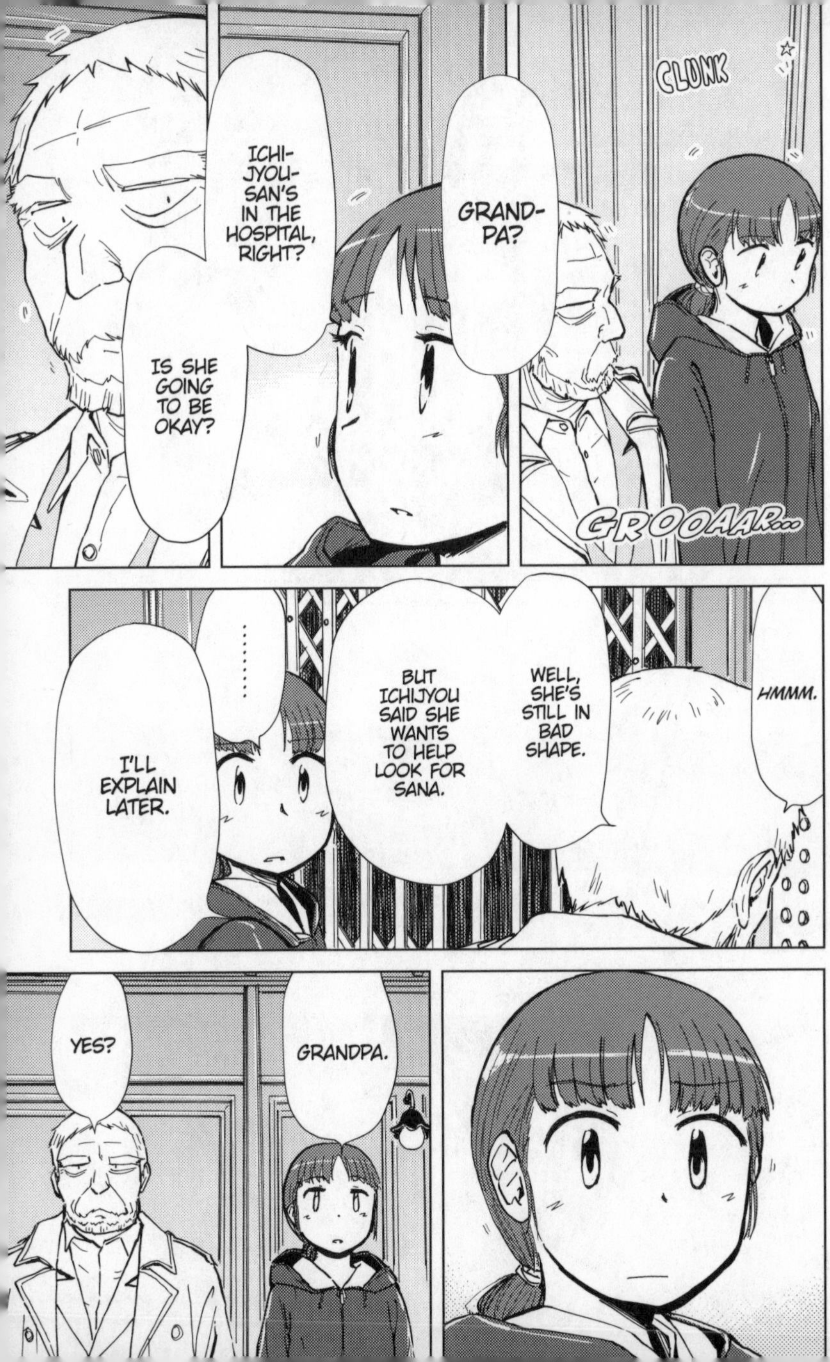
CLUNK
GROOOAAR...
GRAND-PA?
ICHIJYOU-SAN'S IN THE HOSPITAL, RIGHT?
IS SHE GOING TO BE OKAY?
HMMM.
WELL, SHE'S STILL IN BAD SHAPE.
BUT ICHIJYOU SAID SHE WANTS TO HELP LOOK FOR SANA.
......
I'LL EXPLAIN LATER.
GRANDPA.
YES?

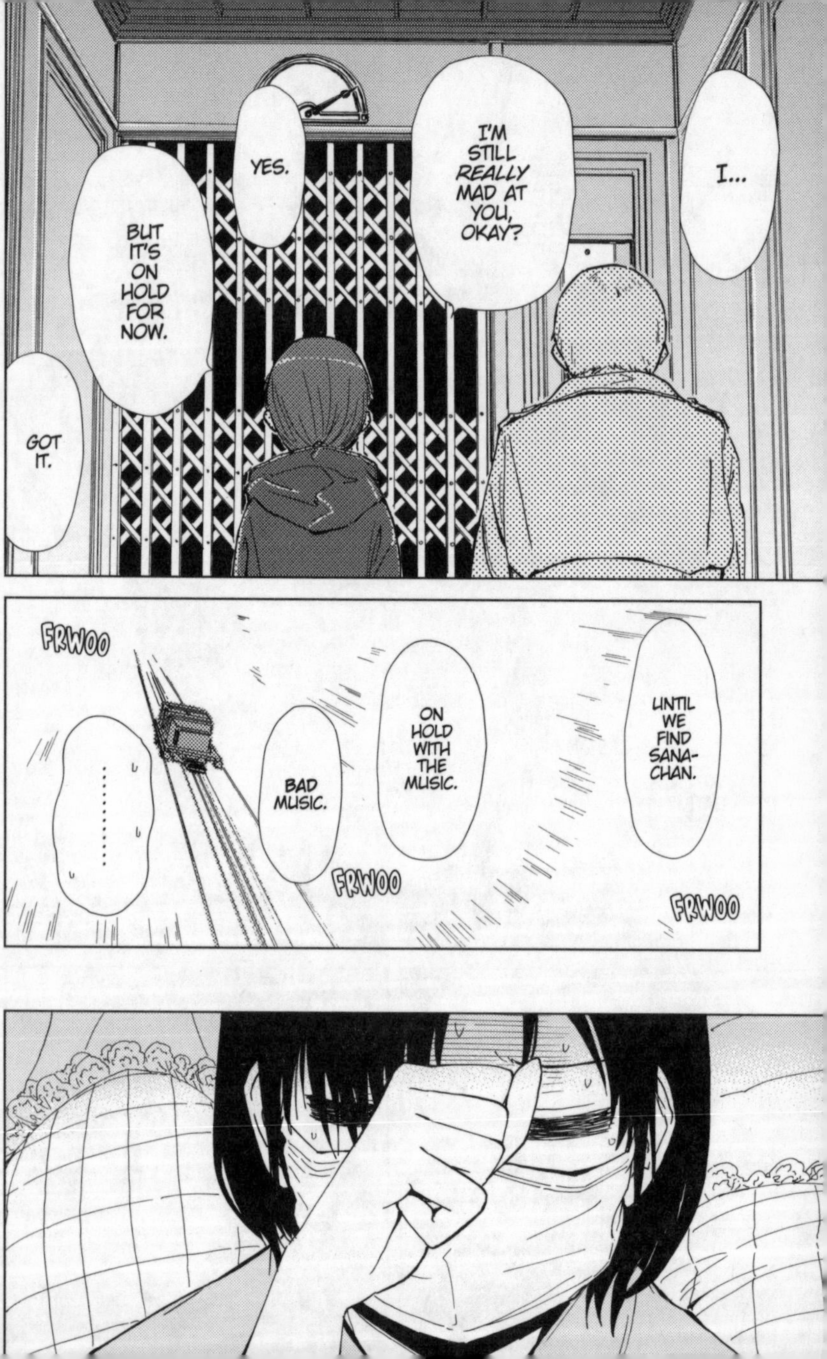
I...
I'M STILL REALLY MAD AT YOU, OKAY?
YES.
BUT IT'S ON HOLD FOR NOW.
GOT IT.
UNTIL WE FIND SANA-CHAN.
FRWOO
ON HOLD WITH THE MUSIC.
BAD MUSIC.
FRWOO
......
FRWOO

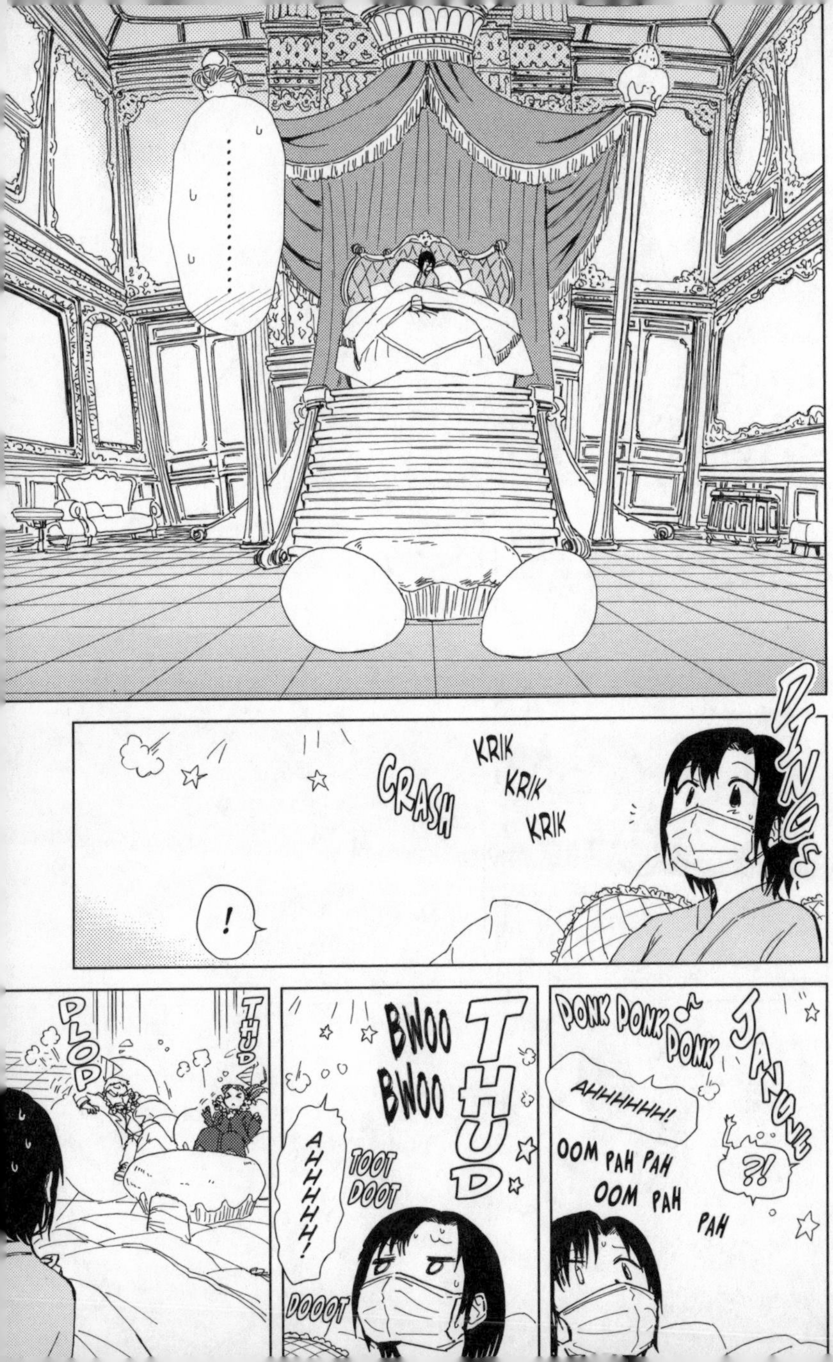
......
DING
CRASH
KRIK
KRIK
KRIK
!
PONK PONK PONK
JANGLE
AHHHHHH!
OOM PAH PAH
OOM PAH
PAH
?!
BWOO
BWOO
THUD
AHHHHHH!
TOOT
DOOT
DOOOT
PLOP
THUD

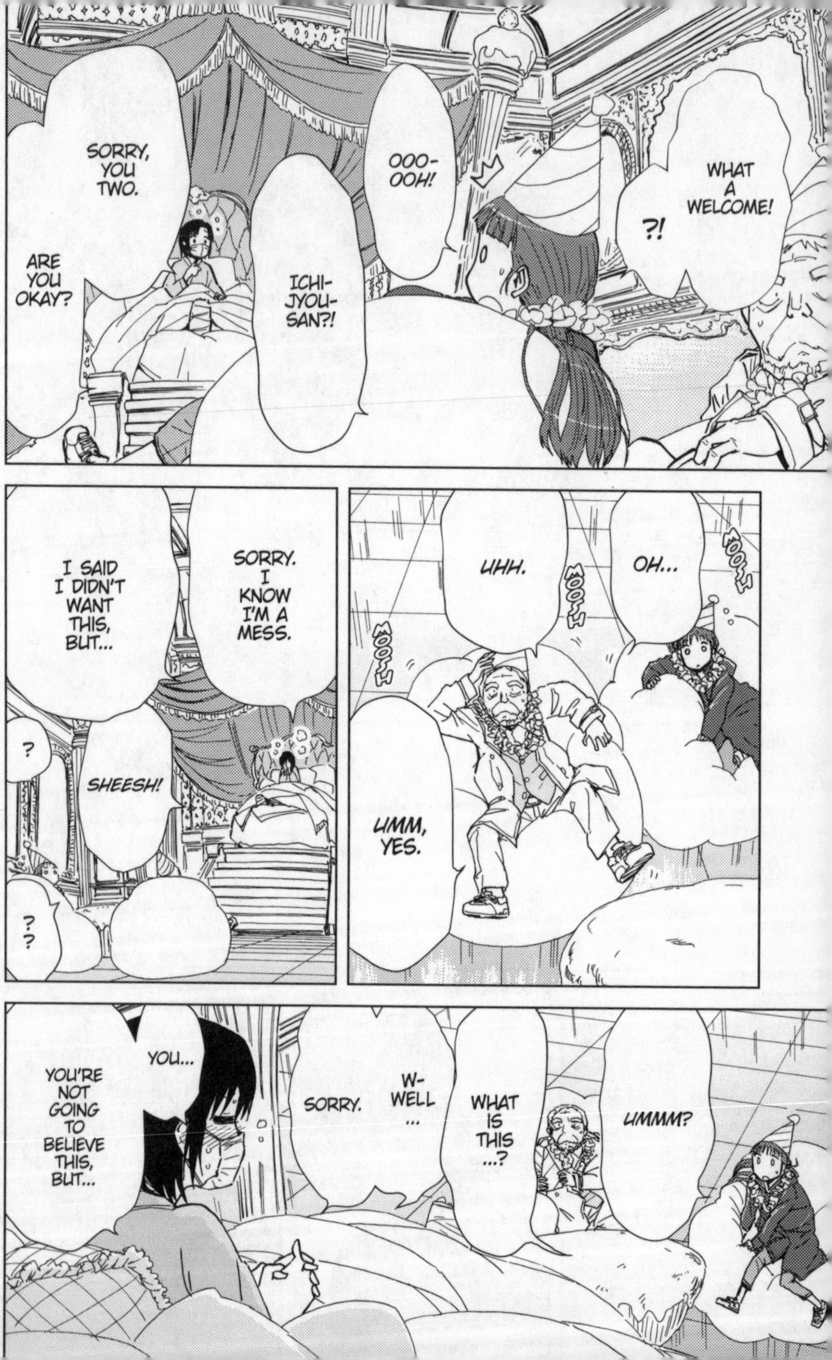

WHAT A WELCOME!
?!
OOO-OOH!
ICHI-JYOU-SAN?!
SORRY, YOU TWO.
ARE YOU OKAY?
OH...
UHH.
UMM, YES.
SORRY. I KNOW I'M A MESS.
I SAID I DIDN'T WANT THIS, BUT...
SHEESH!
?
??
UMMM?
WHAT IS THIS...?
W-WELL...
SORRY.
YOU...
YOU'RE NOT GOING TO BELIEVE THIS, BUT...

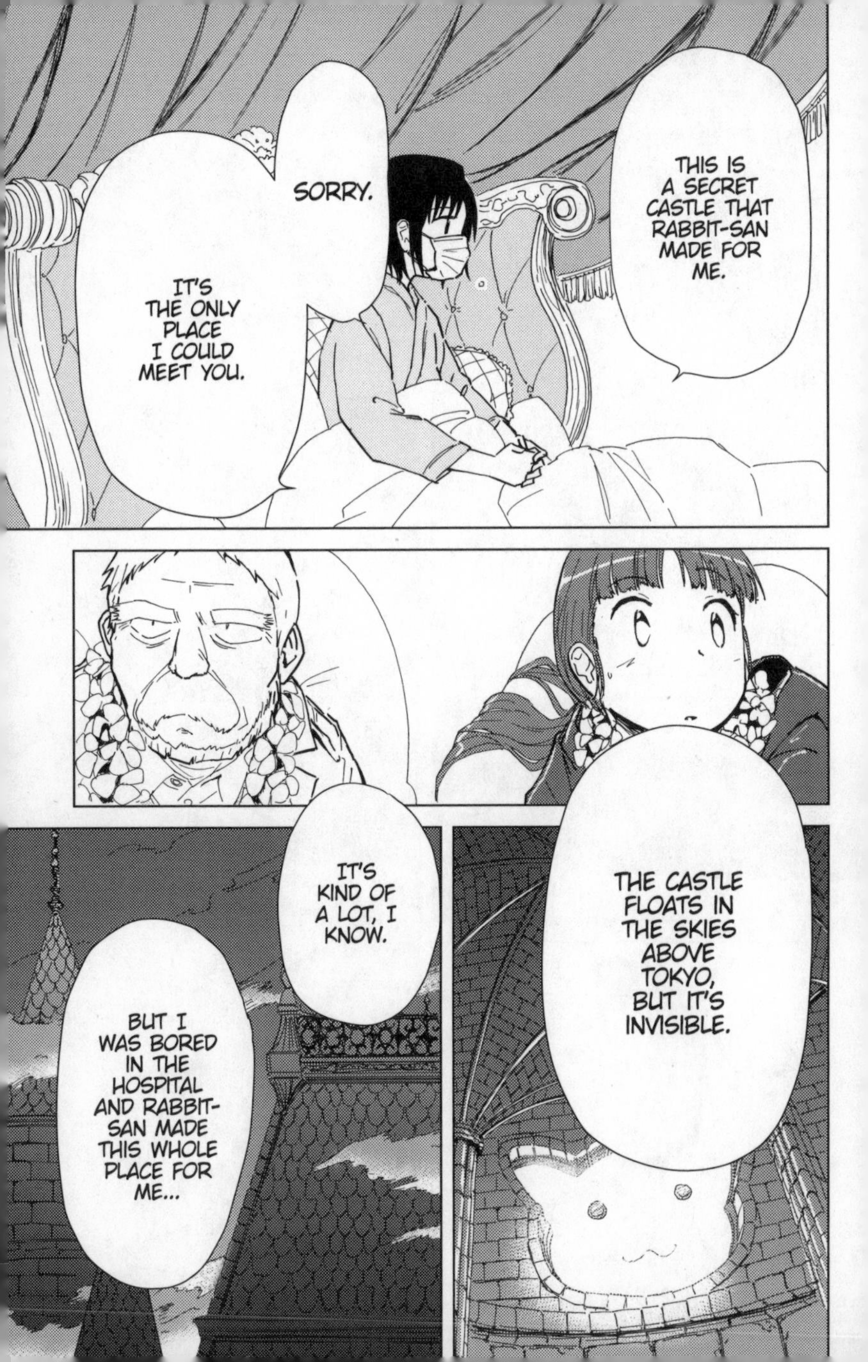
THIS IS A SECRET CASTLE THAT RABBIT-SAN MADE FOR ME.
SORRY.
IT'S THE ONLY PLACE I COULD MEET YOU.
THE CASTLE FLOATS IN THE SKIES ABOVE TOKYO, BUT IT'S INVISIBLE.
IT'S KIND OF A LOT, I KNOW.
BUT I WAS BORED IN THE HOSPITAL AND RABBIT-SAN MADE THIS WHOLE PLACE FOR ME...

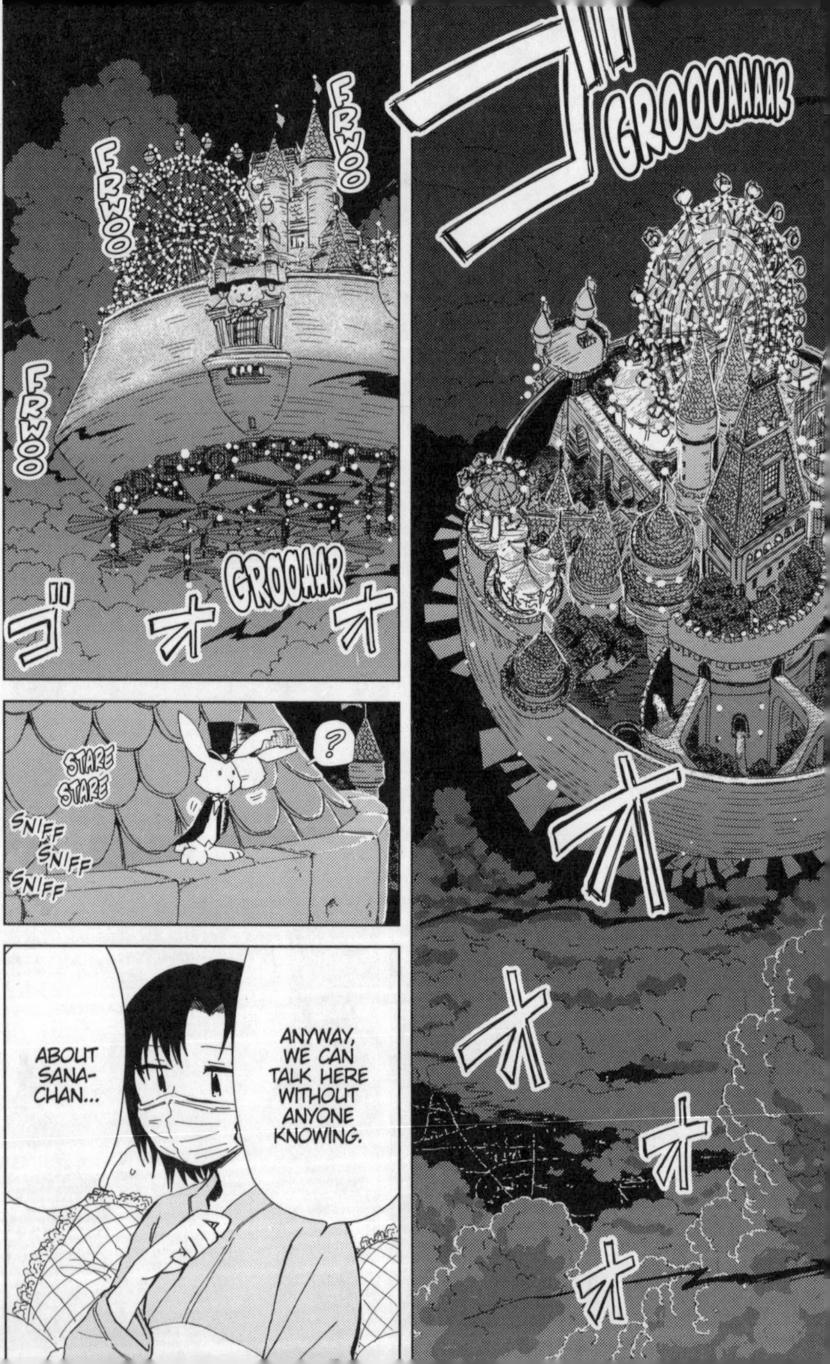
GROOOAAAAR
FRWOO
FRWOO
FRWOO
GROOAAR
?
STARE STARE
SNIFF SNIFF SNIFF
ANYWAY, WE CAN TALK HERE WITHOUT ANYONE KNOWING.
ABOUT SANA-CHAN...

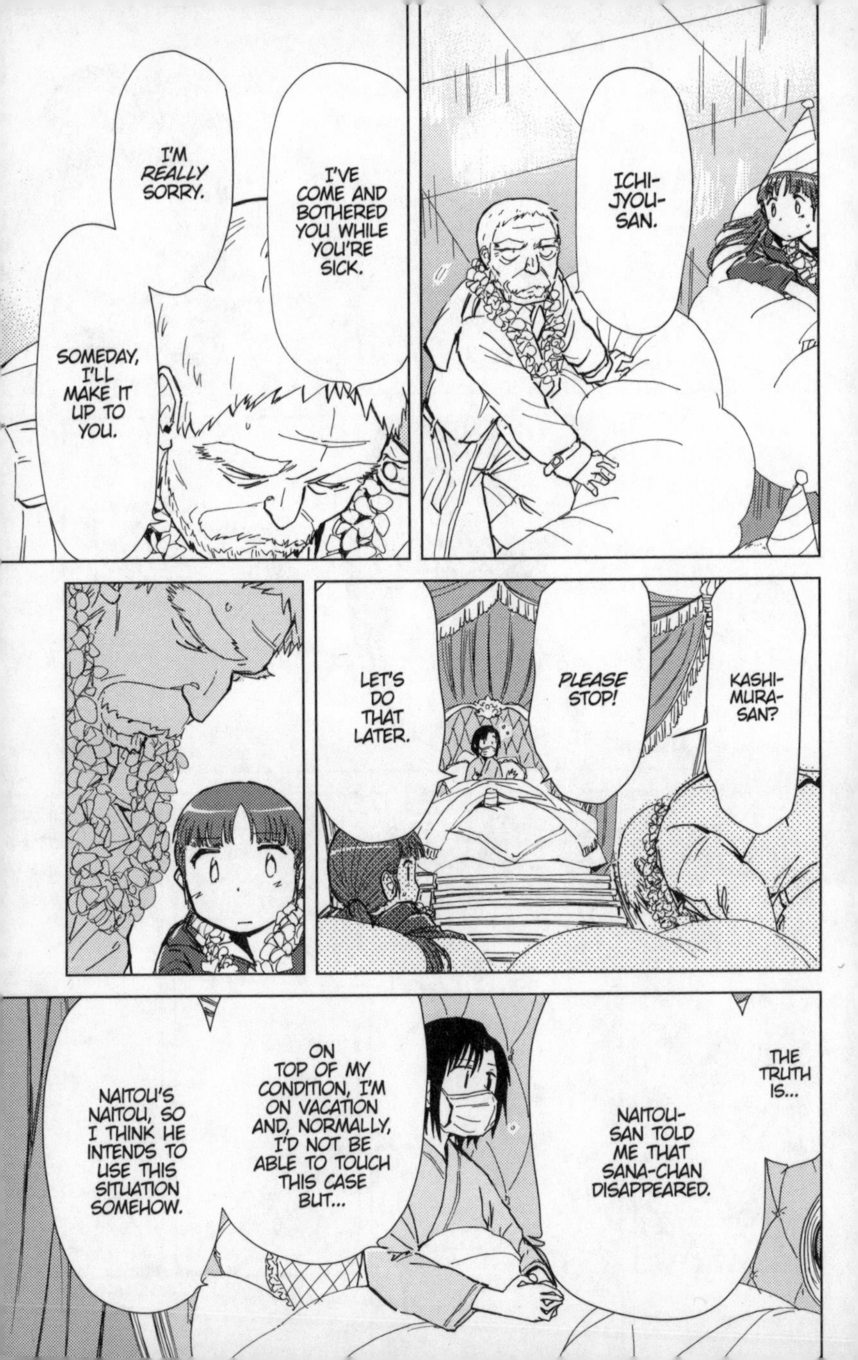
ICHI-JYOU-SAN.
I'VE COME AND BOTHERED YOU WHILE YOU'RE SICK.
I'M *REALLY* SORRY.
SOMEDAY, I'LL MAKE IT UP TO YOU.
KASHI-MURA-SAN?
PLEASE STOP!
LET'S DO THAT LATER.
THE TRUTH IS...
NAITOU-SAN TOLD ME THAT SANA-CHAN DISAPPEARED.
ON TOP OF MY CONDITION, I'M ON VACATION AND, NORMALLY, I'D NOT BE ABLE TO TOUCH THIS CASE BUT...
NAITOU'S NAITOU, SO I THINK HE INTENDS TO USE THIS SITUATION SOMEHOW.

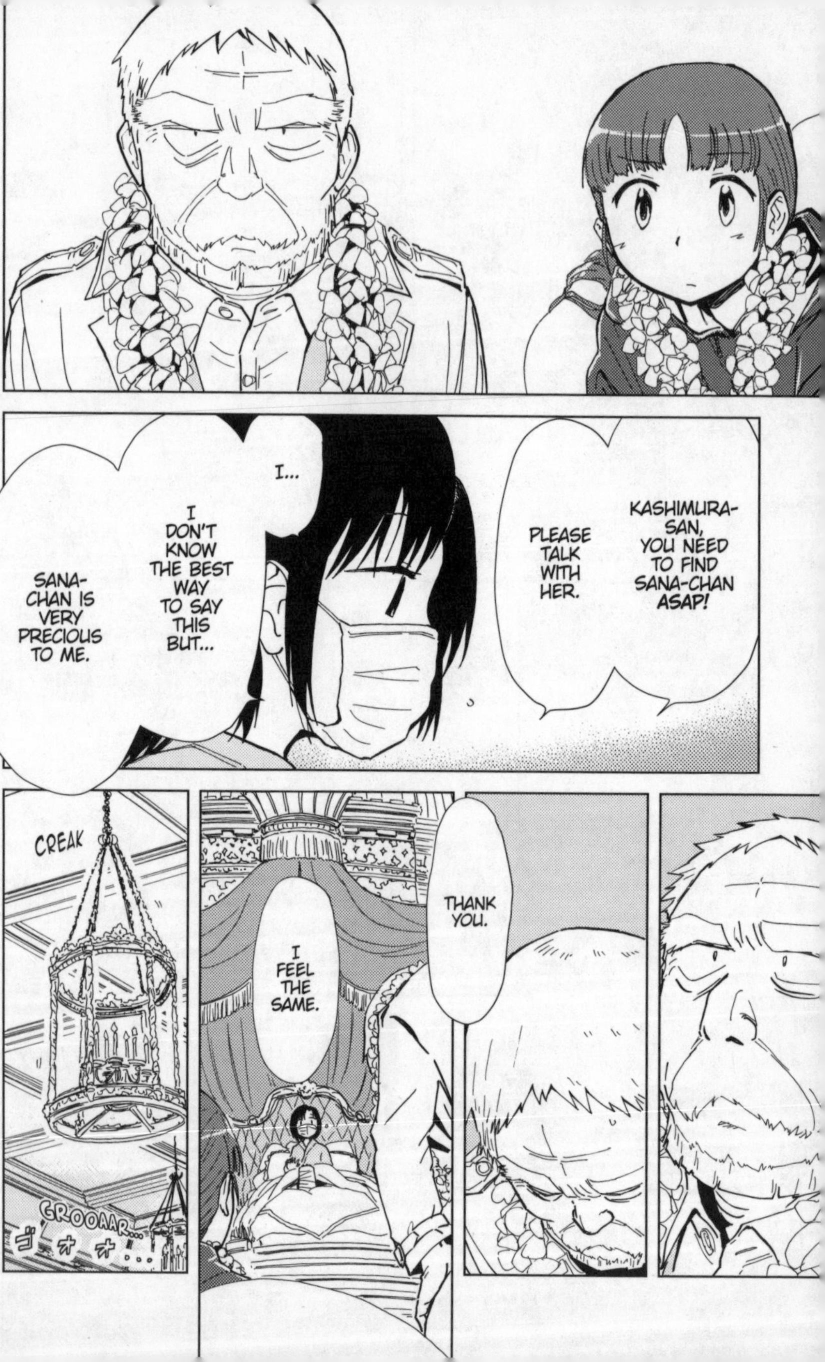
KASHIMURA-SAN, YOU NEED TO FIND SANA-CHAN ASAP!
PLEASE TALK WITH HER.
I...
I DON'T KNOW THE BEST WAY TO SAY THIS BUT...
SANA-CHAN IS VERY PRECIOUS TO ME.
THANK YOU.
I FEEL THE SAME.
CREAK
GROOAAR...
ゴォォ...

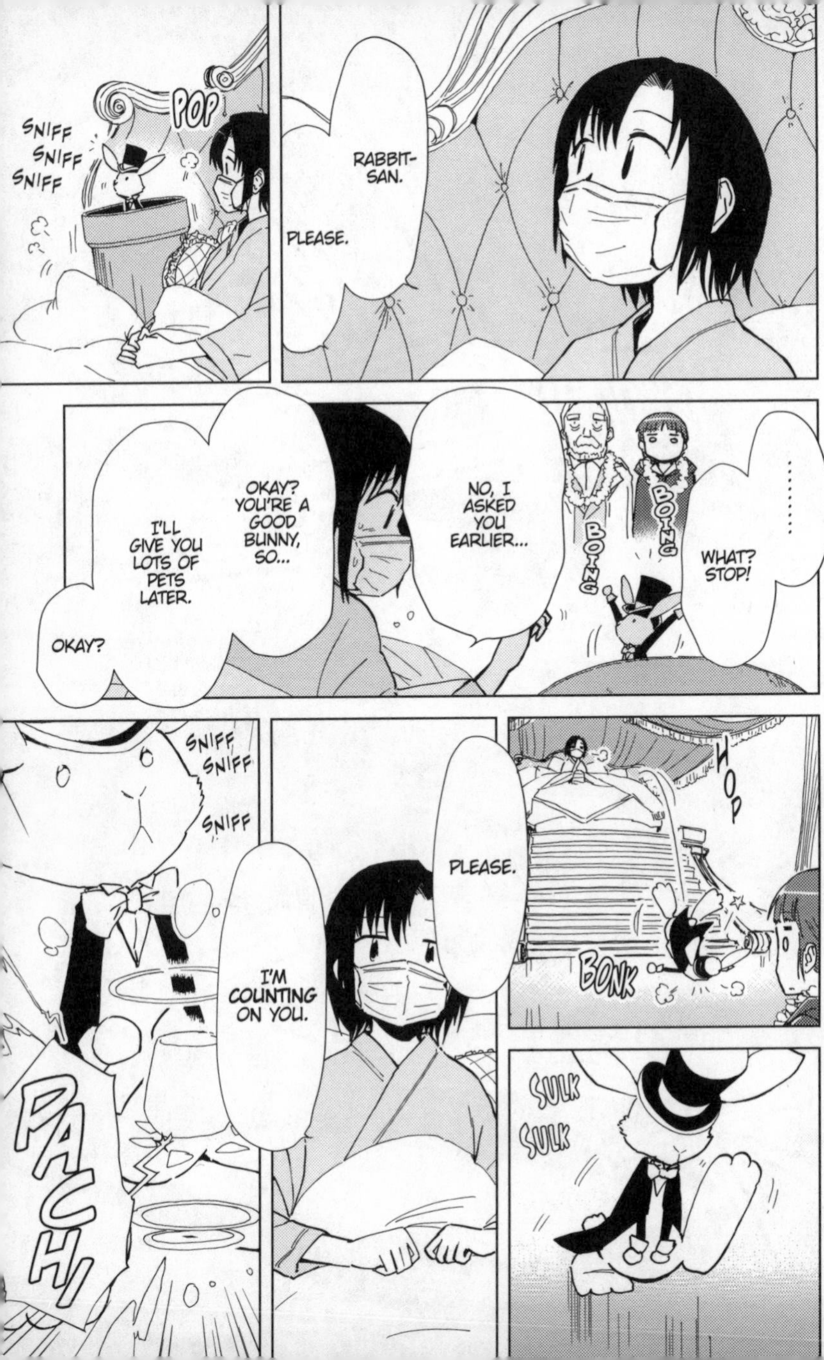
RABBIT-SAN.
PLEASE.
POP
SNIFF SNIFF SNIFF
......
WHAT? STOP!
BOING
BOING
NO, I ASKED YOU EARLIER...
OKAY? YOU'RE A GOOD BUNNY, SO...
I'LL GIVE YOU LOTS OF PETS LATER.
OKAY?
HOP
BONK
SULK SULK
PLEASE.
I'M COUNTING ON YOU.
SNIFF SNIFF
SNIFF
PACHI

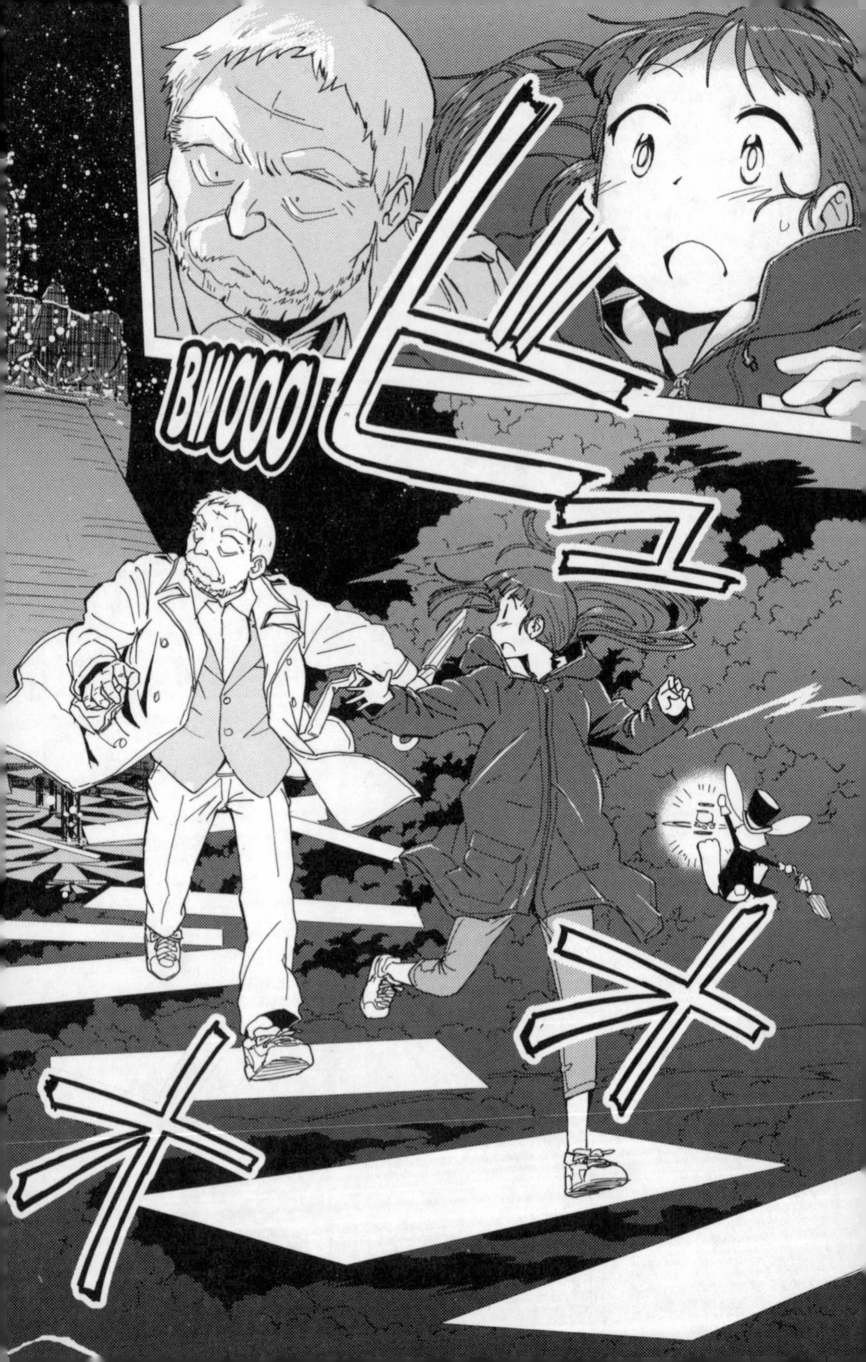

BWOOO
ビュ

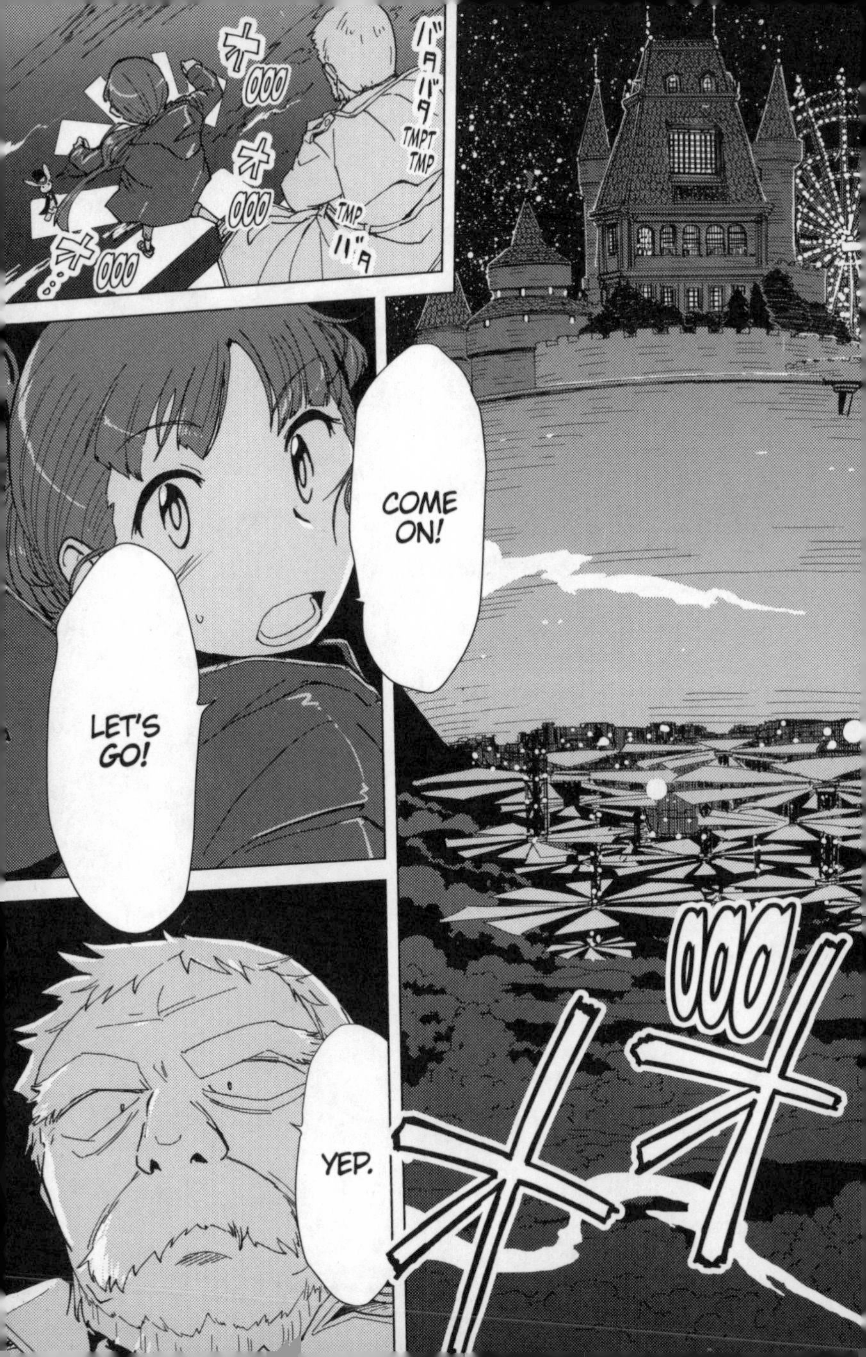
オ
OOO
バタバタ
TMPT TMP
オ OOO
TMP
バタ
オ OOO
オ… OOO
COME ON!
LET'S GO!
YEP.

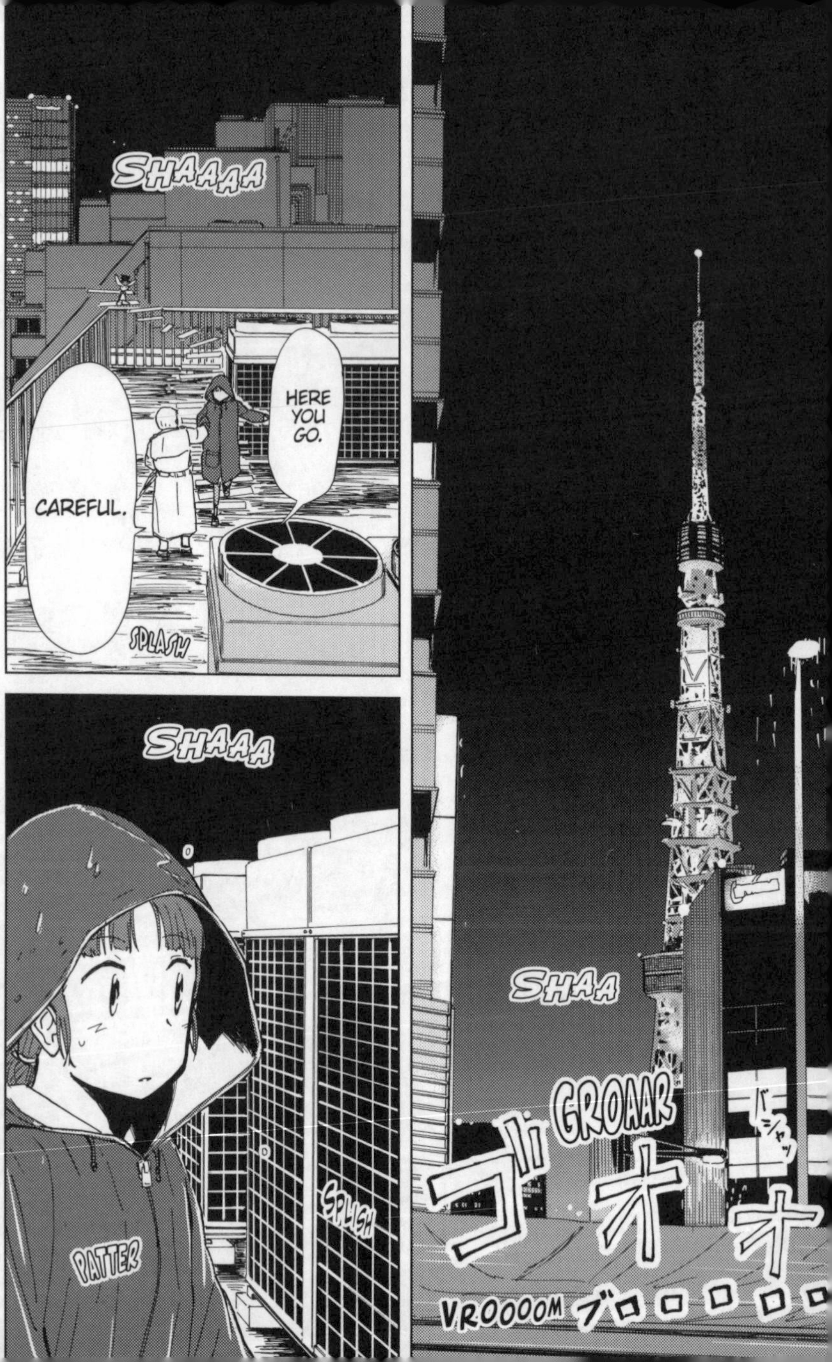
SHAA
GROAAR
ゴオオ
バシャッ
VROOOOM
ブロロロロロ
SHAAAAA
HERE YOU GO.
CAREFUL.
SPLASH
SHAAAA
SPLISH
PATTER

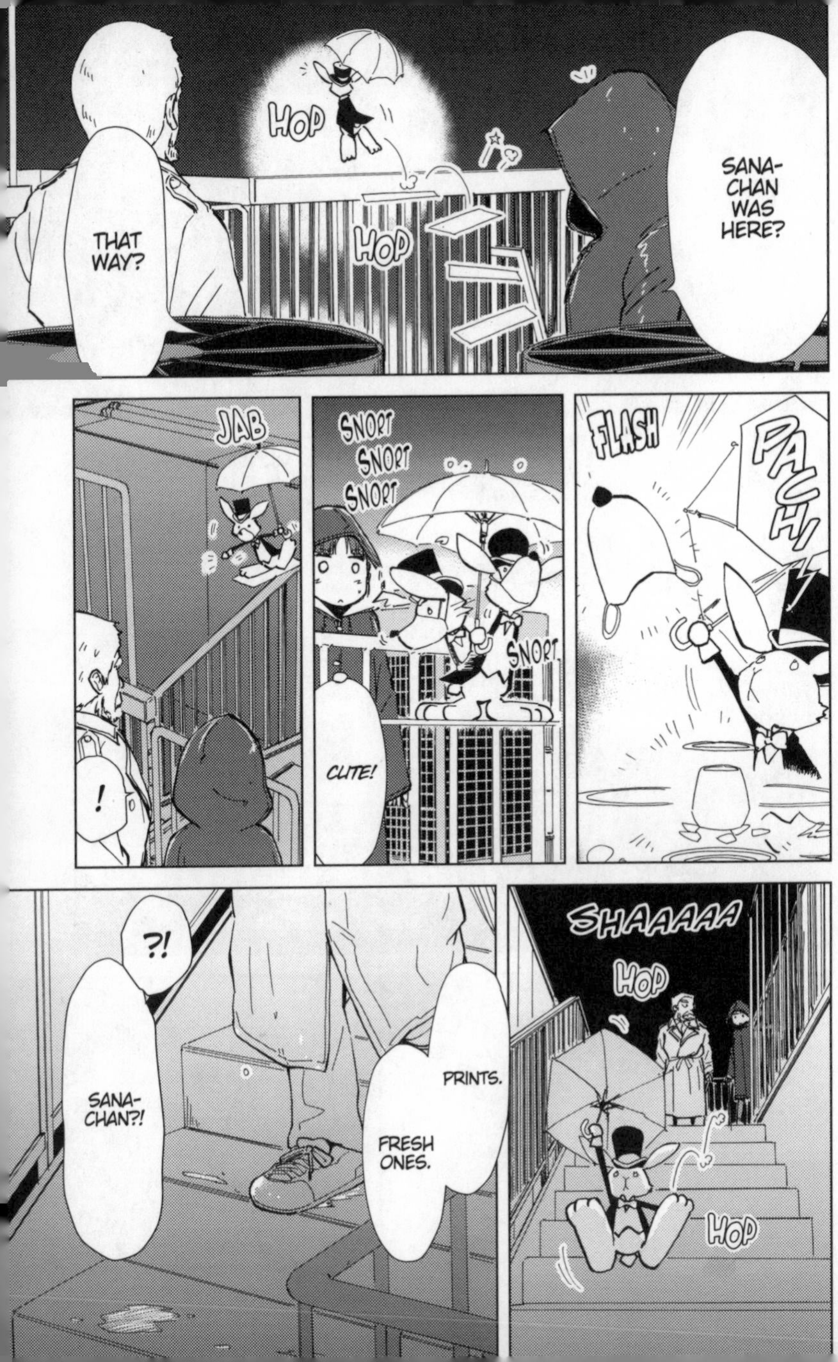
SANA-CHAN WAS HERE?
HOP
HOP
THAT WAY?
FLASH
PACHI
SNORT SNORT SNORT
SNORT
CUTE!
JAB
!
SHAAAAA
HOP
HOP
PRINTS.
FRESH ONES.
?!
SANA-CHAN?!

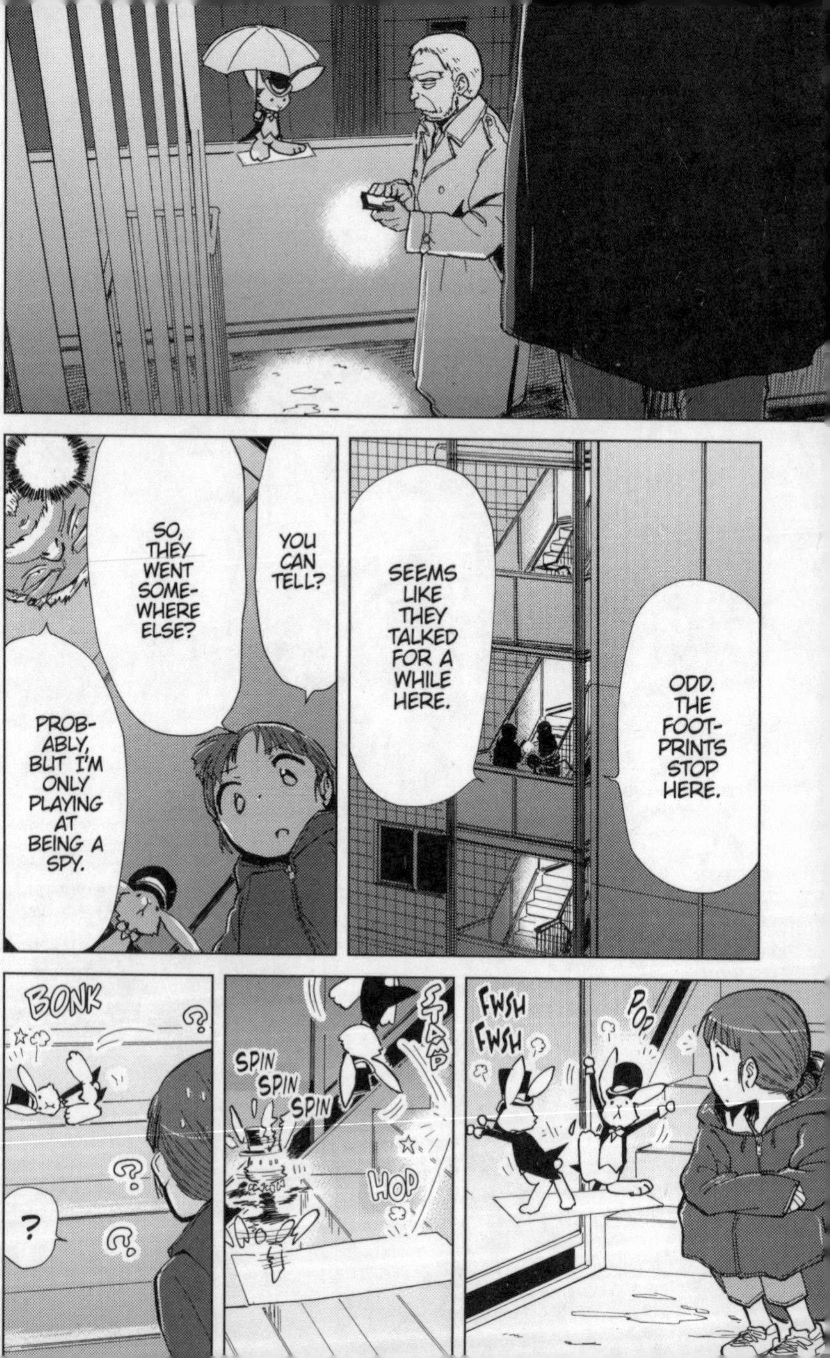
ODD. THE FOOT-PRINTS STOP HERE.
SEEMS LIKE THEY TALKED FOR A WHILE HERE.
YOU CAN TELL?
SO, THEY WENT SOME-WHERE ELSE?
PROB-ABLY, BUT I'M ONLY PLAYING AT BEING A SPY.
POP
FWSH FWSH
STAMP
SPIN SPIN SPIN
HOP
BONK
?

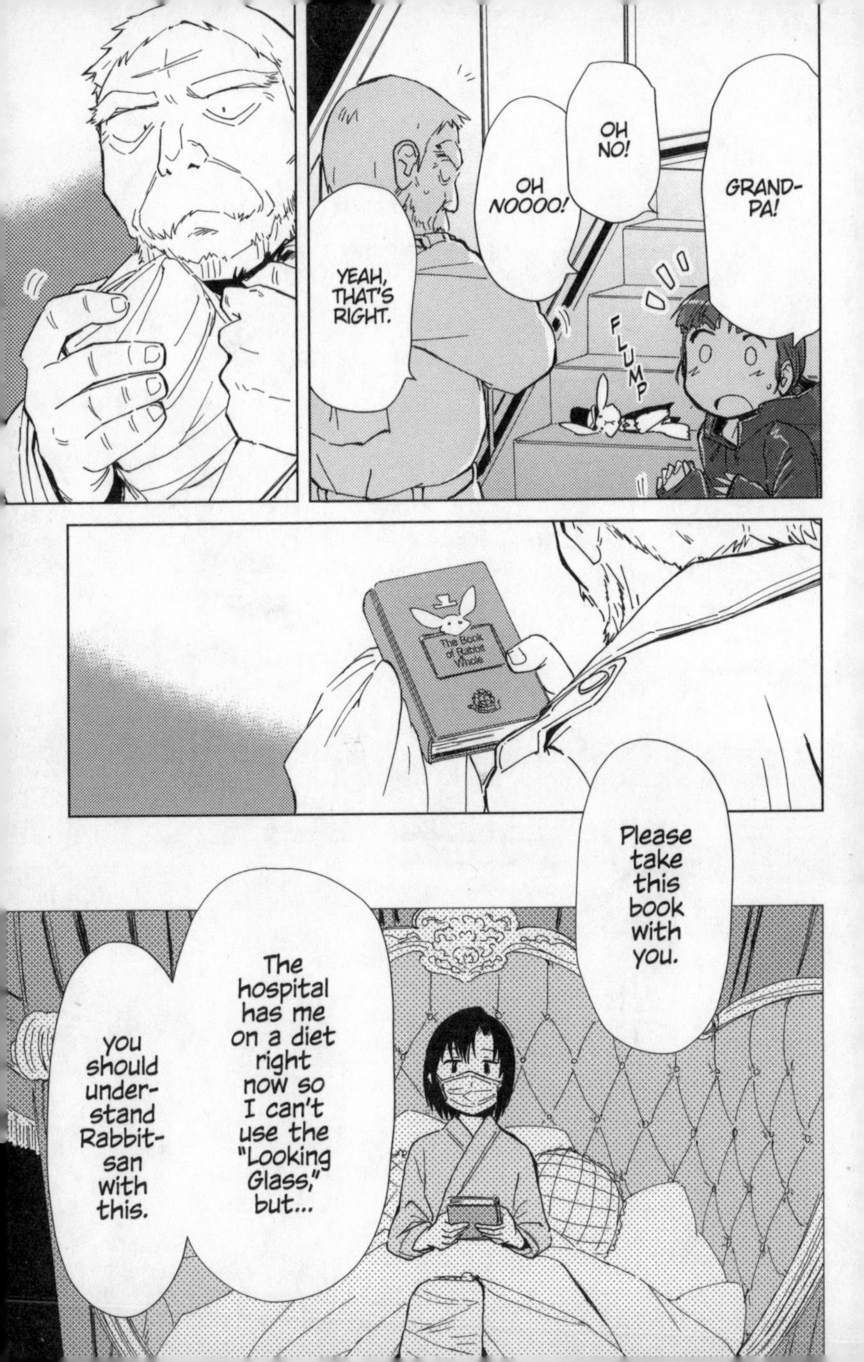
GRAND-PA!
OH NO!
OH NOOOO!
FLUMP
YEAH, THAT'S RIGHT.
The Book of Rabbit Whole
Please take this book with you.
The hospital has me on a diet right now so I can't use the "Looking Glass," but...
you should under-stand Rabbit-san with this.

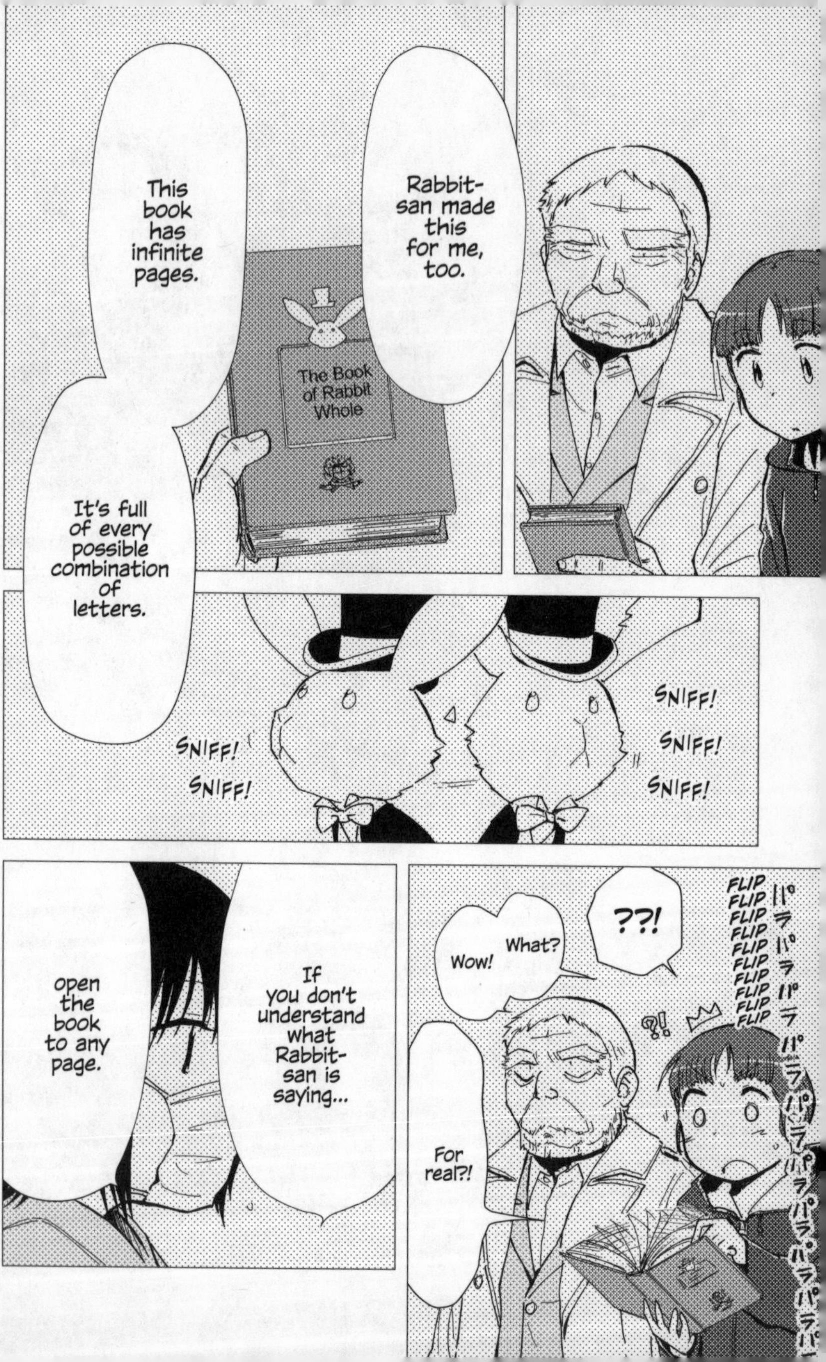

Rabbit-san made this for me, too.
This book has infinite pages.
The Book of Rabbit Whole
It's full of every possible combination of letters.
SNIFF!
SNIFF!
SNIFF!
SNIFF!
SNIFF!
FLIP FLIP FLIP FLIP FLIP FLIP FLIP FLIP FLIP FLIP
??!
What?
Wow!
?!
For real?!
If you don't understand what Rabbit-san is saying...
open the book to any page.

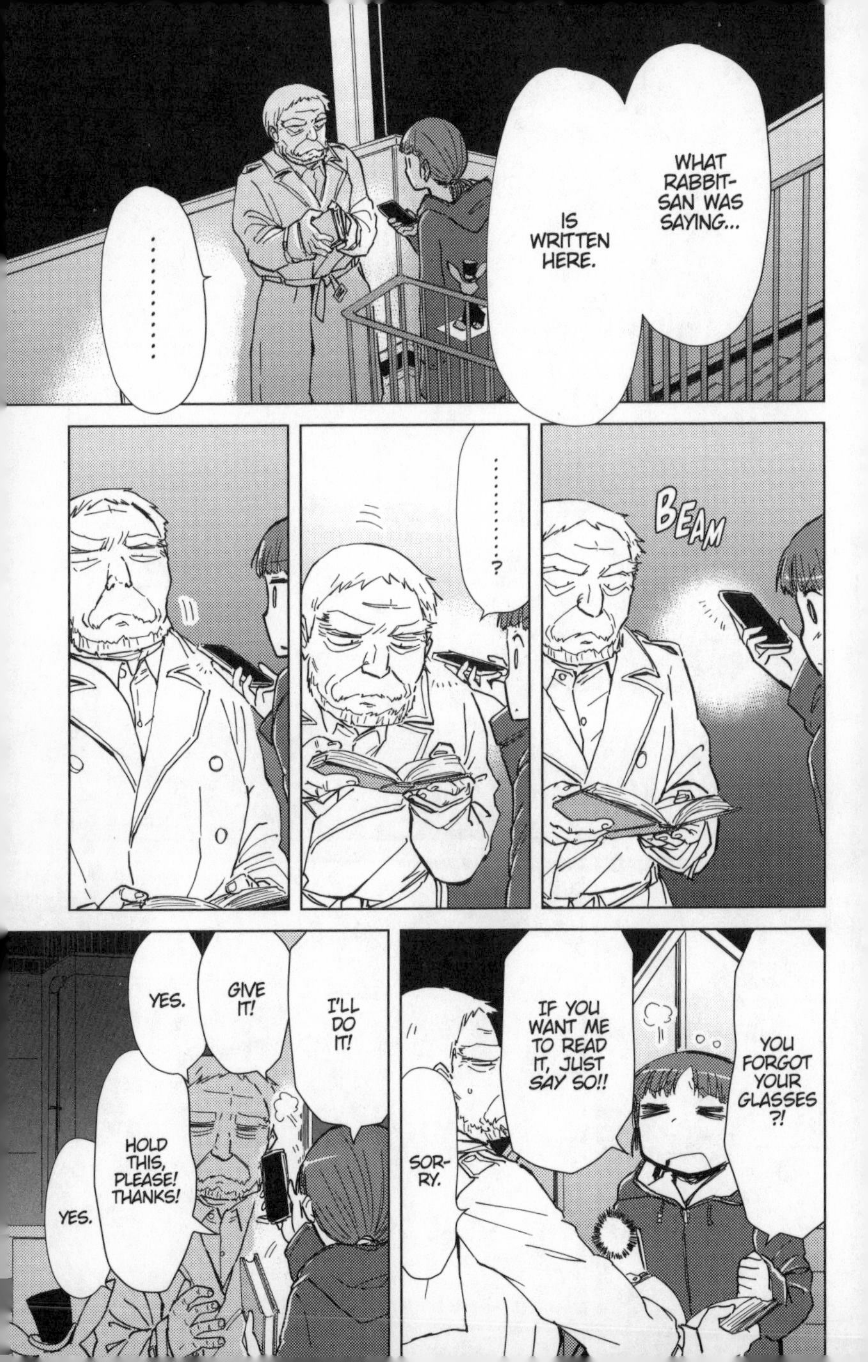
WHAT RABBIT-SAN WAS SAYING...
IS WRITTEN HERE.
......
BEAM
......?
YOU FORGOT YOUR GLASSES?!
IF YOU WANT ME TO READ IT, JUST SAY SO!!
SOR-RY.
I'LL DO IT!
GIVE IT!
YES.
HOLD THIS, PLEASE! THANKS!
YES.

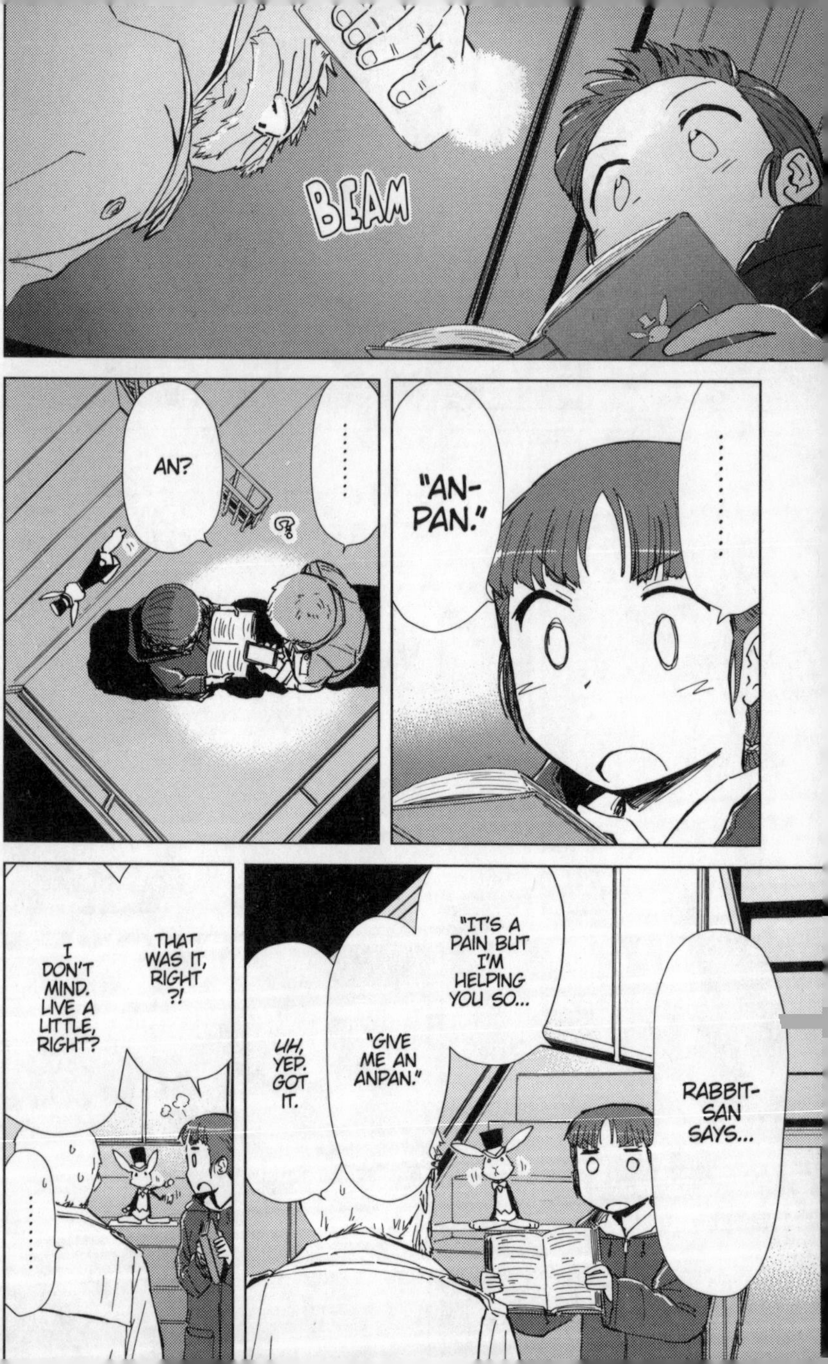
BEAM
......
"AN-PAN."
......
AN?
RABBIT-SAN SAYS...
"IT'S A PAIN BUT I'M HELPING YOU SO...
"GIVE ME AN ANPAN."
UH, YEP. GOT IT.
THAT WAS IT, RIGHT?!
I DON'T MIND. LIVE A LITTLE, RIGHT?
......

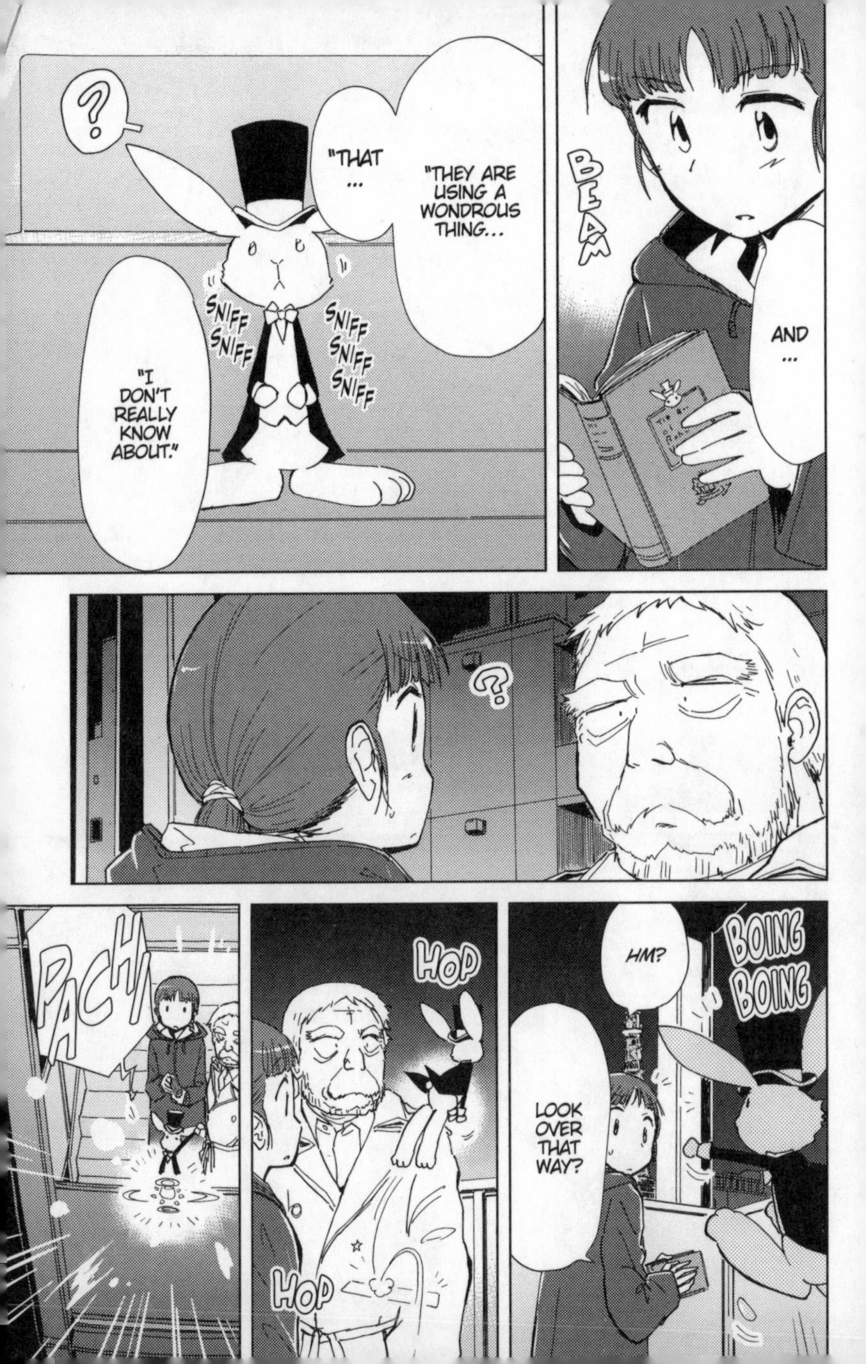
BEAM
AND ...
"THEY ARE USING A WONDROUS THING...
"THAT ...
?
SNIFF SNIFF SNIFF
SNIFF SNIFF
"I DON'T REALLY KNOW ABOUT."
?
BOING BOING
HM?
LOOK OVER THAT WAY?
HOP
HOP
PACHI

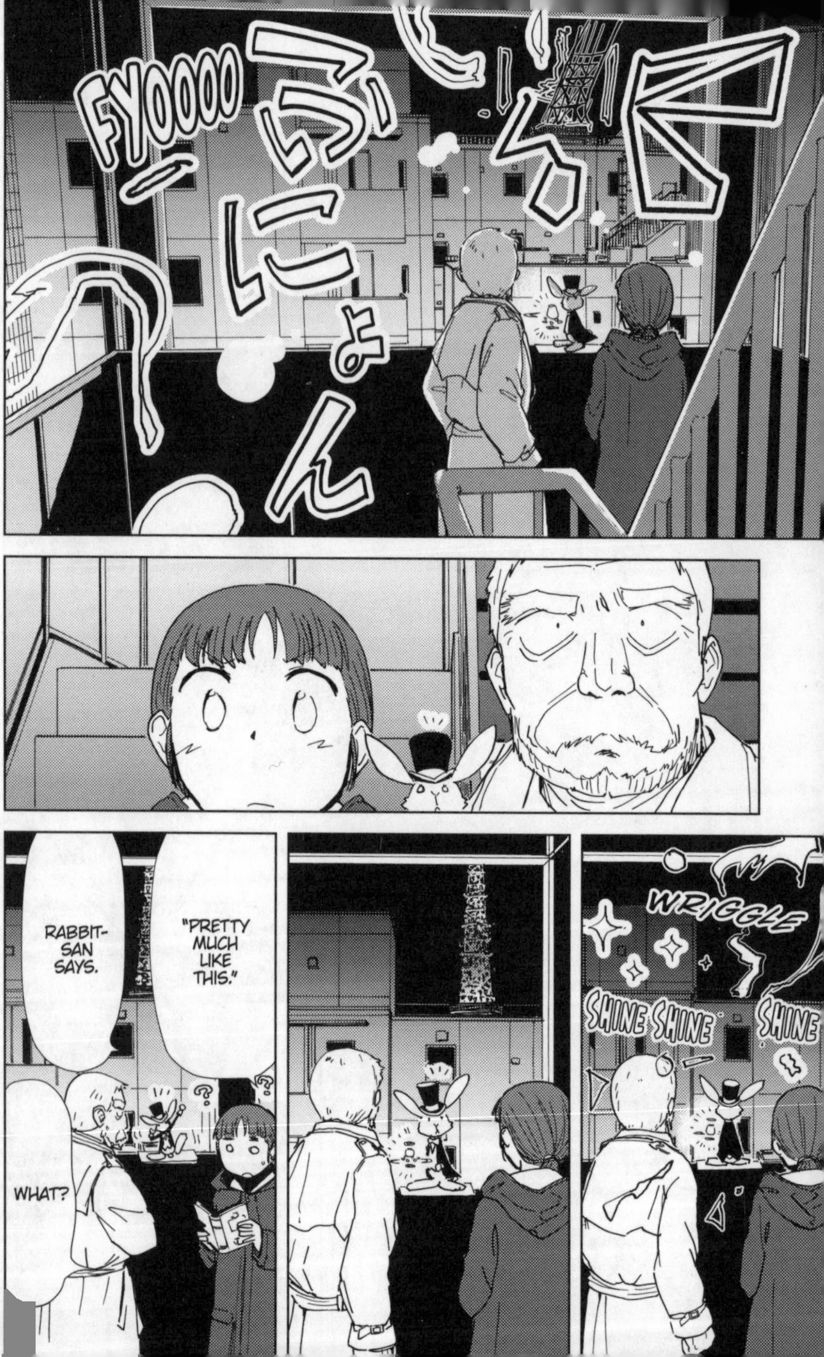

FYOOOO
ふにょん
WRIGGLE
SHINE SHINE
SHINE
"PRETTY MUCH LIKE THIS."
RABBIT-SAN SAYS.
WHAT?

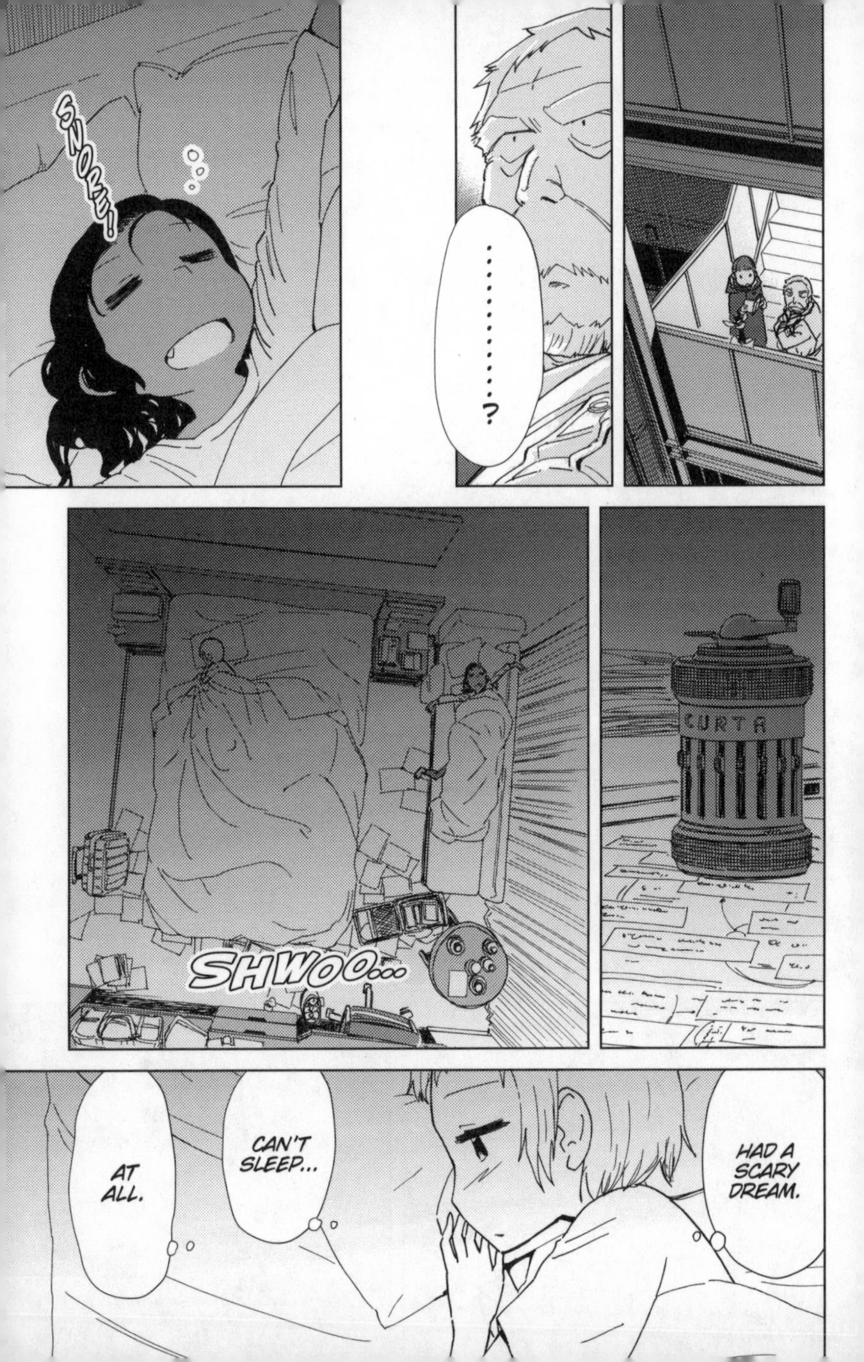

..........?
SNORE!
CURTA
SHWOO...
HAD A SCARY DREAM.
CAN'T SLEEP...
AT ALL.

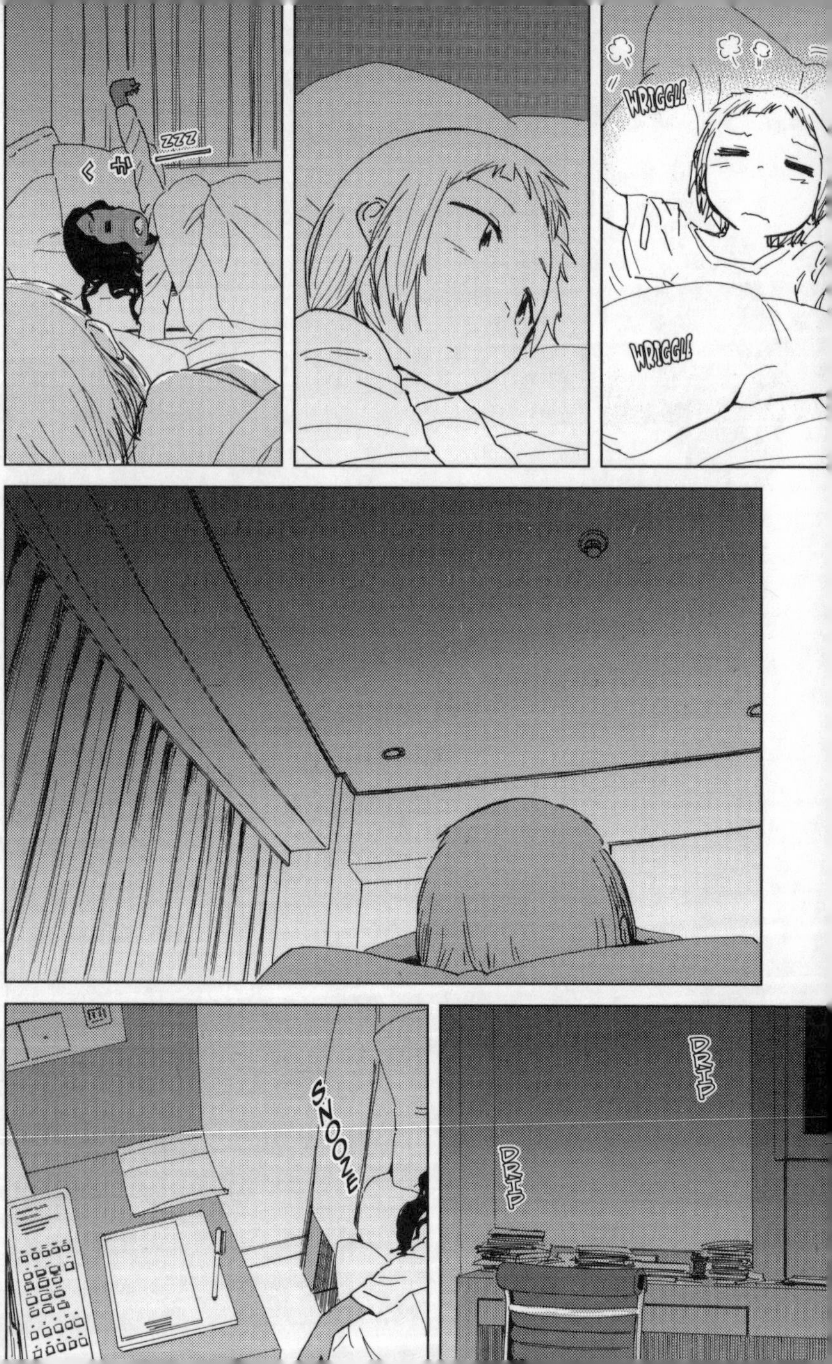
WRIGGLE
WRIGGLE
ZZZ
くか
DRIP
DRIP
SNOOZE

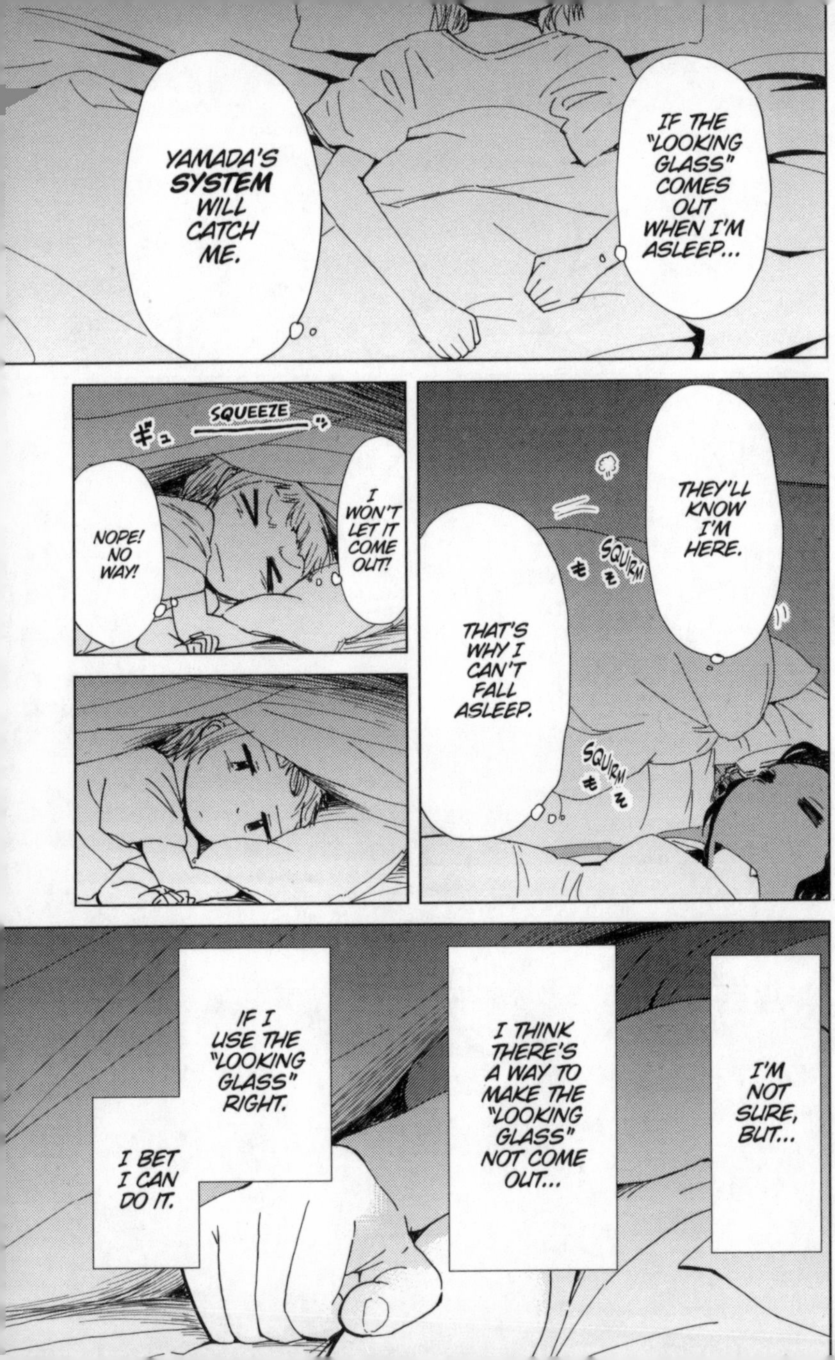
IF THE "LOOKING GLASS" COMES OUT WHEN I'M ASLEEP...
YAMADA'S SYSTEM WILL CATCH ME.
THEY'LL KNOW I'M HERE.
SQUIRM
もぞ
THAT'S WHY I CAN'T FALL ASLEEP.
SQUIRM
もぞ
SQUEEZE
ギュッ
I WON'T LET IT COME OUT!
NOPE! NO WAY!
I'M NOT SURE, BUT...
I THINK THERE'S A WAY TO MAKE THE "LOOKING GLASS" NOT COME OUT...
IF I USE THE "LOOKING GLASS" RIGHT.
I BET I CAN DO IT.

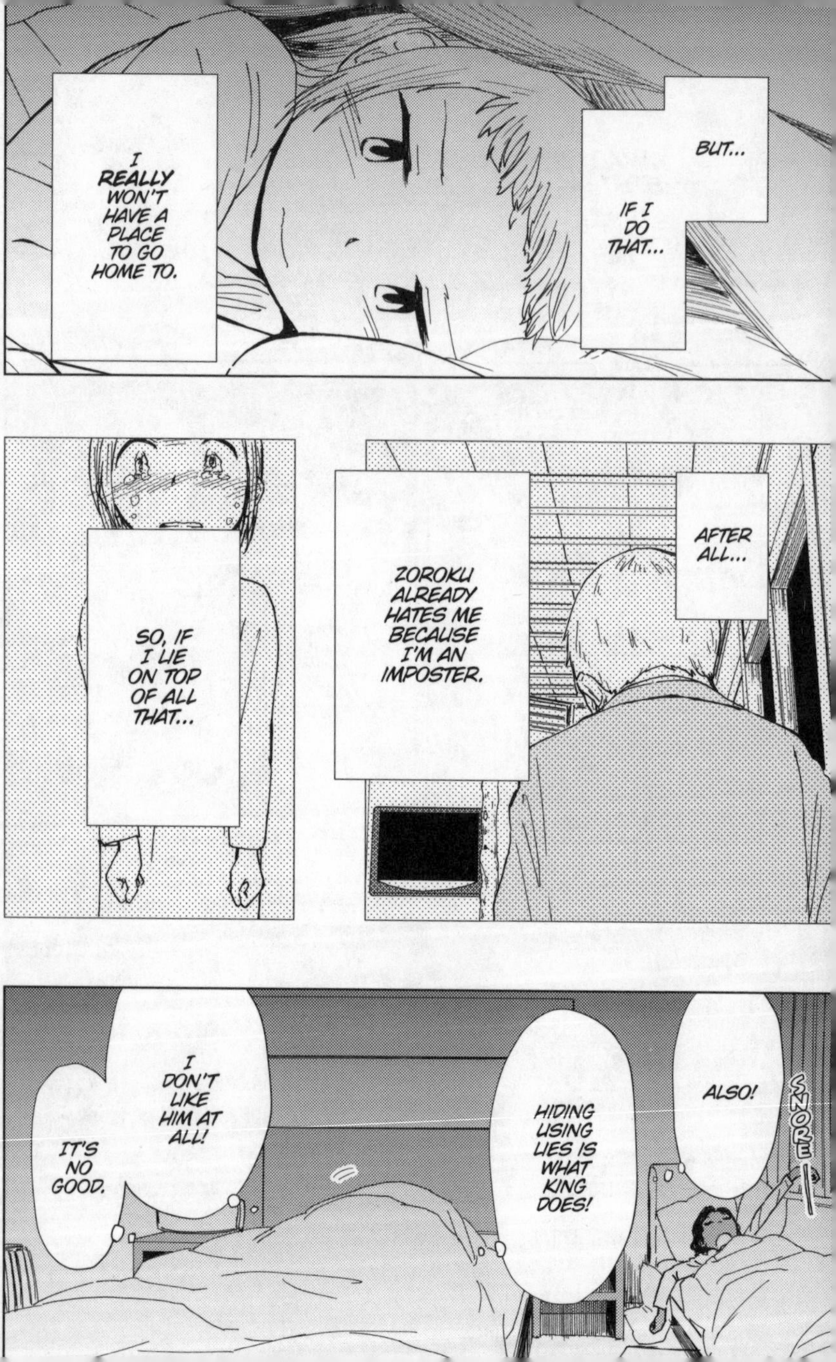
BUT...
IF I DO THAT...
I REALLY WON'T HAVE A PLACE TO GO HOME TO.
AFTER ALL...
ZOROKU ALREADY HATES ME BECAUSE I'M AN IMPOSTER.
SO, IF I LIE ON TOP OF ALL THAT...
SNORE
ALSO!
HIDING USING LIES IS WHAT KING DOES!
I DON'T LIKE HIM AT ALL!
IT'S NO GOOD.

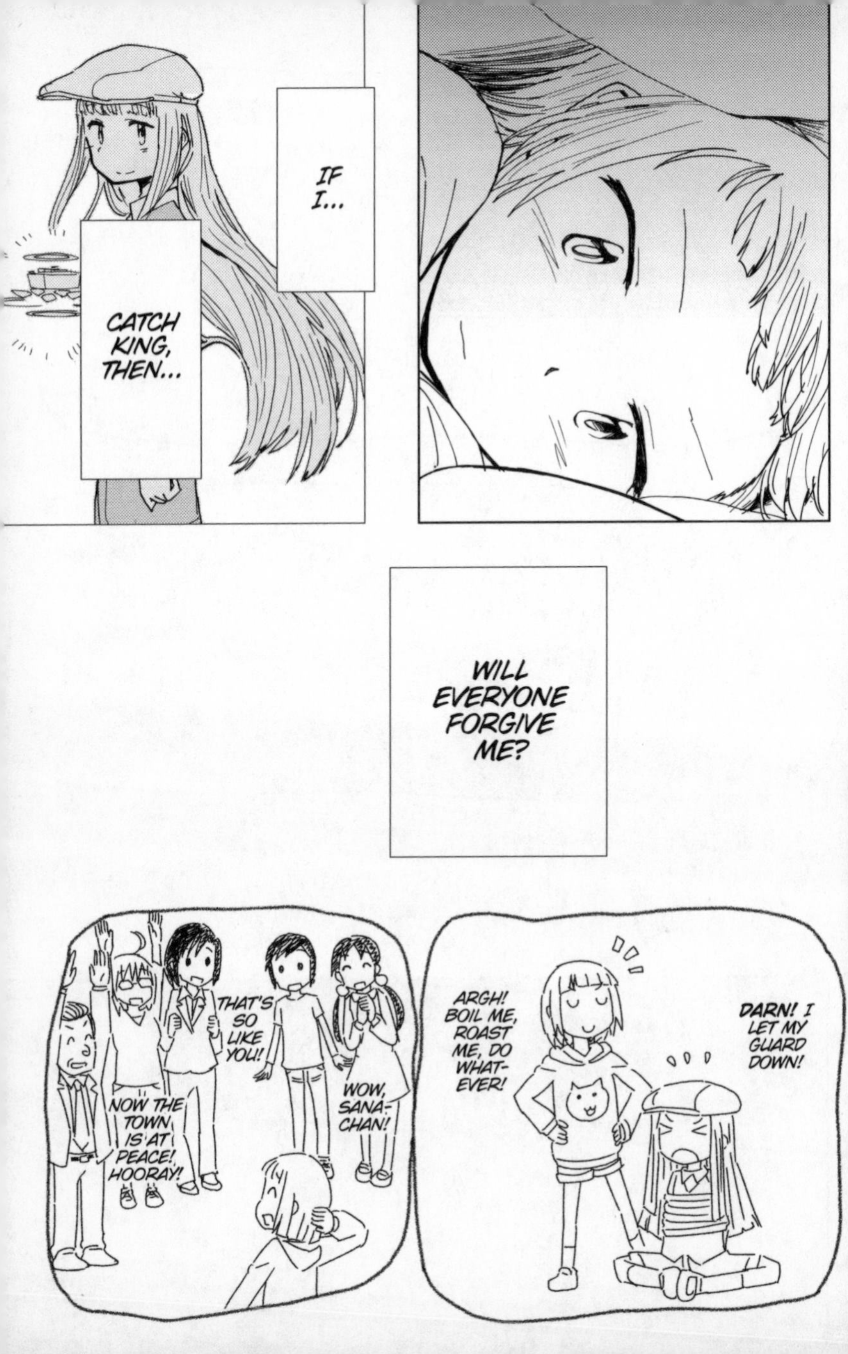
IF I...
CATCH KING, THEN...
WILL EVERYONE FORGIVE ME?
DARN! I LET MY GUARD DOWN!
ARGH! BOIL ME, ROAST ME, DO WHAT-EVER!
THAT'S SO LIKE YOU!
WOW, SANA-CHAN!
NOW THE TOWN IS AT PEACE! HOORAY!

SANA, YOU DID GOOD.
I'M VERY PROUD OF YOU.
ZOROKU!
SNOOZE
SNOOZE
SHAAAAAA

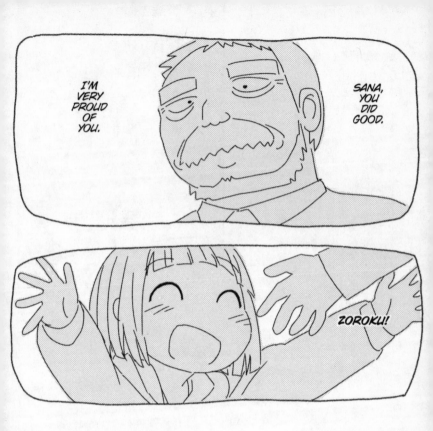

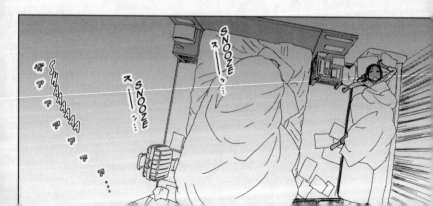

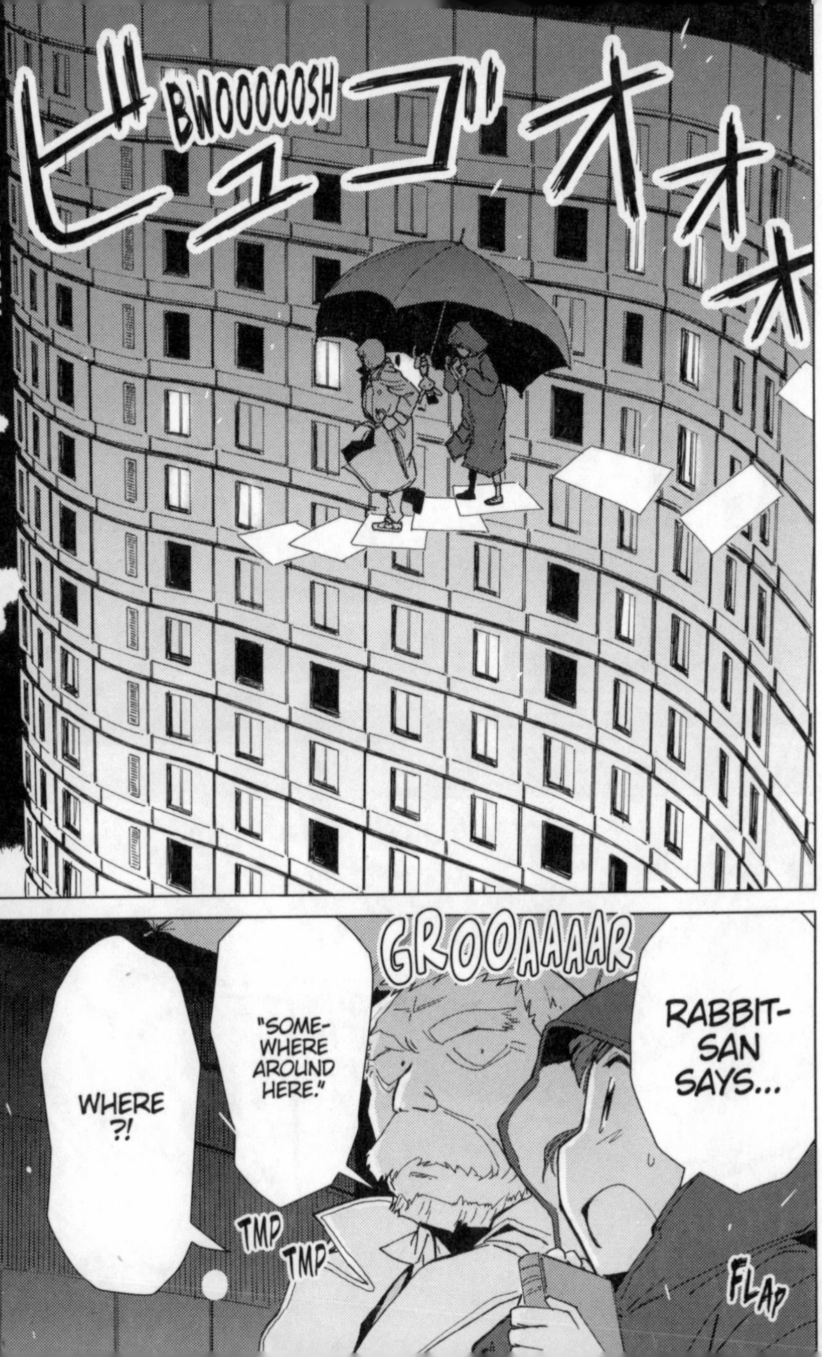
ビュゴオオオ
BWOOOOOSH
GROOAAAAR
RABBIT-SAN SAYS...
"SOME-WHERE AROUND HERE."
WHERE?!
FLAP
TMP
TMP

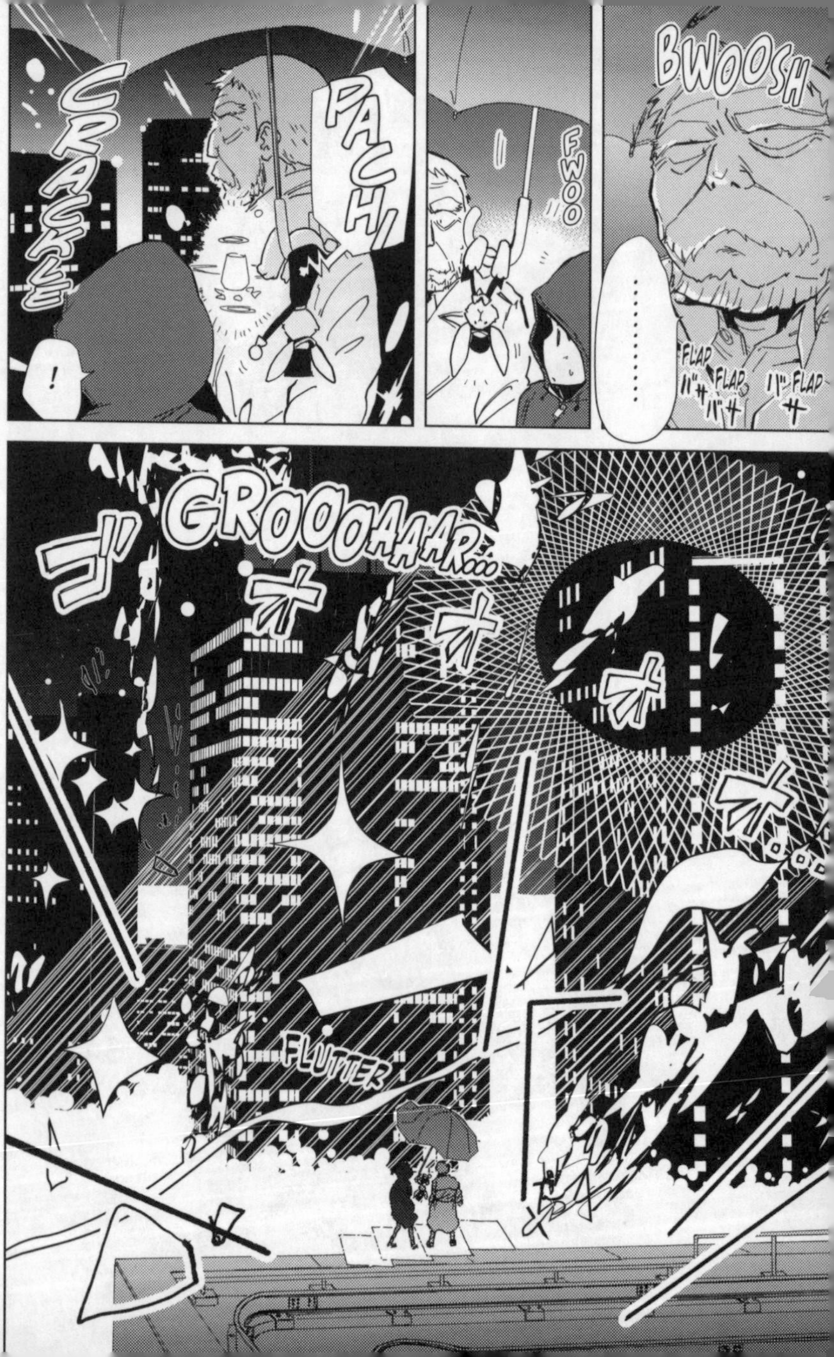
BWOOSH
......
FLAP
バサ
FLAP
バサ
FLAP
バサ
FWOO
PACHI
CRACKLE
!
GROOOAAAAR...
ゴ
オ
オ
オ
オ...
FLUTTER

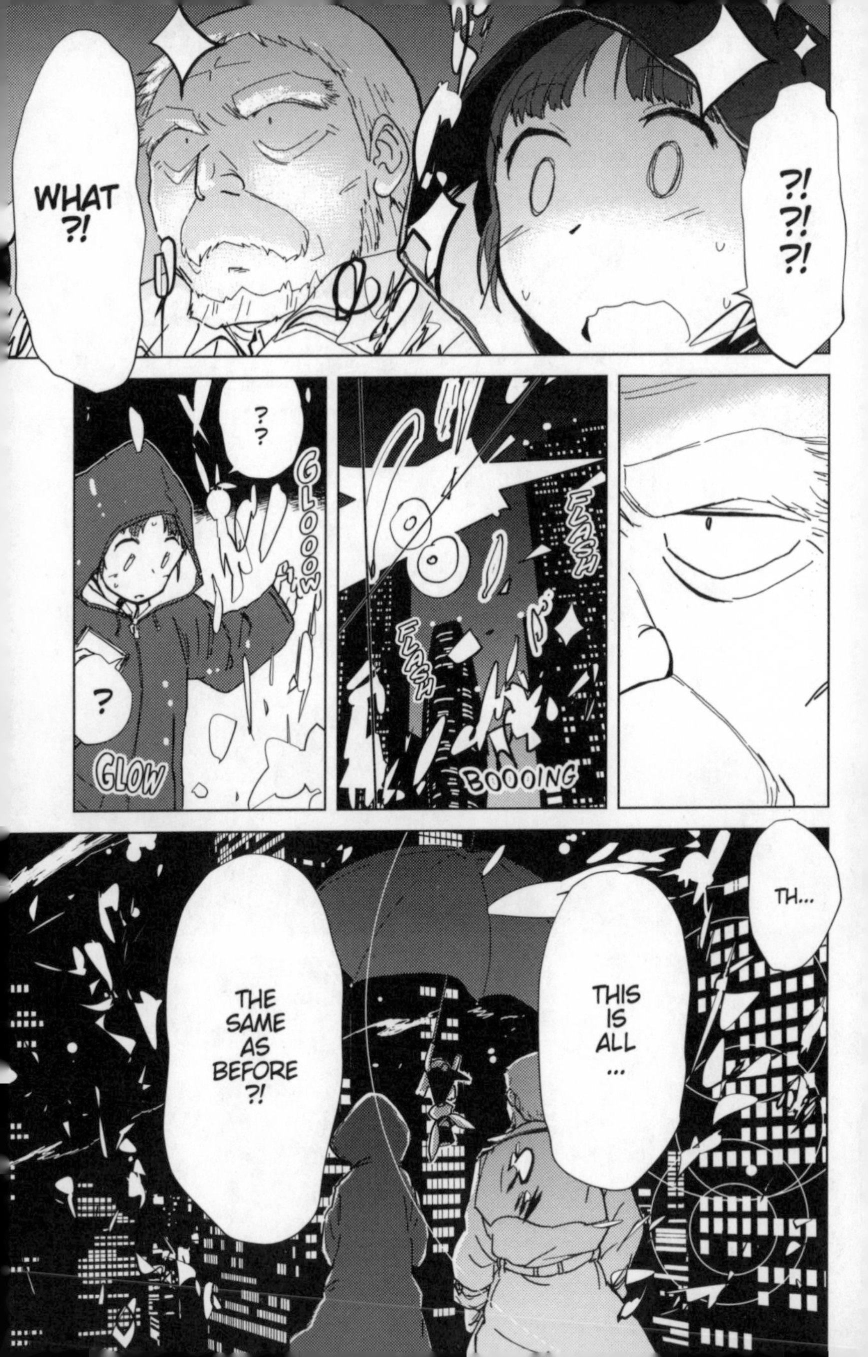
?! ?! ?!
WHAT ?!
FLASH
FLASH
BOOOING
??
GLOOOOW
?
GLOW
TH...
THIS IS ALL ...
THE SAME AS BEFORE ?!

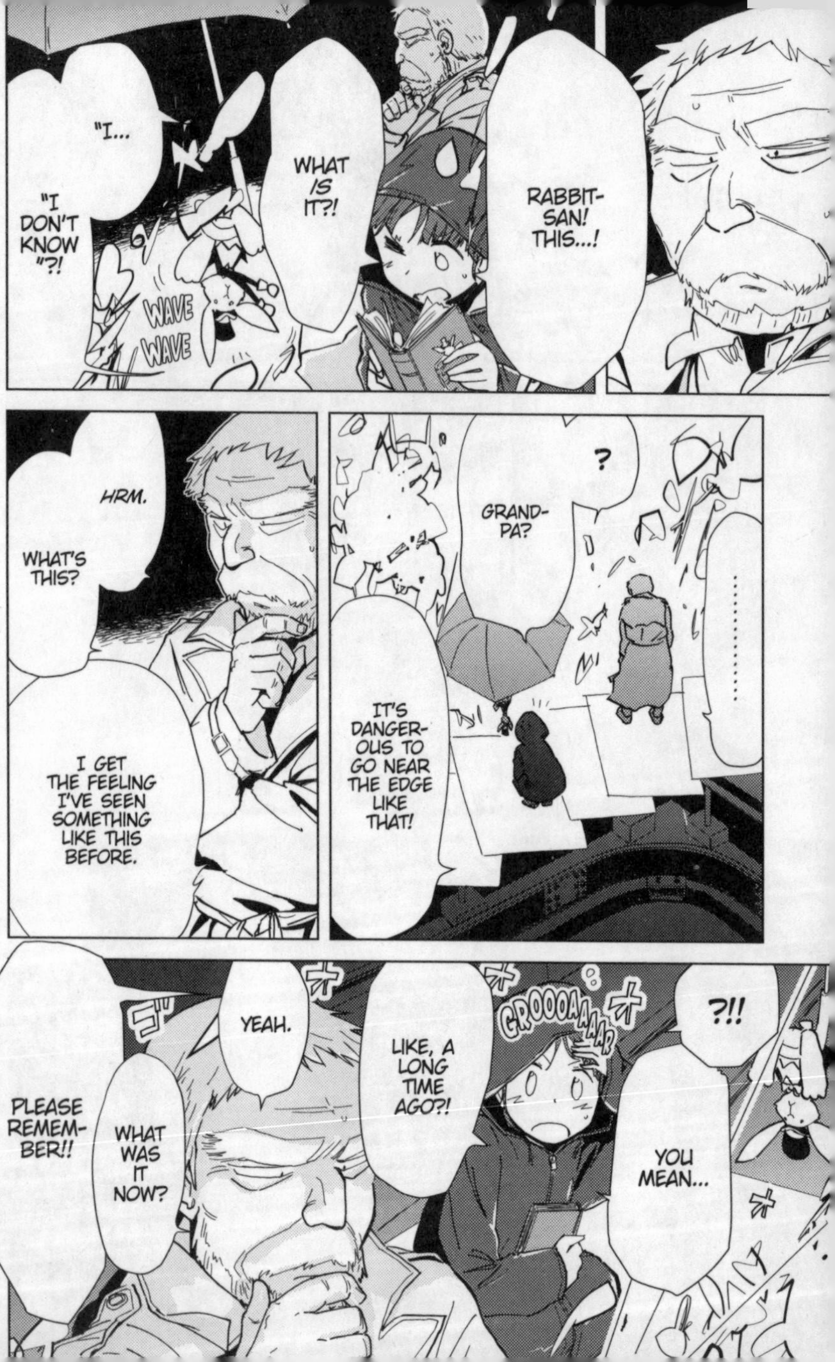
RABBIT-SAN! THIS...!
WHAT IS IT?!
"I...
"I DON'T KNOW"?!
WAVE WAVE
......
?
GRAND-PA?
IT'S DANGER-OUS TO GO NEAR THE EDGE LIKE THAT!
HRM.
WHAT'S THIS?
I GET THE FEELING I'VE SEEN SOMETHING LIKE THIS BEFORE.
?!!
GROOOAAAAR
YOU MEAN...
LIKE, A LONG TIME AGO?!
YEAH.
WHAT WAS IT NOW?
PLEASE REMEM-BER!!

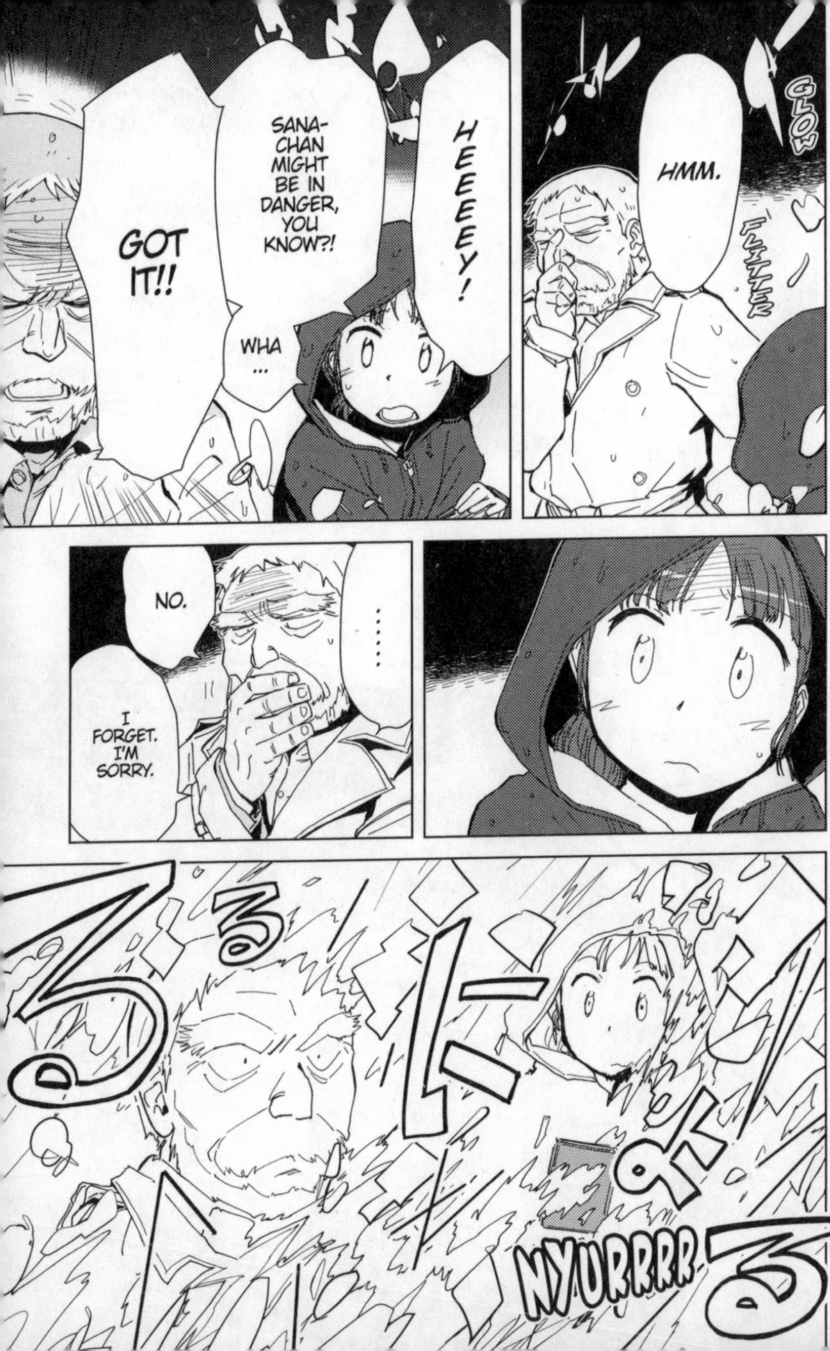
GLOW
HMM.
FLITTER
HEEEEEY!
SANA-CHAN MIGHT BE IN DANGER, YOU KNOW?!
GOT IT!!
WHA ...
......
NO.
I FORGET. I'M SORRY.
NYURRRR

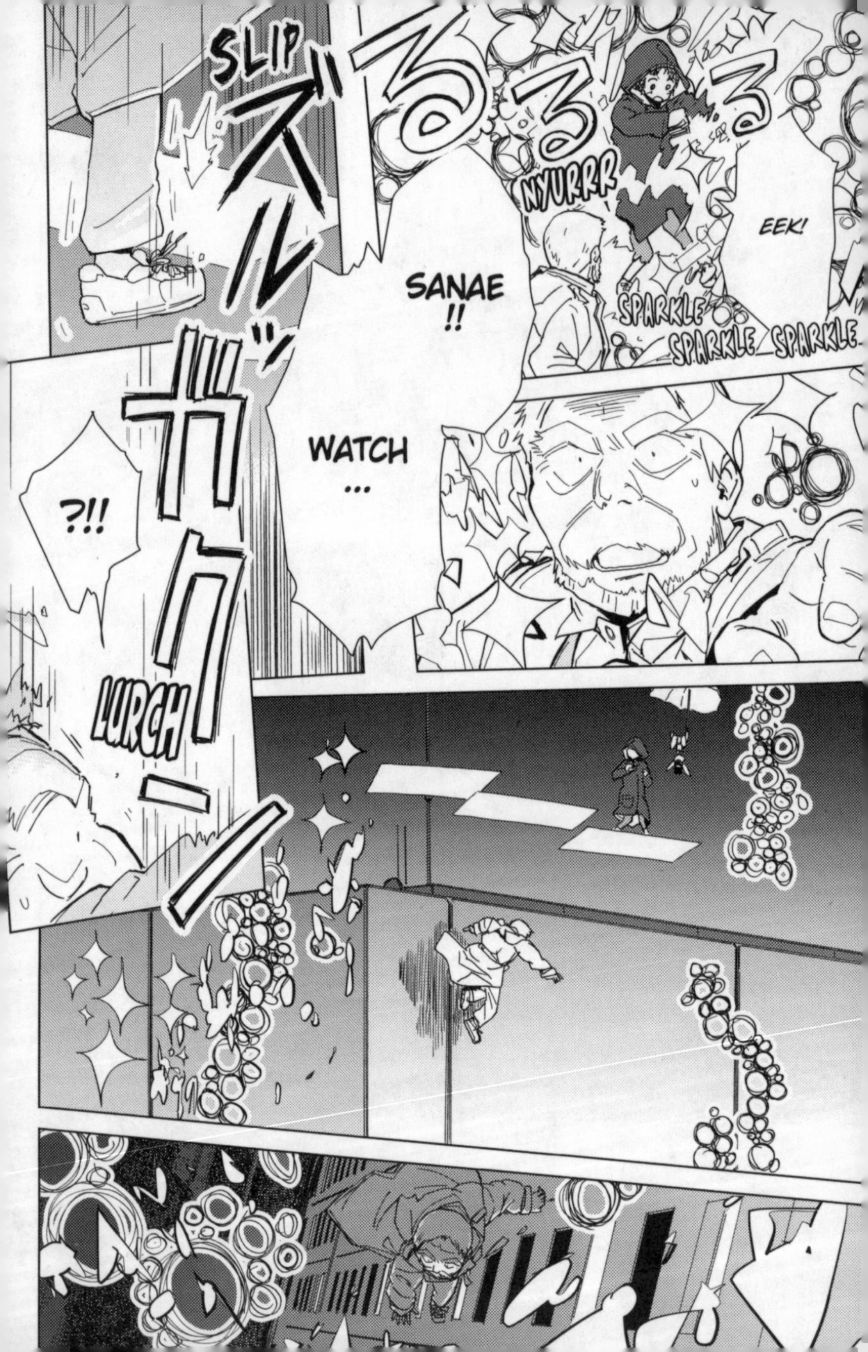
EEK!
NYURRR
SPARKLE SPARKLE SPARKLE
SANAE !!
SLIP
WATCH ...
?!!
LURCH

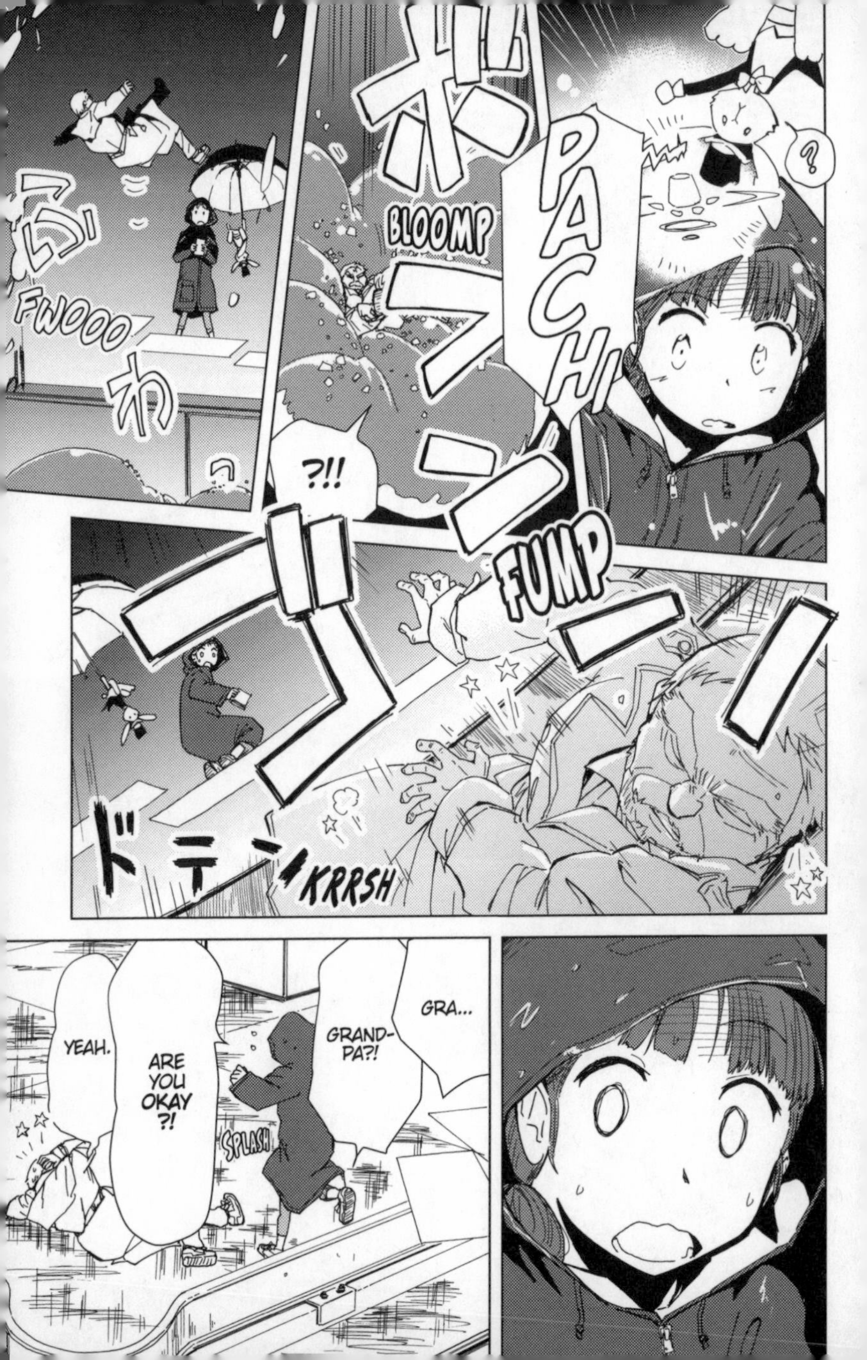
?
PACHI
BLOOMP
?!!
ふわっ
FWOOO
FUMP
ドテーン
KRRSH
GRA...
GRAND-PA?!
SPLASH
ARE YOU OKAY?!
YEAH.

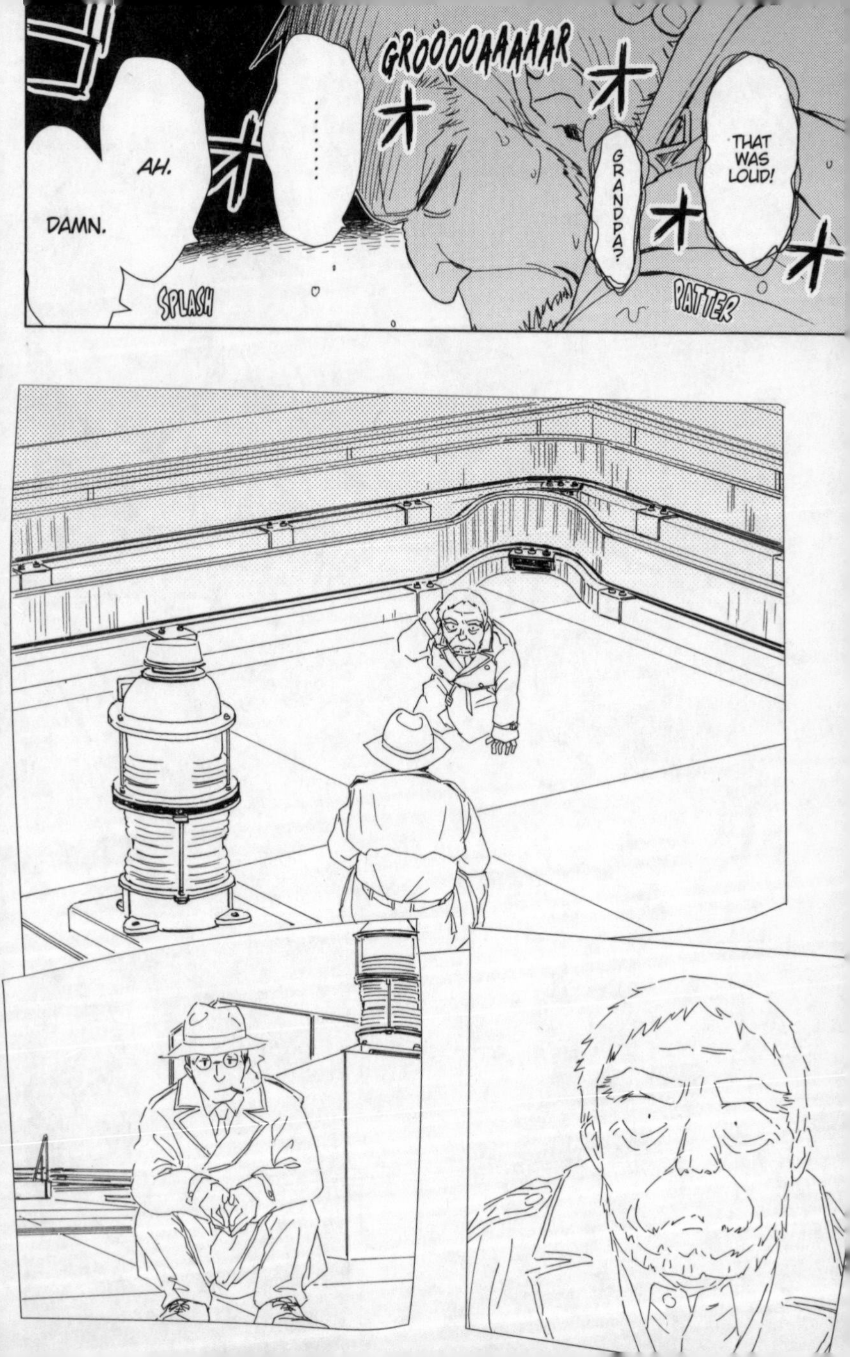
THAT WAS LOUD!
GRANDPA?
GROOOOAAAAR
PATTER
......
AH.
DAMN.
SPLASH

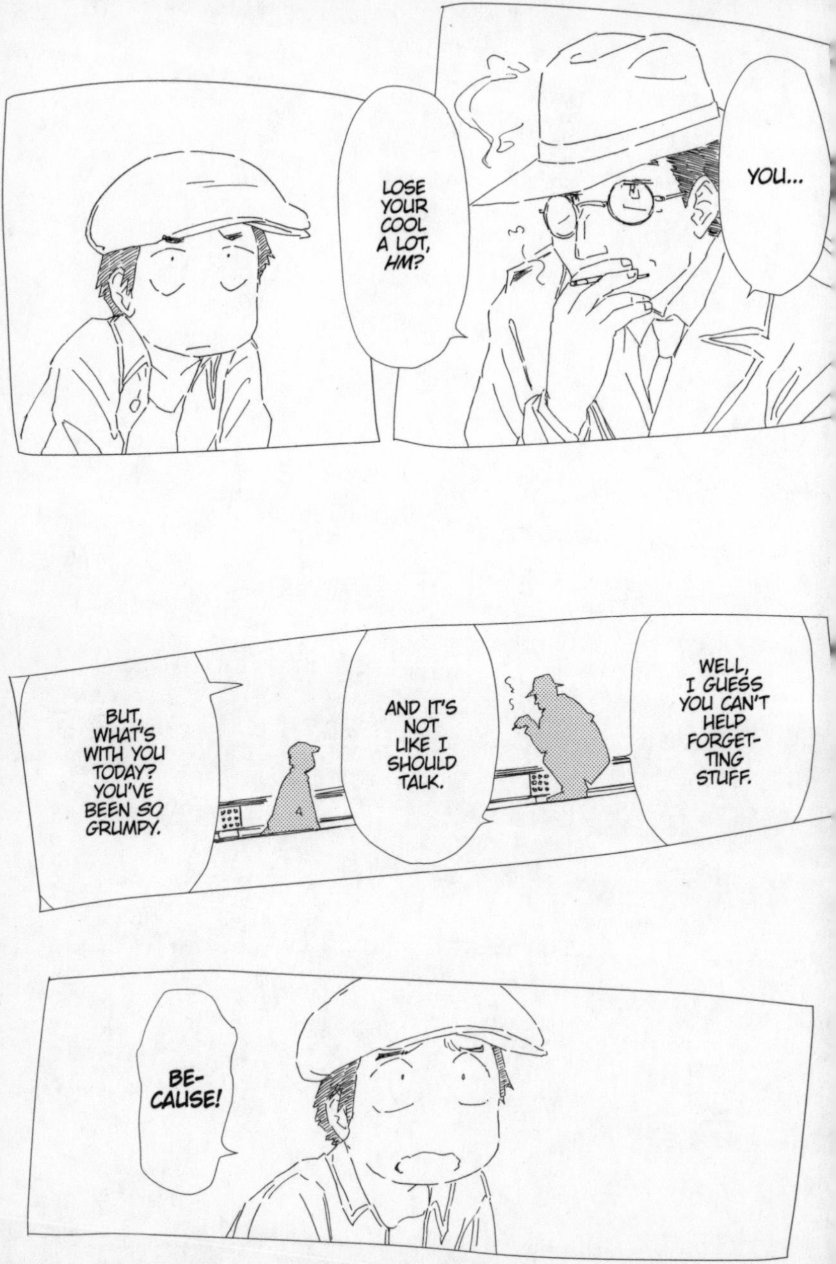
YOU...
LOSE YOUR COOL A LOT, HM?
WELL, I GUESS YOU CAN'T HELP FORGET-TING STUFF.
AND IT'S NOT LIKE I SHOULD TALK.
BUT, WHAT'S WITH YOU TODAY? YOU'VE BEEN SO GRUMPY.
BE-CAUSE!

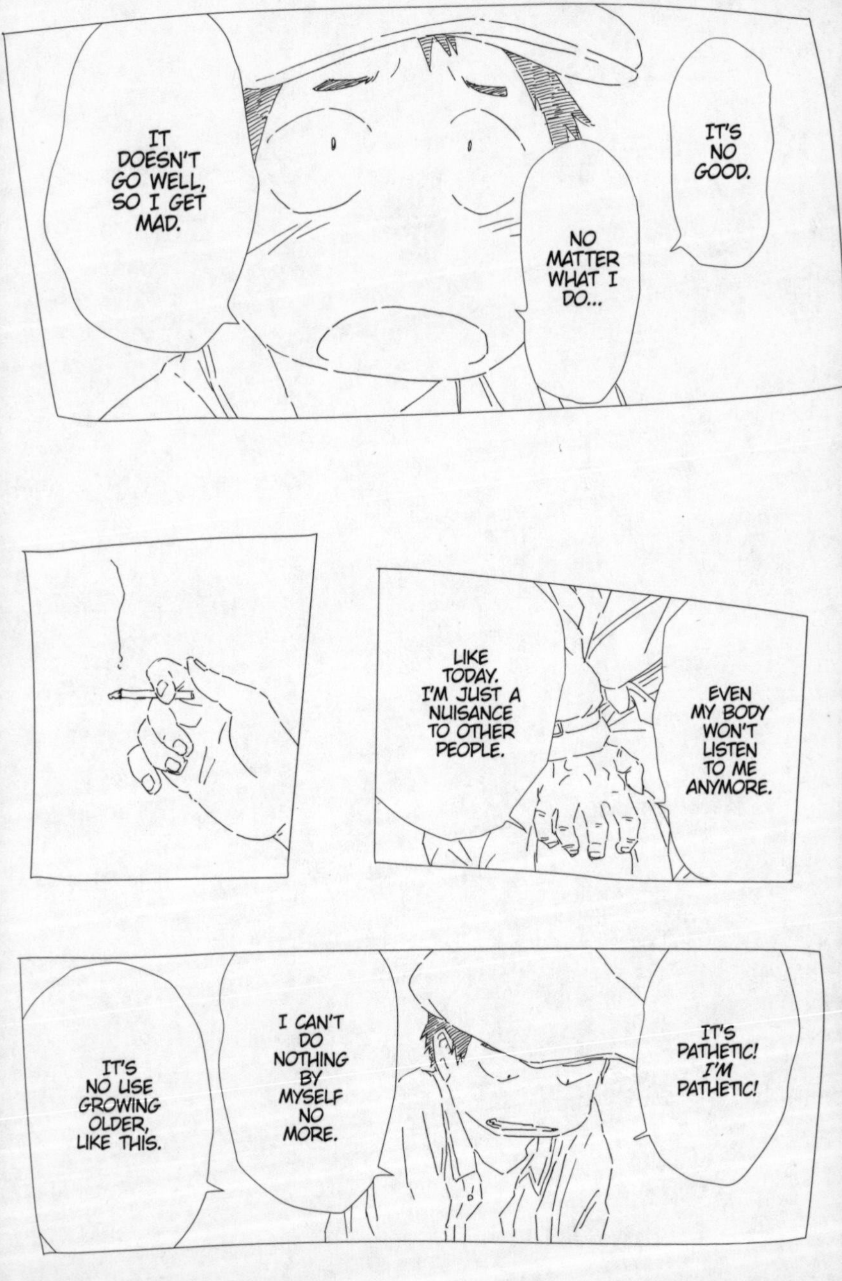
IT'S NO GOOD.
NO MATTER WHAT I DO...
IT DOESN'T GO WELL, SO I GET MAD.
EVEN MY BODY WON'T LISTEN TO ME ANYMORE.
LIKE TODAY. I'M JUST A NUISANCE TO OTHER PEOPLE.
IT'S PATHETIC! *I'M* PATHETIC!
I CAN'T DO NOTHING BY MYSELF NO MORE.
IT'S NO USE GROWING OLDER, LIKE THIS.

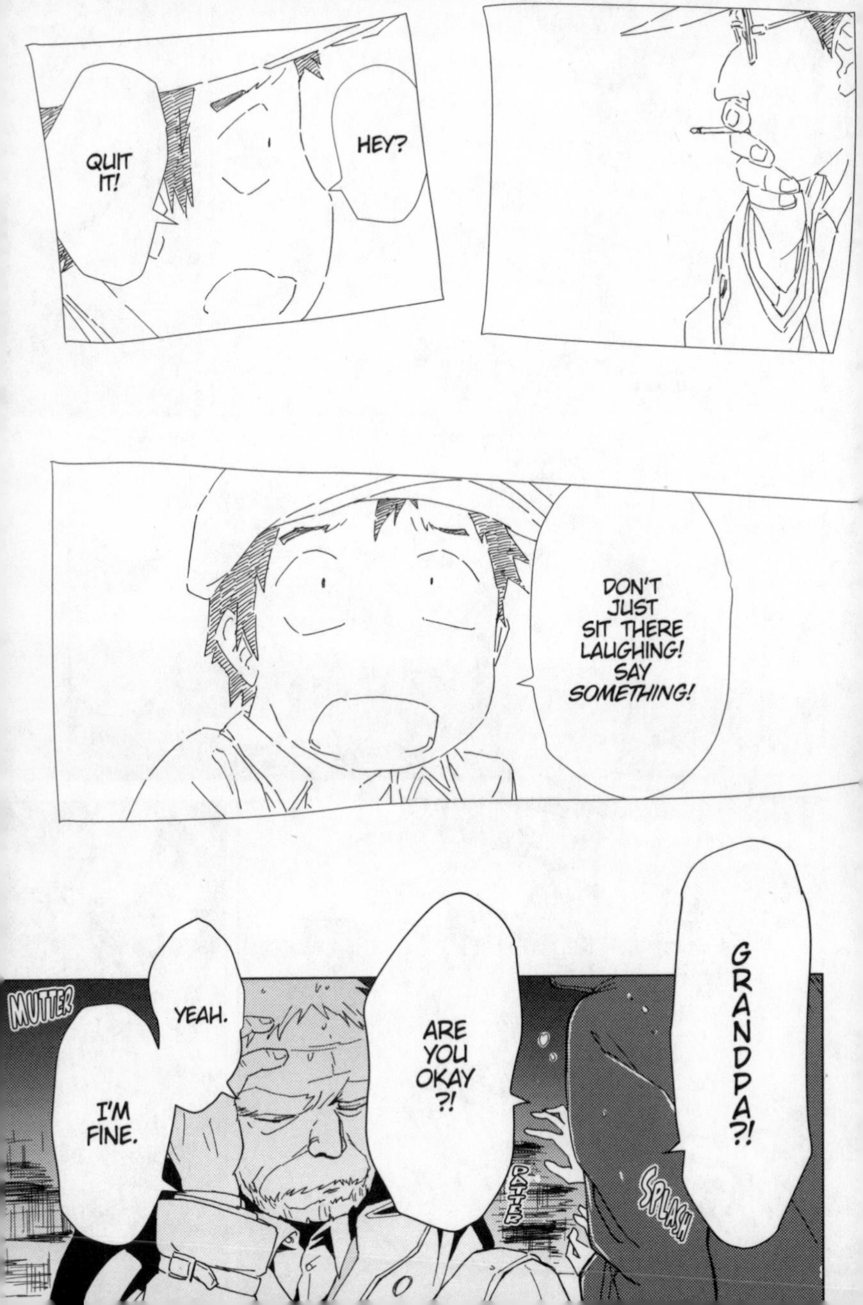
HEY?
QUIT IT!
DON'T JUST SIT THERE LAUGHING! SAY SOMETHING!
GRANDPA?!
SPLASH
ARE YOU OKAY?!
PATTER
YEAH.
I'M FINE.
MUTTER

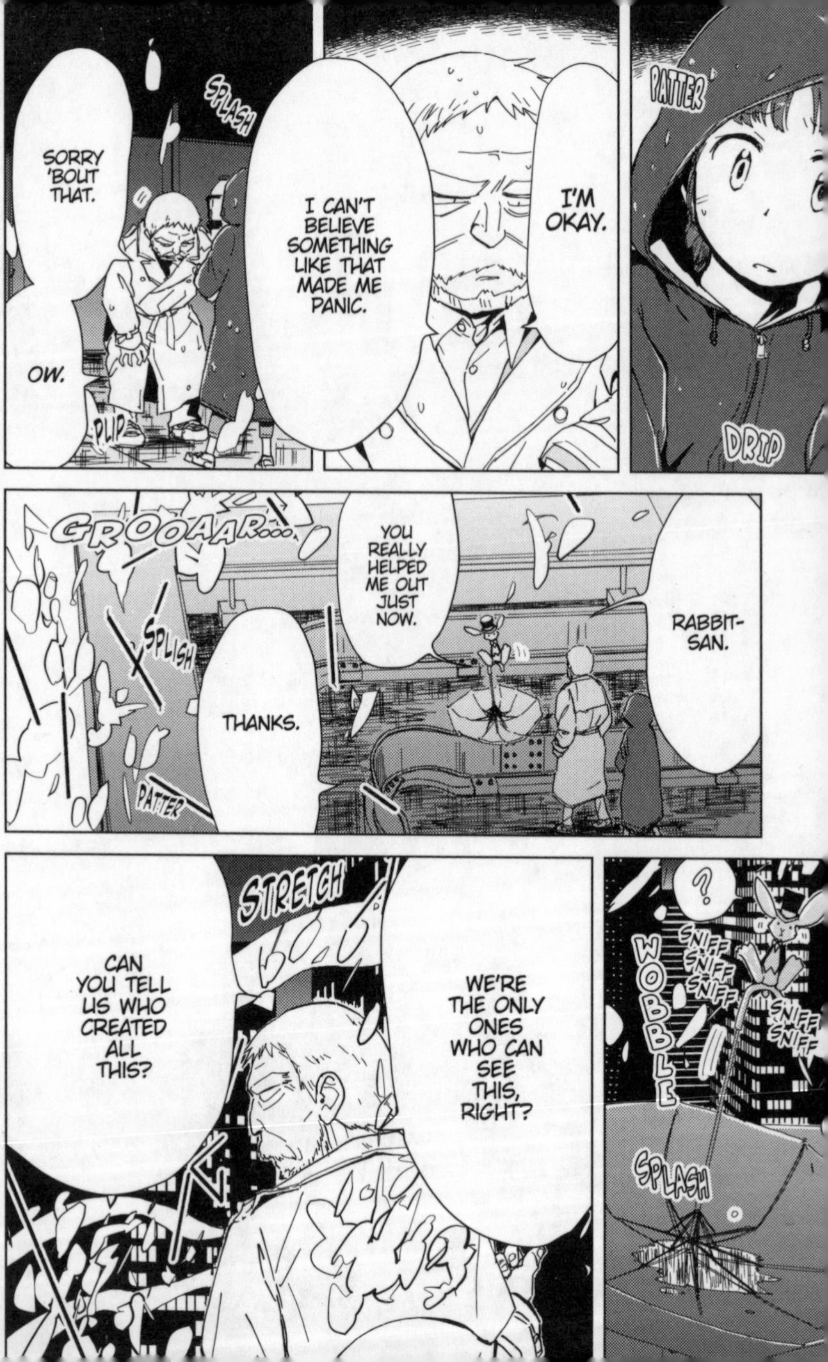
PATTER
DRIP
I'M OKAY.
I CAN'T BELIEVE SOMETHING LIKE THAT MADE ME PANIC.
SPLASH
SORRY 'BOUT THAT.
OW.
PLIP
RABBIT-SAN.
YOU REALLY HELPED ME OUT JUST NOW.
THANKS.
GROOAAR...
SPLISH
PATTER
?
SNIFF SNIFF SNIFF
SNIFF SNIFF
WOBBLE
SPLASH
STRETCH
WE'RE THE ONLY ONES WHO CAN SEE THIS, RIGHT?
CAN YOU TELL US WHO CREATED ALL THIS?

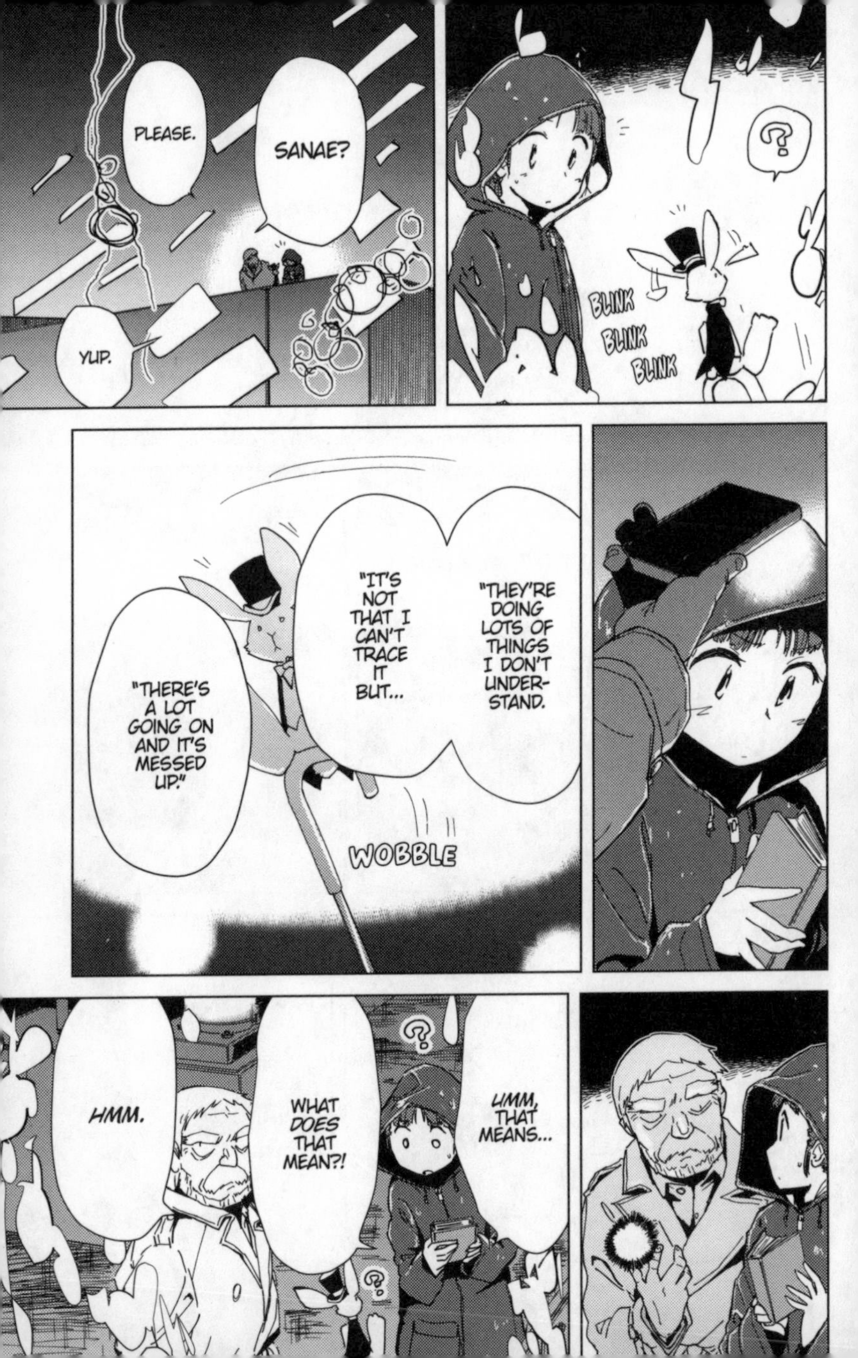
?
BLINK
BLINK
BLINK
SANAE?
PLEASE.
YUP.
"THEY'RE DOING LOTS OF THINGS I DON'T UNDER-STAND.
"IT'S NOT THAT I CAN'T TRACE IT BUT...
"THERE'S A LOT GOING ON AND IT'S MESSED UP."
WOBBLE
UMM, THAT MEANS...
?
WHAT DOES THAT MEAN?!
HMM.

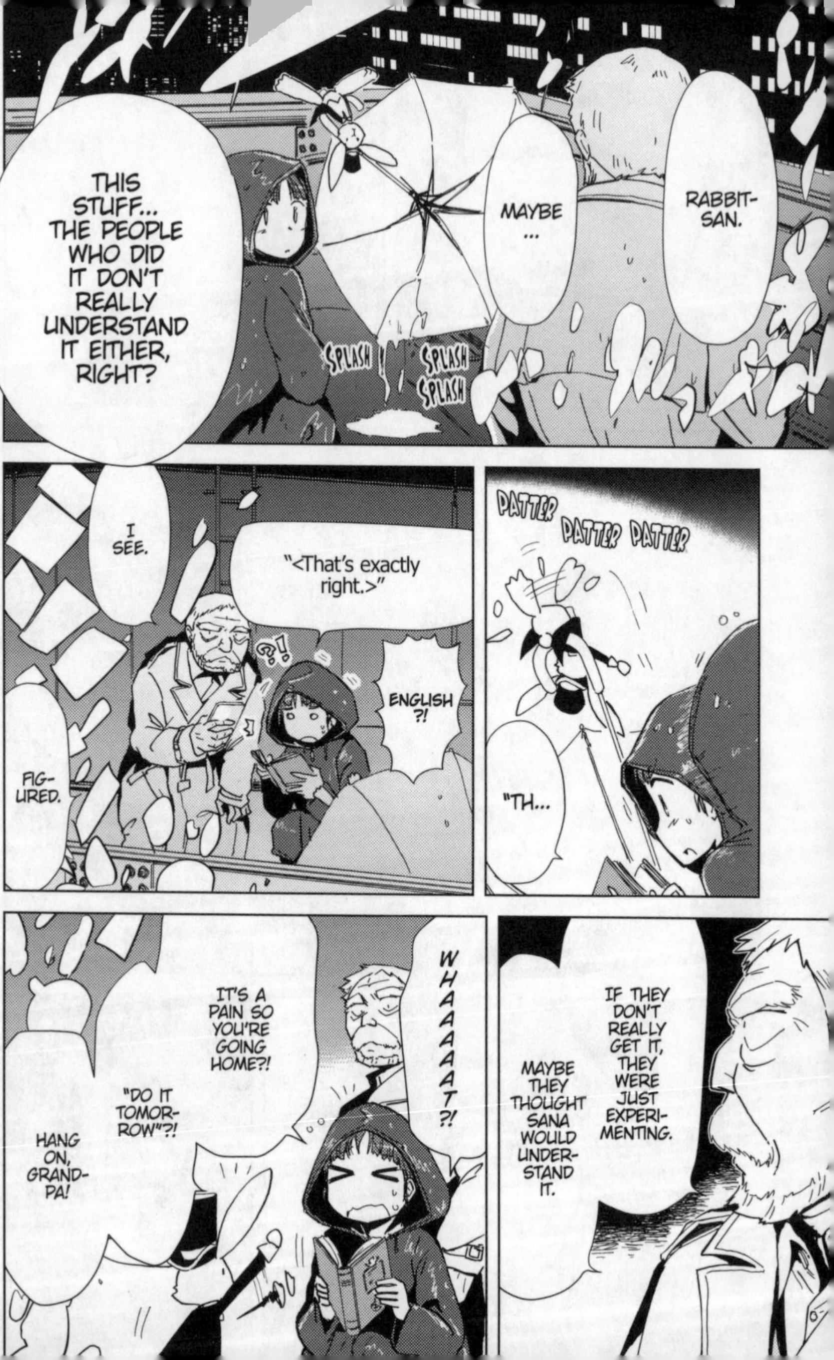
RABBIT-SAN.
MAYBE ...
SPLASH
SPLASH SPLASH
SPLASH
THIS STUFF... THE PEOPLE WHO DID IT DON'T REALLY UNDERSTAND IT EITHER, RIGHT?
PATTER PATTER PATTER
"TH...
ENGLISH?!
"<That's exactly right.>"
I SEE.
FIGURED.
IF THEY DON'T REALLY GET IT, THEY WERE JUST EXPERIMENTING.
MAYBE THEY THOUGHT SANA WOULD UNDERSTAND IT.
WHAAAAAAT?!
IT'S A PAIN SO YOU'RE GOING HOME?!
"DO IT TOMORROW"?!
HANG ON, GRANDPA!

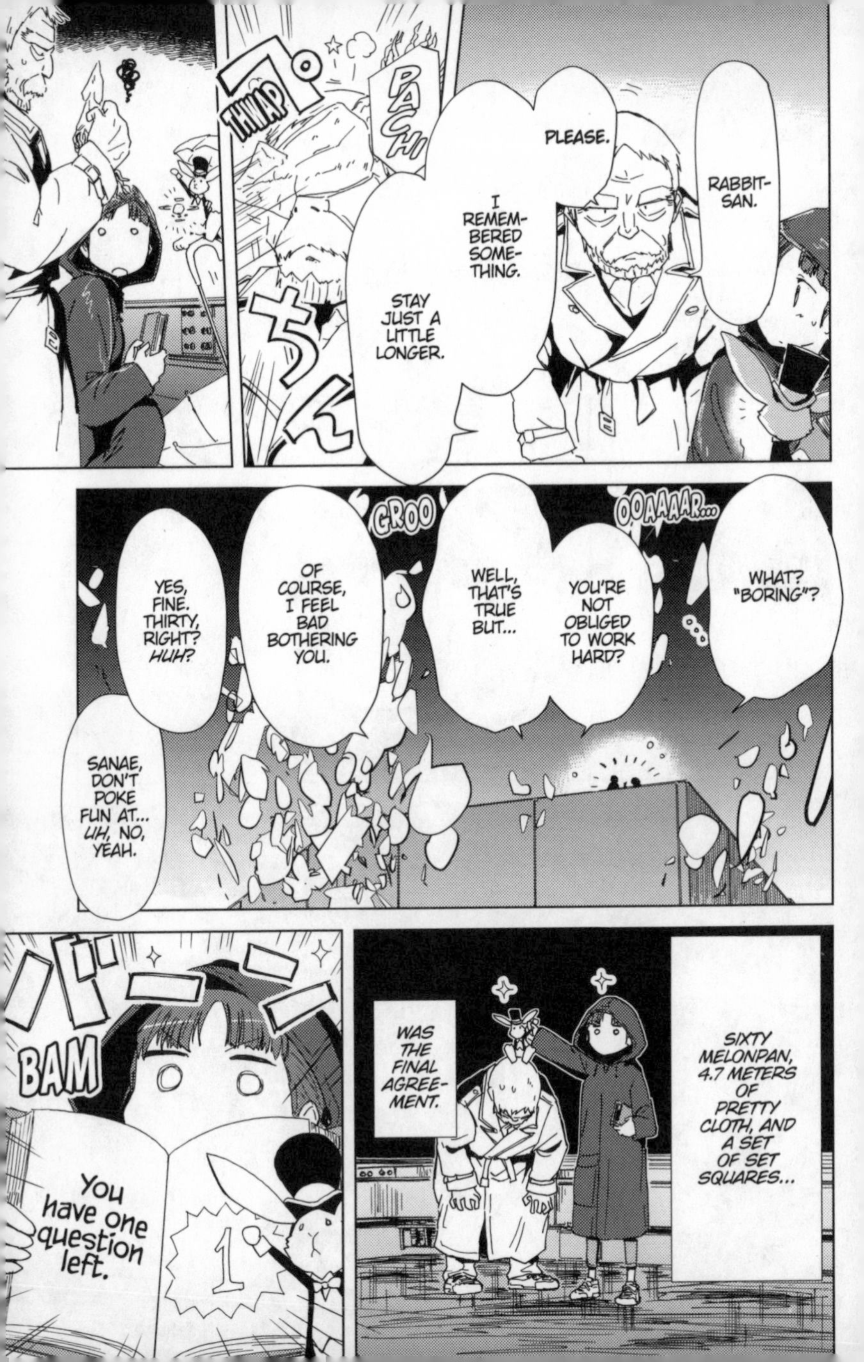
RABBIT-SAN.
PLEASE.
I REMEMBERED SOMETHING.
STAY JUST A LITTLE LONGER.
PACHI
THWAP
OOAAAAR...
WHAT? "BORING"?
YOU'RE NOT OBLIGED TO WORK HARD?
WELL, THAT'S TRUE BUT...
GROO
OF COURSE, I FEEL BAD BOTHERING YOU.
YES, FINE. THIRTY, RIGHT? HUH?
SANAE, DON'T POKE FUN AT... UH, NO, YEAH.
SIXTY MELONPAN, 4.7 METERS OF PRETTY CLOTH, AND A SET OF SET SQUARES...
WAS THE FINAL AGREEMENT.
BAM
You have one question left.
1

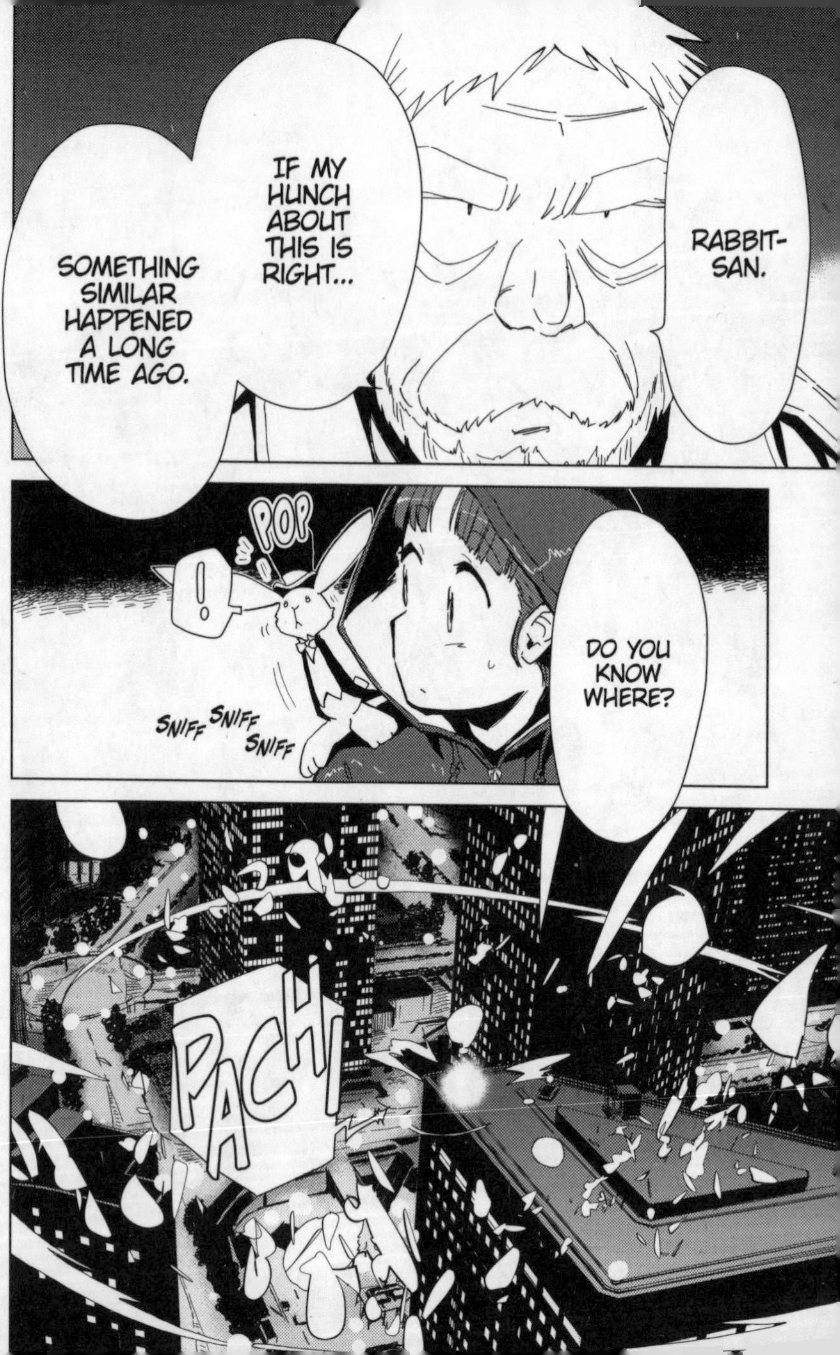
RABBIT-SAN.
IF MY HUNCH ABOUT THIS IS RIGHT...
SOMETHING SIMILAR HAPPENED A LONG TIME AGO.
DO YOU KNOW WHERE?
POP
!
SNIFF SNIFF SNIFF
PACHI

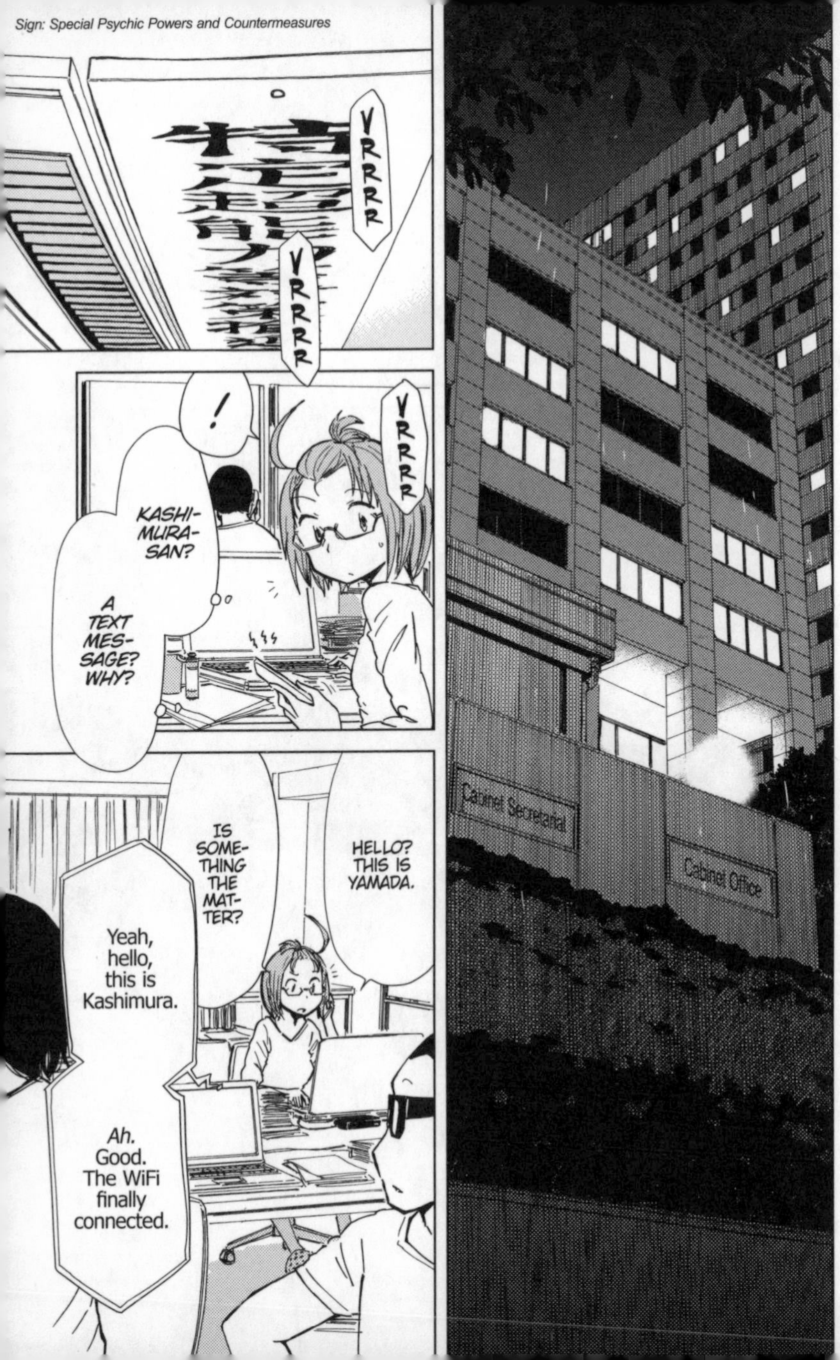
Cabinet Secretariat
Cabinet Office
Sign: Special Psychic Powers and Countermeasures
VRRRR
VRRRR
VRRRR
!
KASHIMURA-SAN?
A TEXT MESSAGE? WHY?
HELLO? THIS IS YAMADA.
IS SOMETHING THE MATTER?
Yeah, hello, this is Kashimura.
Ah. Good. The WiFi finally connected.

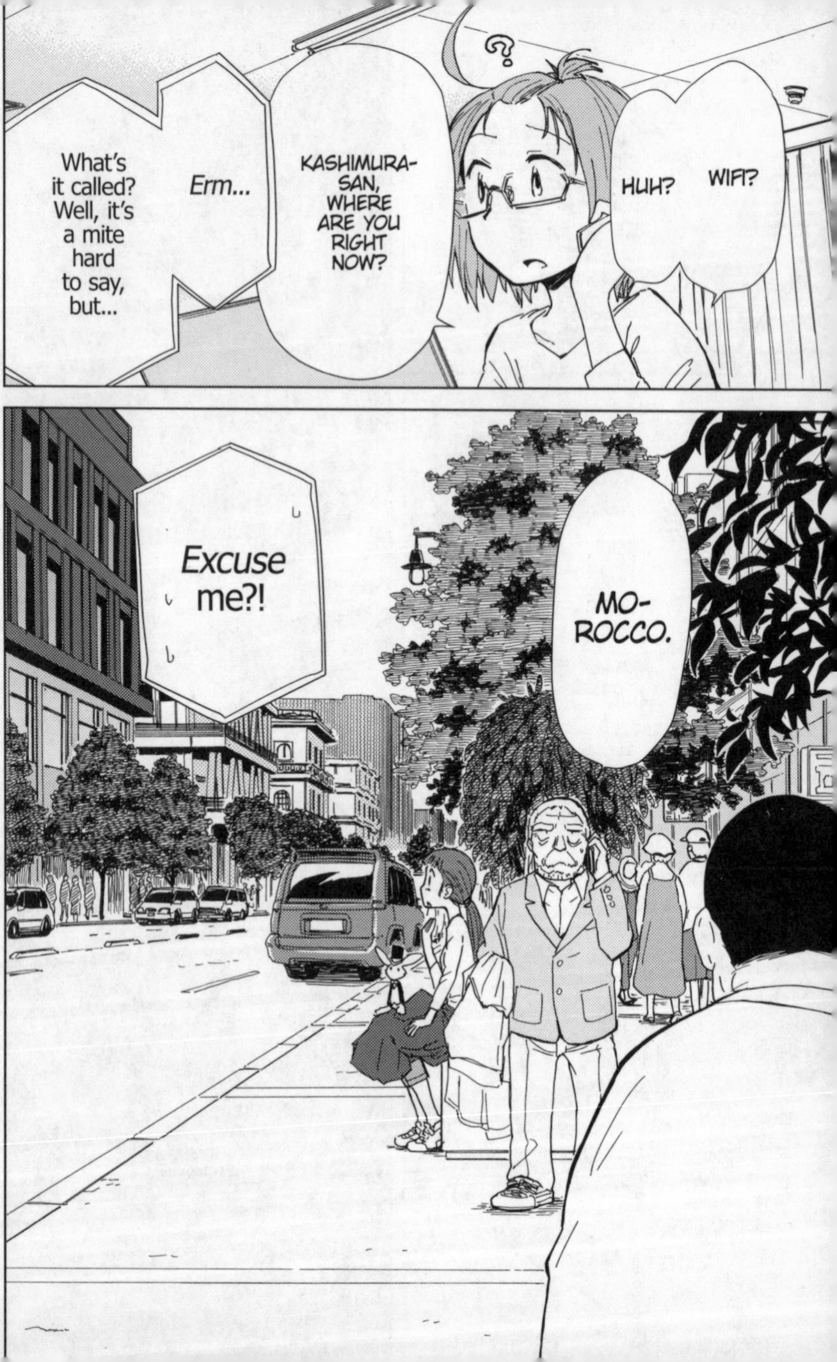
HUH? WIFI?
KASHIMURA-SAN, WHERE ARE YOU RIGHT NOW?
Erm...
What's it called? Well, it's a mite hard to say, but...
MO-ROCCO.
Excuse me?!

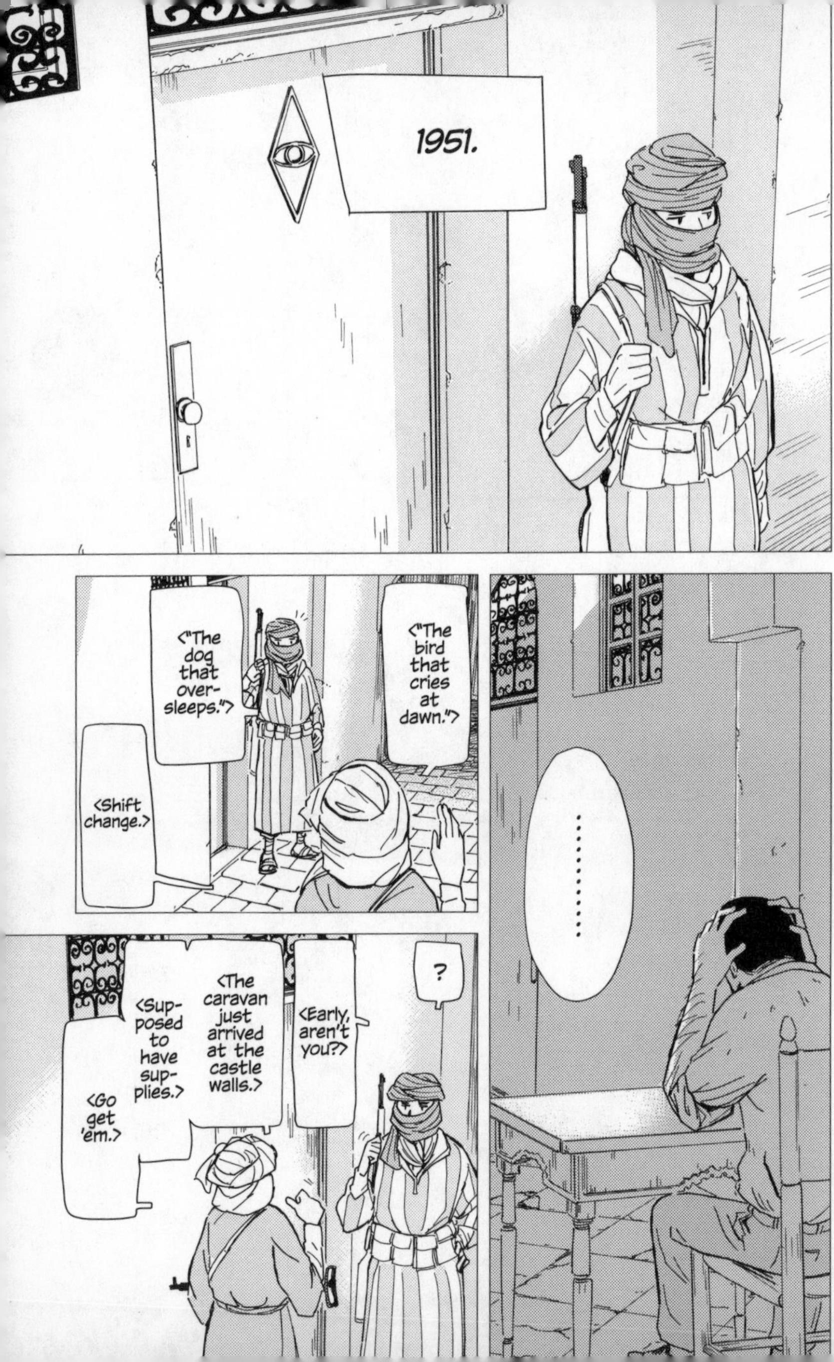
1951.
……
<"The bird that cries at dawn.">
<"The dog that oversleeps.">
<Shift change.>
?
<Early, aren't you?>
<The caravan just arrived at the castle walls.>
<Supposed to have supplies.>
<Go get 'em.>

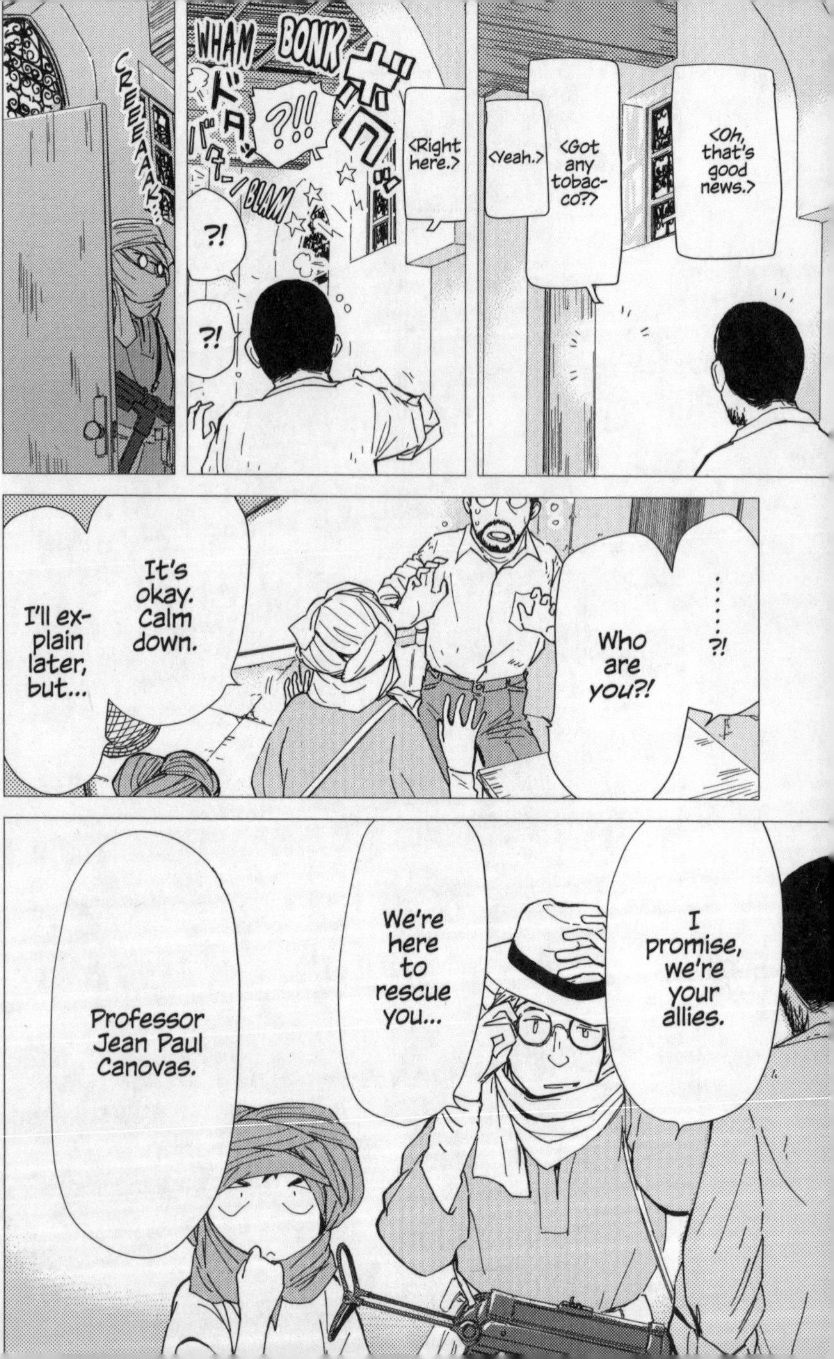
<Oh, that's good news.>
<Got any tobacco?>
<Yeah.>
<Right here.>
BONK
WHAM
?!!
BLAM
?!
?!
CREEEAAAK
......?!
Who are you?!
It's okay. Calm down.
I'll explain later, but...
I promise, we're your allies.
We're here to rescue you...
Professor Jean Paul Canovas.

Alice & Zoroku

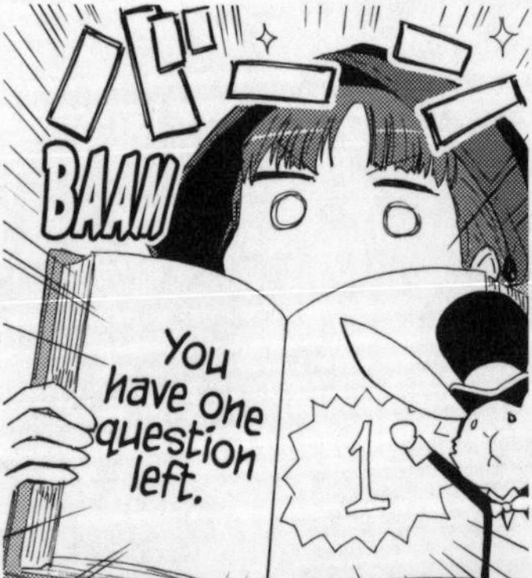
BAAM
You have one question left.
1

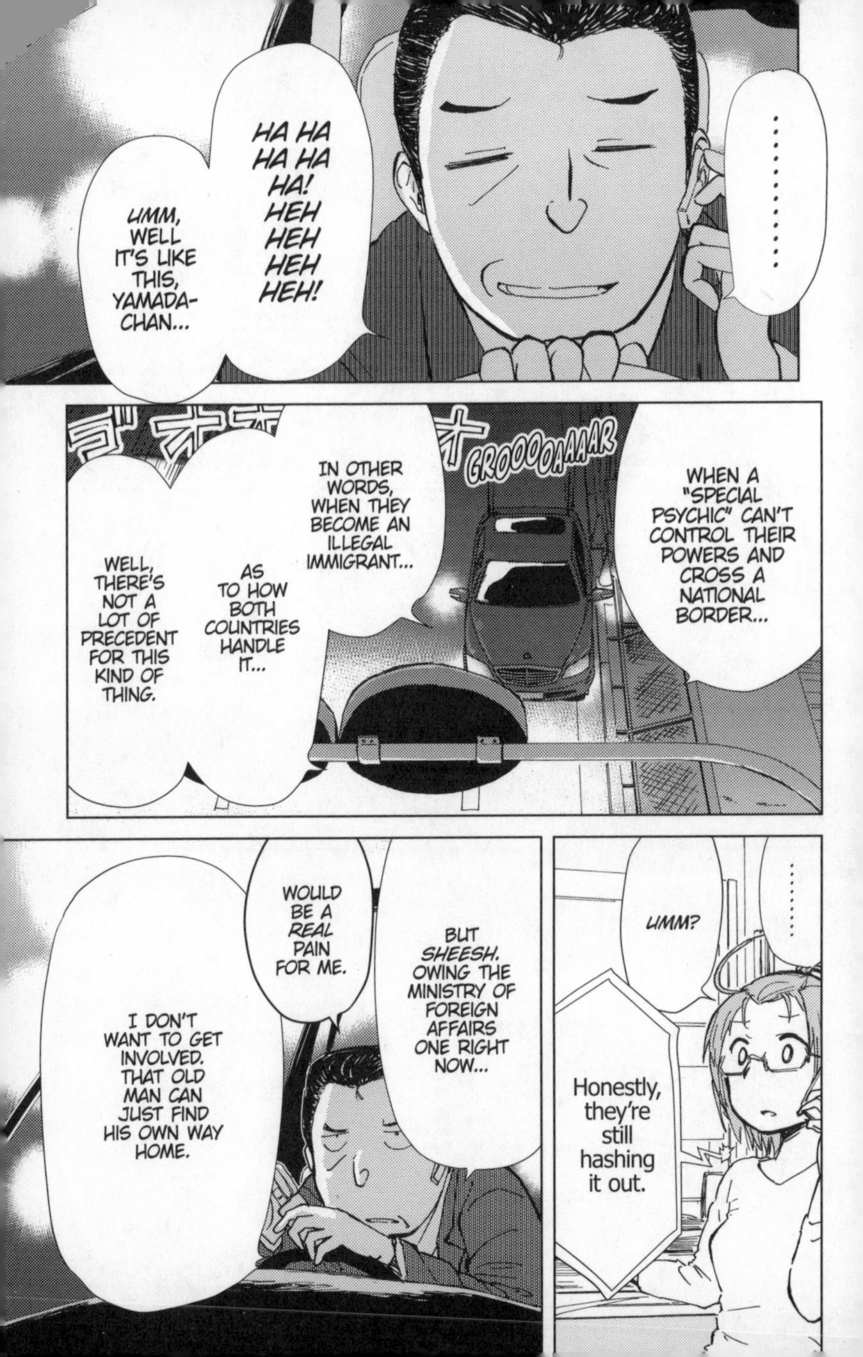
......
HA HA HA HA HA! HEH HEH HEH HEH!
UMM, WELL IT'S LIKE THIS, YAMADA-CHAN...
WHEN A "SPECIAL PSYCHIC" CAN'T CONTROL THEIR POWERS AND CROSS A NATIONAL BORDER...
GROOOOAAAAR
IN OTHER WORDS, WHEN THEY BECOME AN ILLEGAL IMMIGRANT...
AS TO HOW BOTH COUNTRIES HANDLE IT...
WELL, THERE'S NOT A LOT OF PRECEDENT FOR THIS KIND OF THING.
......
UMM?
Honestly, they're still hashing it out.
BUT SHEESH. OWING THE MINISTRY OF FOREIGN AFFAIRS ONE RIGHT NOW...
WOULD BE A REAL PAIN FOR ME.
I DON'T WANT TO GET INVOLVED. THAT OLD MAN CAN JUST FIND HIS OWN WAY HOME.

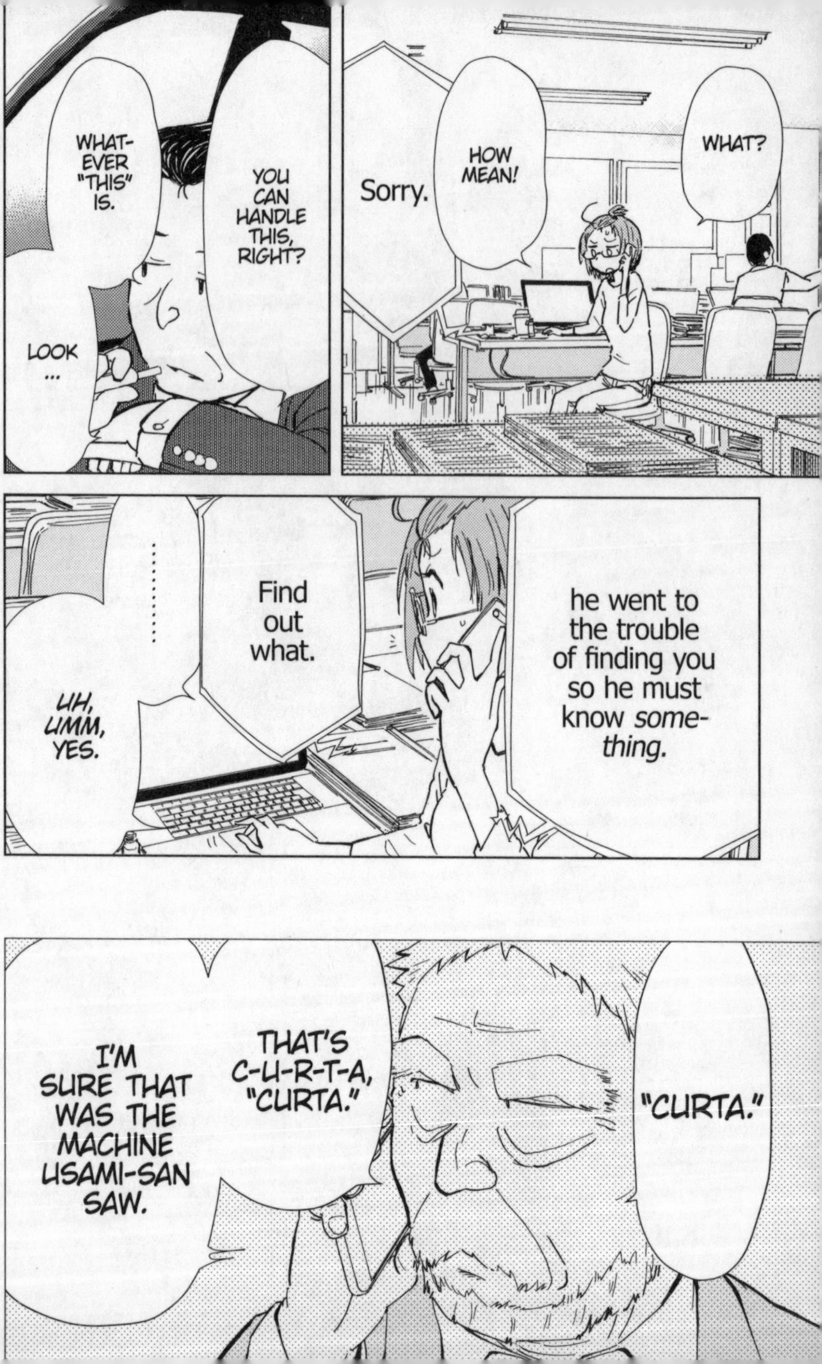
WHAT?
HOW MEAN!
Sorry.
YOU CAN HANDLE THIS, RIGHT?
WHAT-EVER "THIS" IS.
LOOK ...
he went to the trouble of finding you so he must know *some-thing.*
Find out what.
......
UH, UMM, YES.
"CURTA."
THAT'S C-U-R-T-A, "CURTA."
I'M SURE THAT WAS THE MACHINE USAMI-SAN SAW.

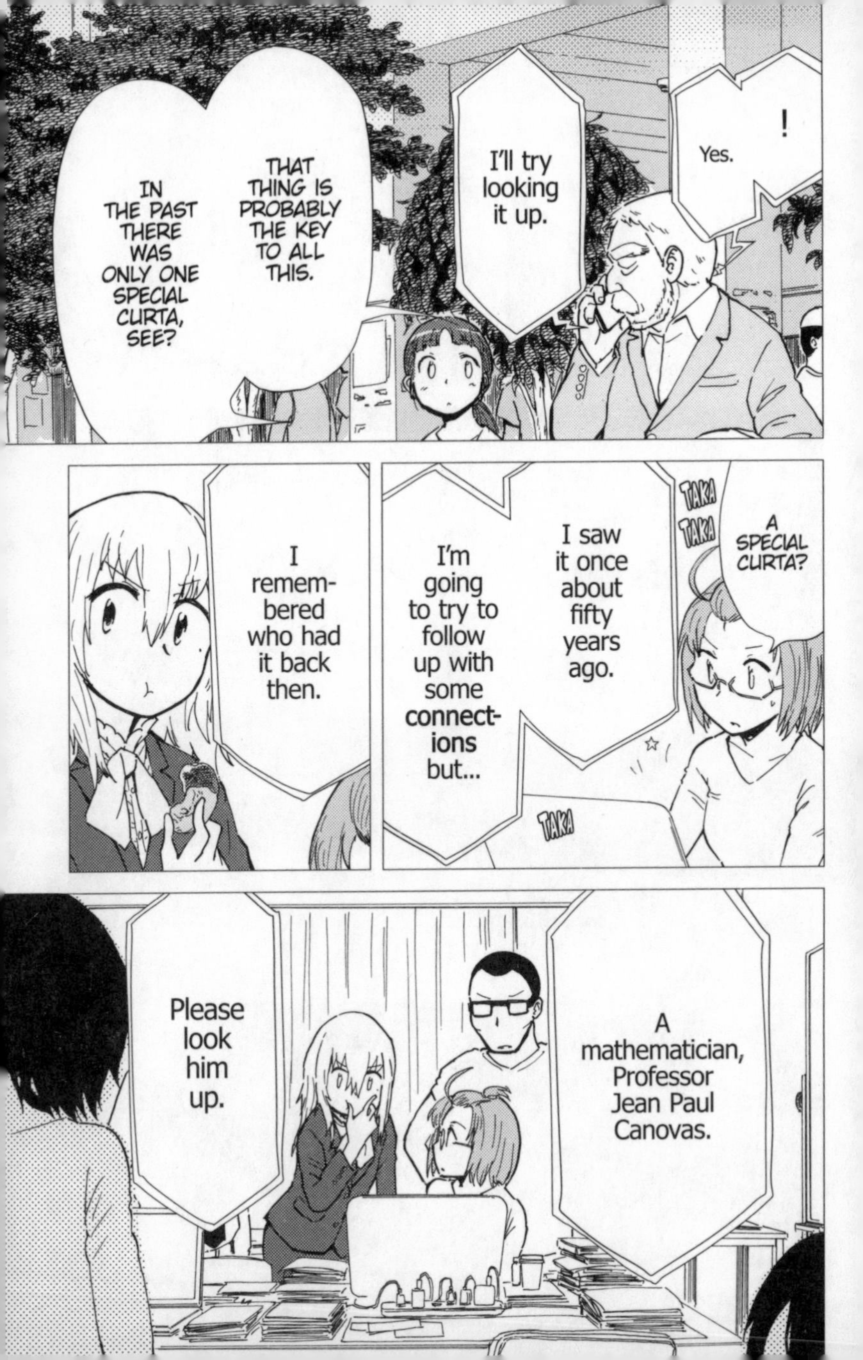
!
Yes.
I'll try looking it up.
THAT THING IS PROBABLY THE KEY TO ALL THIS.
IN THE PAST THERE WAS ONLY ONE SPECIAL CURTA, SEE?
TAKA TAKA
A SPECIAL CURTA?
I saw it once about fifty years ago.
I'm going to try to follow up with some connections but...
TAKA
I remembered who had it back then.
A mathematician, Professor Jean Paul Canovas.
Please look him up.

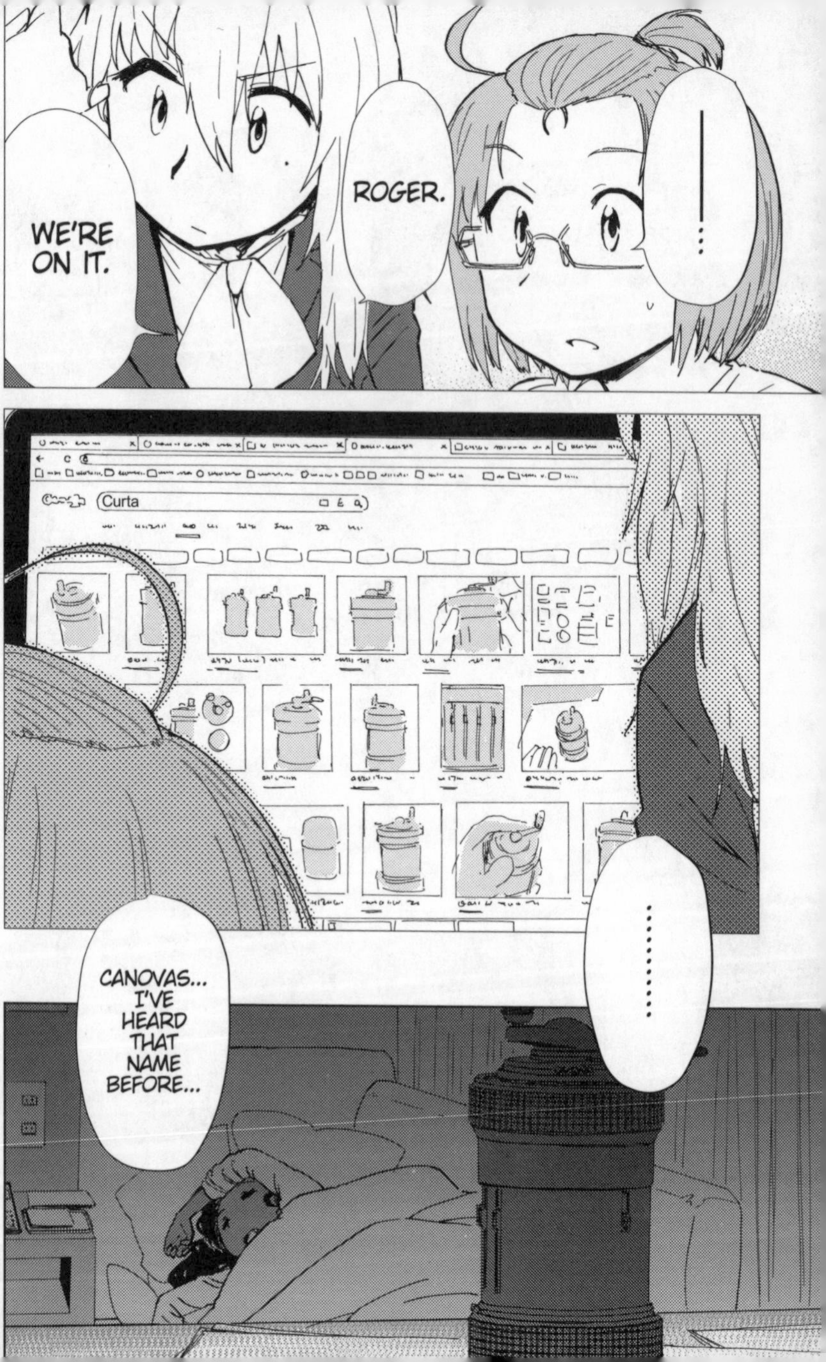
!......
ROGER.
WE'RE ON IT.
Curta
....
CANOVAS... I'VE HEARD THAT NAME BEFORE...

Chapter 36: And Then Days of Adventure

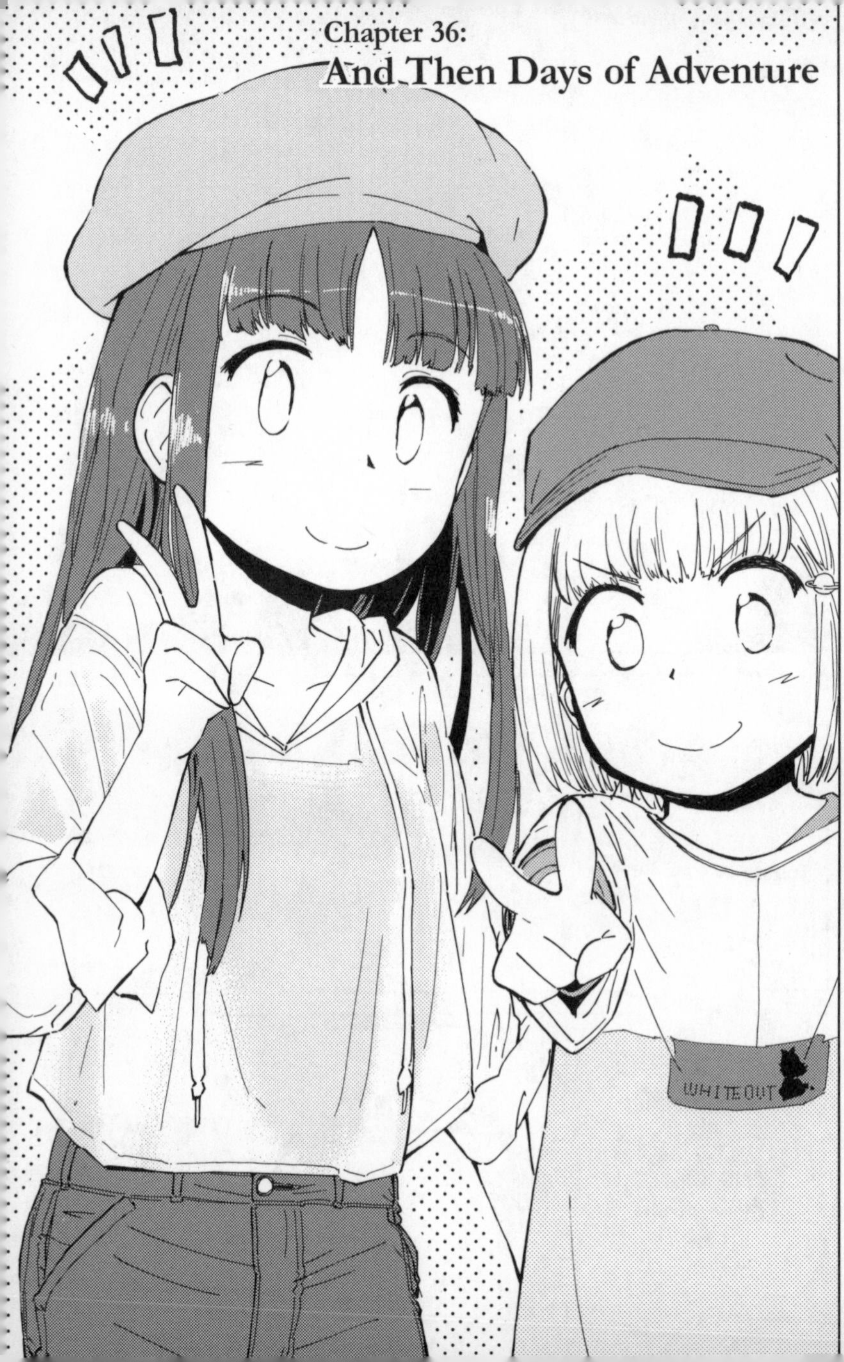
WHITEOUT

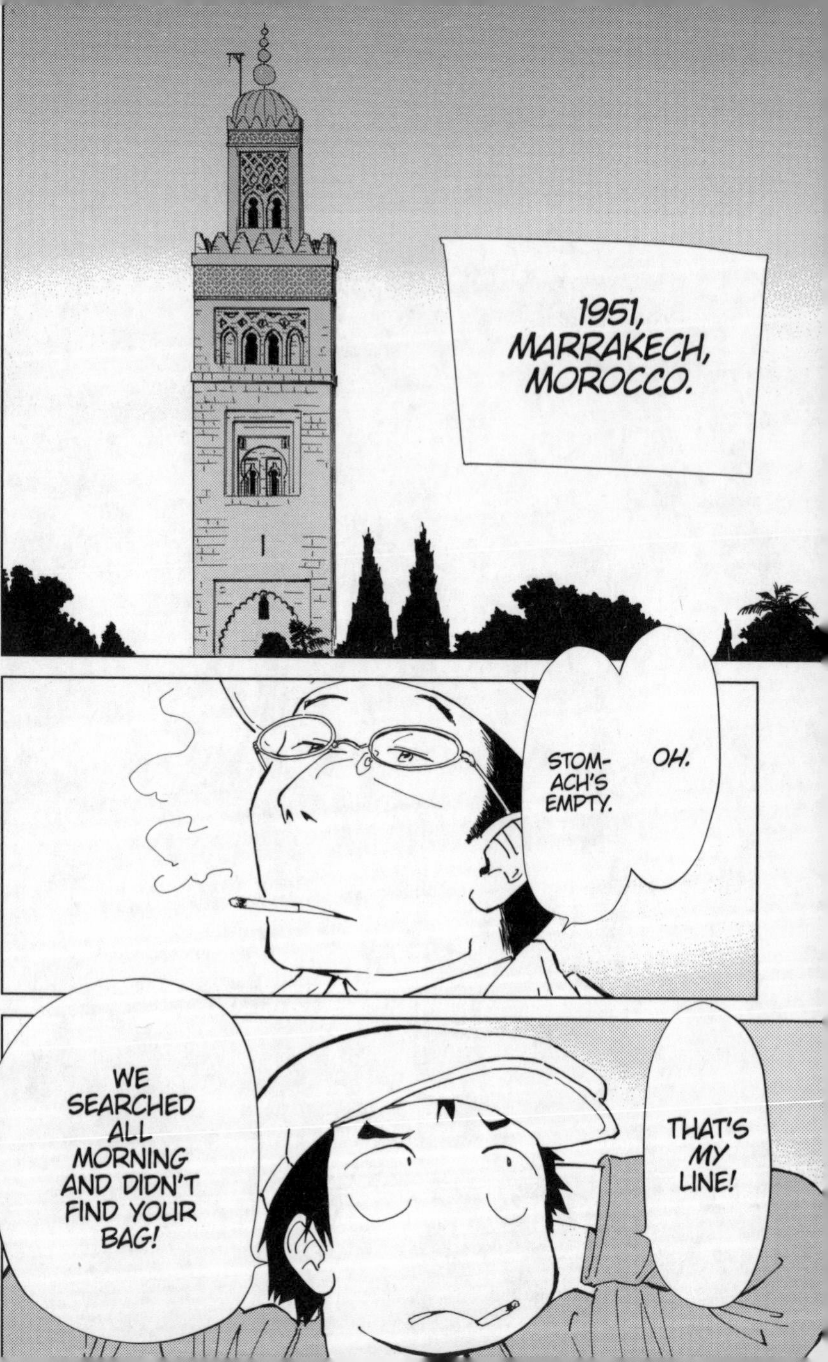
1951, MARRAKECH, MOROCCO.
OH.
STOM-ACH'S EMPTY.
THAT'S MY LINE!
WE SEARCHED ALL MORNING AND DIDN'T FIND YOUR BAG!

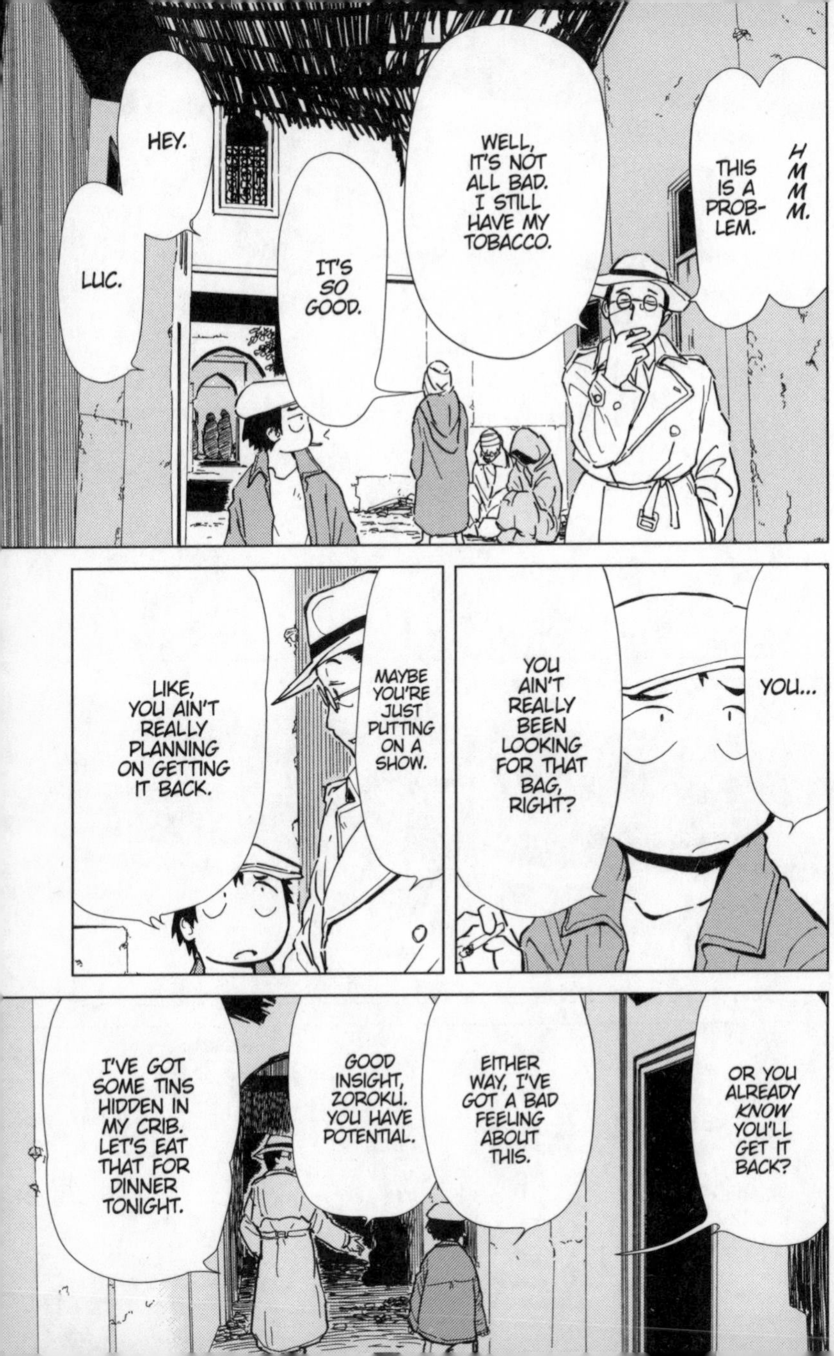
HMMM.
THIS IS A PROBLEM.
WELL, IT'S NOT ALL BAD. I STILL HAVE MY TOBACCO.
IT'S SO GOOD.
HEY.
LUC.
YOU...
YOU AIN'T REALLY BEEN LOOKING FOR THAT BAG, RIGHT?
MAYBE YOU'RE JUST PUTTING ON A SHOW.
LIKE, YOU AIN'T REALLY PLANNING ON GETTING IT BACK.
OR YOU ALREADY *KNOW* YOU'LL GET IT BACK?
EITHER WAY, I'VE GOT A BAD FEELING ABOUT THIS.
GOOD INSIGHT, ZOROKU. YOU HAVE POTENTIAL.
I'VE GOT SOME TINS HIDDEN IN MY CRIB. LET'S EAT THAT FOR DINNER TONIGHT.

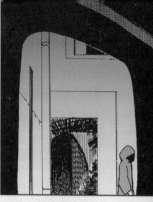

SO, THIS, IS YOUR HIDEOUT?

I'VE BEEN WAITING. WELL, SIT DOWN.

LUC, YOU LET THEM HAVE IT ON PURPOSE, DIDN'T YOU?!

SEE? I KNEW IT!

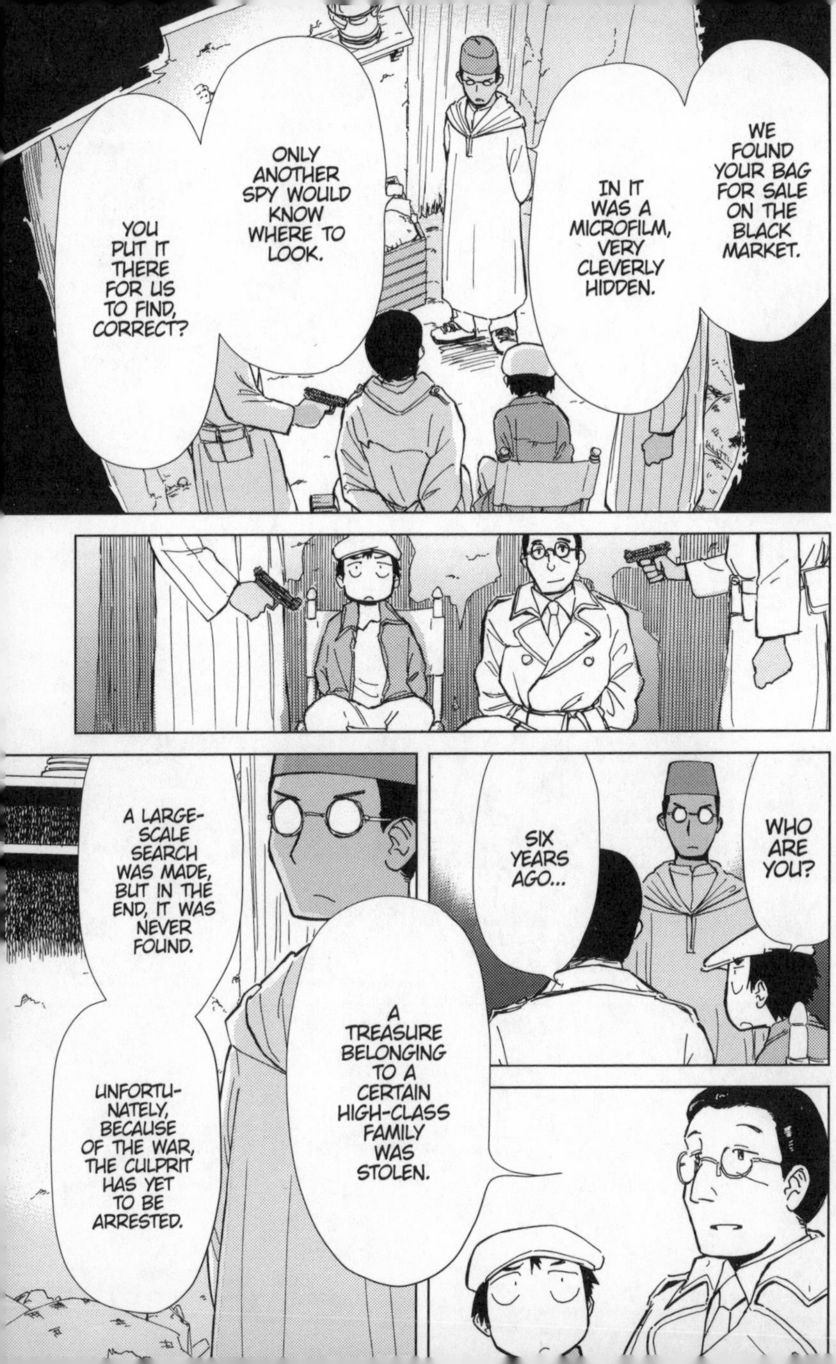

WE FOUND YOUR BAG FOR SALE ON THE BLACK MARKET.
IN IT WAS A MICROFILM, VERY CLEVERLY HIDDEN.
ONLY ANOTHER SPY WOULD KNOW WHERE TO LOOK.
YOU PUT IT THERE FOR US TO FIND, CORRECT?
WHO ARE YOU?
SIX YEARS AGO...
A TREASURE BELONGING TO A CERTAIN HIGH-CLASS FAMILY WAS STOLEN.
A LARGE-SCALE SEARCH WAS MADE, BUT IN THE END, IT WAS NEVER FOUND.
UNFORTUNATELY, BECAUSE OF THE WAR, THE CULPRIT HAS YET TO BE ARRESTED.

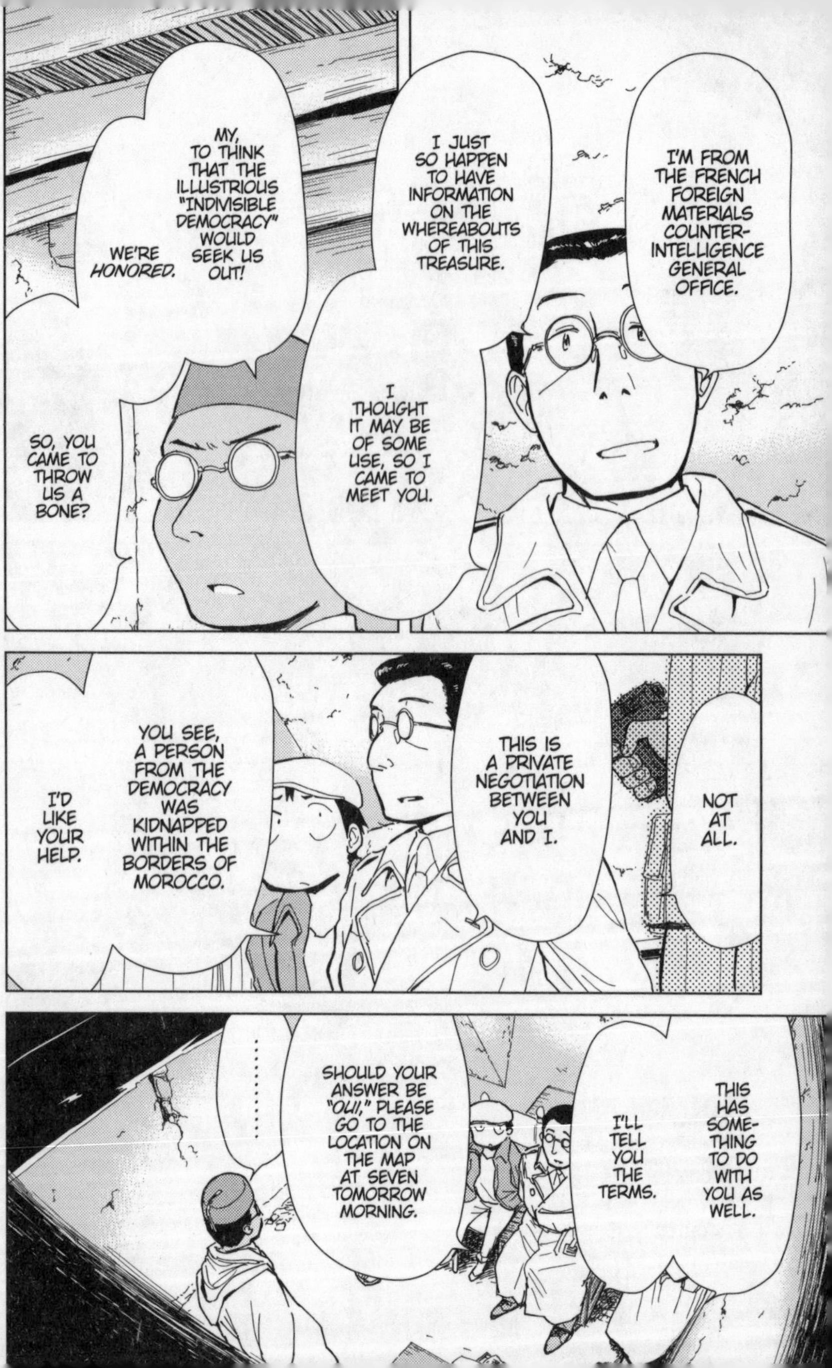
I'M FROM THE FRENCH FOREIGN MATERIALS COUNTER-INTELLIGENCE GENERAL OFFICE.
I JUST SO HAPPEN TO HAVE INFORMATION ON THE WHEREABOUTS OF THIS TREASURE.
I THOUGHT IT MAY BE OF SOME USE, SO I CAME TO MEET YOU.
MY, TO THINK THAT THE ILLUSTRIOUS "INDIVISIBLE DEMOCRACY" WOULD SEEK US OUT!
WE'RE *HONORED.*
SO, YOU CAME TO THROW US A BONE?
NOT AT ALL.
THIS IS A PRIVATE NEGOTIATION BETWEEN YOU AND I.
YOU SEE, A PERSON FROM THE DEMOCRACY WAS KIDNAPPED WITHIN THE BORDERS OF MOROCCO.
I'D LIKE YOUR HELP.
THIS HAS SOMETHING TO DO WITH YOU AS WELL.
I'LL TELL YOU THE TERMS.
SHOULD YOUR ANSWER BE "*OUI!*," PLEASE GO TO THE LOCATION ON THE MAP AT SEVEN TOMORROW MORNING.
......

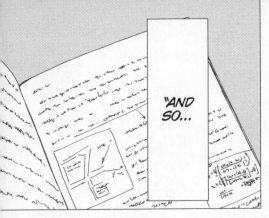

FROM PROFESSOR JEAN PAUL CANOVAS'S RESEARCH NOTES.

"AND SO...

"I'VE BEEN TEACHING MATHEMATICS AT THE UNIVERSITY SINCE THE WAR...

"STUDYING STRANGE PHENOMENA THAT CAN'T BE EXPLAINED BY TODAY'S SCIENCE.

"I EVEN DISCOVER THINGS ONCE IN A WHILE."

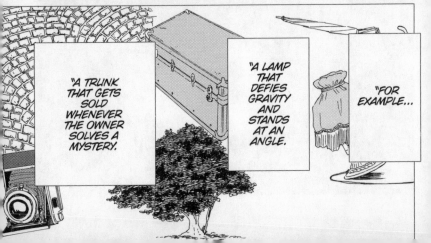

"FOR EXAMPLE...

"A LAMP THAT DEFIES GRAVITY AND STANDS AT AN ANGLE.

"A TRUNK THAT GETS SOLD WHENEVER THE OWNER SOLVES A MYSTERY.

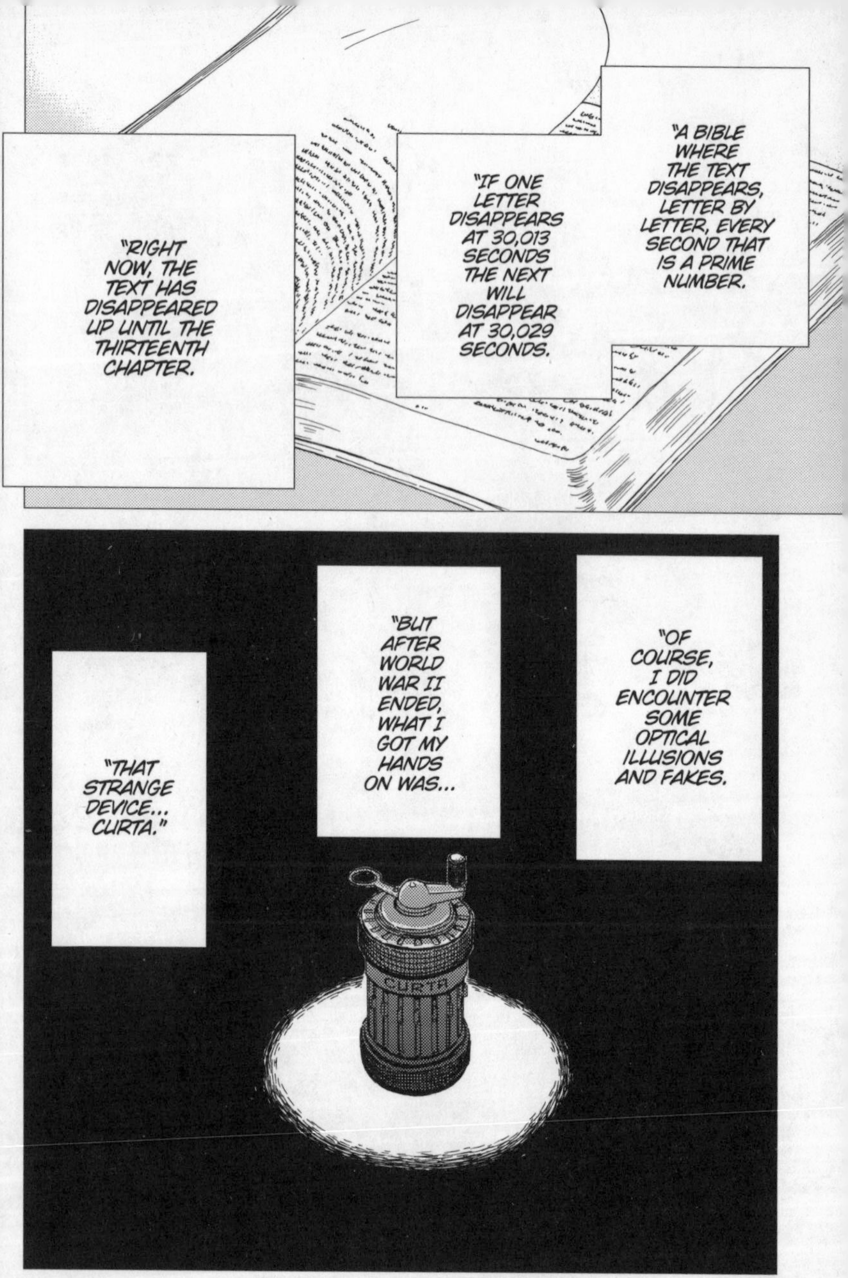
"A BIBLE WHERE THE TEXT DISAPPEARS, LETTER BY LETTER, EVERY SECOND THAT IS A PRIME NUMBER.
"IF ONE LETTER DISAPPEARS AT 30,013 SECONDS THE NEXT WILL DISAPPEAR AT 30,029 SECONDS.
"RIGHT NOW, THE TEXT HAS DISAPPEARED UP UNTIL THE THIRTEENTH CHAPTER.
"OF COURSE, I DID ENCOUNTER SOME OPTICAL ILLUSIONS AND FAKES.
"BUT AFTER WORLD WAR II ENDED, WHAT I GOT MY HANDS ON WAS...
"THAT STRANGE DEVICE... CURTA."
CURTA

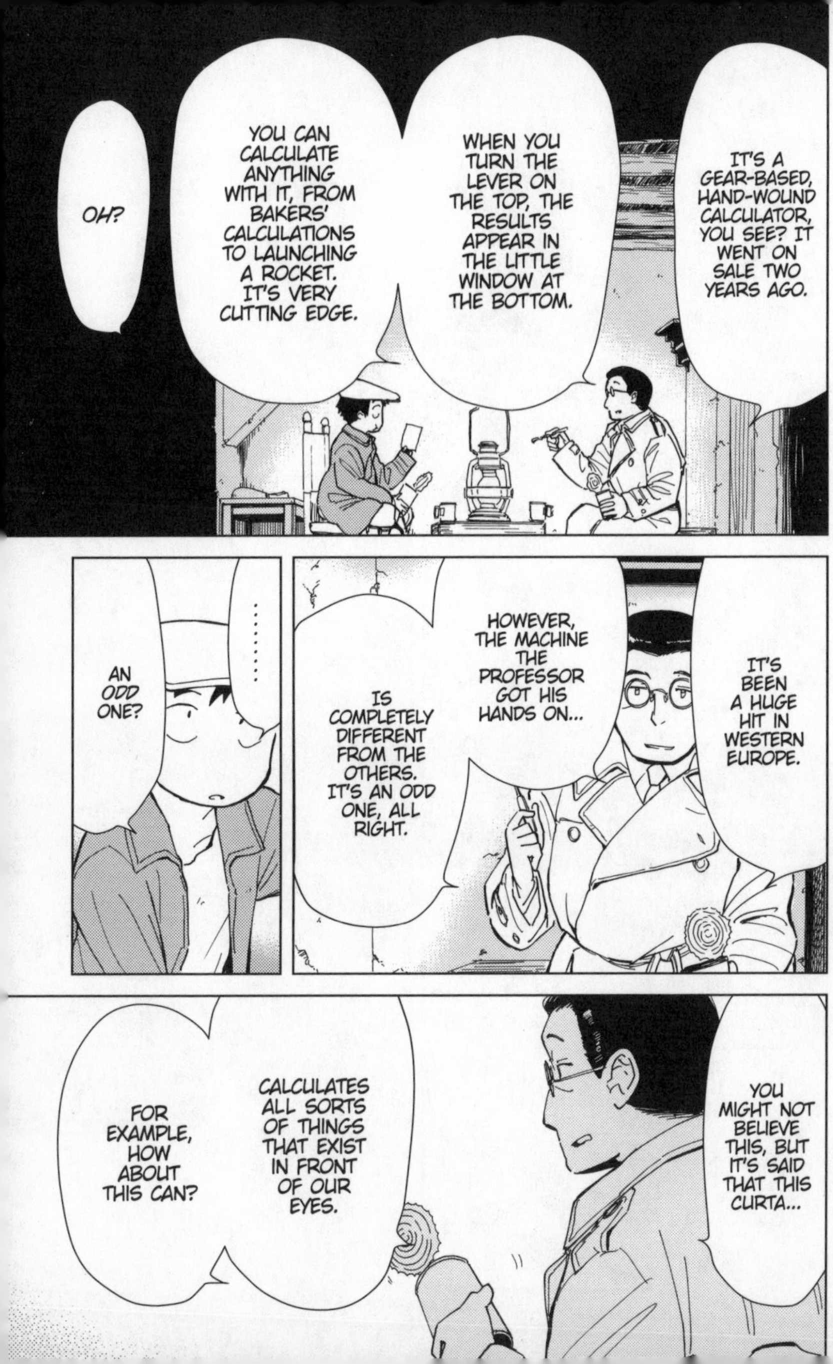
IT'S A GEAR-BASED, HAND-WOUND CALCULATOR, YOU SEE? IT WENT ON SALE TWO YEARS AGO.
WHEN YOU TURN THE LEVER ON THE TOP, THE RESULTS APPEAR IN THE LITTLE WINDOW AT THE BOTTOM.
YOU CAN CALCULATE ANYTHING WITH IT, FROM BAKERS' CALCULATIONS TO LAUNCHING A ROCKET. IT'S VERY CUTTING EDGE.
OH?
IT'S BEEN A HUGE HIT IN WESTERN EUROPE.
HOWEVER, THE MACHINE THE PROFESSOR GOT HIS HANDS ON...
IS COMPLETELY DIFFERENT FROM THE OTHERS. IT'S AN ODD ONE, ALL RIGHT.
....
AN ODD ONE?
YOU MIGHT NOT BELIEVE THIS, BUT IT'S SAID THAT THIS CURTA...
CALCULATES ALL SORTS OF THINGS THAT EXIST IN FRONT OF OUR EYES.
FOR EXAMPLE, HOW ABOUT THIS CAN?

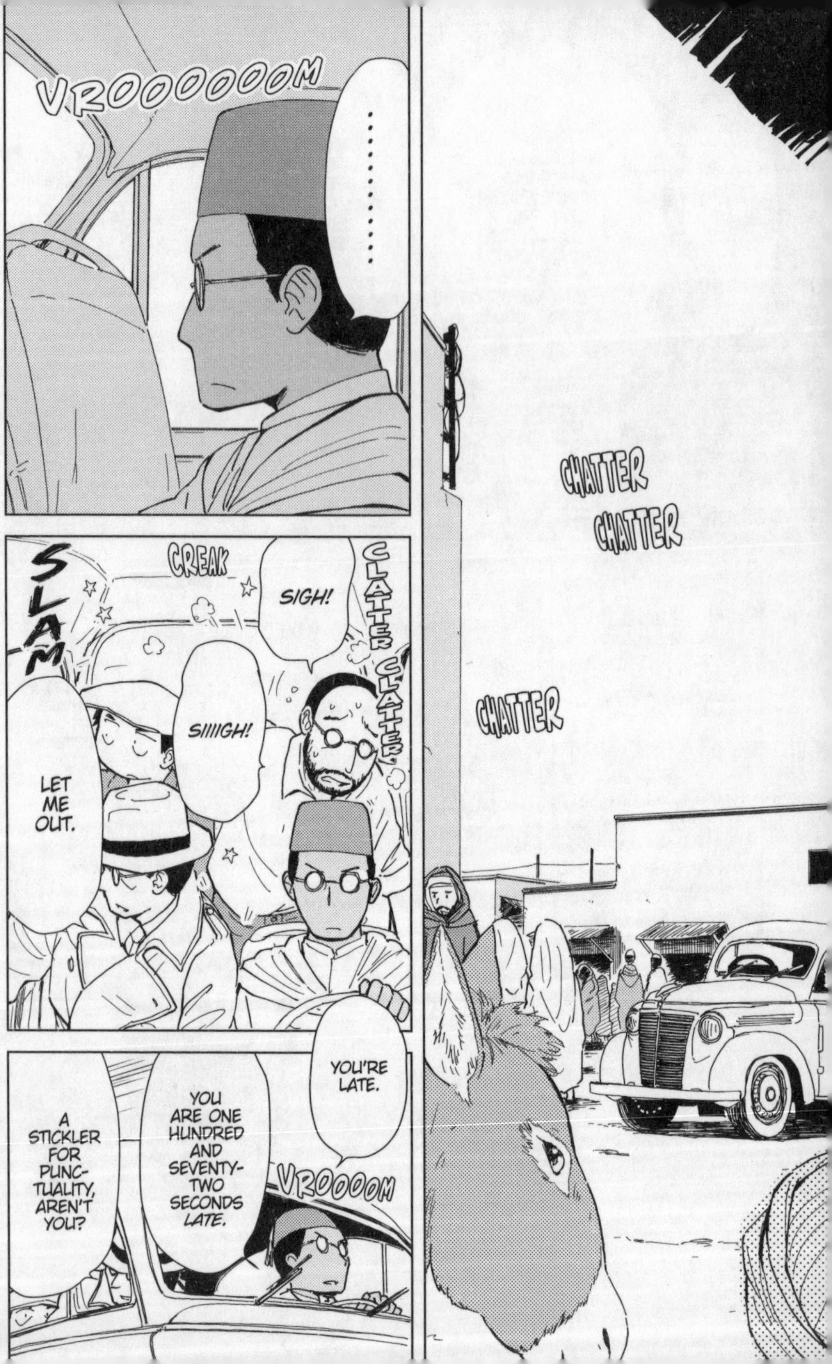
CHATTER
CHATTER
CHATTER
VROOOOOOOM
......
CLATTER CLATTER
SIGH!
CREAK
SLAM
SIIIGH!
LET ME OUT.
YOU'RE LATE.
VROOOOM
YOU ARE ONE HUNDRED AND SEVENTY-TWO SECONDS LATE.
A STICKLER FOR PUNC-TUALITY, AREN'T YOU?

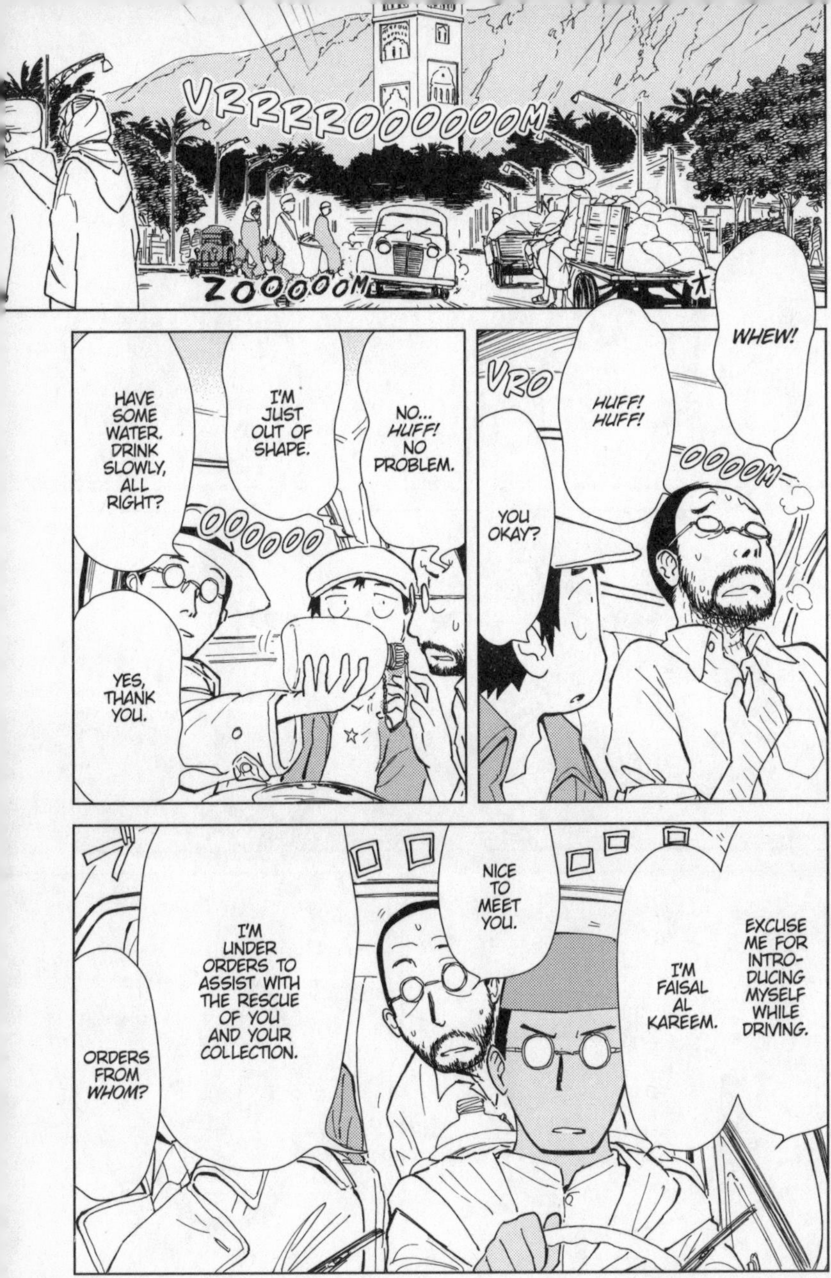
VRRRROOOOOOOM
ZOOOOOOM
WHEW!
VRO
OOOOM
HUFF! HUFF!
YOU OKAY?
NO... HUFF! NO PROBLEM.
I'M JUST OUT OF SHAPE.
HAVE SOME WATER. DRINK SLOWLY, ALL RIGHT?
OOOOOO
YES, THANK YOU.
EXCUSE ME FOR INTRO-DUCING MYSELF WHILE DRIVING.
I'M FAISAL AL KAREEM.
NICE TO MEET YOU.
I'M UNDER ORDERS TO ASSIST WITH THE RESCUE OF YOU AND YOUR COLLECTION.
ORDERS FROM WHOM?

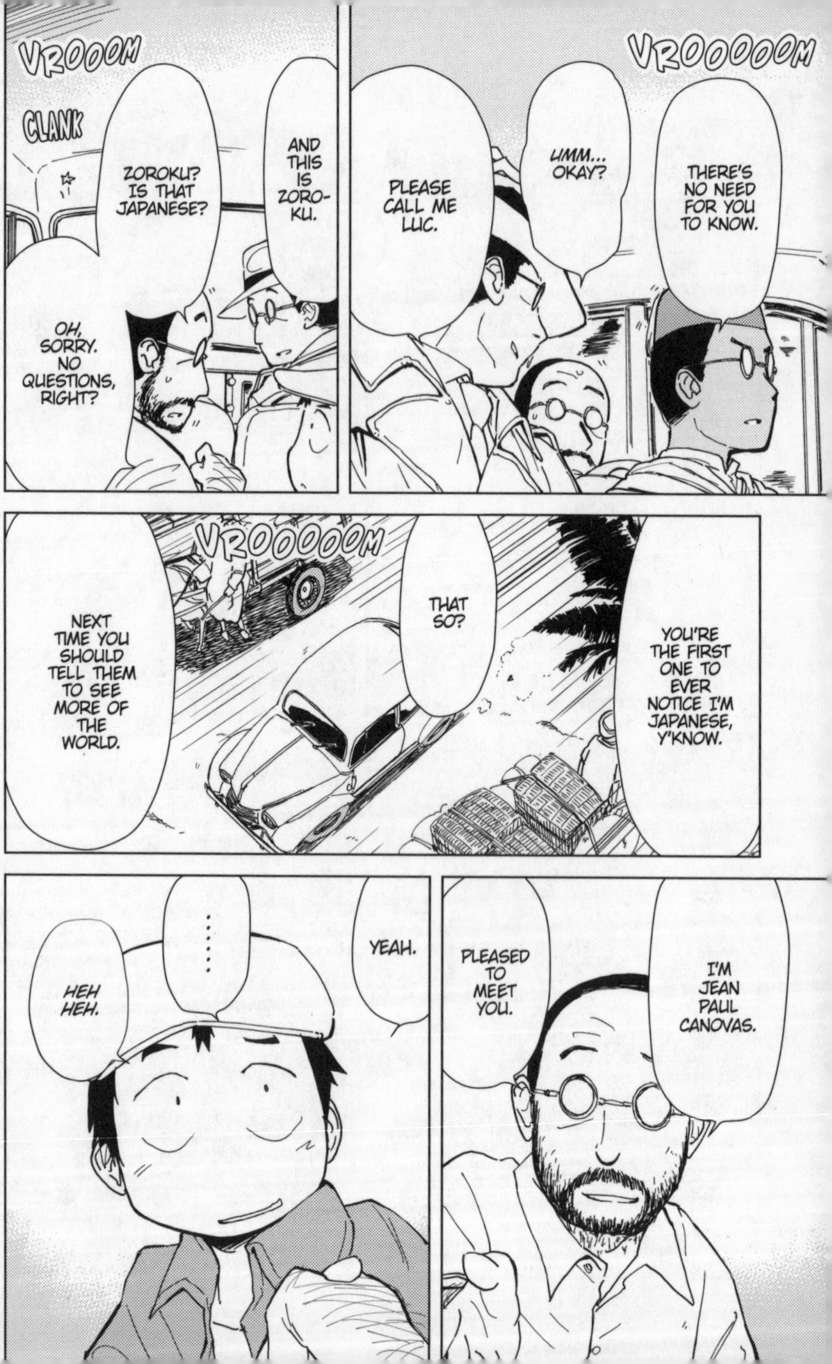
VROOOOOM
THERE'S NO NEED FOR YOU TO KNOW.
UMM... OKAY?
PLEASE CALL ME LUC.
AND THIS IS ZORO-KU.
ZOROKU? IS THAT JAPANESE?
VROOOM
CLANK
OH, SORRY. NO QUESTIONS, RIGHT?
YOU'RE THE FIRST ONE TO EVER NOTICE I'M JAPANESE, Y'KNOW.
THAT SO?
VROOOOOM
NEXT TIME YOU SHOULD TELL THEM TO SEE MORE OF THE WORLD.
I'M JEAN PAUL CANOVAS.
PLEASED TO MEET YOU.
YEAH.
......
HEH HEH.

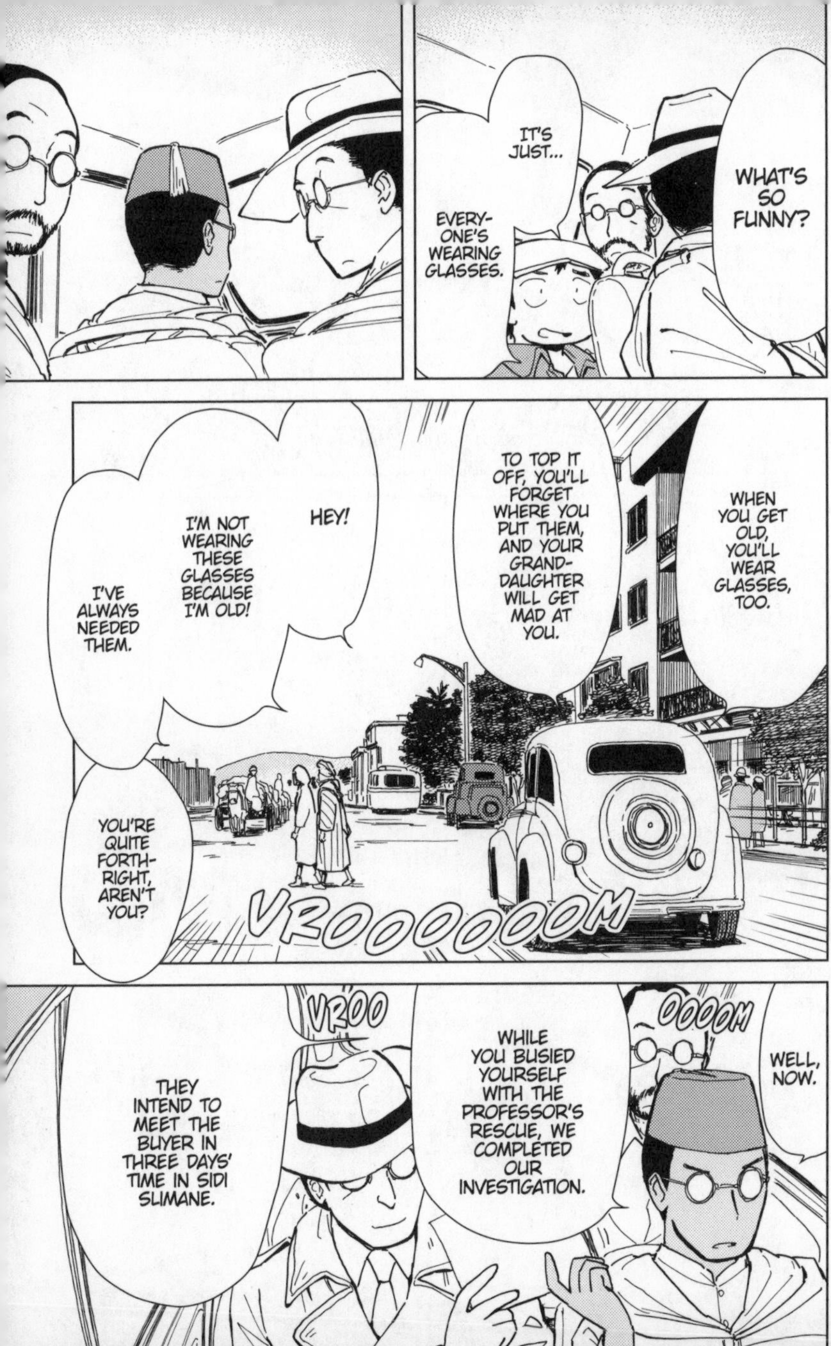
WHAT'S SO FUNNY?
IT'S JUST...
EVERYONE'S WEARING GLASSES.
WHEN YOU GET OLD, YOU'LL WEAR GLASSES, TOO.
TO TOP IT OFF, YOU'LL FORGET WHERE YOU PUT THEM, AND YOUR GRANDDAUGHTER WILL GET MAD AT YOU.
HEY!
I'M NOT WEARING THESE GLASSES BECAUSE I'M OLD!
I'VE ALWAYS NEEDED THEM.
YOU'RE QUITE FORTHRIGHT, AREN'T YOU?
VROOOOOOOM
WELL, NOW.
VROO
OOOOM
WHILE YOU BUSIED YOURSELF WITH THE PROFESSOR'S RESCUE, WE COMPLETED OUR INVESTIGATION.
THEY INTEND TO MEET THE BUYER IN THREE DAYS' TIME IN SIDI SLIMANE.

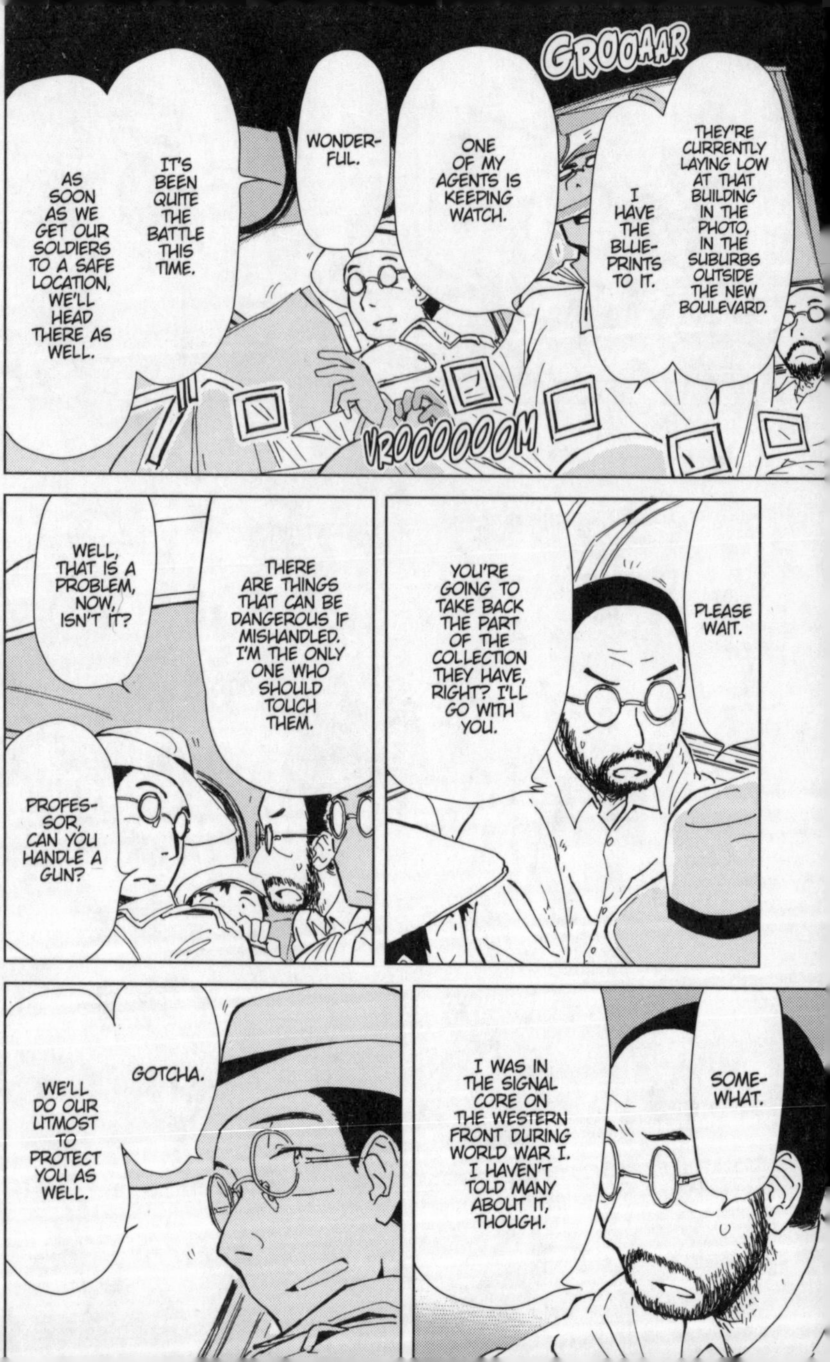
GROOAAR
THEY'RE CURRENTLY LAYING LOW AT THAT BUILDING IN THE PHOTO, IN THE SUBURBS OUTSIDE THE NEW BOULEVARD.
I HAVE THE BLUE-PRINTS TO IT.
ONE OF MY AGENTS IS KEEPING WATCH.
WONDER-FUL.
IT'S BEEN QUITE THE BATTLE THIS TIME.
AS SOON AS WE GET OUR SOLDIERS TO A SAFE LOCATION, WE'LL HEAD THERE AS WELL.
VROOOOOOOM
PLEASE WAIT.
YOU'RE GOING TO TAKE BACK THE PART OF THE COLLECTION THEY HAVE, RIGHT? I'LL GO WITH YOU.
THERE ARE THINGS THAT CAN BE DANGEROUS IF MISHANDLED. I'M THE ONLY ONE WHO SHOULD TOUCH THEM.
WELL, THAT IS A PROBLEM, NOW, ISN'T IT?
PROFES-SOR, CAN YOU HANDLE A GUN?
SOME-WHAT.
I WAS IN THE SIGNAL CORE ON THE WESTERN FRONT DURING WORLD WAR I. I HAVEN'T TOLD MANY ABOUT IT, THOUGH.
GOTCHA.
WE'LL DO OUR UTMOST TO PROTECT YOU AS WELL.

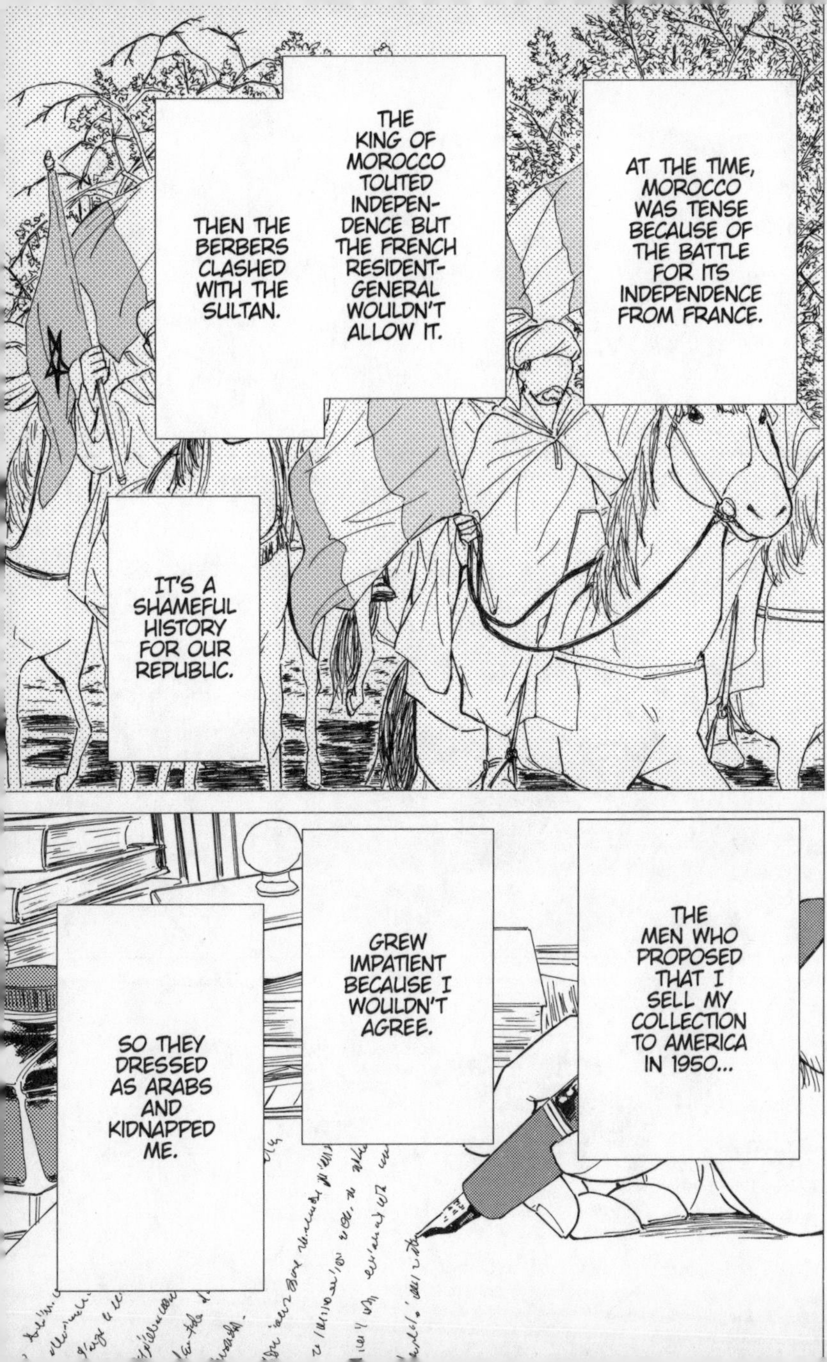
AT THE TIME, MOROCCO WAS TENSE BECAUSE OF THE BATTLE FOR ITS INDEPENDENCE FROM FRANCE.
THE KING OF MOROCCO TOUTED INDEPENDENCE BUT THE FRENCH RESIDENT-GENERAL WOULDN'T ALLOW IT.
THEN THE BERBERS CLASHED WITH THE SULTAN.
IT'S A SHAMEFUL HISTORY FOR OUR REPUBLIC.
THE MEN WHO PROPOSED THAT I SELL MY COLLECTION TO AMERICA IN 1950...
GREW IMPATIENT BECAUSE I WOULDN'T AGREE.
SO THEY DRESSED AS ARABS AND KIDNAPPED ME.

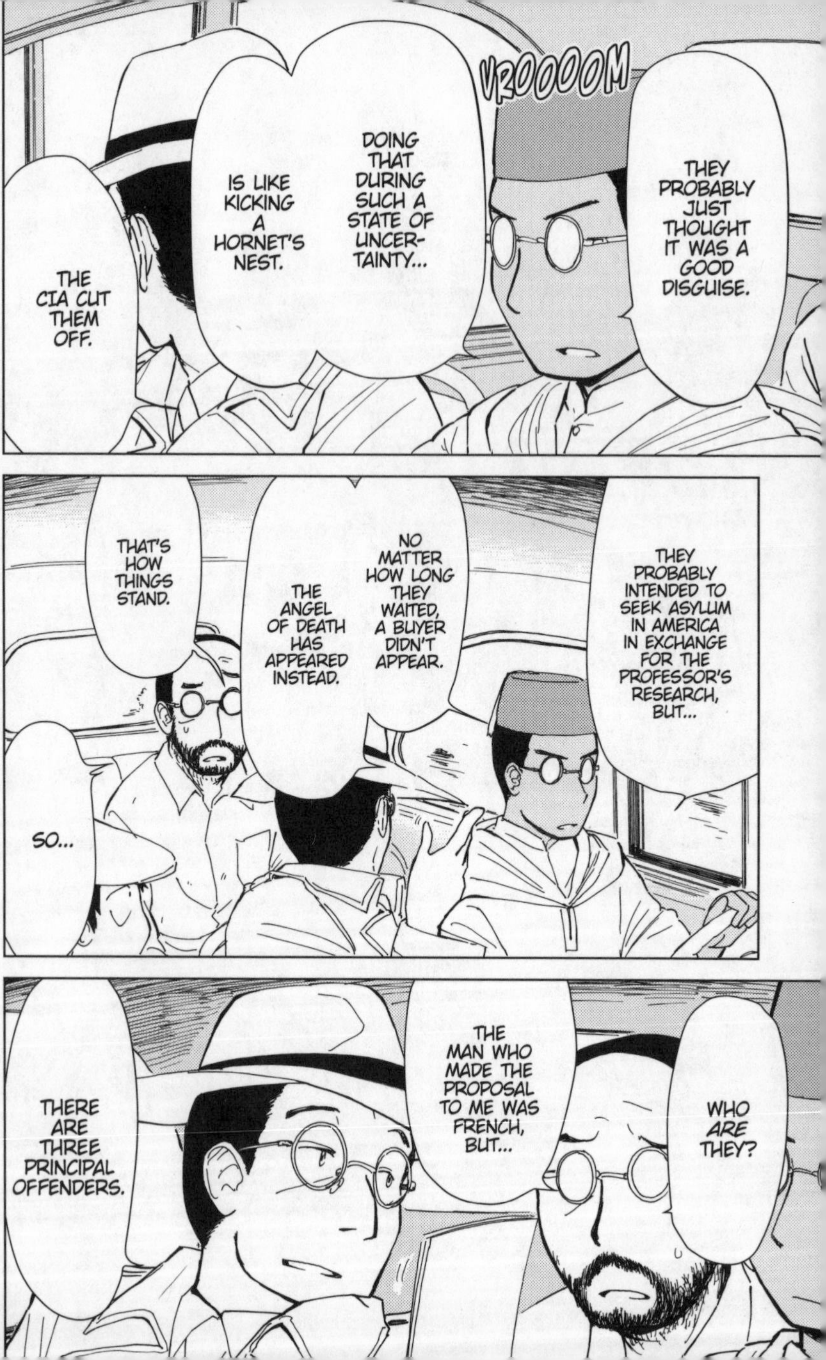
VROOOOM
THEY PROBABLY JUST THOUGHT IT WAS A GOOD DISGUISE.
DOING THAT DURING SUCH A STATE OF UNCER-TAINTY...
IS LIKE KICKING A HORNET'S NEST.
THE CIA CUT THEM OFF.
THEY PROBABLY INTENDED TO SEEK ASYLUM IN AMERICA IN EXCHANGE FOR THE PROFESSOR'S RESEARCH, BUT...
NO MATTER HOW LONG THEY WAITED, A BUYER DIDN'T APPEAR.
THE ANGEL OF DEATH HAS APPEARED INSTEAD.
THAT'S HOW THINGS STAND.
SO...
WHO *ARE* THEY?
THE MAN WHO MADE THE PROPOSAL TO ME WAS FRENCH, BUT...
THERE ARE THREE PRINCIPAL OFFENDERS.

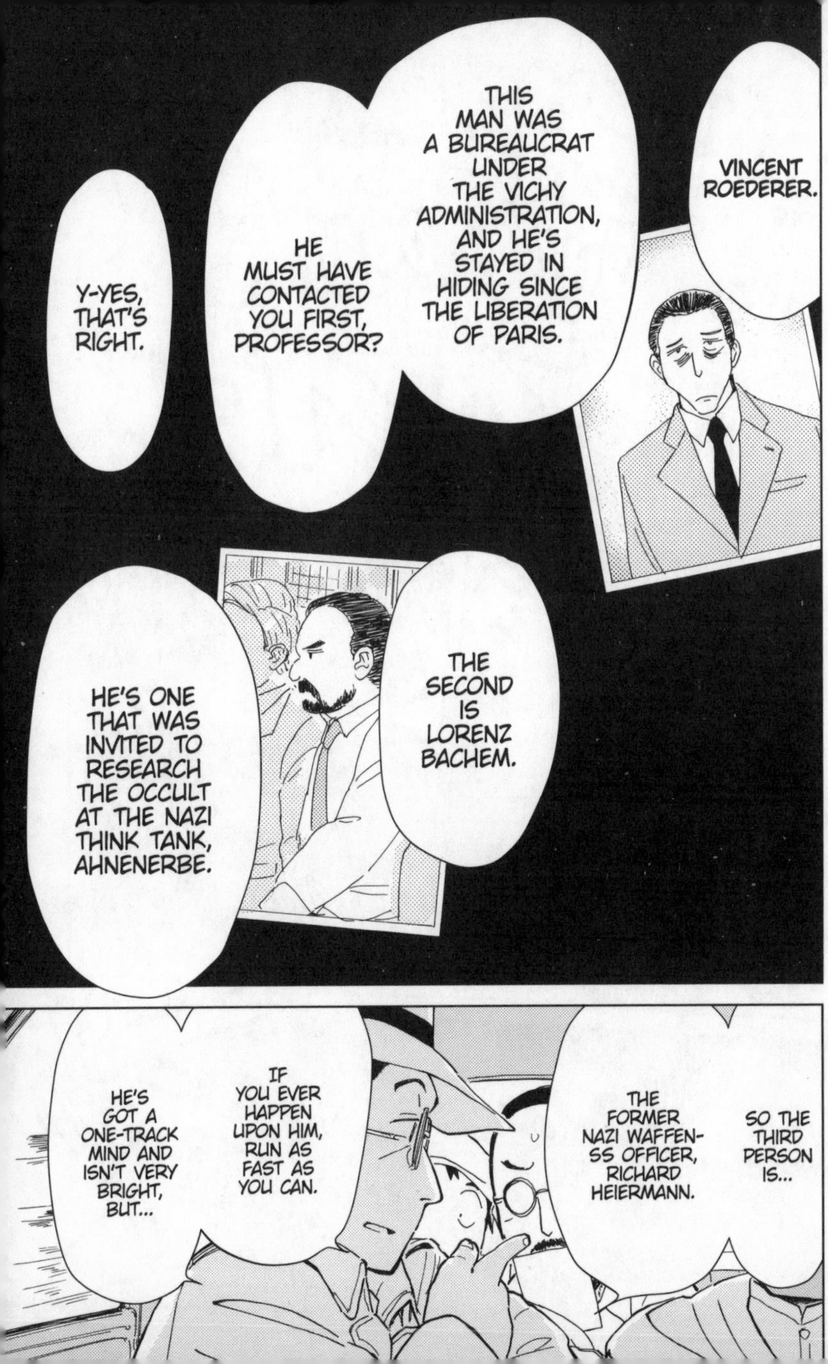
VINCENT ROEDERER.
THIS MAN WAS A BUREAUCRAT UNDER THE VICHY ADMINISTRATION, AND HE'S STAYED IN HIDING SINCE THE LIBERATION OF PARIS.
HE MUST HAVE CONTACTED YOU FIRST, PROFESSOR?
Y-YES, THAT'S RIGHT.
THE SECOND IS LORENZ BACHEM.
HE'S ONE THAT WAS INVITED TO RESEARCH THE OCCULT AT THE NAZI THINK TANK, AHNENERBE.
SO THE THIRD PERSON IS...
THE FORMER NAZI WAFFEN-SS OFFICER, RICHARD HEIERMANN.
IF YOU EVER HAPPEN UPON HIM, RUN AS FAST AS YOU CAN.
HE'S GOT A ONE-TRACK MIND AND ISN'T VERY BRIGHT, BUT...

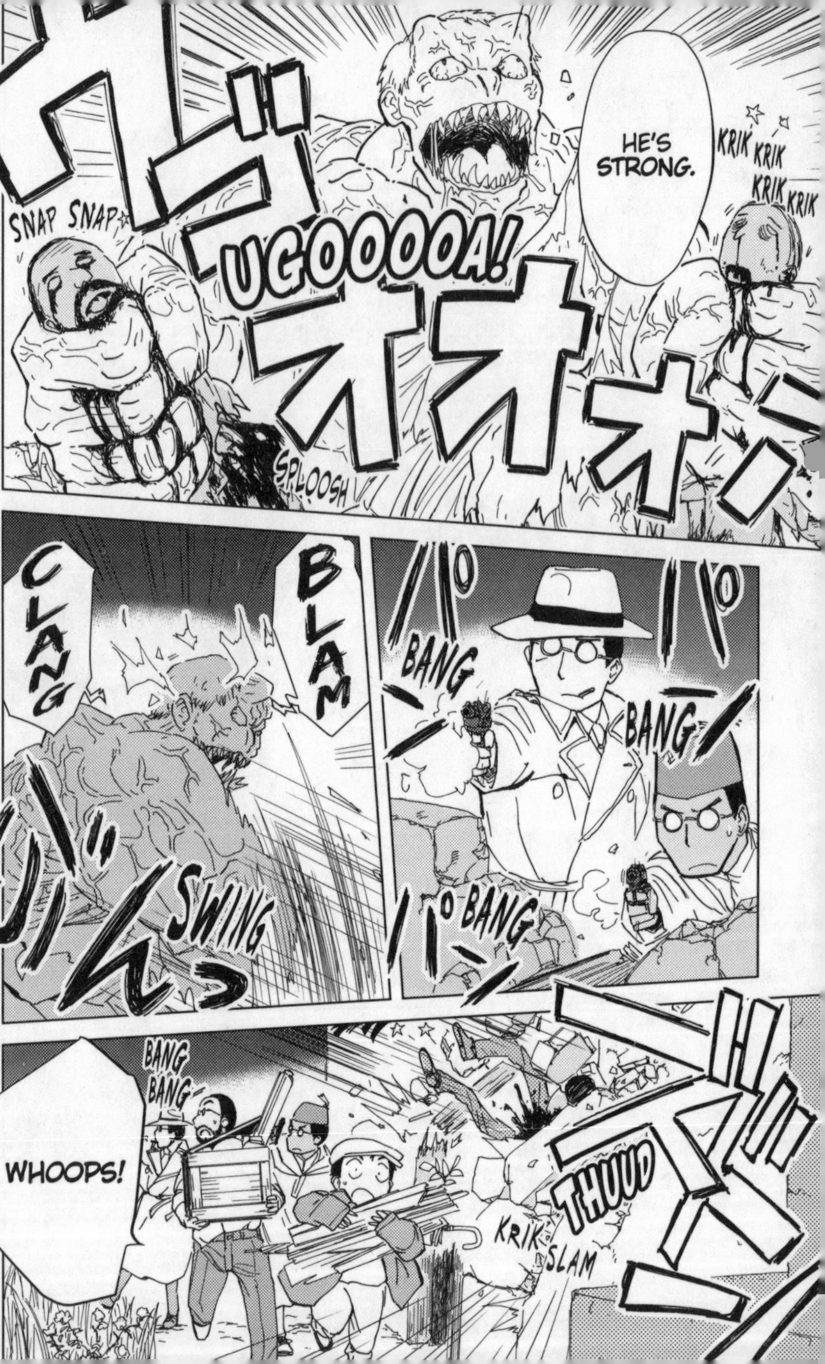
KRIK KRIK KRIK KRIK
HE'S STRONG.
UGOOOOA!
SNAP SNAP
SPLOOSH
BANG
BANG
BANG
BLAM
CLANG
SWING
THUUD
KRIK
SLAM
BANG BANG
WHOOPS!

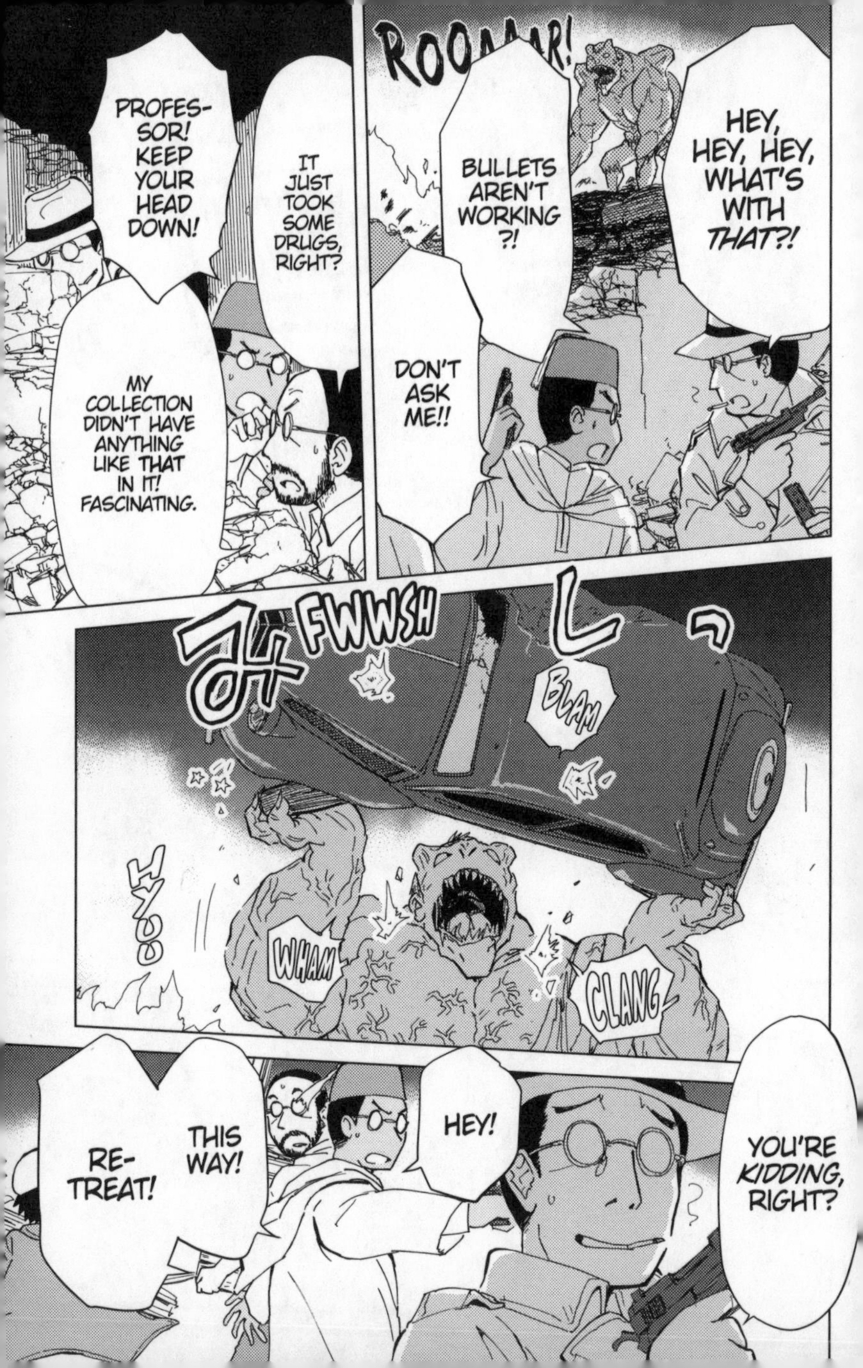
ROOAAR!
HEY, HEY, HEY, WHAT'S WITH THAT?!
BULLETS AREN'T WORKING?!
DON'T ASK ME!!
IT JUST TOOK SOME DRUGS, RIGHT?
PROFES-SOR! KEEP YOUR HEAD DOWN!
MY COLLECTION DIDN'T HAVE ANYTHING LIKE THAT IN IT! FASCINATING.
FWWSH
BLAM
WHAM
CLANG
YOU'RE KIDDING, RIGHT?
HEY!
THIS WAY!
RE-TREAT!

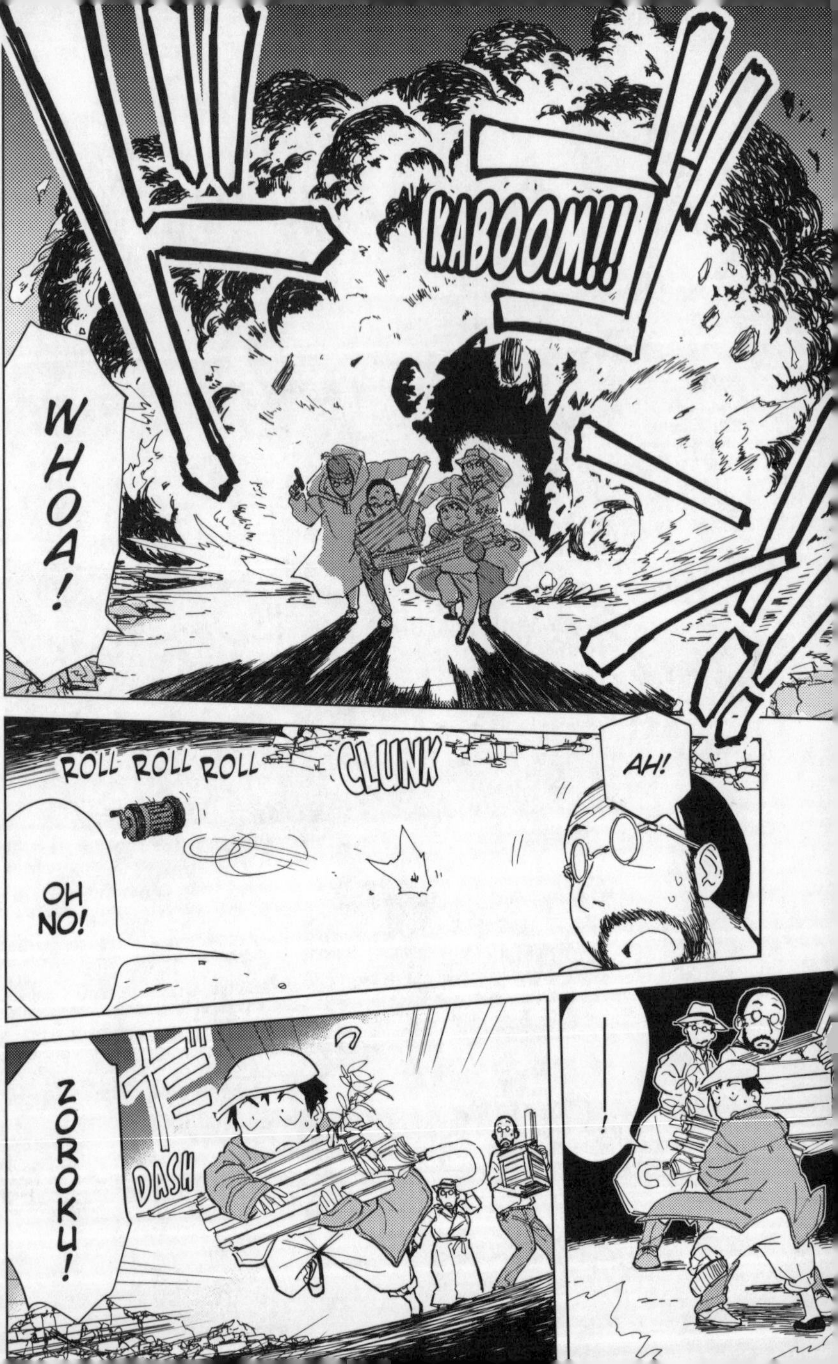
KABOOM!!
WHOA!
AH!
CLUNK
ROLL ROLL ROLL
OH NO!
!
ZOROKU!
DASH

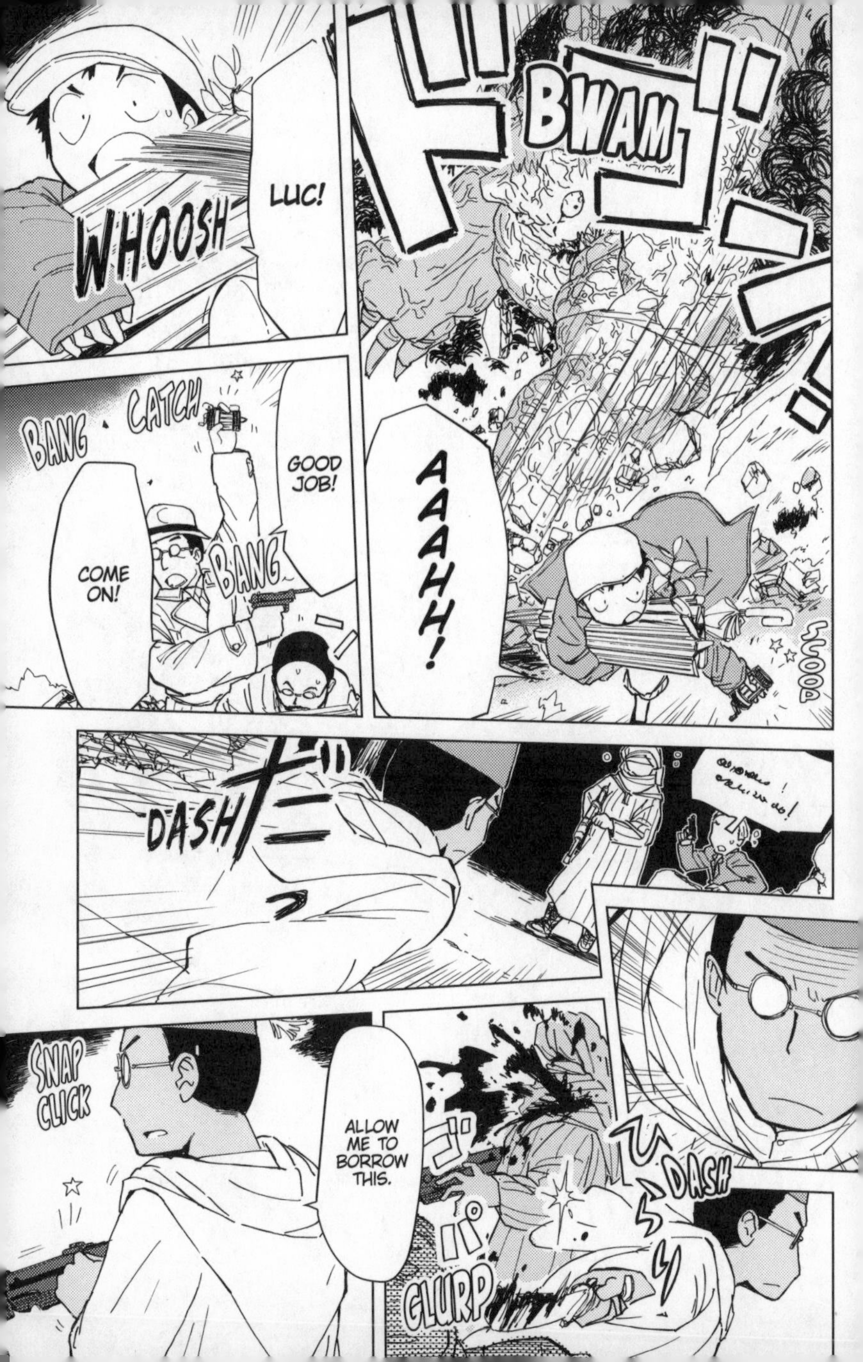
BWAM
AAAHH!
SCOOP
WHOOSH
LUC!
GOOD JOB!
CATCH
BANG
COME ON!
BANG
DASH
DASH
GLURP
ALLOW ME TO BORROW THIS.
SNAP CLICK

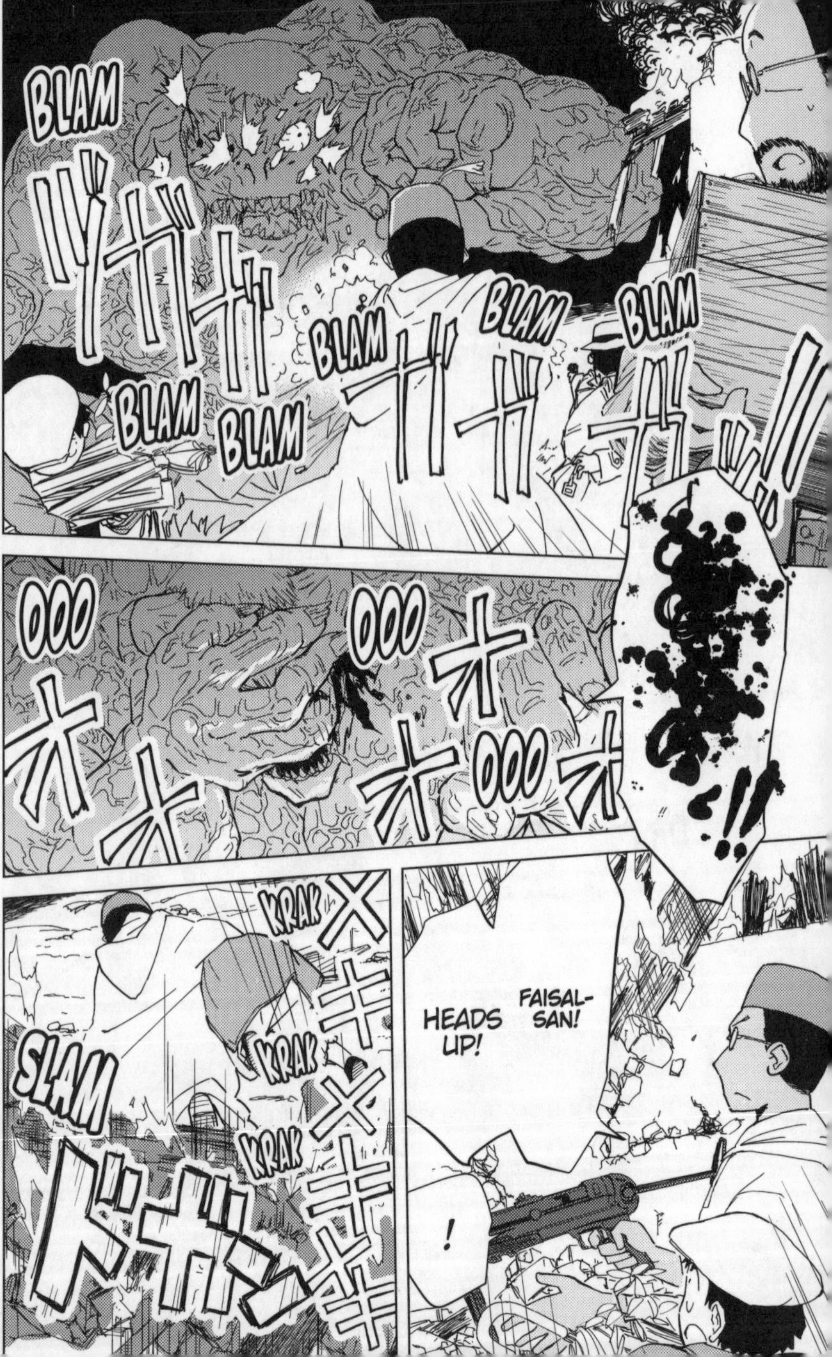

BLAM
BLAM
BLAM
BLAM
BLAM
BLAM
BLAM
OOO
OOO
OOO
FAISAL-SAN!
HEADS UP!
!
KRAK
KRAK
KRAK
SLAM

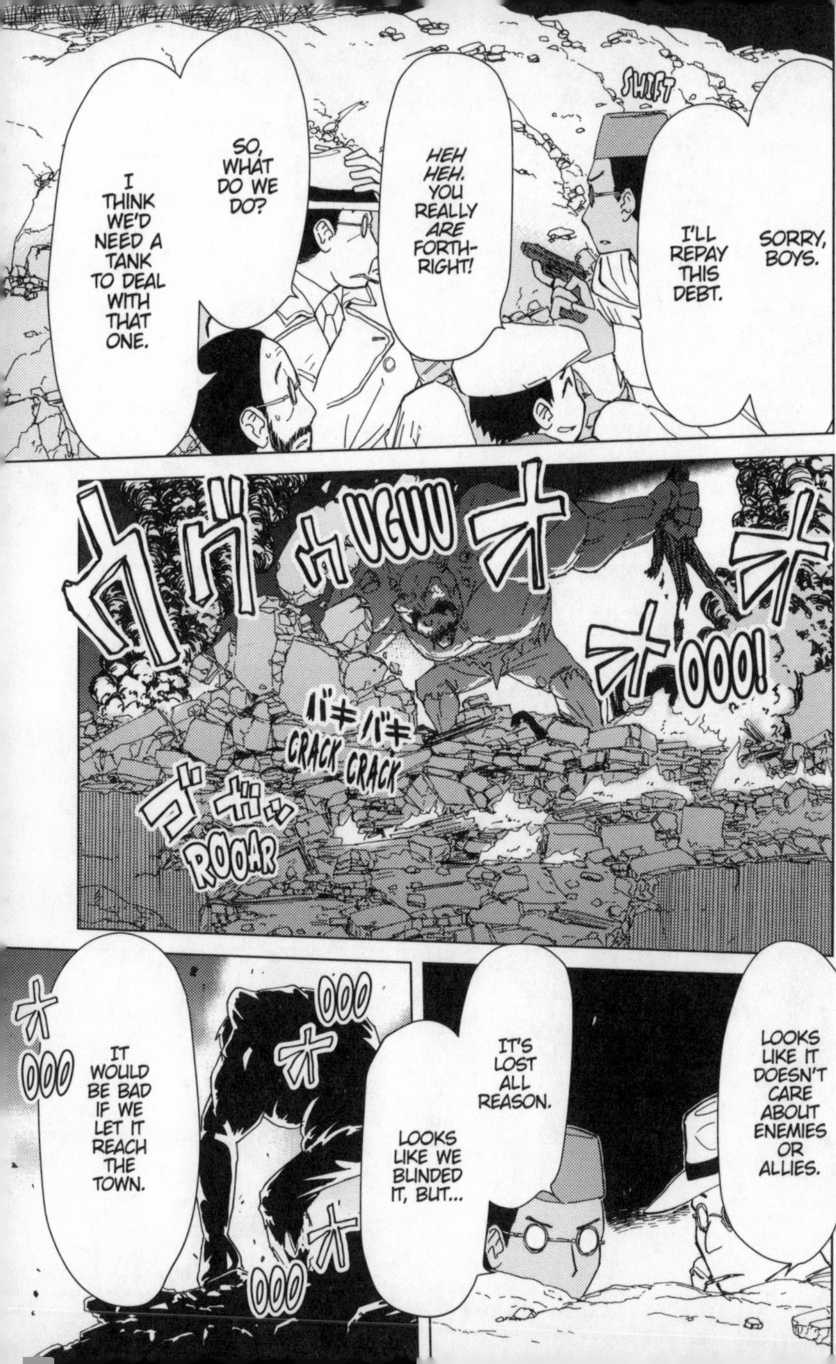
SHIFT
SORRY, BOYS.
I'LL REPAY THIS DEBT.
HEH HEH. YOU REALLY ARE FORTHRIGHT!
SO, WHAT DO WE DO?
I THINK WE'D NEED A TANK TO DEAL WITH THAT ONE.
ウヴゥ UGUU
オオオ OOO!
バキバキ CRACK CRACK
ゴガッ ROOAR
LOOKS LIKE IT DOESN'T CARE ABOUT ENEMIES OR ALLIES.
IT'S LOST ALL REASON.
LOOKS LIKE WE BLINDED IT, BUT...
OOO オ
オ OOO
IT WOULD BE BAD IF WE LET IT REACH THE TOWN.
オ OOO

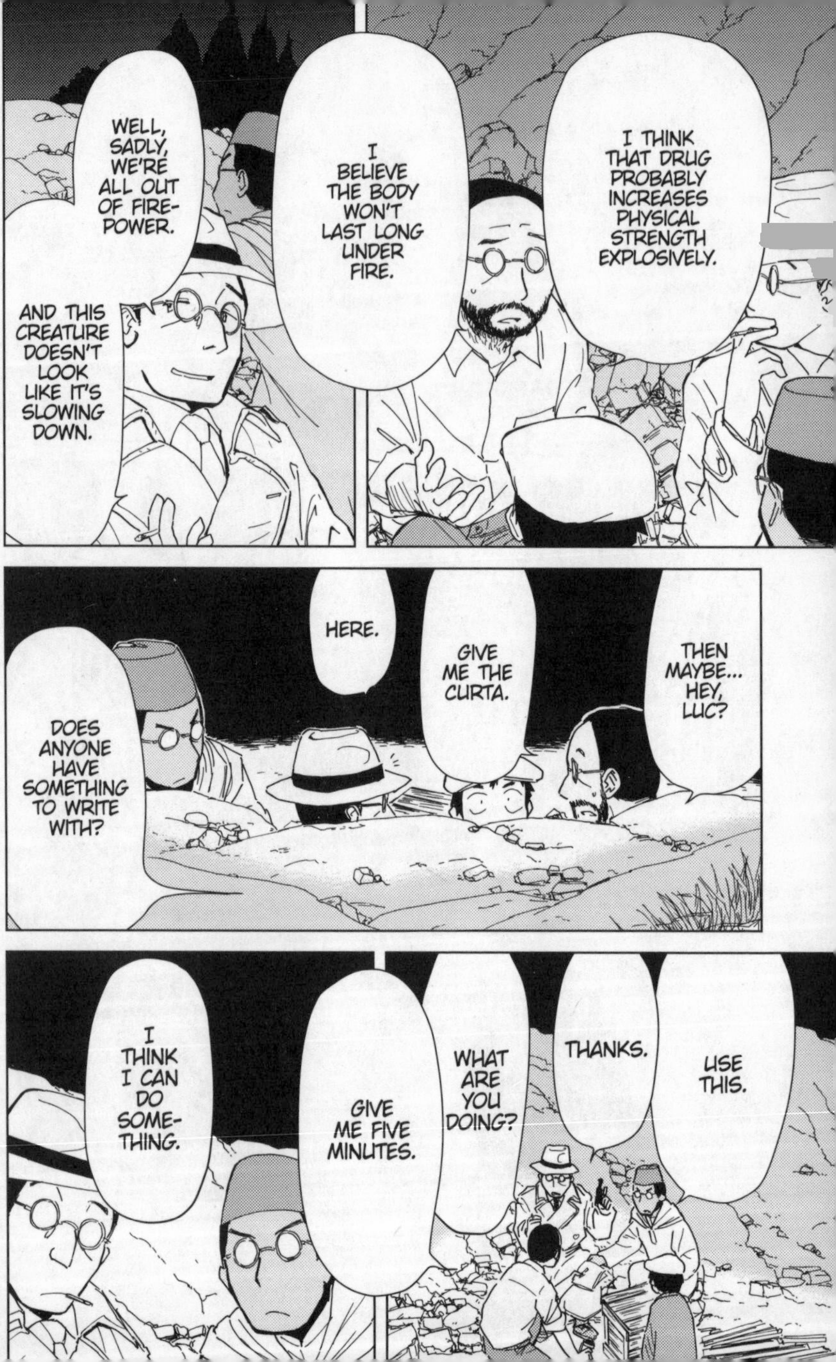
I THINK THAT DRUG PROBABLY INCREASES PHYSICAL STRENGTH EXPLOSIVELY.
I BELIEVE THE BODY WON'T LAST LONG UNDER FIRE.
WELL, SADLY, WE'RE ALL OUT OF FIRE-POWER.
AND THIS CREATURE DOESN'T LOOK LIKE IT'S SLOWING DOWN.
THEN MAYBE... HEY, LUC?
GIVE ME THE CURTA.
HERE.
DOES ANYONE HAVE SOMETHING TO WRITE WITH?
USE THIS.
THANKS.
WHAT ARE YOU DOING?
GIVE ME FIVE MINUTES.
I THINK I CAN DO SOME-THING.

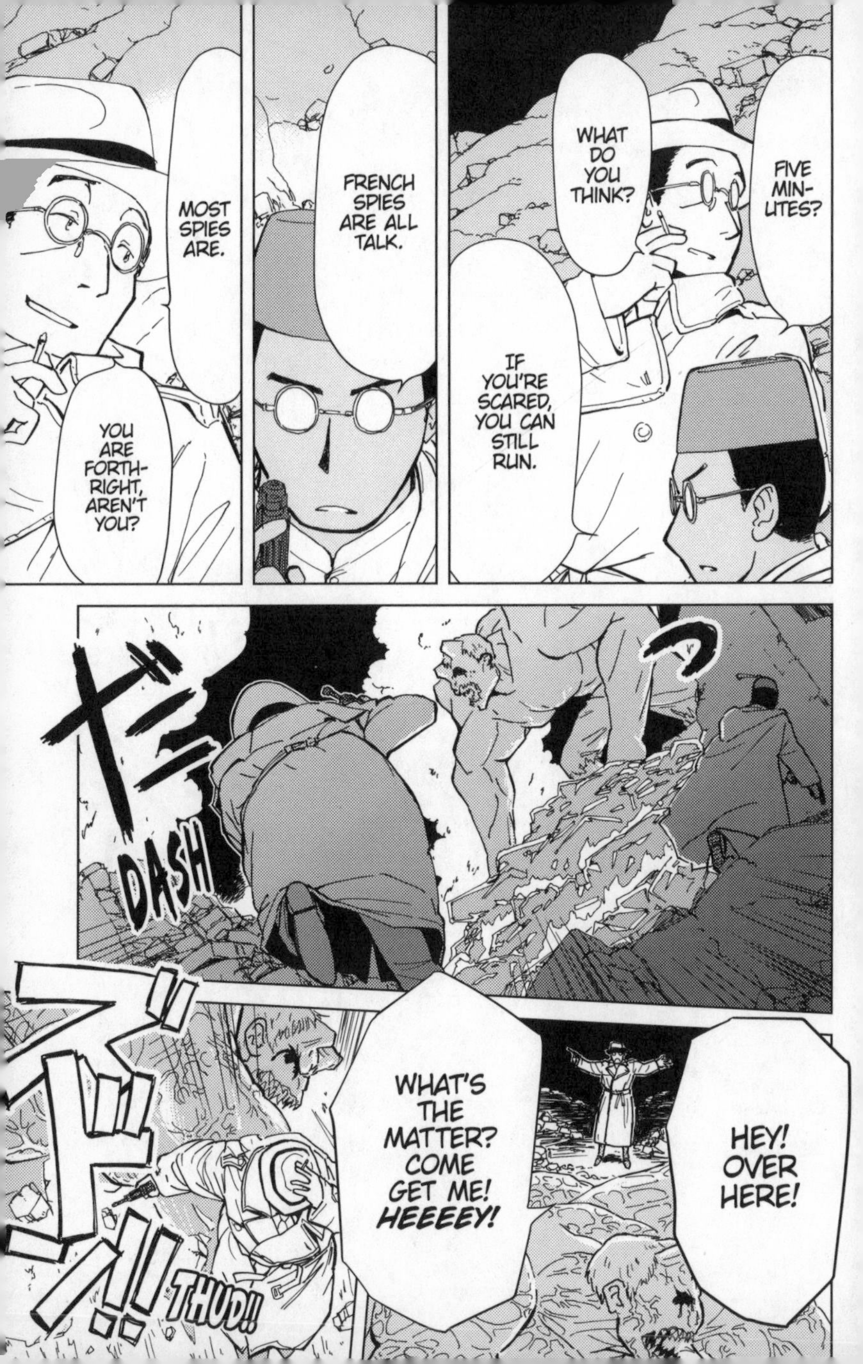

FIVE MIN-UTES?
WHAT DO YOU THINK?
IF YOU'RE SCARED, YOU CAN STILL RUN.
FRENCH SPIES ARE ALL TALK.
MOST SPIES ARE.
YOU ARE FORTH-RIGHT, AREN'T YOU?
DASH
HEY! OVER HERE!
WHAT'S THE MATTER? COME GET ME! *HEEEEY!*
THUD!!

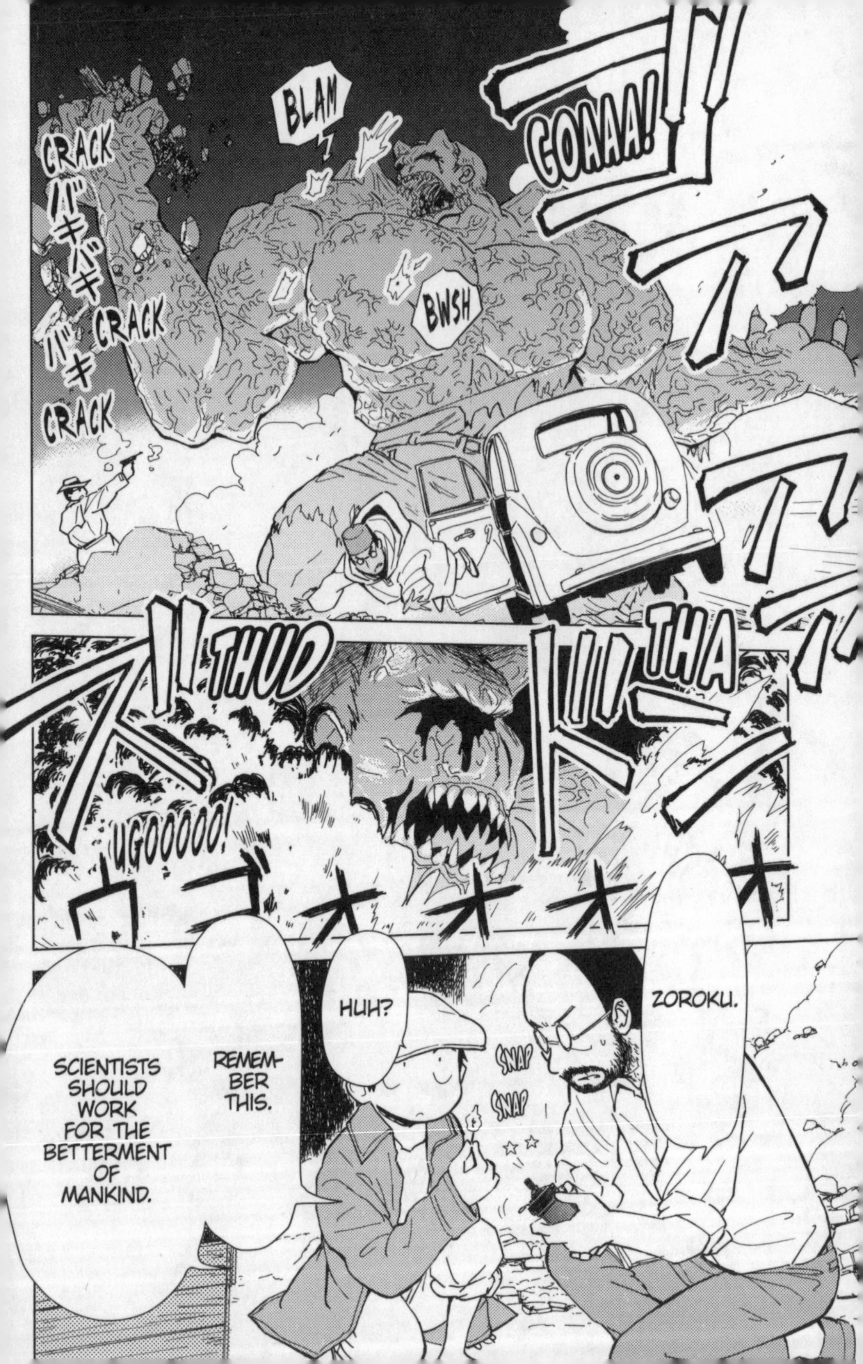

GOAAA!
BLAM
BWSH
CRACK
バキバキ
CRACK
バキ
CRACK
THA
THUD
UGOOOOO!
ZOROKU.
HUH?
SNAP
SNAP
REMEMBER THIS.
SCIENTISTS SHOULD WORK FOR THE BETTERMENT OF MANKIND.

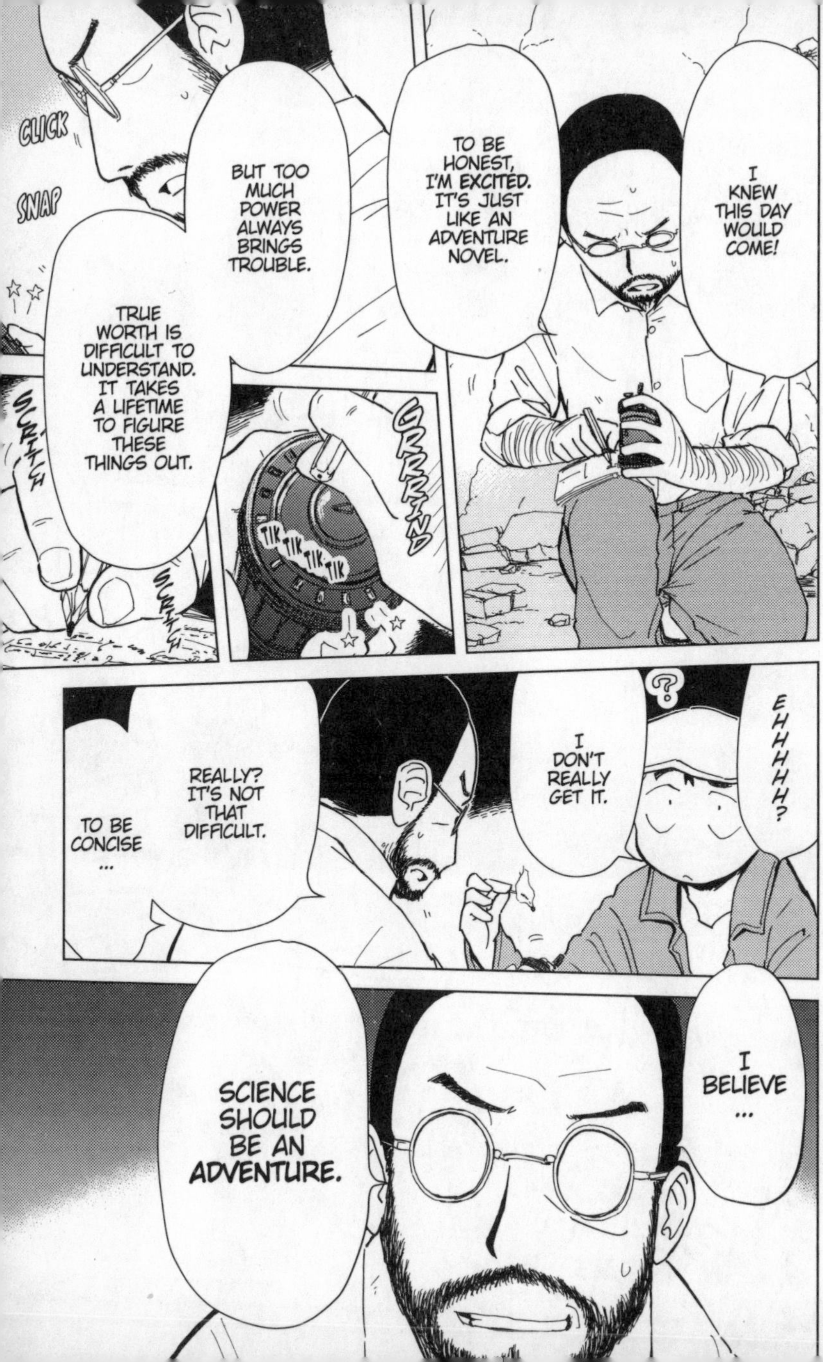
I KNEW THIS DAY WOULD COME!
TO BE HONEST, I'M EXCITED. IT'S JUST LIKE AN ADVENTURE NOVEL.
BUT TOO MUCH POWER ALWAYS BRINGS TROUBLE.
CLICK
SNAP
GRRRIND
TIK TIK TIK TIK
TRUE WORTH IS DIFFICULT TO UNDERSTAND. IT TAKES A LIFETIME TO FIGURE THESE THINGS OUT.
SCRITCH
SCRITCH
EHHHHHH?
?
I DON'T REALLY GET IT.
REALLY? IT'S NOT THAT DIFFICULT.
TO BE CONCISE ...
I BELIEVE ...
SCIENCE SHOULD BE AN ADVENTURE.

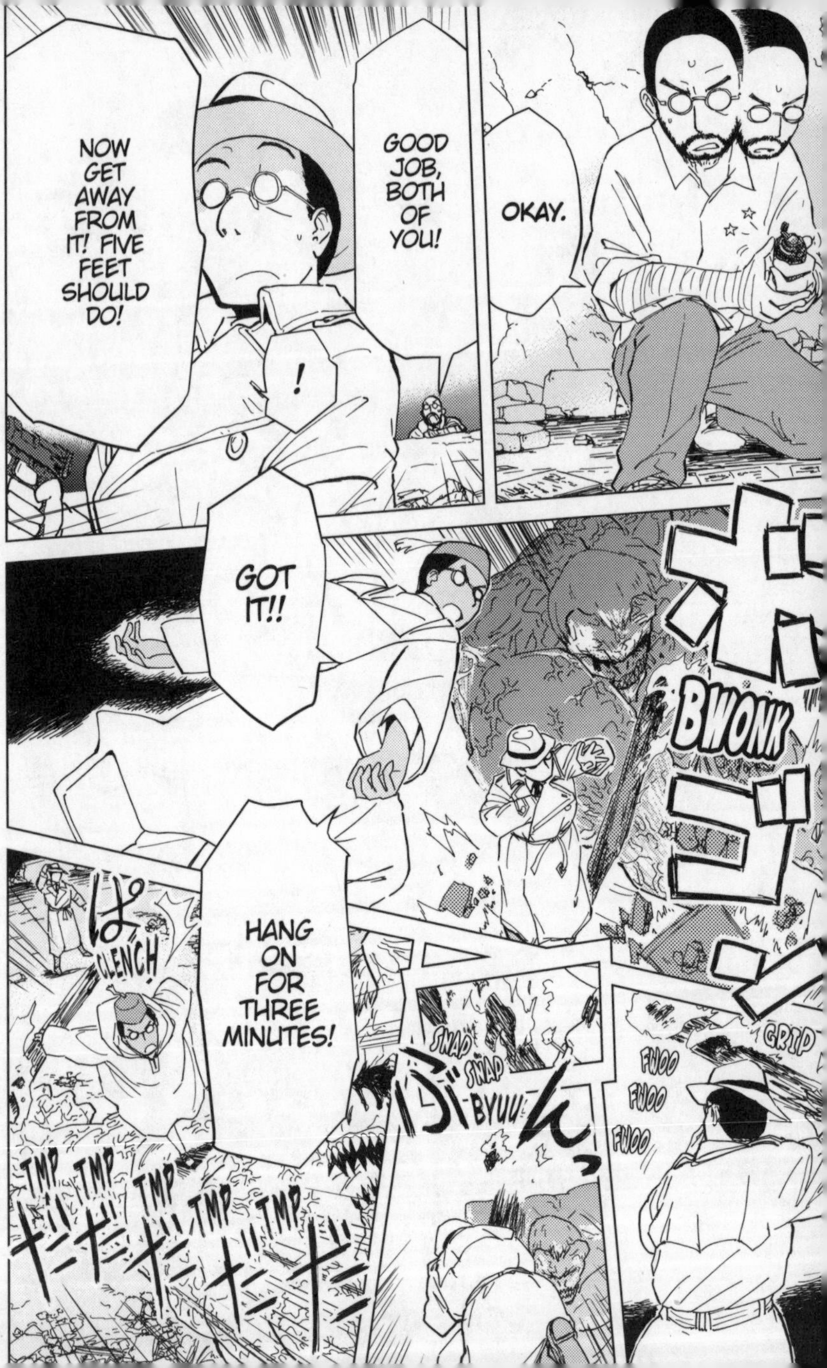
OKAY.
GOOD JOB, BOTH OF YOU!
NOW GET AWAY FROM IT! FIVE FEET SHOULD DO!
!
BWONK
GOT IT!!
GRIP
FWOO
FWOO
FWOO
SNAP
SNAP
BYUU
HANG ON FOR THREE MINUTES!
CLENCH
TMP TMP TMP TMP TMP TMP

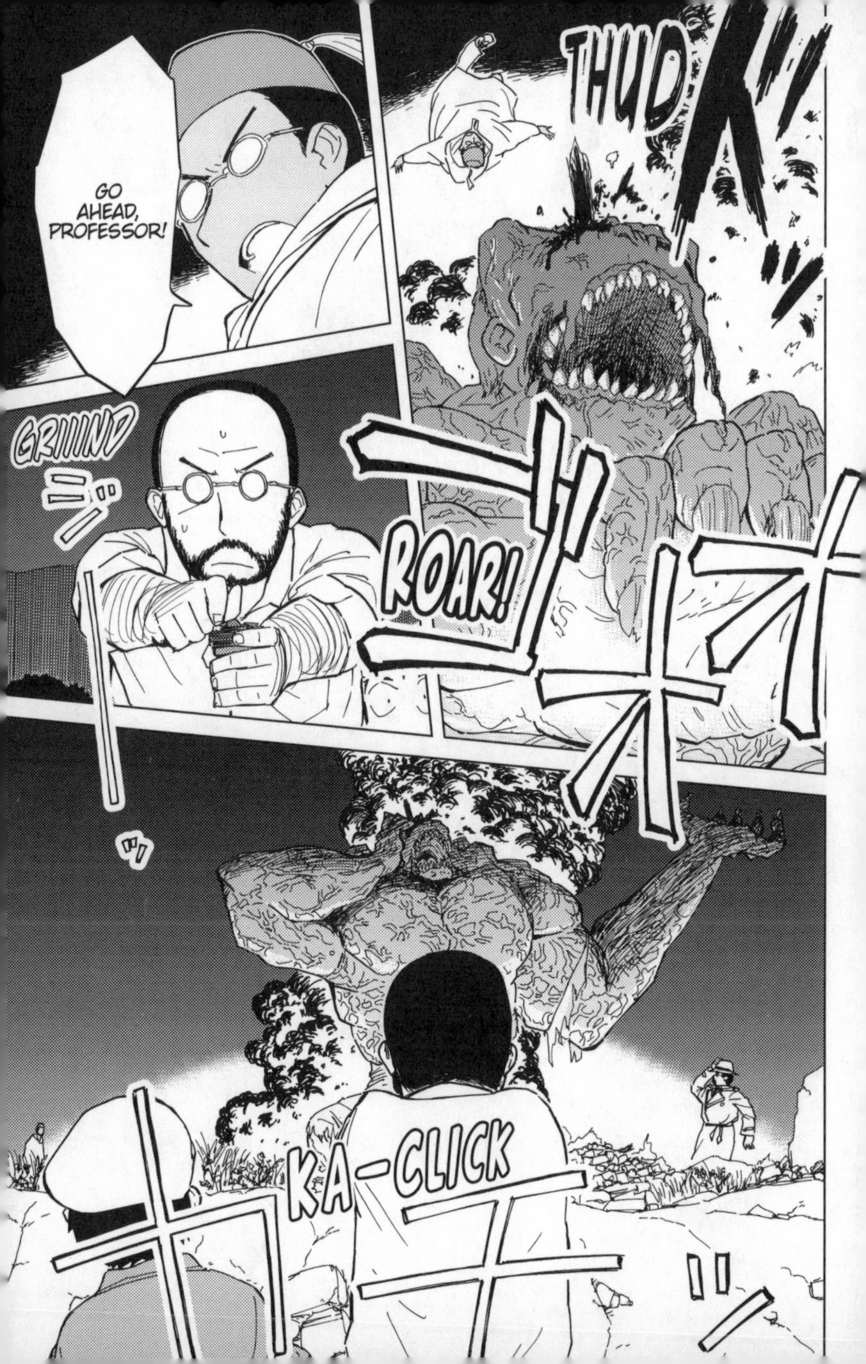
THUD
GO AHEAD, PROFESSOR!
ROAR!
GRIIIND
KA-CLICK

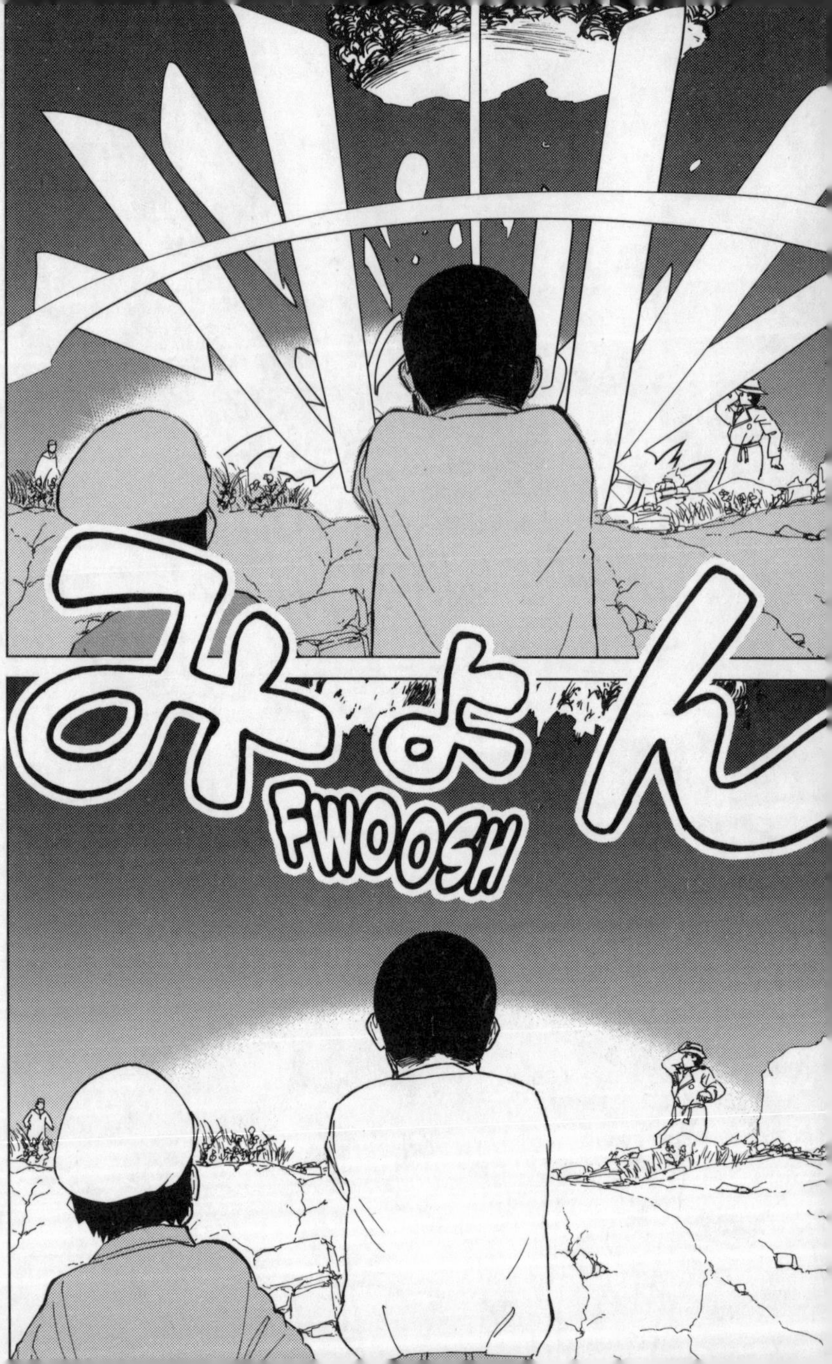
みょん
FWOOSH

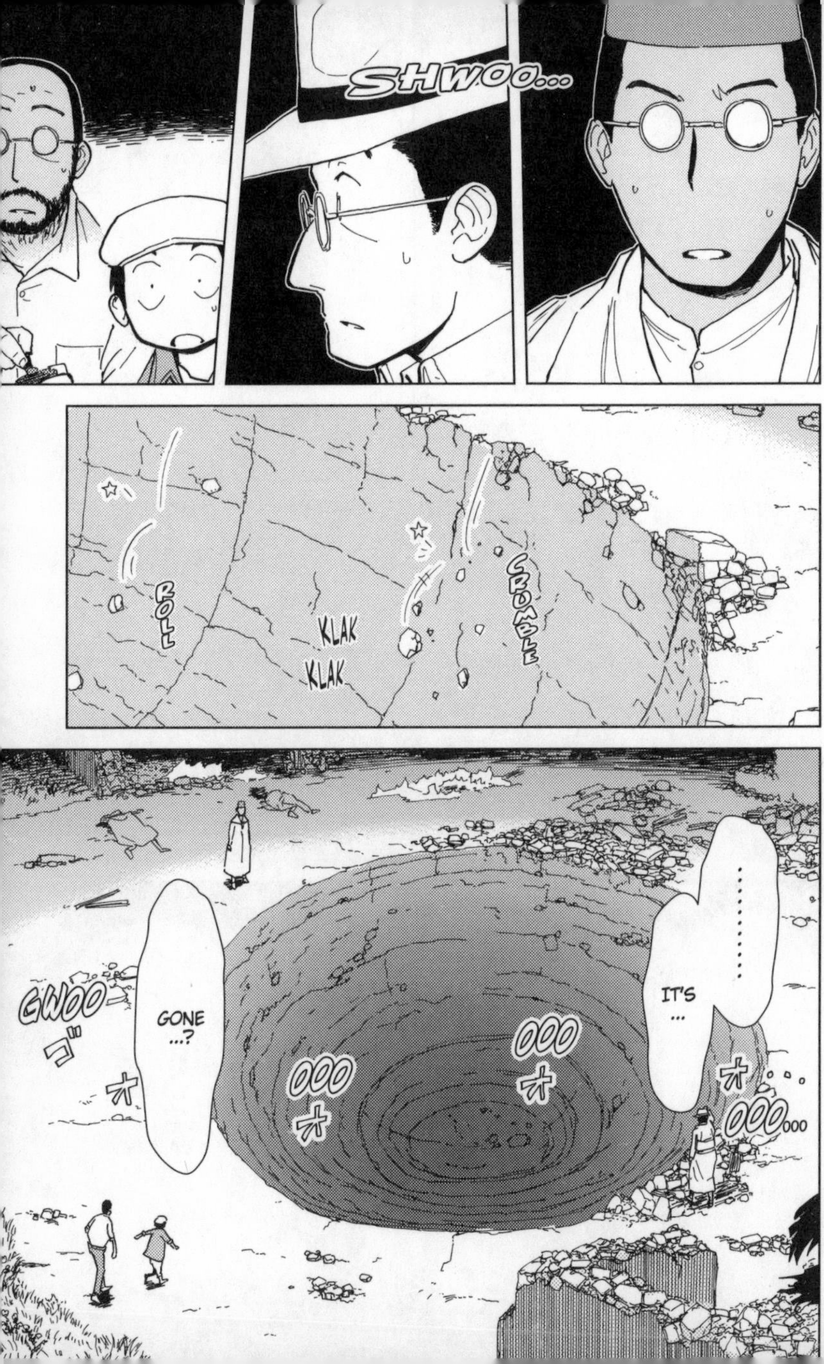
SHWOO...
CRUMBLE
KLAK
KLAK
ROLL
......
IT'S ...
OOO...
オ
OOO
オ
OOO
オ
GONE ...?
GWOO
ゴオ

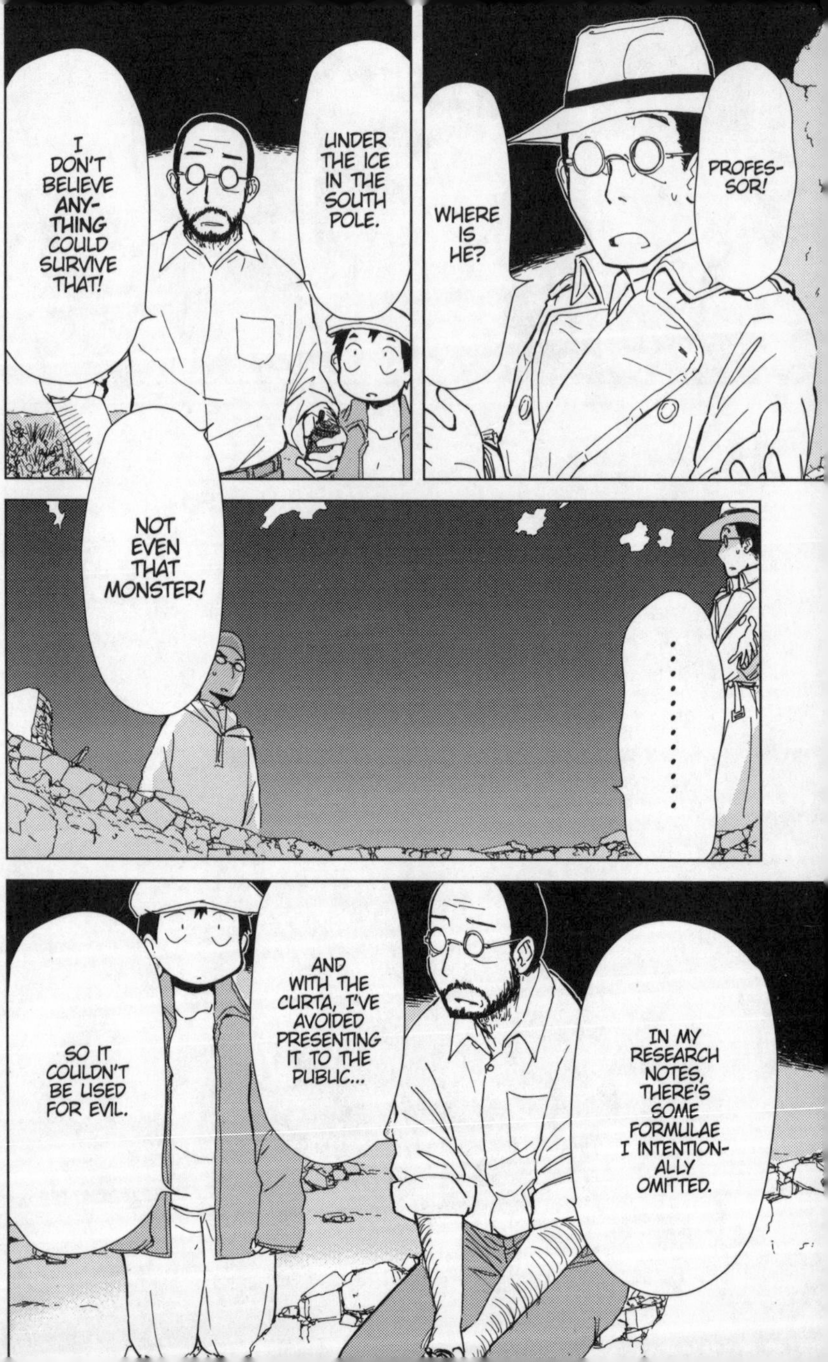
PROFESSOR!
WHERE IS HE?
UNDER THE ICE IN THE SOUTH POLE.
I DON'T BELIEVE ANYTHING COULD SURVIVE THAT!
NOT EVEN THAT MONSTER!
......
IN MY RESEARCH NOTES, THERE'S SOME FORMULAE I INTENTIONALLY OMITTED.
AND WITH THE CURTA, I'VE AVOIDED PRESENTING IT TO THE PUBLIC...
SO IT COULDN'T BE USED FOR EVIL.

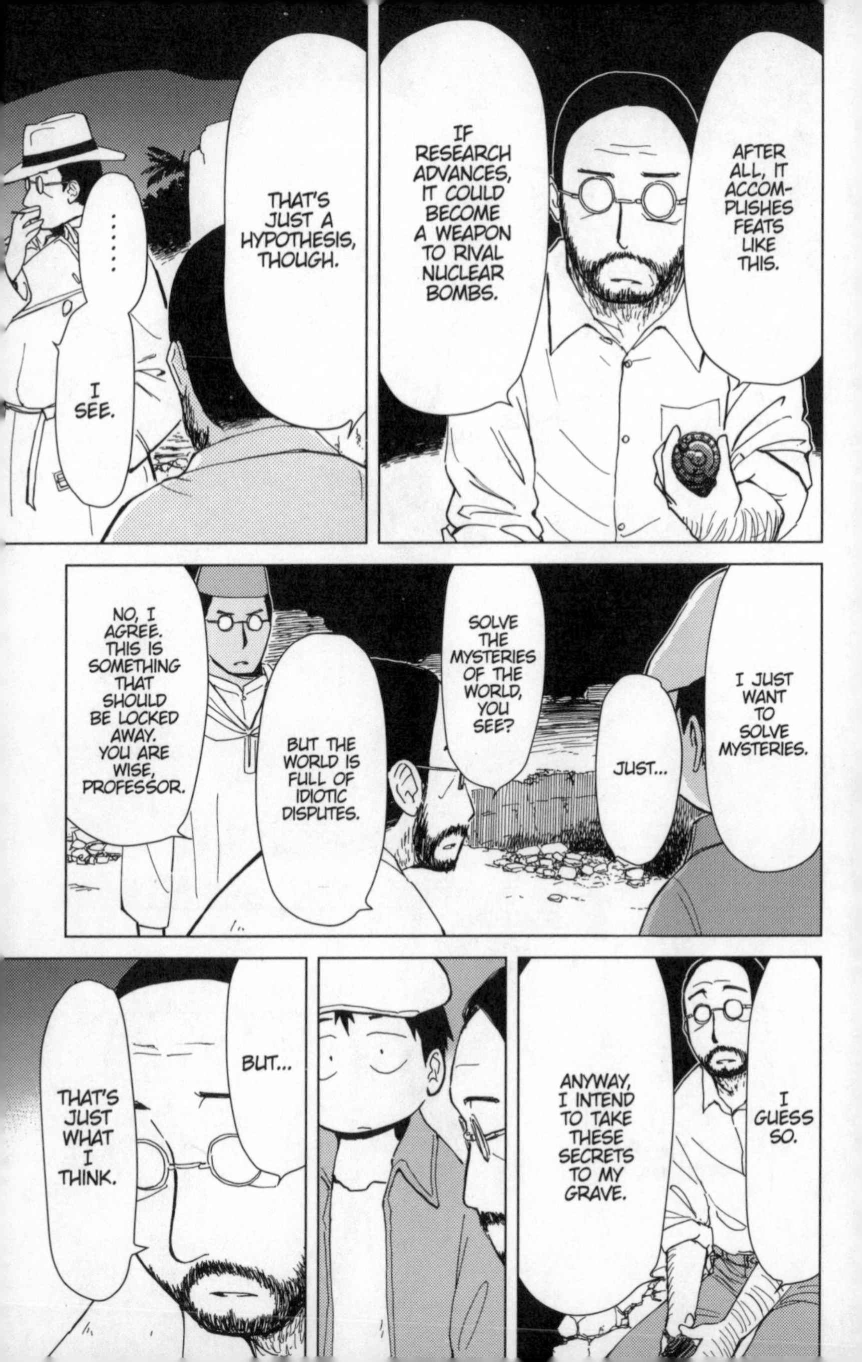
AFTER ALL, IT ACCOMPLISHES FEATS LIKE THIS.
IF RESEARCH ADVANCES, IT COULD BECOME A WEAPON TO RIVAL NUCLEAR BOMBS.
THAT'S JUST A HYPOTHESIS, THOUGH.
......
I SEE.
I JUST WANT TO SOLVE MYSTERIES.
JUST...
SOLVE THE MYSTERIES OF THE WORLD, YOU SEE?
BUT THE WORLD IS FULL OF IDIOTIC DISPUTES.
NO, I AGREE. THIS IS SOMETHING THAT SHOULD BE LOCKED AWAY. YOU ARE WISE, PROFESSOR.
I GUESS SO.
ANYWAY, I INTEND TO TAKE THESE SECRETS TO MY GRAVE.
BUT...
THAT'S JUST WHAT I THINK.

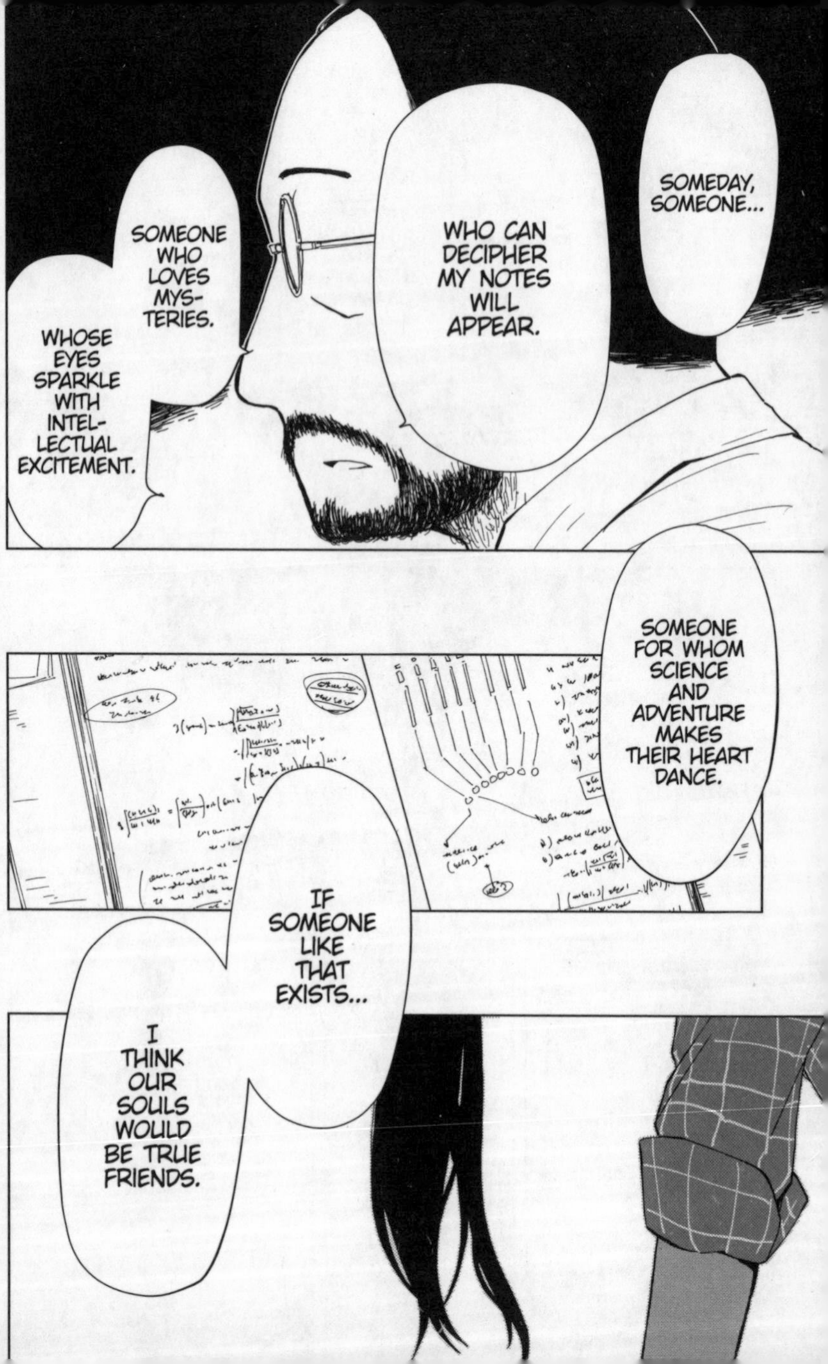
SOMEDAY, SOMEONE...
WHO CAN DECIPHER MY NOTES WILL APPEAR.
SOMEONE WHO LOVES MYSTERIES.
WHOSE EYES SPARKLE WITH INTELLECTUAL EXCITEMENT.
SOMEONE FOR WHOM SCIENCE AND ADVENTURE MAKES THEIR HEART DANCE.
IF SOMEONE LIKE THAT EXISTS...
I THINK OUR SOULS WOULD BE TRUE FRIENDS.

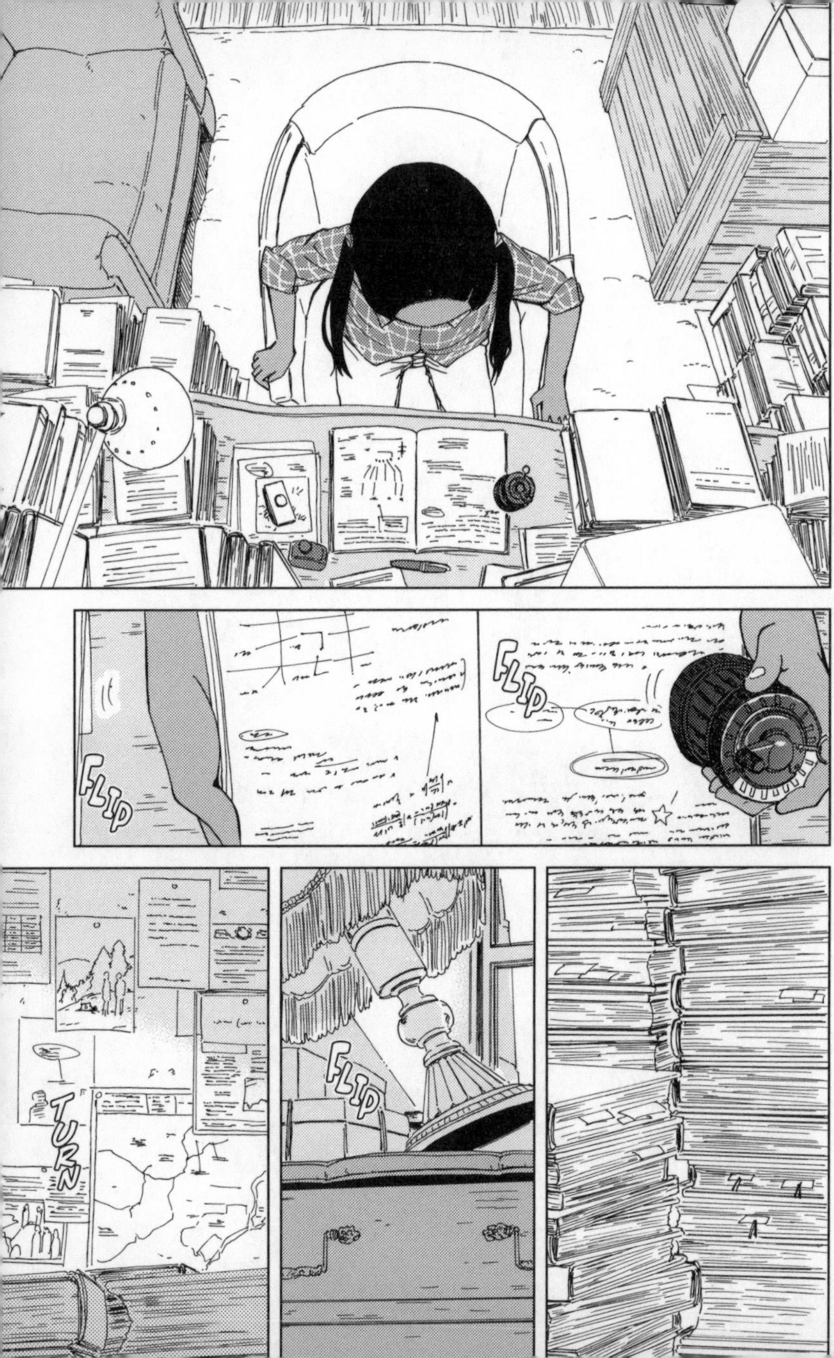
FLIP
FLIP
FLIP
TURN

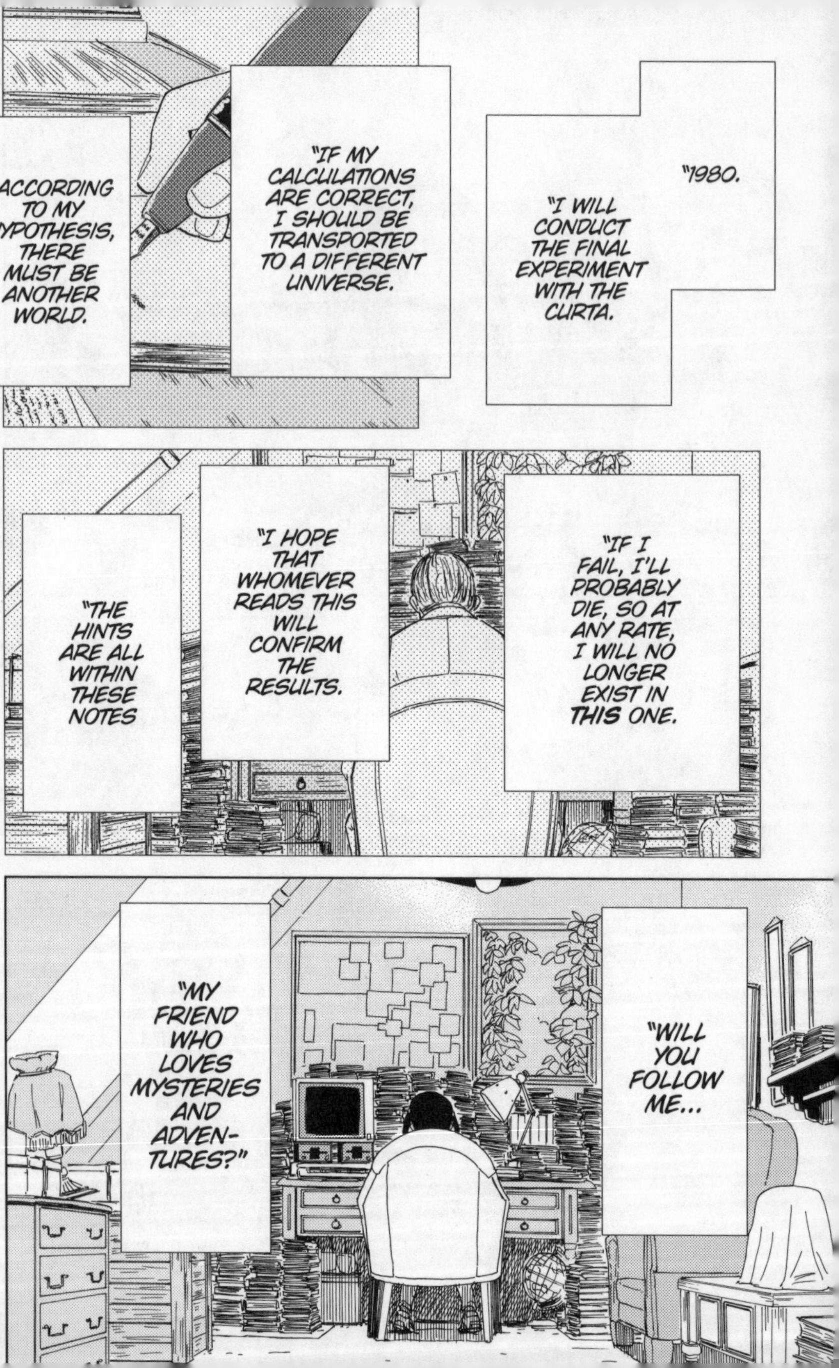
"1980.
"I WILL CONDUCT THE FINAL EXPERIMENT WITH THE CURTA.
"IF MY CALCULATIONS ARE CORRECT, I SHOULD BE TRANSPORTED TO A DIFFERENT UNIVERSE.
"ACCORDING TO MY HYPOTHESIS, THERE MUST BE ANOTHER WORLD.
"IF I FAIL, I'LL PROBABLY DIE, SO AT ANY RATE, I WILL NO LONGER EXIST IN THIS ONE.
"I HOPE THAT WHOMEVER READS THIS WILL CONFIRM THE RESULTS.
"THE HINTS ARE ALL WITHIN THESE NOTES
"WILL YOU FOLLOW ME...
"MY FRIEND WHO LOVES MYSTERIES AND ADVEN-TURES?"

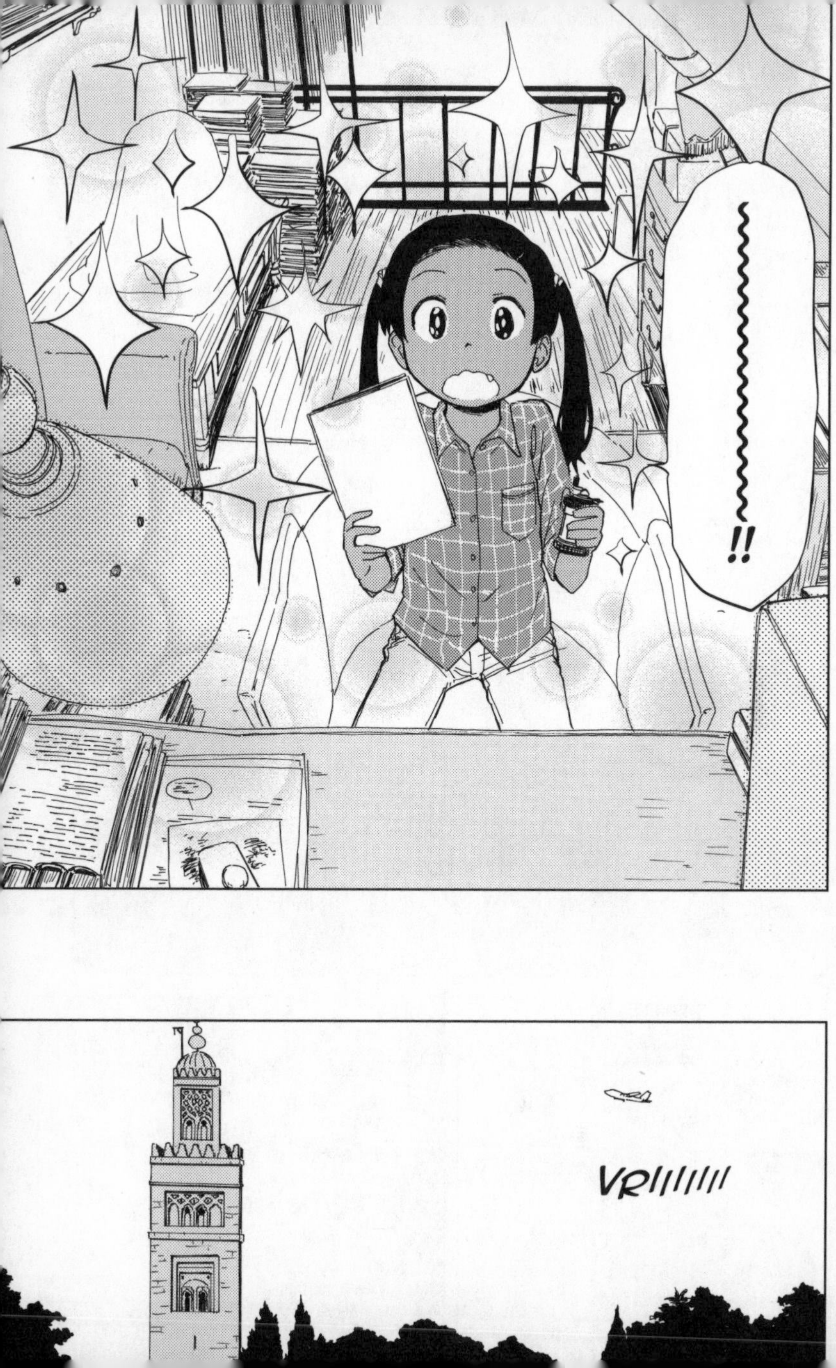
!!
VRIIIIIII

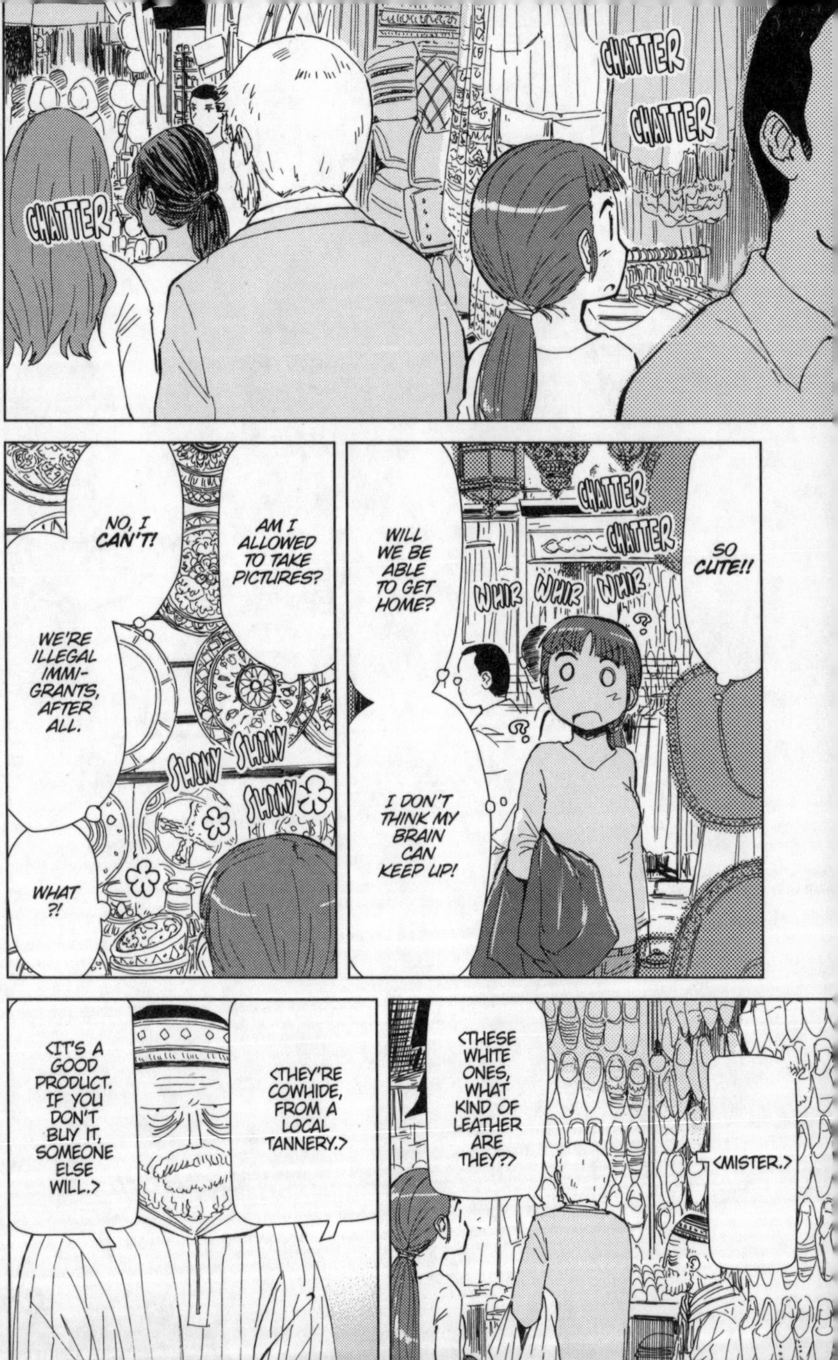
CHATTER
CHATTER
CHATTER
SO CUTE!!
CHATTER
CHATTER
WHIR WHIR WHIR
?
?
WILL WE BE ABLE TO GET HOME?
I DON'T THINK MY BRAIN CAN KEEP UP!
AM I ALLOWED TO TAKE PICTURES?
NO, I CAN'T!
WE'RE ILLEGAL IMMI-GRANTS, AFTER ALL.
SHINY SHINY
SHINY
WHAT?!
<MISTER.>
<THESE WHITE ONES, WHAT KIND OF LEATHER ARE THEY?>
<THEY'RE COWHIDE, FROM A LOCAL TANNERY.>
<IT'S A GOOD PRODUCT. IF YOU DON'T BUY IT, SOMEONE ELSE WILL.>

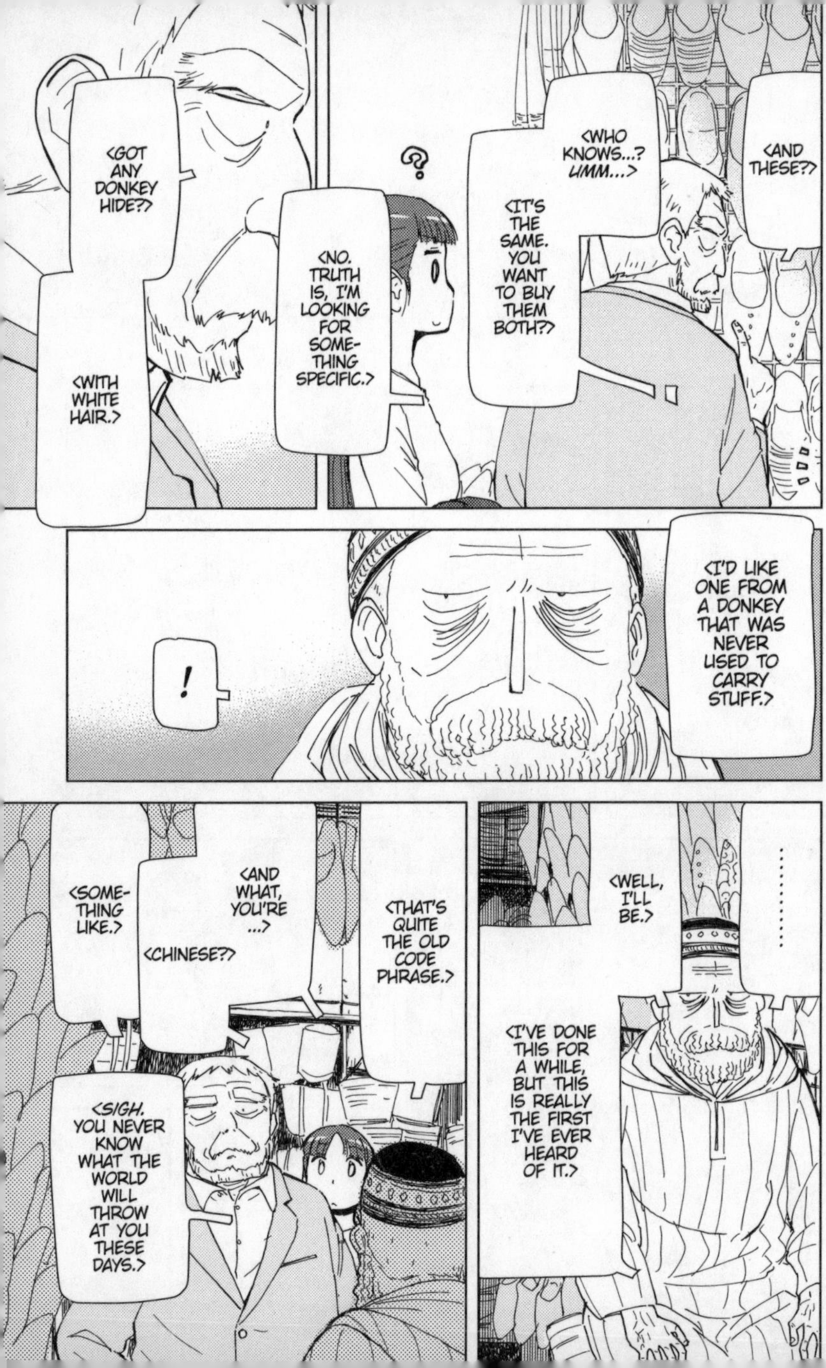
<AND THESE?>
<WHO KNOWS...? UMM...>
<IT'S THE SAME. YOU WANT TO BUY THEM BOTH?>
?
<NO. TRUTH IS, I'M LOOKING FOR SOME-THING SPECIFIC.>
<GOT ANY DONKEY HIDE?>
<WITH WHITE HAIR.>
<I'D LIKE ONE FROM A DONKEY THAT WAS NEVER USED TO CARRY STUFF.>
!
......
<WELL, I'LL BE.>
<I'VE DONE THIS FOR A WHILE, BUT THIS IS REALLY THE FIRST I'VE EVER HEARD OF IT.>
<THAT'S QUITE THE OLD CODE PHRASE.>
<AND WHAT, YOU'RE ...>
<CHINESE?>
<SOME-THING LIKE.>
<SIGH. YOU NEVER KNOW WHAT THE WORLD WILL THROW AT YOU THESE DAYS.>

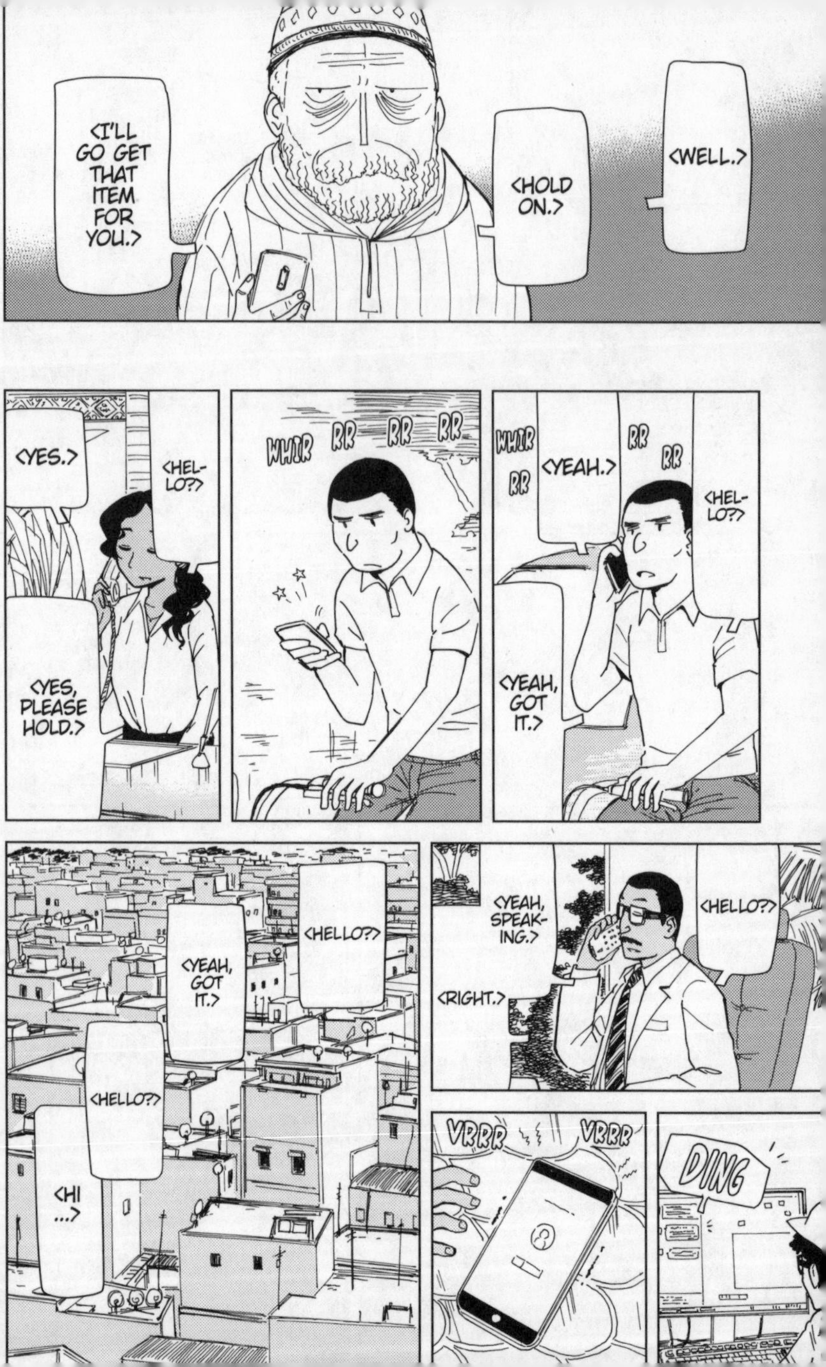
<WELL.>
<HOLD ON.>
<I'LL GO GET THAT ITEM FOR YOU.>
RR
RR
<YEAH.>
<HEL-LO?>
WHIR
RR
<YEAH, GOT IT.>
RR
RR
RR
WHIR
<HEL-LO?>
<YES.>
<YES, PLEASE HOLD.>
<HELLO?>
<YEAH, SPEAK-ING.>
<RIGHT.>
DING
VRRR
VRRR
<HELLO?>
<YEAH, GOT IT.>
<HELLO?>
<HI ...>

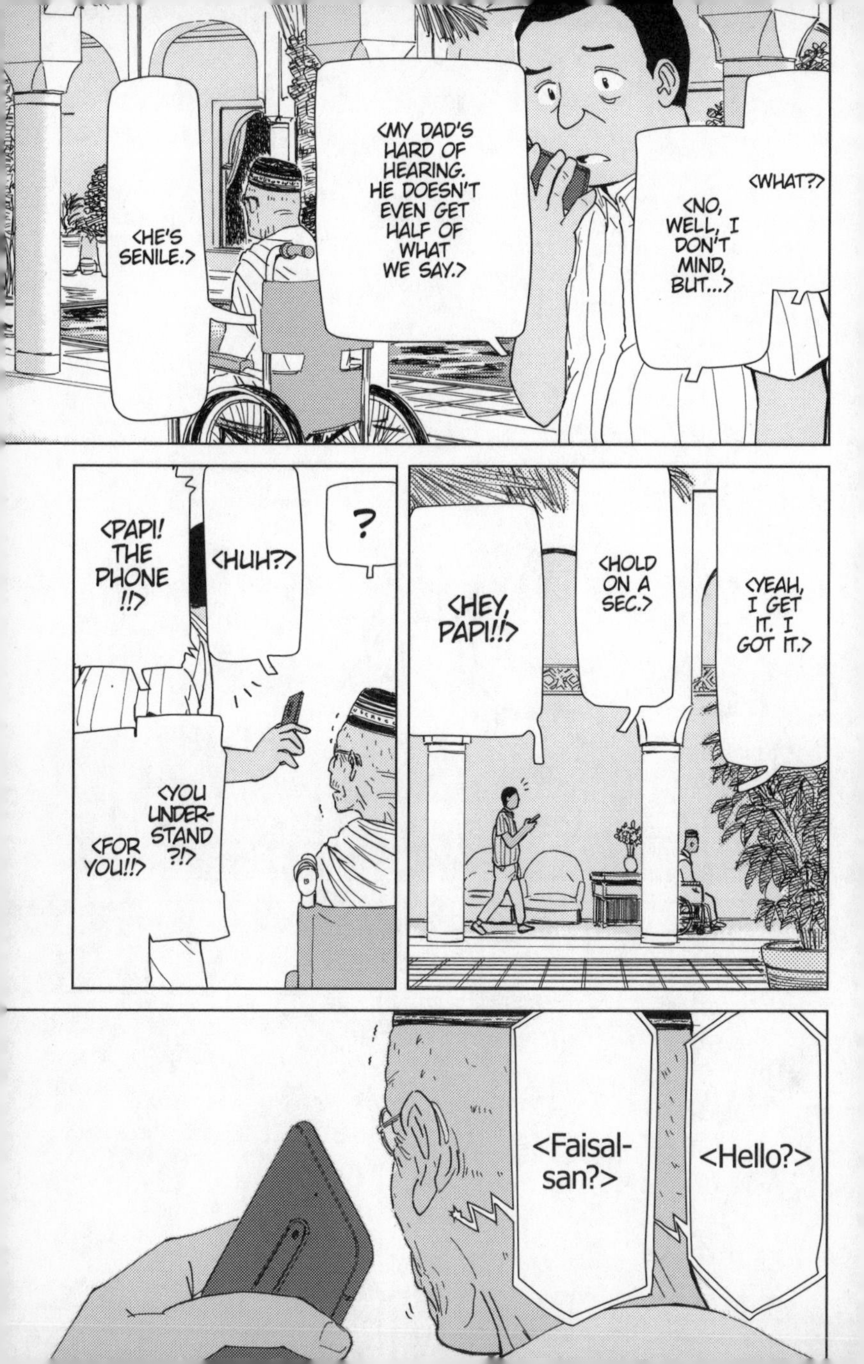
<WHAT?>
<NO, WELL, I DON'T MIND, BUT...>
<MY DAD'S HARD OF HEARING. HE DOESN'T EVEN GET HALF OF WHAT WE SAY.>
<HE'S SENILE.>
<YEAH, I GET IT. I GOT IT.>
<HOLD ON A SEC.>
<HEY, PAPI!!>
?
<HUH?>
<PAPI! THE PHONE!!>
<YOU UNDER-STAND?!>
<FOR YOU!!>
<Hello?>
<Faisal-san?>

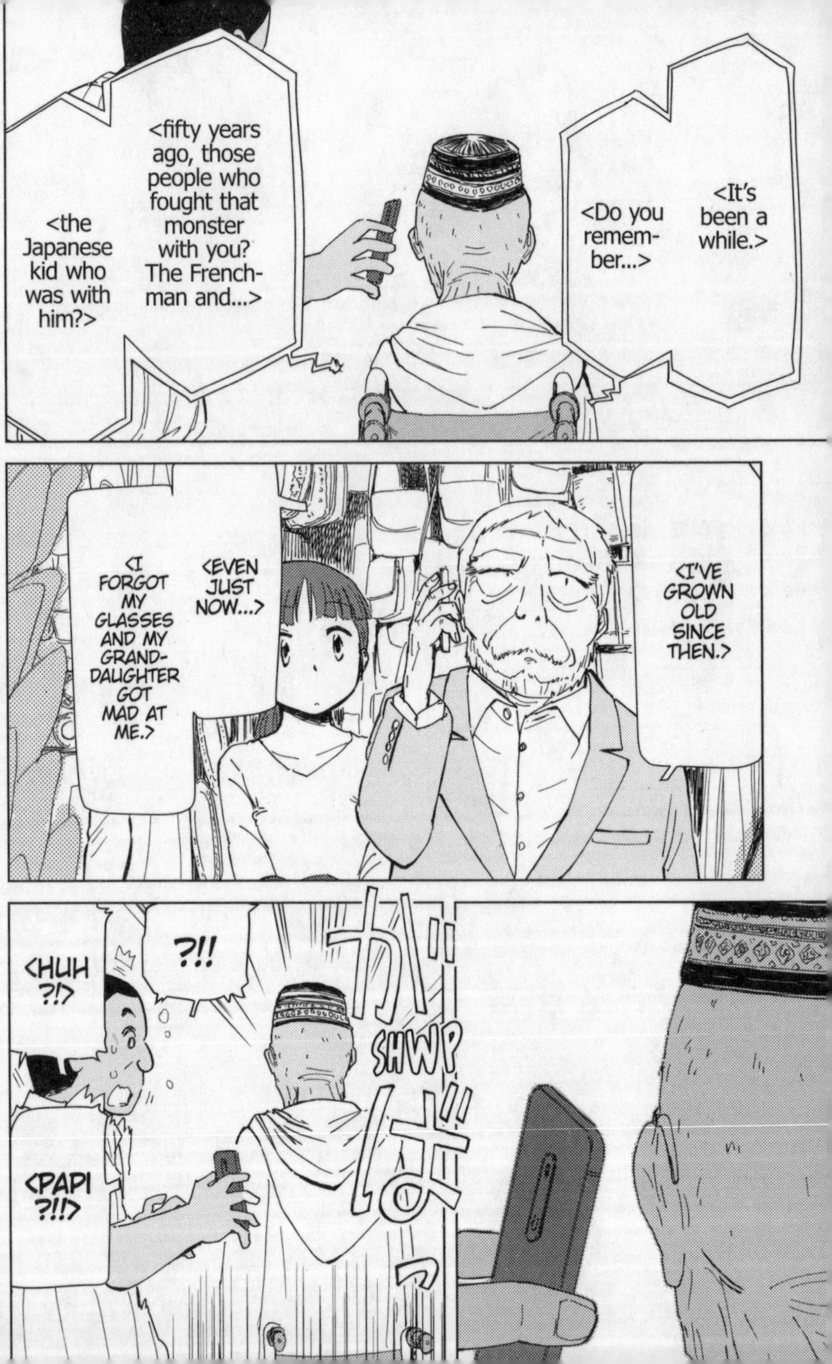

<It's been a while.>
<Do you remember...>
<fifty years ago, those people who fought that monster with you? The Frenchman and...>
<the Japanese kid who was with him?>
<I'VE GROWN OLD SINCE THEN.>
<EVEN JUST NOW...>
<I FORGOT MY GLASSES AND MY GRANDDAUGHTER GOT MAD AT ME.>
SHWP
ばっ
?!!
<HUH ?!>
<PAPI ?!!>

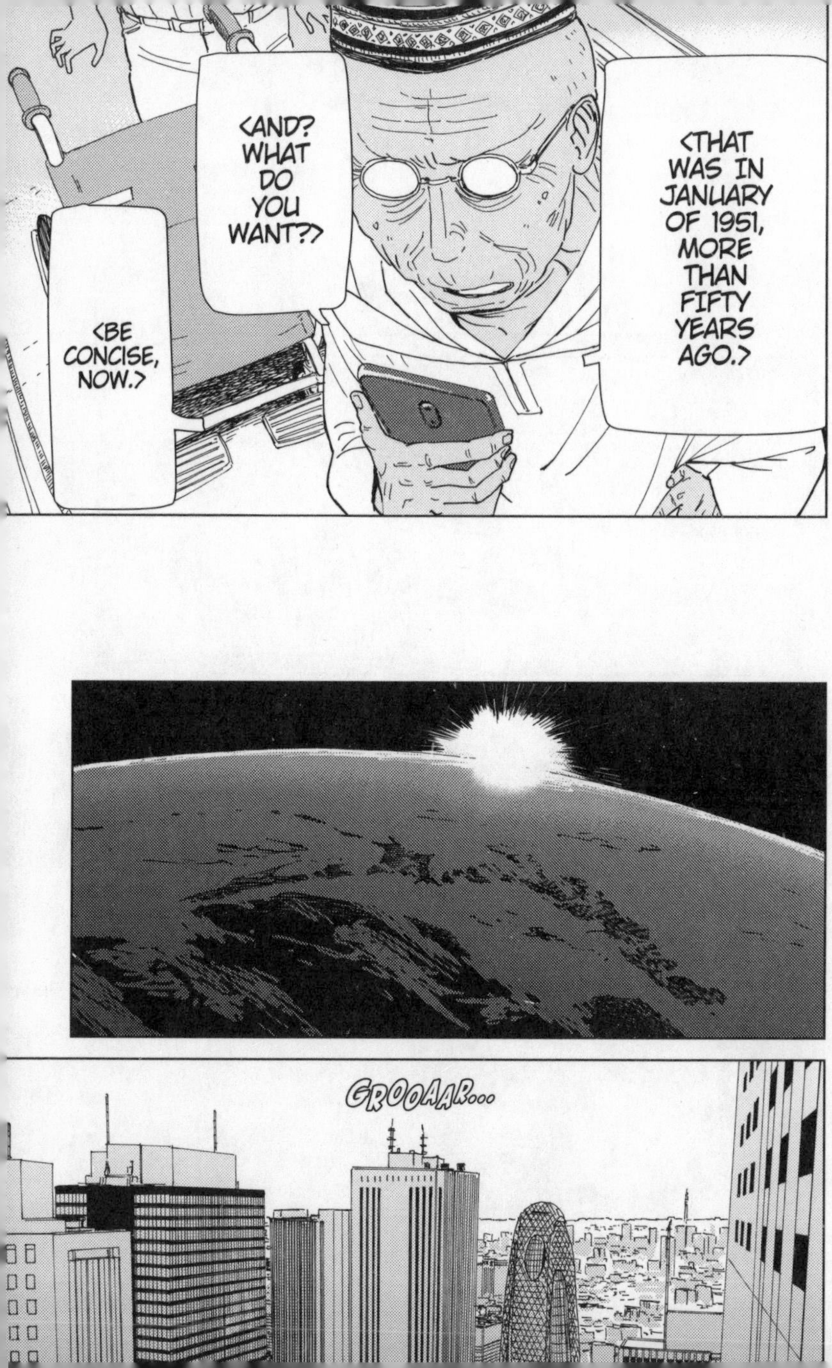
<THAT WAS IN JANUARY OF 1951, MORE THAN FIFTY YEARS AGO.>
<AND? WHAT DO YOU WANT?>
<BE CONCISE, NOW.>
GROOAAR...

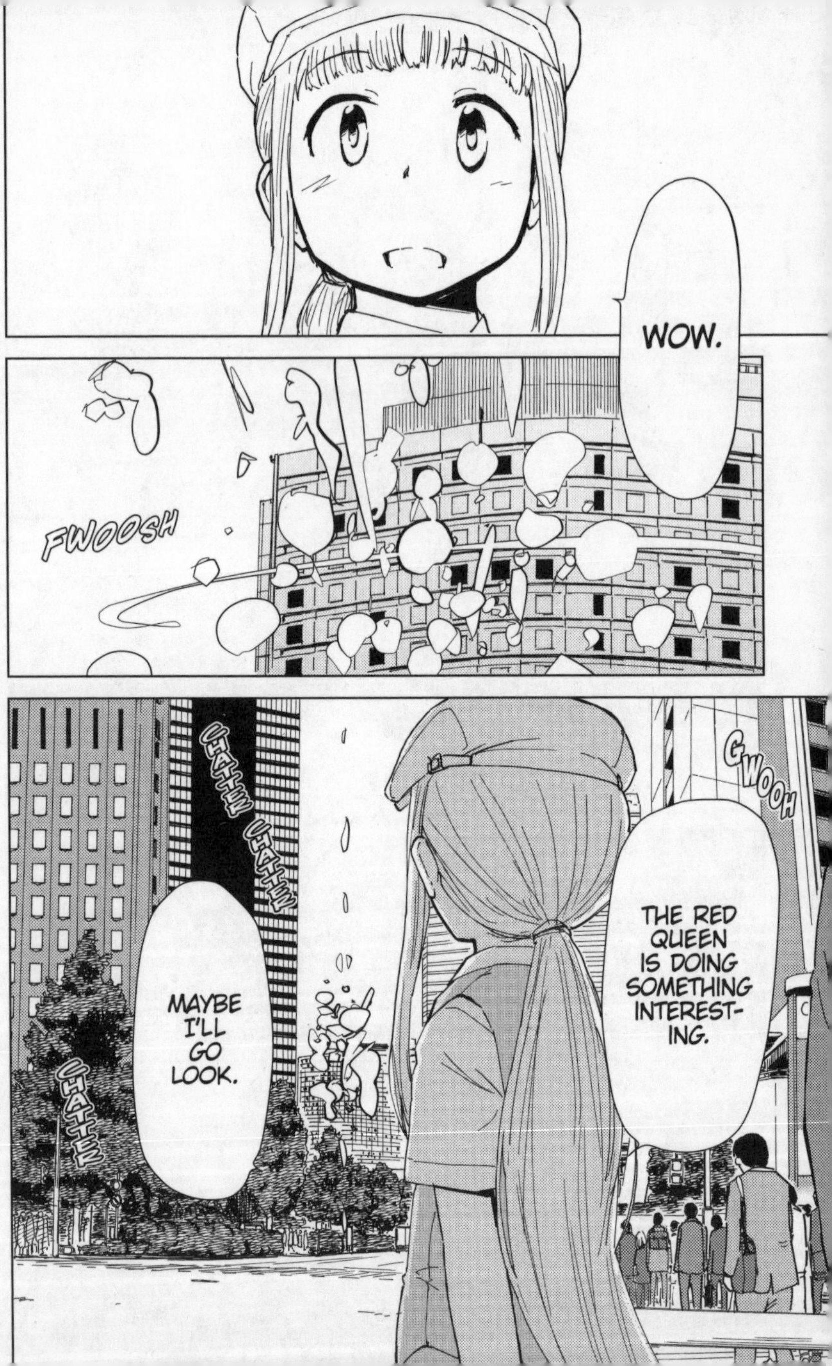
WOW.
FWOOSH
GWOOH
THE RED QUEEN IS DOING SOMETHING INTEREST-ING.
CHATTER CHATTER
MAYBE I'LL GO LOOK.
CHATTER

Alice & Zoroku

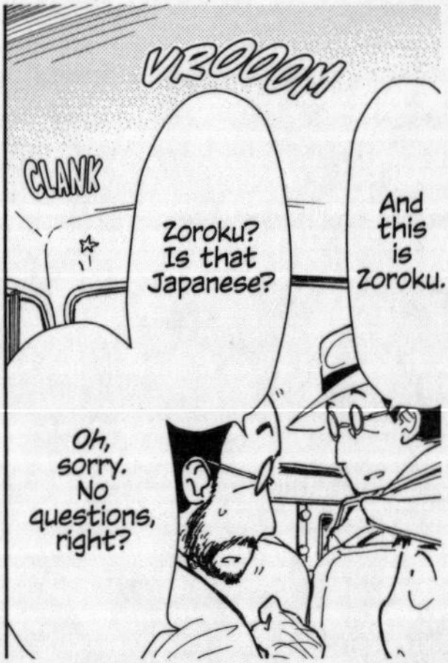
VROOOM
And this is Zoroku.
Zoroku? Is that Japanese?
CLANK
Oh, sorry. No questions, right?

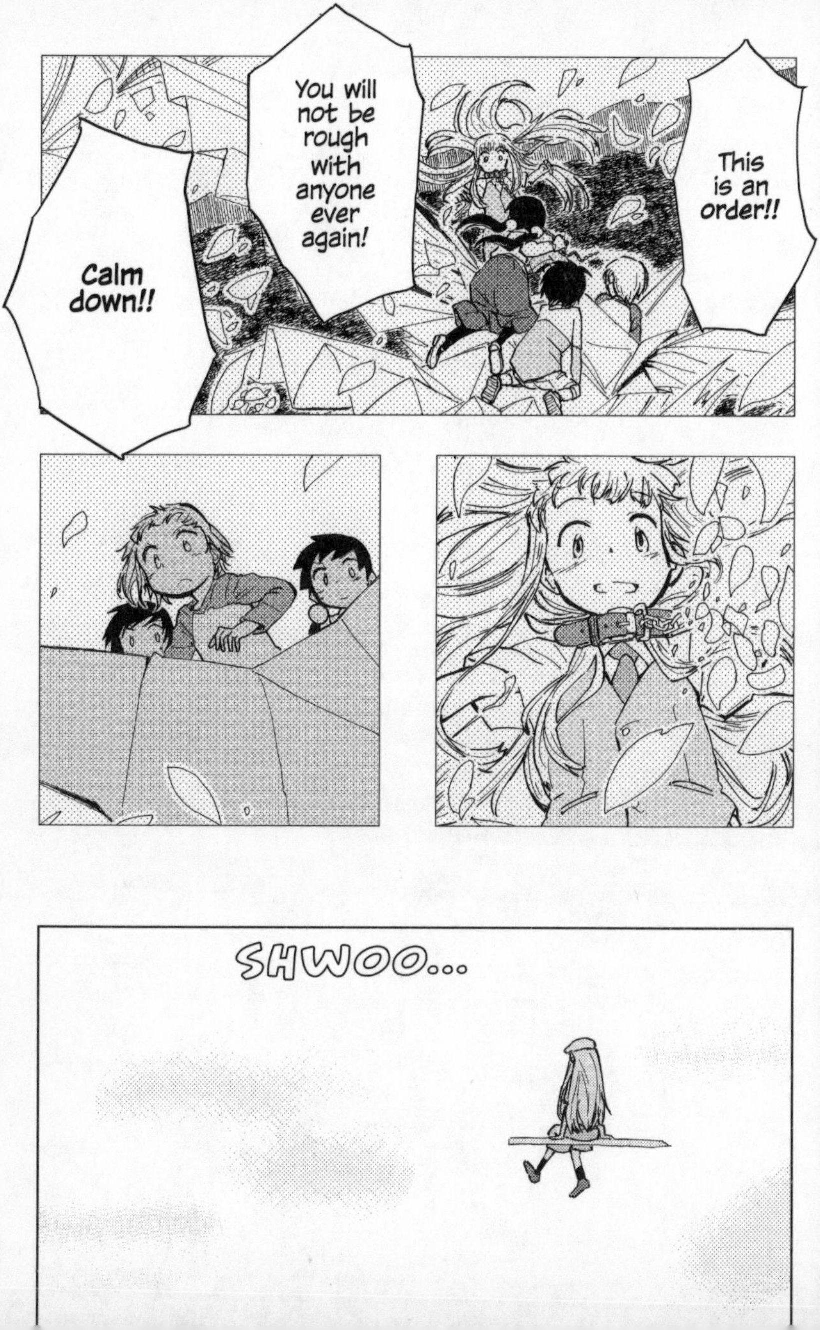
This is an order!!
You will not be rough with anyone ever again!
Calm down!!
SHWOO...

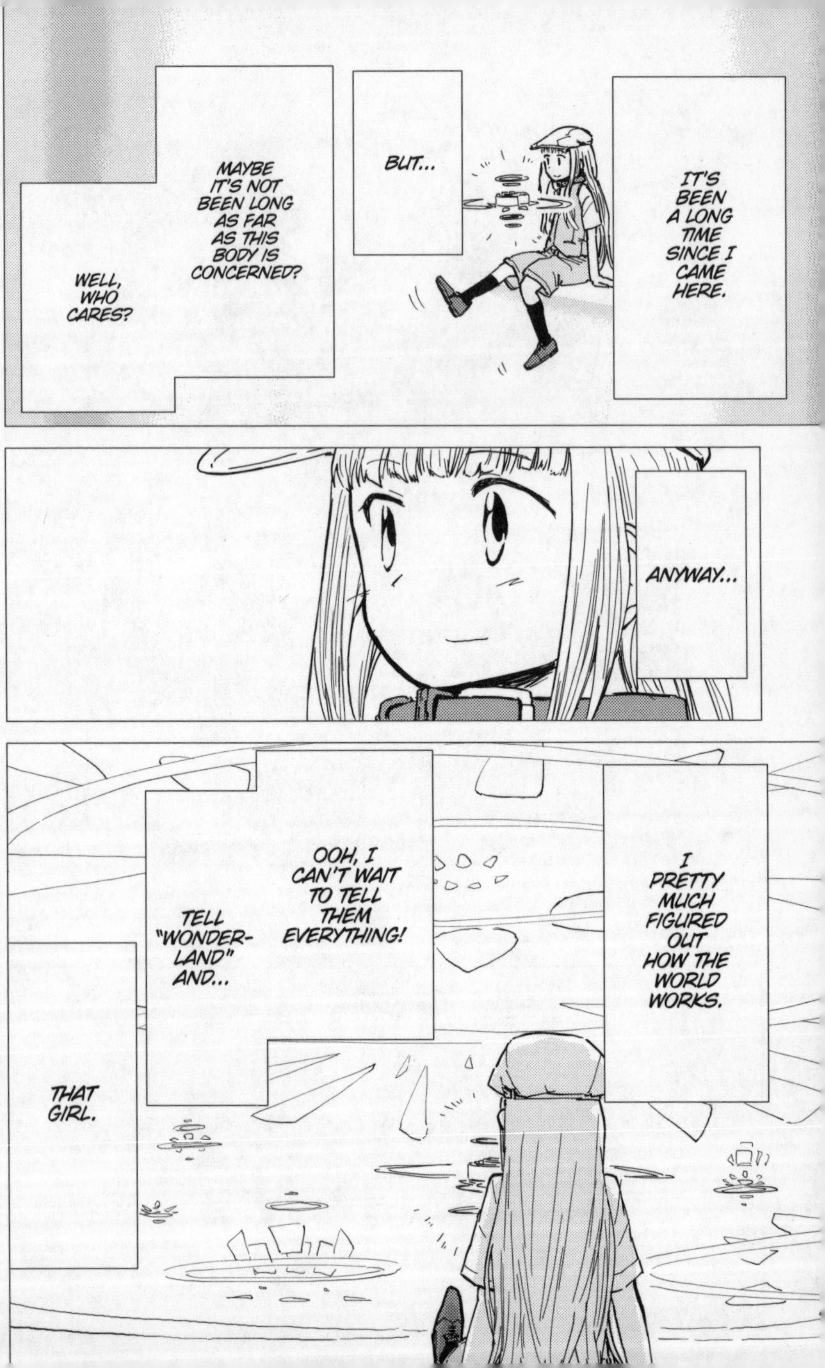
IT'S BEEN A LONG TIME SINCE I CAME HERE.
BUT...
MAYBE IT'S NOT BEEN LONG AS FAR AS THIS BODY IS CONCERNED?
WELL, WHO CARES?
ANYWAY...
I PRETTY MUCH FIGURED OUT HOW THE WORLD WORKS.
OOH, I CAN'T WAIT TO TELL THEM EVERYTHING!
TELL "WONDER-LAND" AND...
THAT GIRL.

Chapter 37:
The Story Ever After

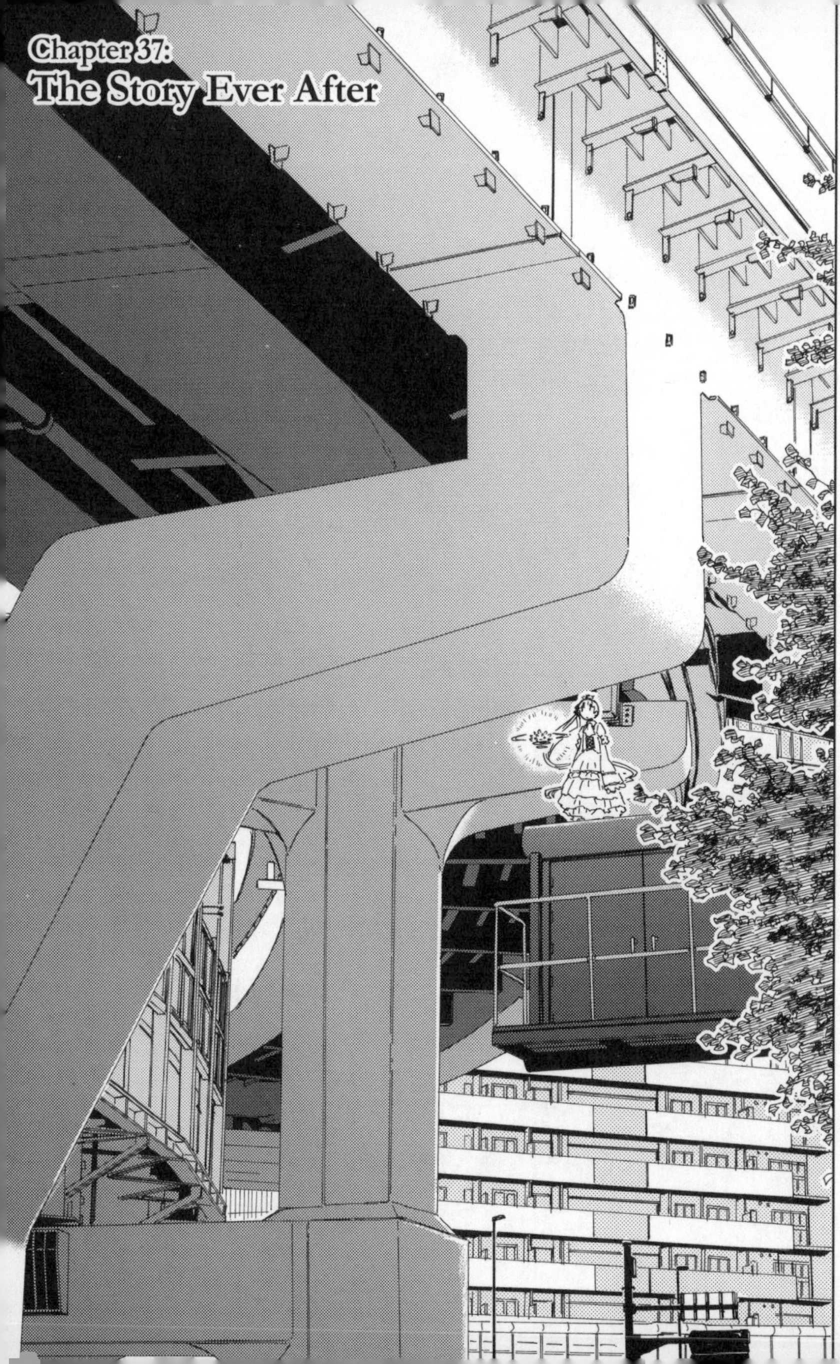

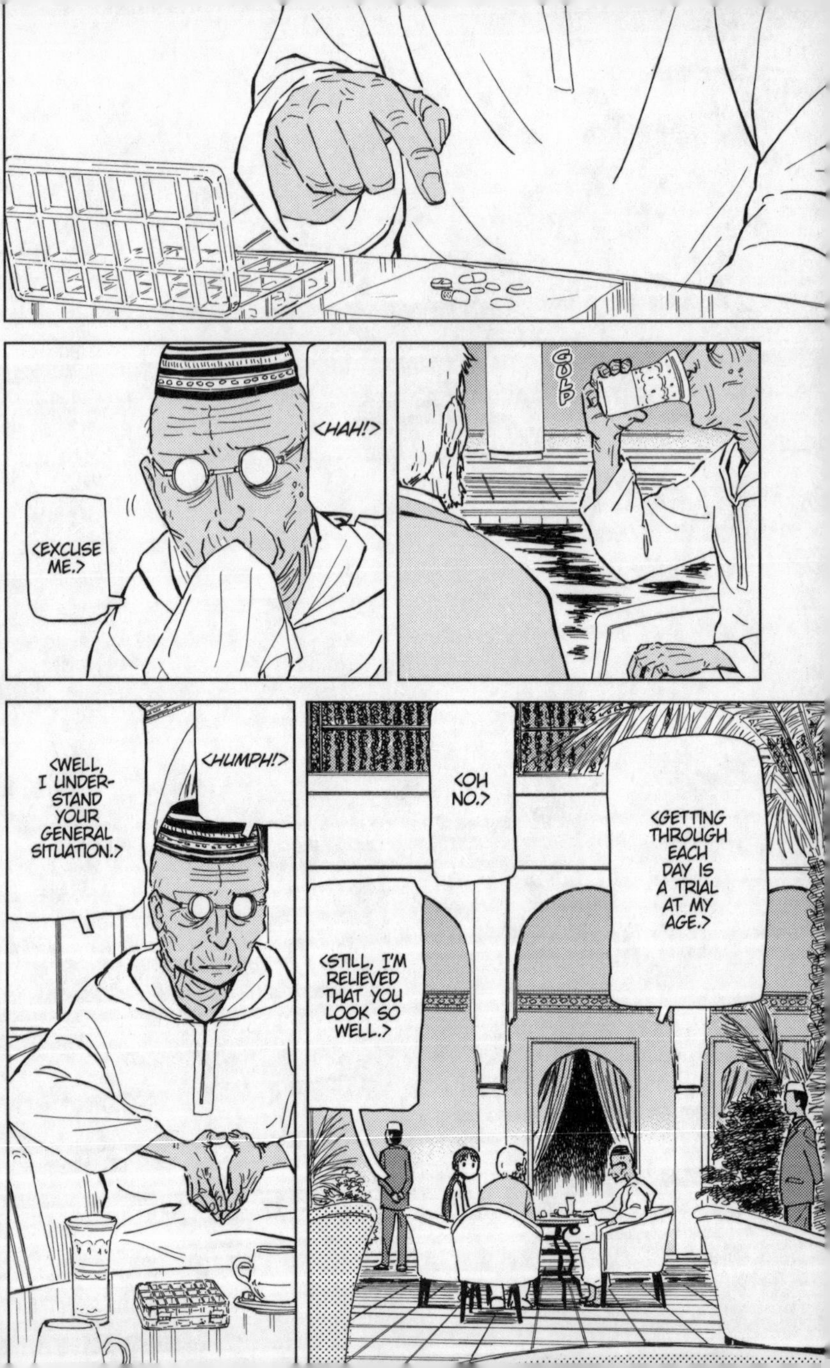
GULP
<HAH!>
<EXCUSE ME.>
<GETTING THROUGH EACH DAY IS A TRIAL AT MY AGE.>
<OH NO.>
<STILL, I'M RELIEVED THAT YOU LOOK SO WELL.>
<HUMPH!>
<WELL, I UNDER-STAND YOUR GENERAL SITUATION.>

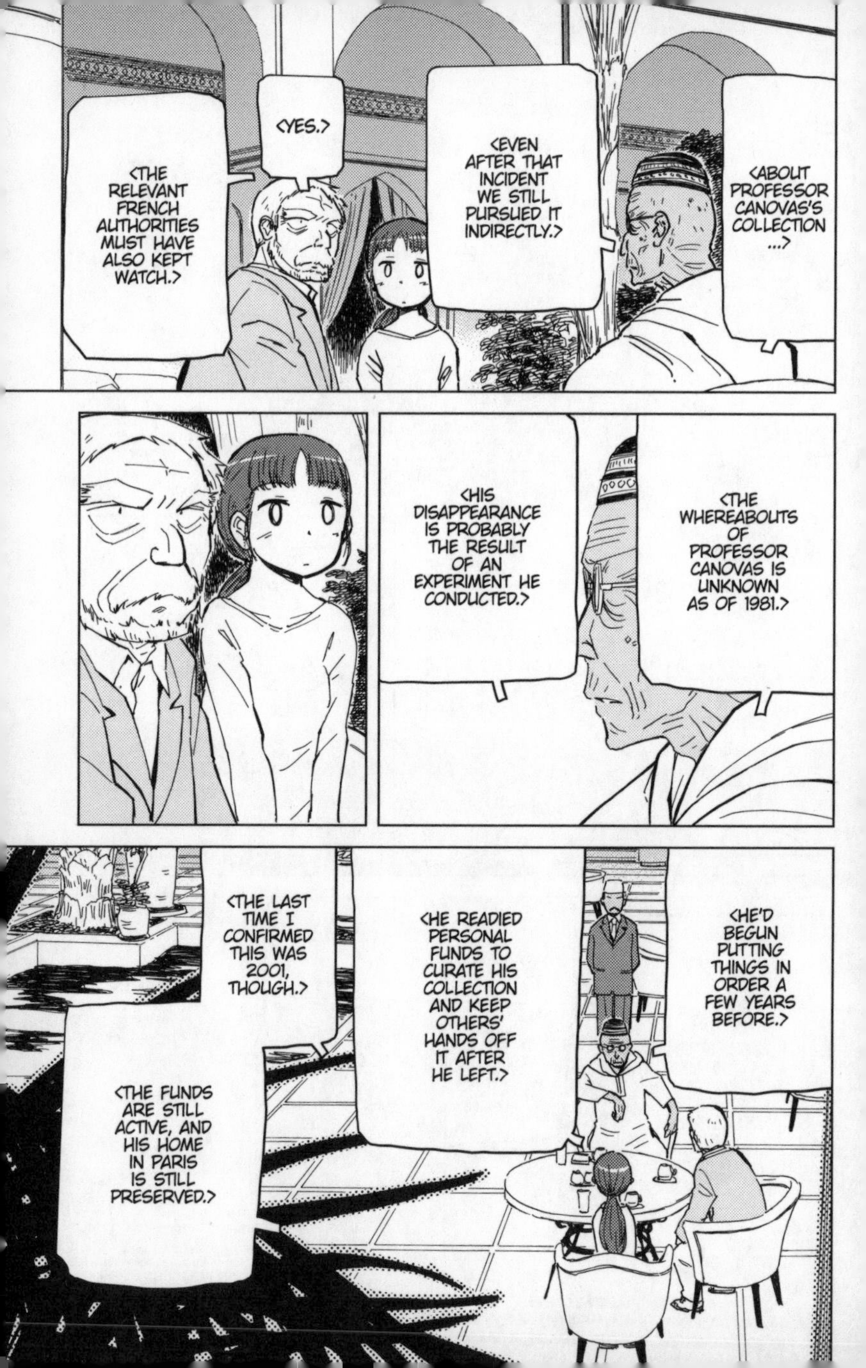
<ABOUT PROFESSOR CANOVAS'S COLLECTION ...>
<EVEN AFTER THAT INCIDENT WE STILL PURSUED IT INDIRECTLY.>
<YES.>
<THE RELEVANT FRENCH AUTHORITIES MUST HAVE ALSO KEPT WATCH.>
<THE WHEREABOUTS OF PROFESSOR CANOVAS IS UNKNOWN AS OF 1981.>
<HIS DISAPPEARANCE IS PROBABLY THE RESULT OF AN EXPERIMENT HE CONDUCTED.>
<HE'D BEGUN PUTTING THINGS IN ORDER A FEW YEARS BEFORE.>
<HE READIED PERSONAL FUNDS TO CURATE HIS COLLECTION AND KEEP OTHERS' HANDS OFF IT AFTER HE LEFT.>
<THE LAST TIME I CONFIRMED THIS WAS 2001, THOUGH.>
<THE FUNDS ARE STILL ACTIVE, AND HIS HOME IN PARIS IS STILL PRESERVED.>

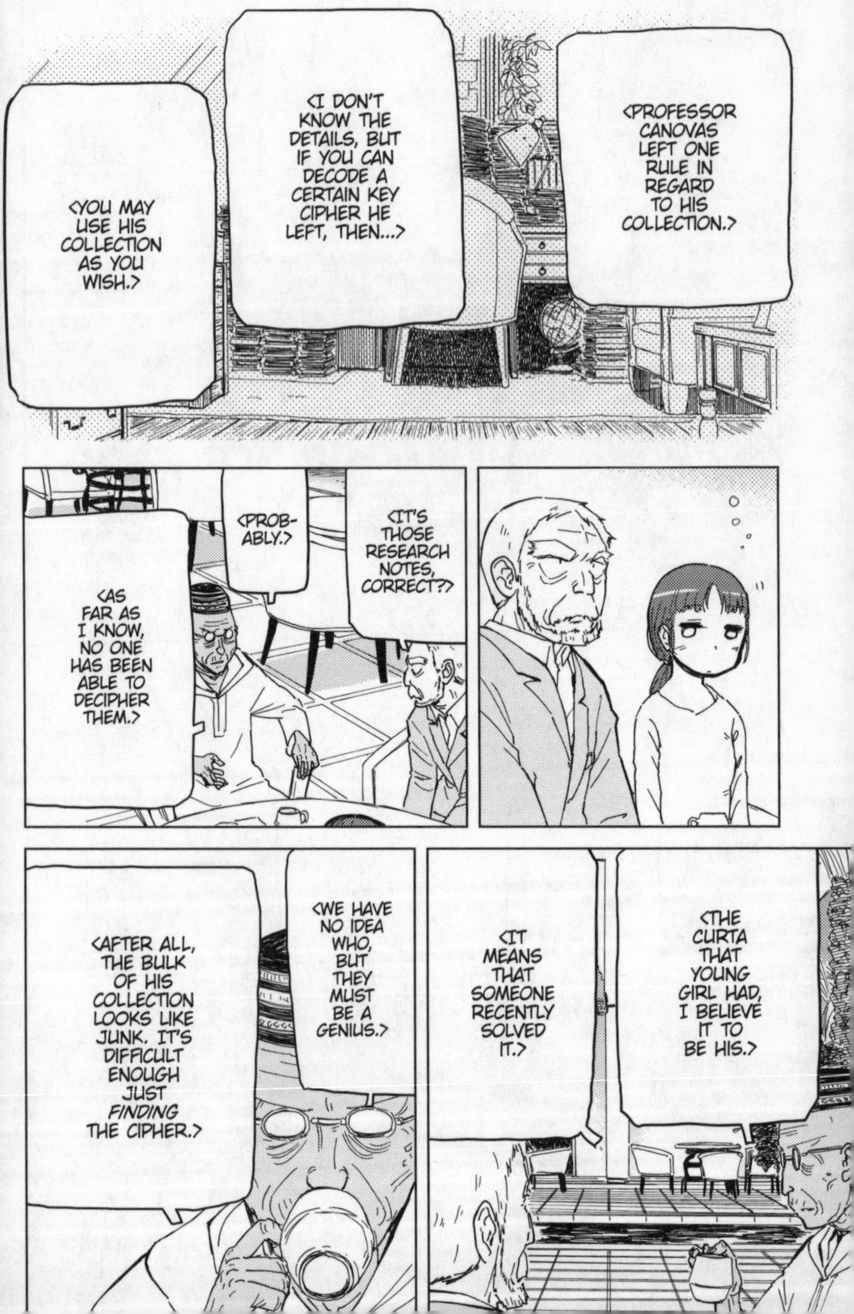
<PROFESSOR CANOVAS LEFT ONE RULE IN REGARD TO HIS COLLECTION.>
<I DON'T KNOW THE DETAILS, BUT IF YOU CAN DECODE A CERTAIN KEY CIPHER HE LEFT, THEN...>
<YOU MAY USE HIS COLLECTION AS YOU WISH.>
<IT'S THOSE RESEARCH NOTES, CORRECT?>
<PROB-ABLY.>
<AS FAR AS I KNOW, NO ONE HAS BEEN ABLE TO DECIPHER THEM.>
<THE CURTA THAT YOUNG GIRL HAD, I BELIEVE IT TO BE HIS.>
<IT MEANS THAT SOMEONE RECENTLY SOLVED IT.>
<WE HAVE NO IDEA WHO, BUT THEY MUST BE A GENIUS.>
<AFTER ALL, THE BULK OF HIS COLLECTION LOOKS LIKE JUNK. IT'S DIFFICULT ENOUGH JUST *FINDING* THE CIPHER.>

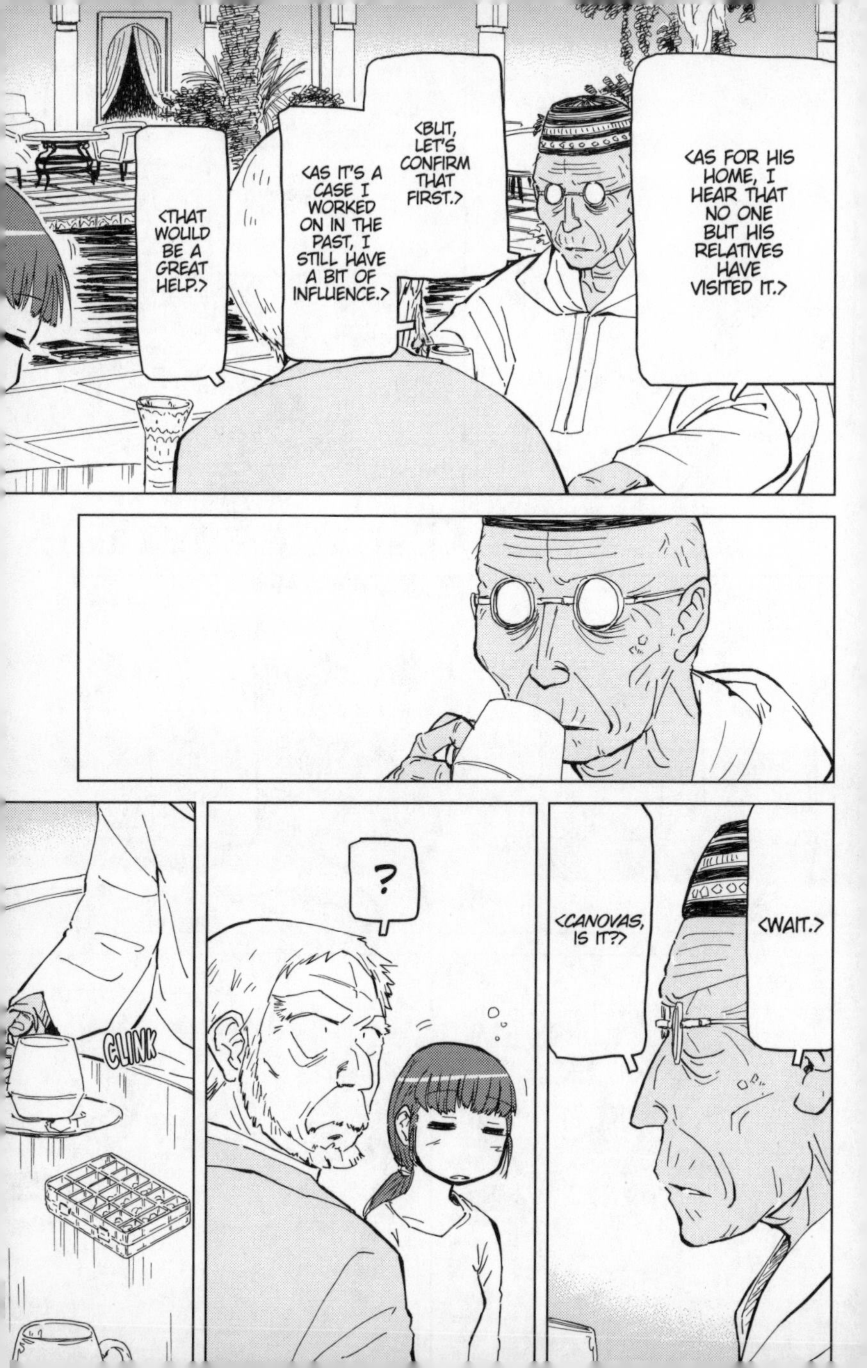
<AS FOR HIS HOME, I HEAR THAT NO ONE BUT HIS RELATIVES HAVE VISITED IT.>
<BUT, LET'S CONFIRM THAT FIRST.>
<AS IT'S A CASE I WORKED ON IN THE PAST, I STILL HAVE A BIT OF INFLUENCE.>
<THAT WOULD BE A GREAT HELP.>
<WAIT.>
<CANOVAS, IS IT?>
?
CLINK

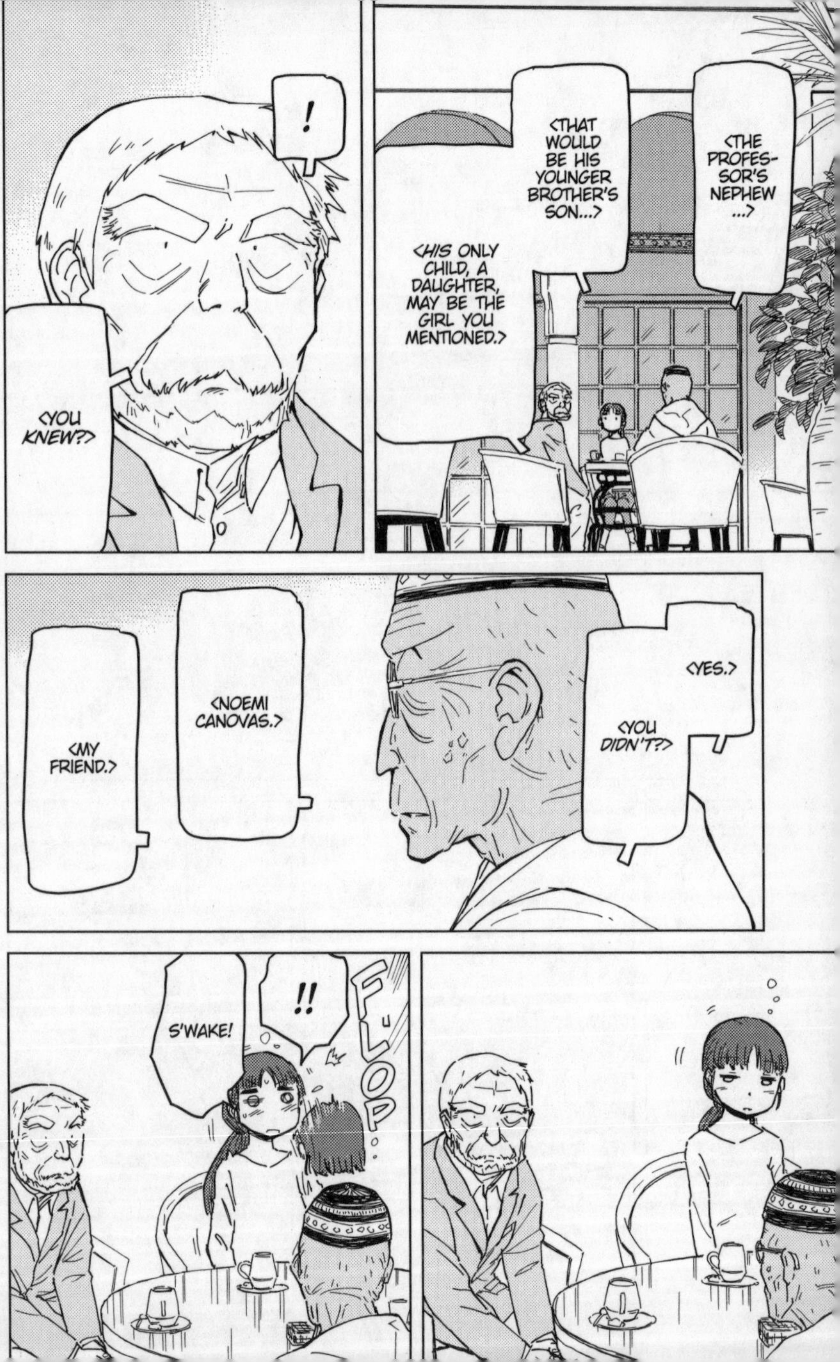
<THE PROFESSOR'S NEPHEW ...>
<THAT WOULD BE HIS YOUNGER BROTHER'S SON...>
<HIS ONLY CHILD, A DAUGHTER, MAY BE THE GIRL YOU MENTIONED.>
!
<YOU KNEW?>
<YES.>
<YOU DIDN'T?>
<NOEMI CANOVAS.>
<MY FRIEND.>
FLOP
!!
S'WAKE!

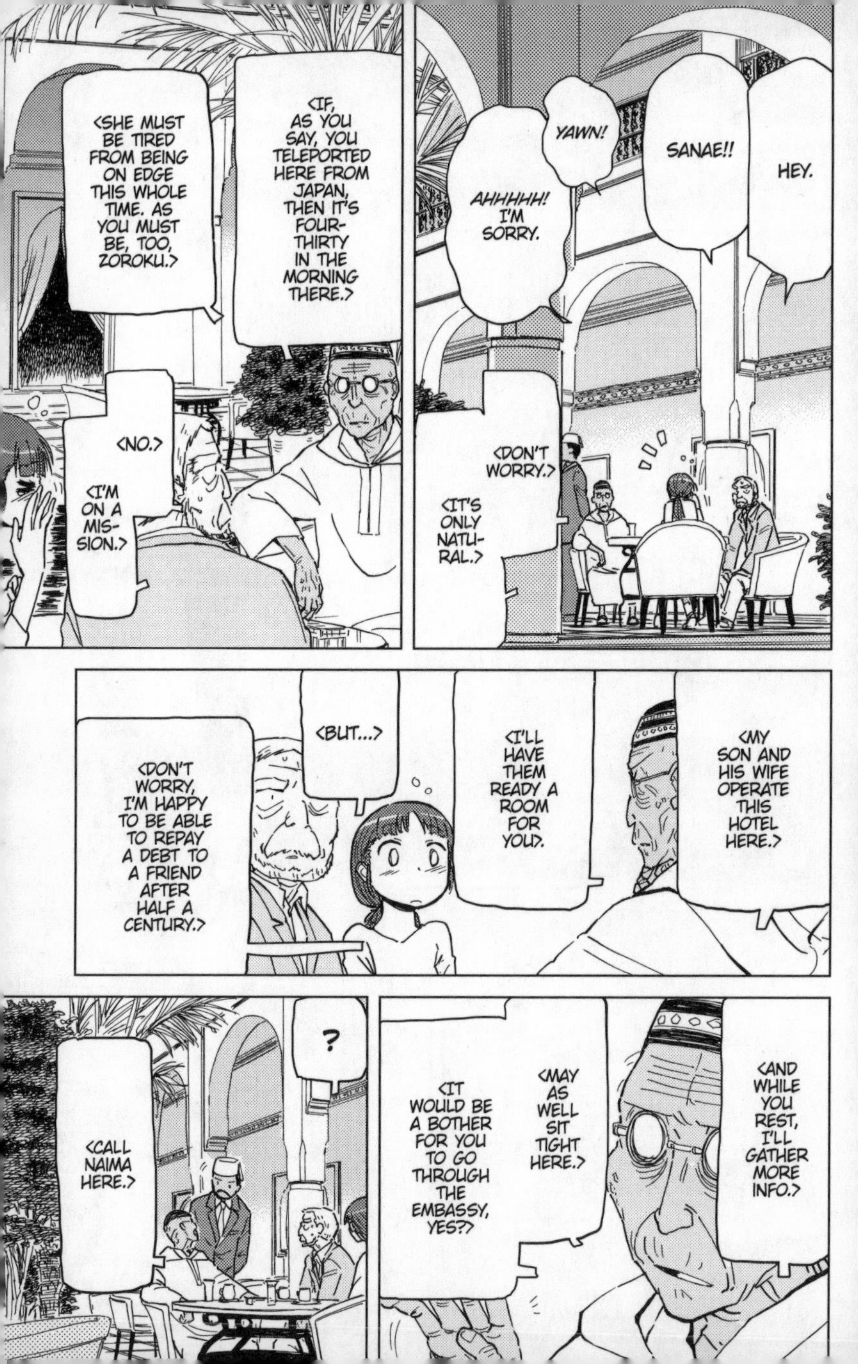
HEY.
SANAE!!
YAWN!
AHHHHH! I'M SORRY.
<DON'T WORRY.>
<IT'S ONLY NATURAL.>
<IF, AS YOU SAY, YOU TELEPORTED HERE FROM JAPAN, THEN IT'S FOUR-THIRTY IN THE MORNING THERE.>
<SHE MUST BE TIRED FROM BEING ON EDGE THIS WHOLE TIME. AS YOU MUST BE, TOO, ZOROKU.>
<NO.>
<I'M ON A MISSION.>
<MY SON AND HIS WIFE OPERATE THIS HOTEL HERE.>
<I'LL HAVE THEM READY A ROOM FOR YOU>.
<BUT...>
<DON'T WORRY, I'M HAPPY TO BE ABLE TO REPAY A DEBT TO A FRIEND AFTER HALF A CENTURY.>
<AND WHILE YOU REST, I'LL GATHER MORE INFO.>
<MAY AS WELL SIT TIGHT HERE.>
<IT WOULD BE A BOTHER FOR YOU TO GO THROUGH THE EMBASSY, YES?>
?
<CALL NAIMA HERE.>

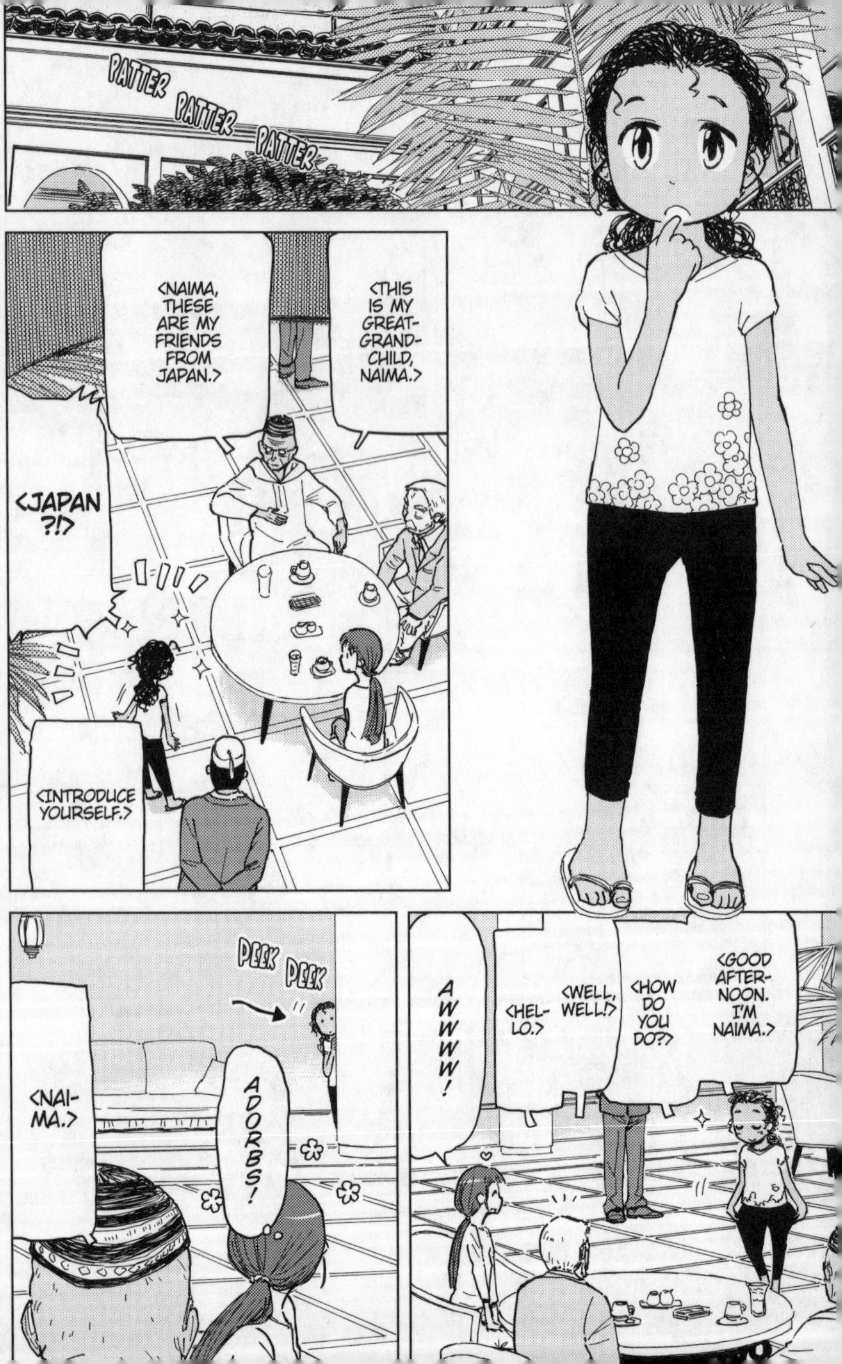
PATTER PATTER PATTER
<THIS IS MY GREAT-GRANDCHILD, NAIMA.>
<NAIMA, THESE ARE MY FRIENDS FROM JAPAN.>
<JAPAN ?!>
<INTRODUCE YOURSELF.>
<GOOD AFTERNOON. I'M NAIMA.>
<HOW DO YOU DO?>
<WELL, WELL!>
<HEL-LO.>
AWWWW!
PEEK PEEK
ADORBS!
<NAI-MA.>

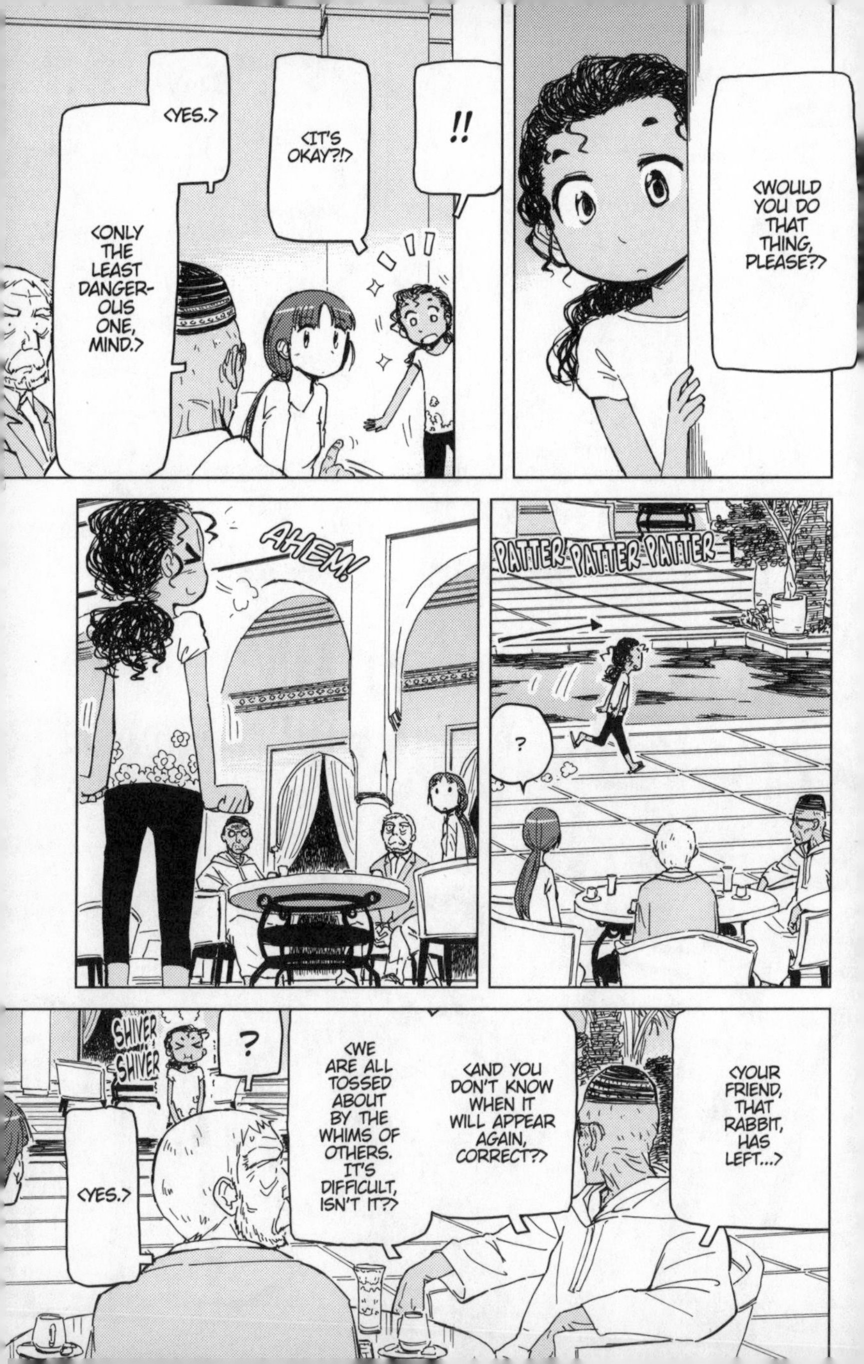
<WOULD YOU DO THAT THING, PLEASE?>
!!
<IT'S OKAY?!>
<YES.>
<ONLY THE LEAST DANGER-OUS ONE, MIND.>
PATTER PATTER PATTER
?
AHEM!
<YOUR FRIEND, THAT RABBIT, HAS LEFT...>
<AND YOU DON'T KNOW WHEN IT WILL APPEAR AGAIN, CORRECT?>
<WE ARE ALL TOSSED ABOUT BY THE WHIMS OF OTHERS. IT'S DIFFICULT, ISN'T IT?>
?
SHIVER SHIVER
<YES.>

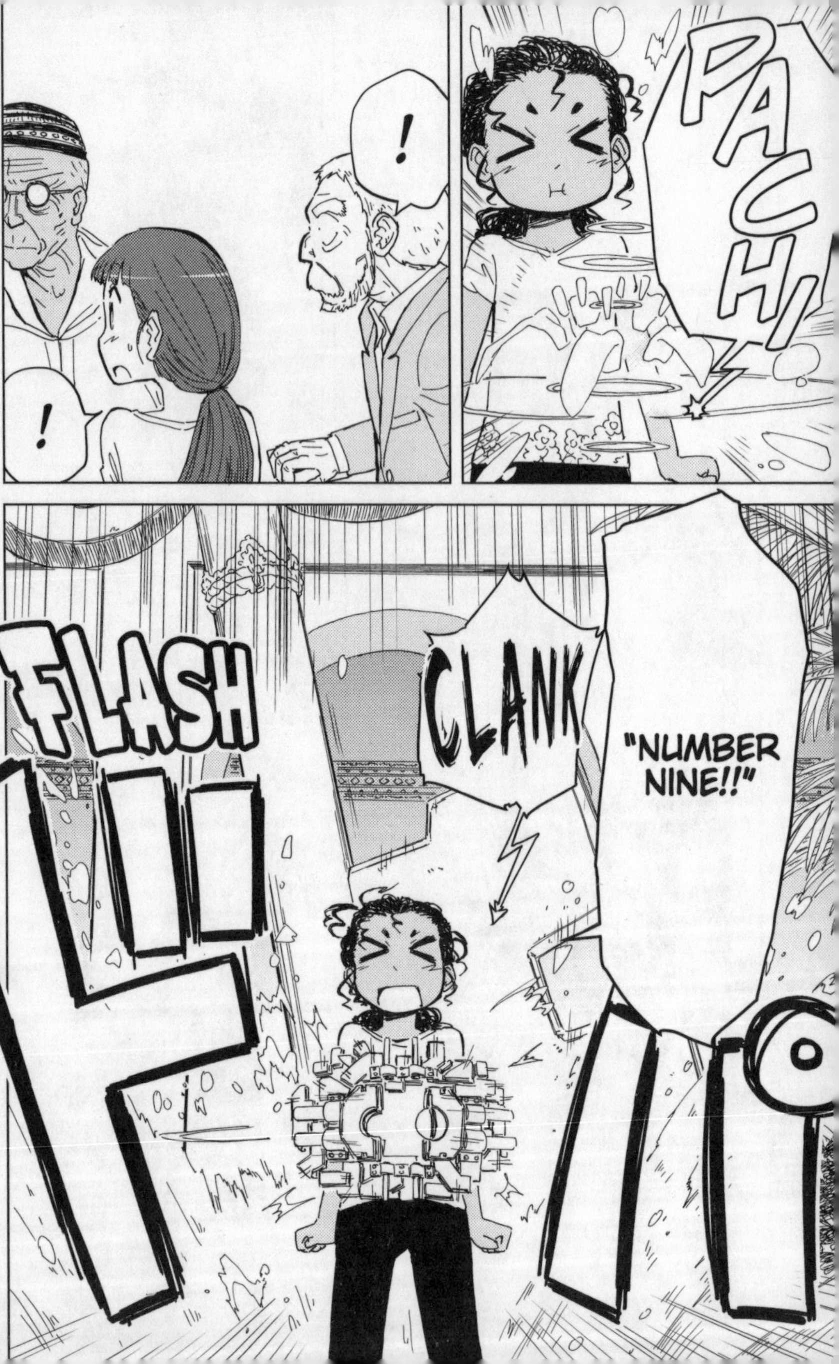
PACHI
!
!
"NUMBER NINE!!"
CLANK
FLASH

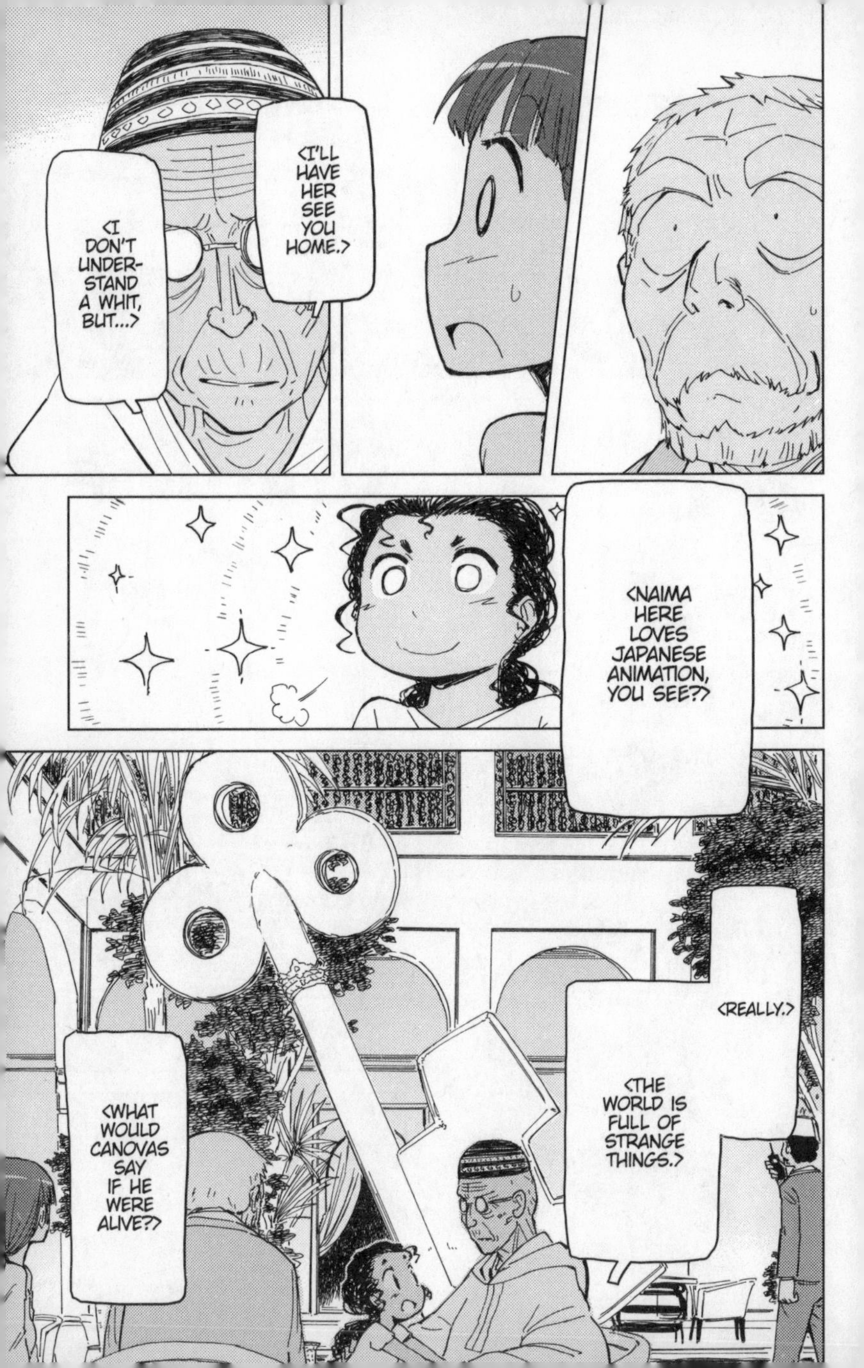
<I'LL HAVE HER SEE YOU HOME.>
<I DON'T UNDERSTAND A WHIT, BUT...>
<NAIMA HERE LOVES JAPANESE ANIMATION, YOU SEE?>
<REALLY.>
<THE WORLD IS FULL OF STRANGE THINGS.>
<WHAT WOULD CANOVAS SAY IF HE WERE ALIVE?>

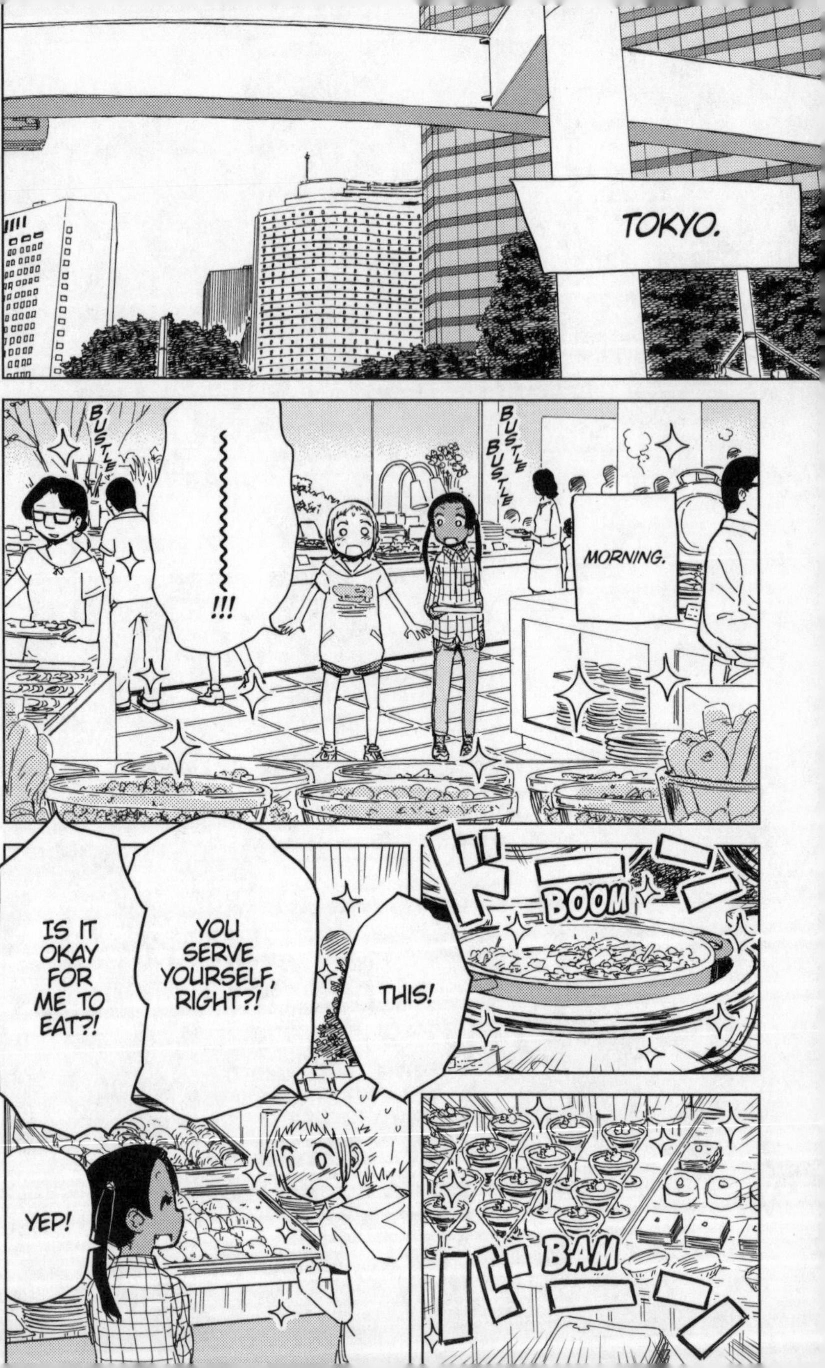
TOKYO.
MORNING.
BUSTLE BUSTLE
!!!
BUSTLE
ド
BOOM
ド
BAM
THIS!
YOU SERVE YOURSELF, RIGHT?!
IS IT OKAY FOR ME TO EAT?!
YEP!

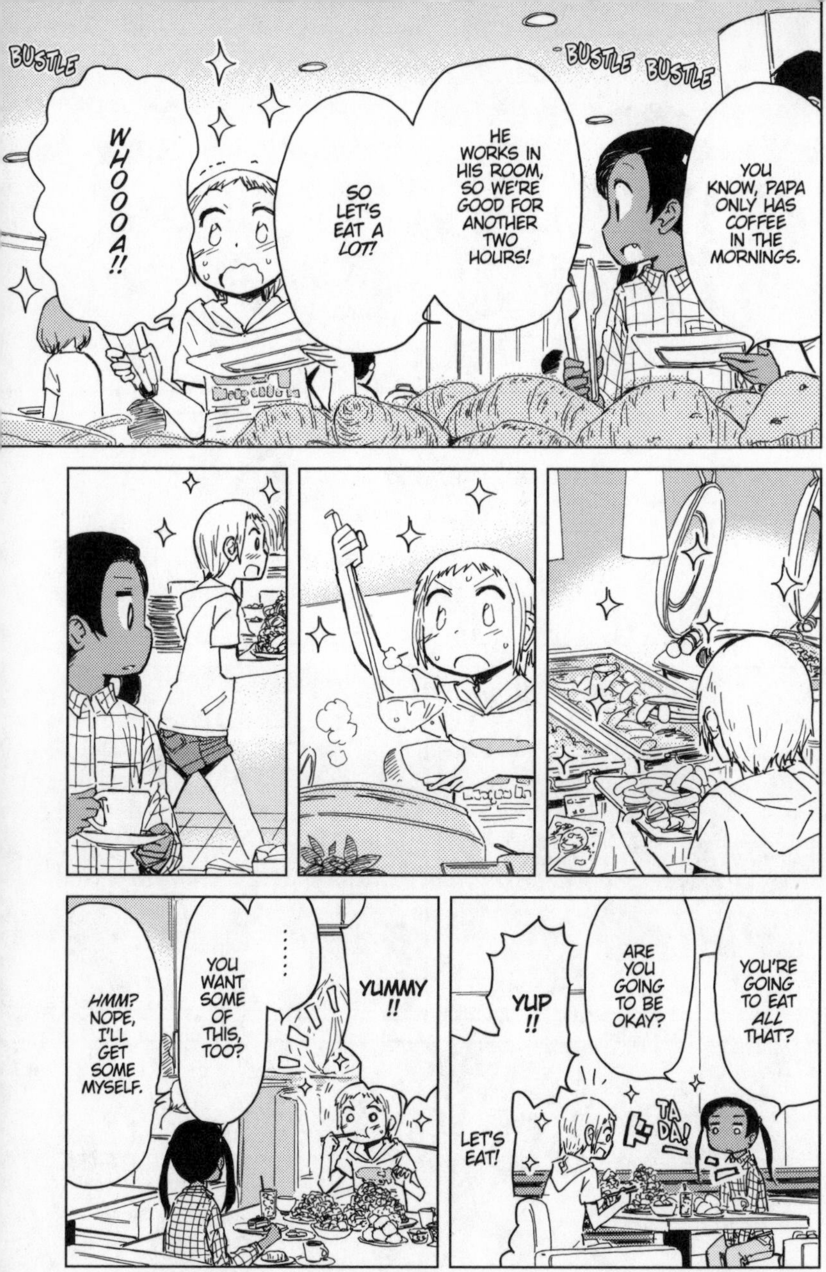
BUSTLE BUSTLE
YOU KNOW, PAPA ONLY HAS COFFEE IN THE MORNINGS.
HE WORKS IN HIS ROOM, SO WE'RE GOOD FOR ANOTHER TWO HOURS!
SO LET'S EAT A *LOT!*
WHOOOOA!!
BUSTLE
YOU'RE GOING TO EAT *ALL* THAT?
ARE YOU GOING TO BE OKAY?
YUP!!
TA DA!
LET'S EAT!
YUMMY!!
......
YOU WANT SOME OF THIS, TOO?
HMM? NOPE, I'LL GET SOME MYSELF.

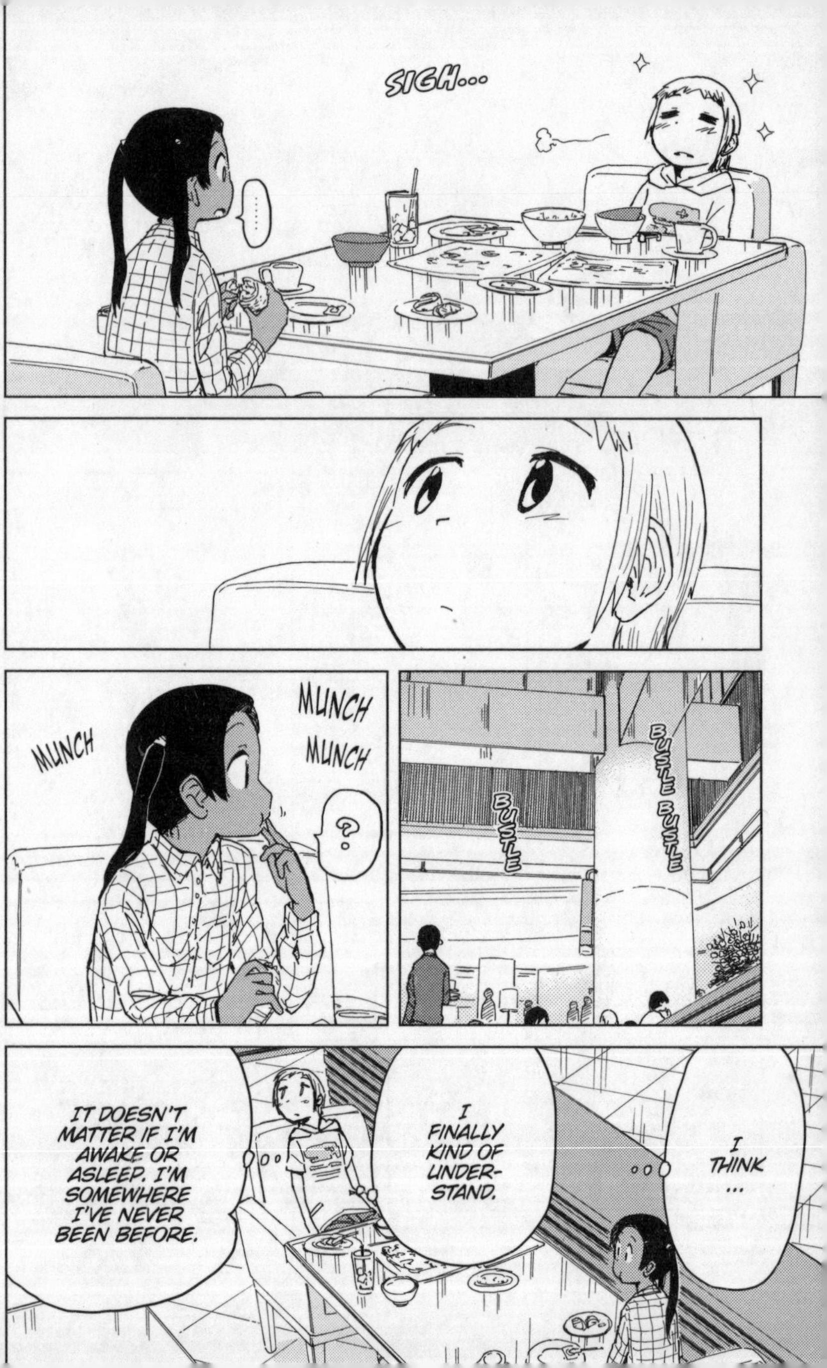
SIGH...
......
BUSTLE BUSTLE
BUSTLE
MUNCH
MUNCH
MUNCH
?
I THINK ...
I FINALLY KIND OF UNDER-STAND.
IT DOESN'T MATTER IF I'M AWAKE OR ASLEEP. I'M SOMEWHERE I'VE NEVER BEEN BEFORE.

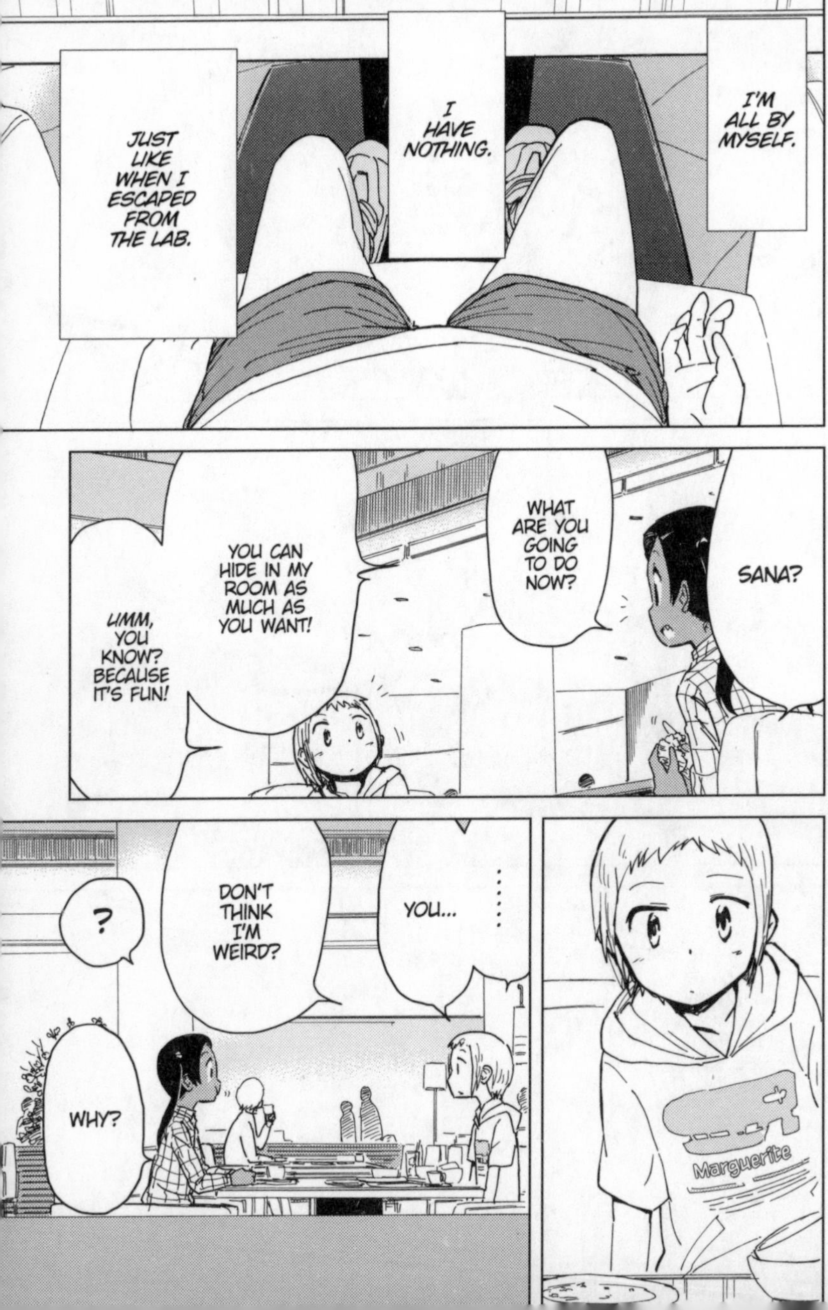
I'M ALL BY MYSELF.
I HAVE NOTHING.
JUST LIKE WHEN I ESCAPED FROM THE LAB.
SANA?
WHAT ARE YOU GOING TO DO NOW?
YOU CAN HIDE IN MY ROOM AS MUCH AS YOU WANT!
UMM, YOU KNOW? BECAUSE IT'S FUN!
Marguerite
......
YOU...
DON'T THINK I'M WEIRD?
?
WHY?

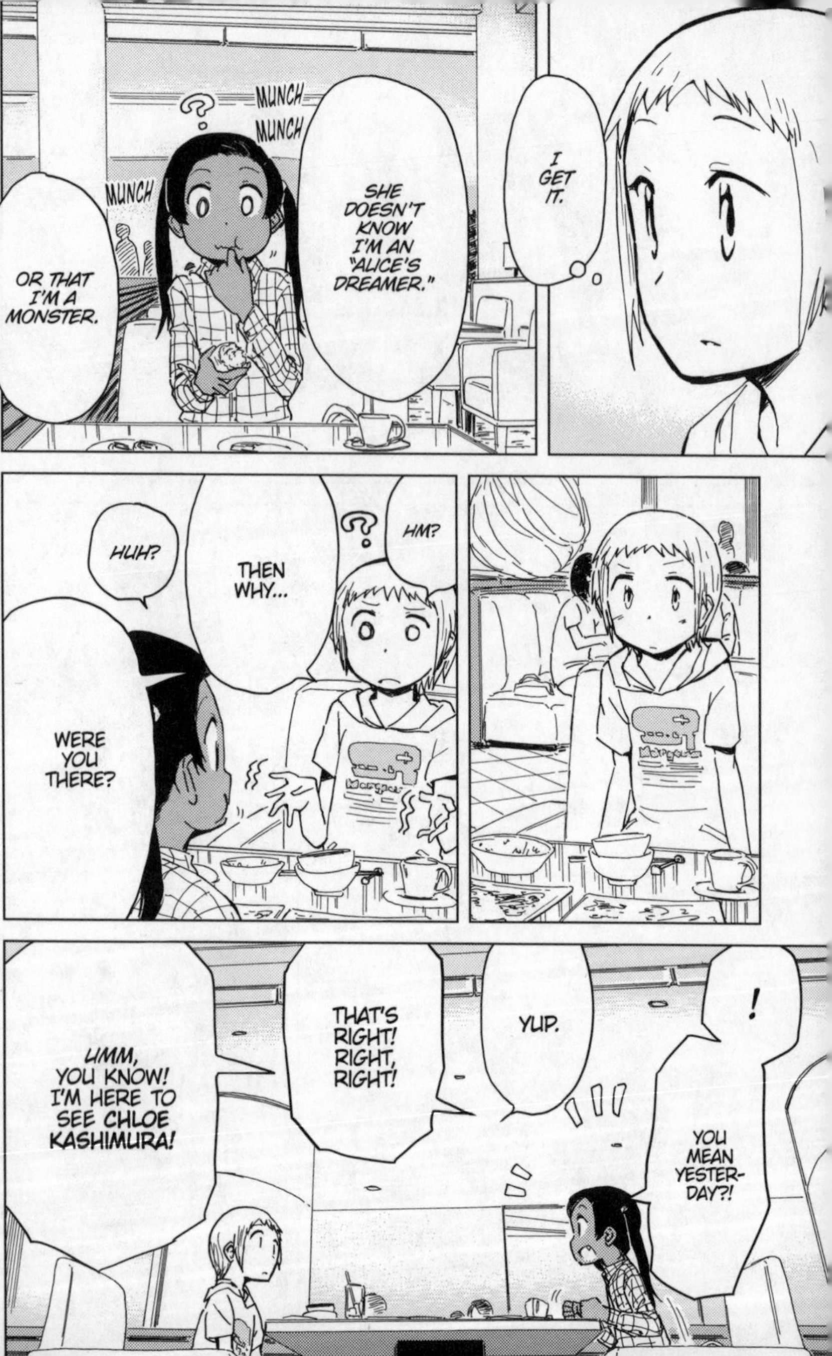
I GET IT.
SHE DOESN'T KNOW I'M AN "ALICE'S DREAMER."
MUNCH
MUNCH
MUNCH
OR THAT I'M A MONSTER.
HM?
THEN WHY...
HUH?
WERE YOU THERE?
!
YOU MEAN YESTER-DAY?!
YUP.
THAT'S RIGHT! RIGHT, RIGHT!
UMM, YOU KNOW! I'M HERE TO SEE CHLOE KASHIMURA!

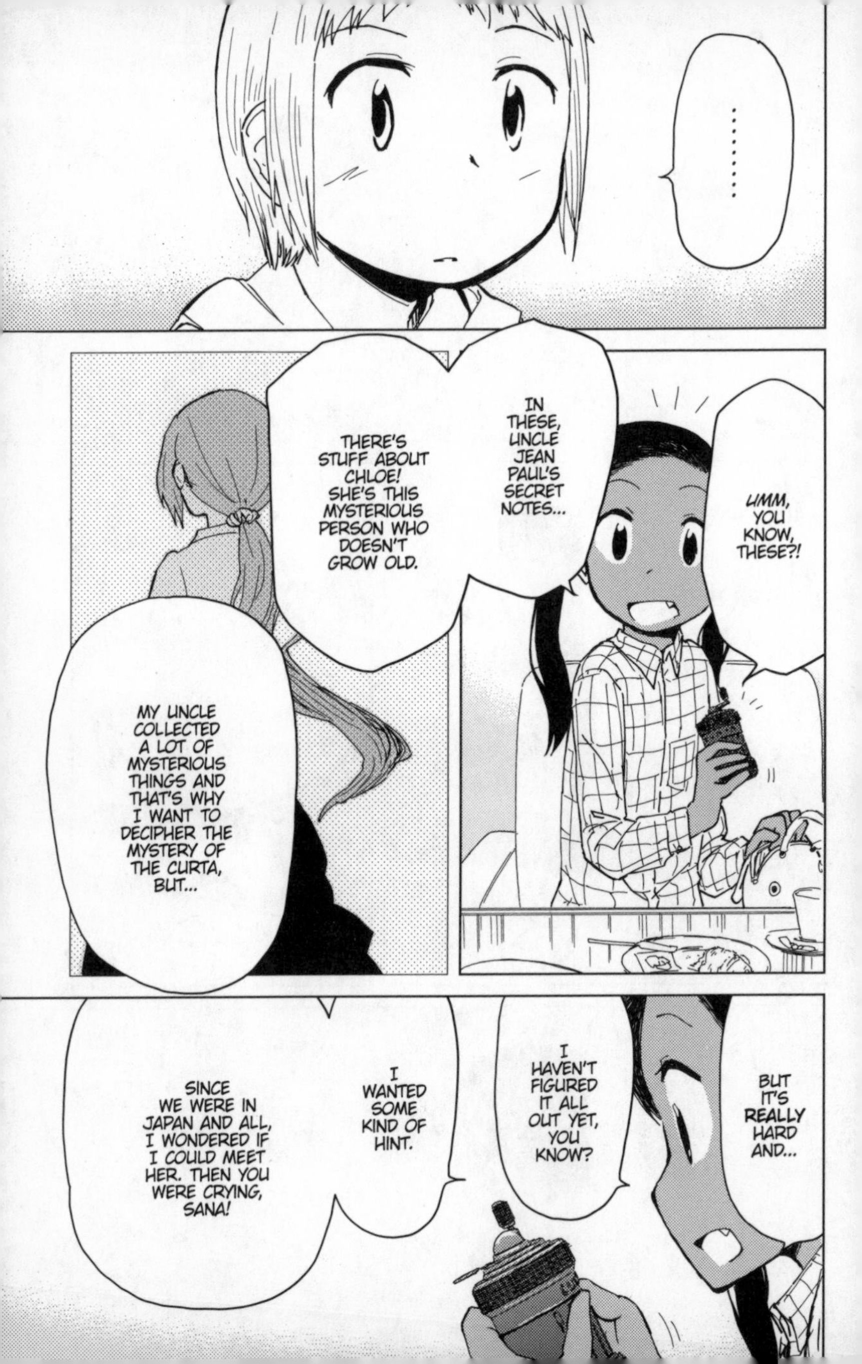
......
UMM, YOU KNOW, THESE?!
IN THESE, UNCLE JEAN PAUL'S SECRET NOTES...
THERE'S STUFF ABOUT CHLOE! SHE'S THIS MYSTERIOUS PERSON WHO DOESN'T GROW OLD.
MY UNCLE COLLECTED A LOT OF MYSTERIOUS THINGS AND THAT'S WHY I WANT TO DECIPHER THE MYSTERY OF THE CURTA, BUT...
BUT IT'S REALLY HARD AND...
I HAVEN'T FIGURED IT ALL OUT YET, YOU KNOW?
I WANTED SOME KIND OF HINT.
SINCE WE WERE IN JAPAN AND ALL, I WONDERED IF I COULD MEET HER. THEN YOU WERE CRYING, SANA!

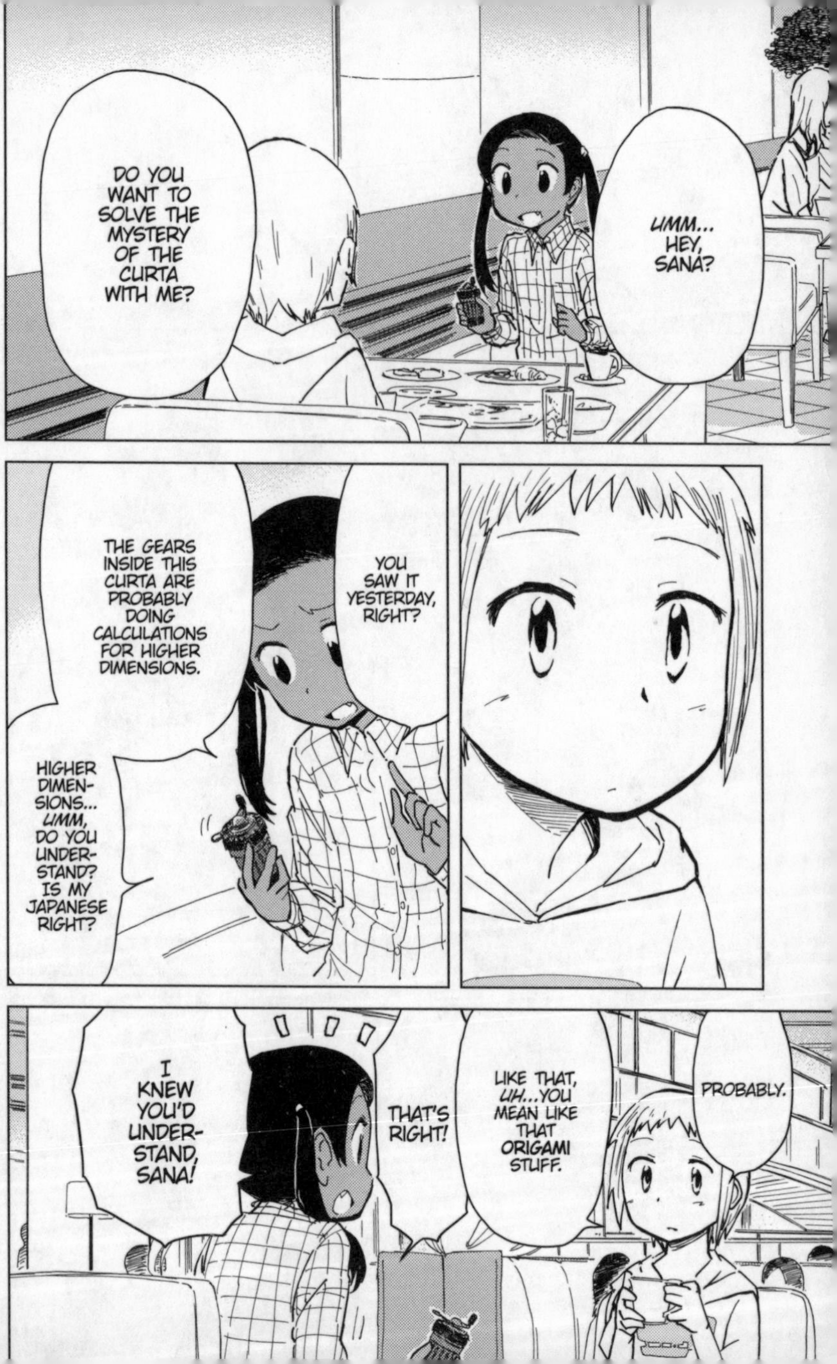
UMM... HEY, SANA?
DO YOU WANT TO SOLVE THE MYSTERY OF THE CURTA WITH ME?
YOU SAW IT YESTERDAY, RIGHT?
THE GEARS INSIDE THIS CURTA ARE PROBABLY DOING CALCULATIONS FOR HIGHER DIMENSIONS.
HIGHER DIMEN-SIONS... UMM, DO YOU UNDER-STAND? IS MY JAPANESE RIGHT?
PROBABLY.
LIKE THAT, UH...YOU MEAN LIKE THAT ORIGAMI STUFF.
THAT'S RIGHT!
I KNEW YOU'D UNDER-STAND, SANA!

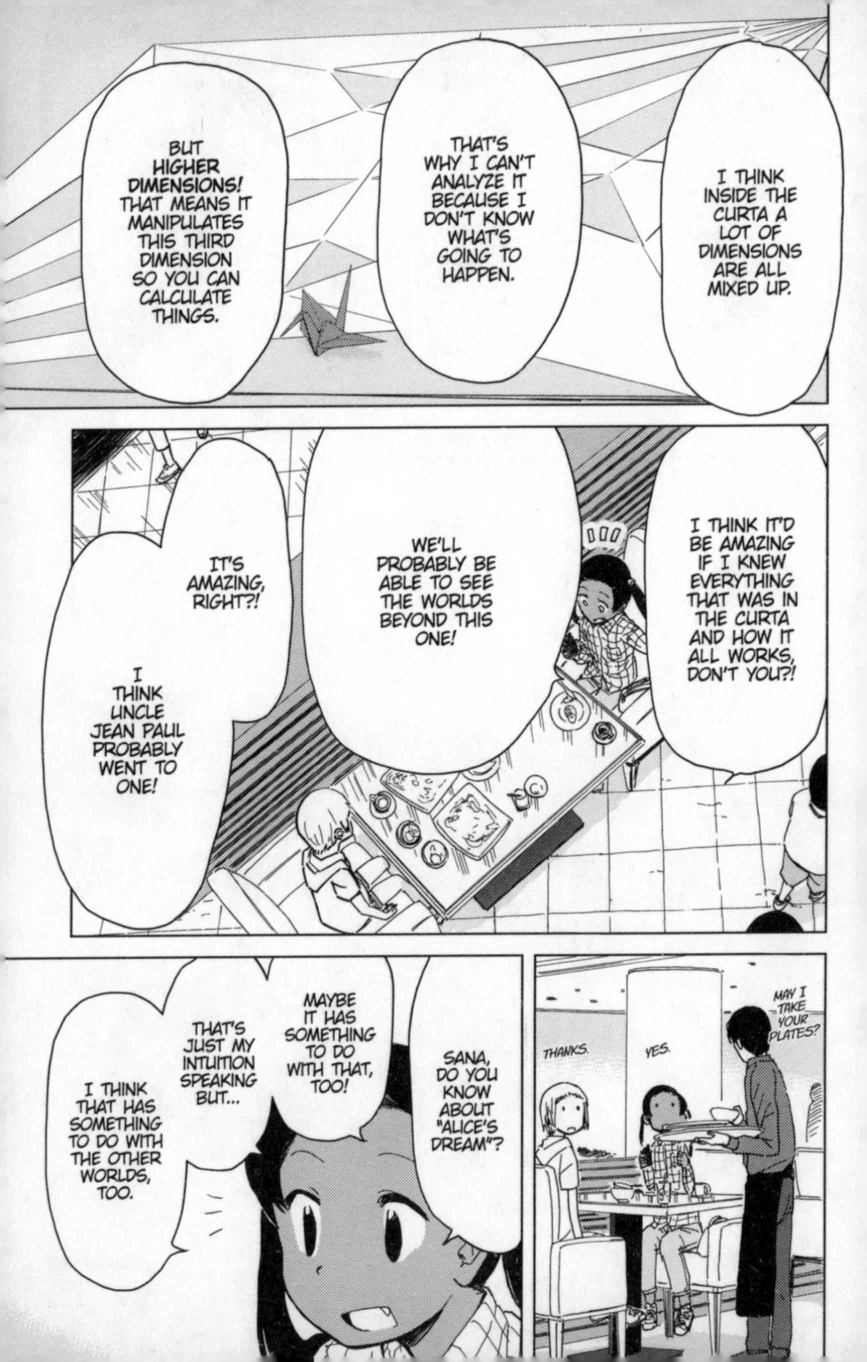
I THINK INSIDE THE CURTA A LOT OF DIMENSIONS ARE ALL MIXED UP.
THAT'S WHY I CAN'T ANALYZE IT BECAUSE I DON'T KNOW WHAT'S GOING TO HAPPEN.
BUT HIGHER DIMENSIONS! THAT MEANS IT MANIPULATES THIS THIRD DIMENSION SO YOU CAN CALCULATE THINGS.
I THINK IT'D BE AMAZING IF I KNEW EVERYTHING THAT WAS IN THE CURTA AND HOW IT ALL WORKS, DON'T YOU?!
WE'LL PROBABLY BE ABLE TO SEE THE WORLDS BEYOND THIS ONE!
IT'S AMAZING, RIGHT?!
I THINK UNCLE JEAN PAUL PROBABLY WENT TO ONE!
MAY I TAKE YOUR PLATES?
YES.
THANKS.
SANA, DO YOU KNOW ABOUT "ALICE'S DREAM"?
MAYBE IT HAS SOMETHING TO DO WITH THAT, TOO!
THAT'S JUST MY INTUITION SPEAKING BUT...
I THINK THAT HAS SOMETHING TO DO WITH THE OTHER WORLDS, TOO.

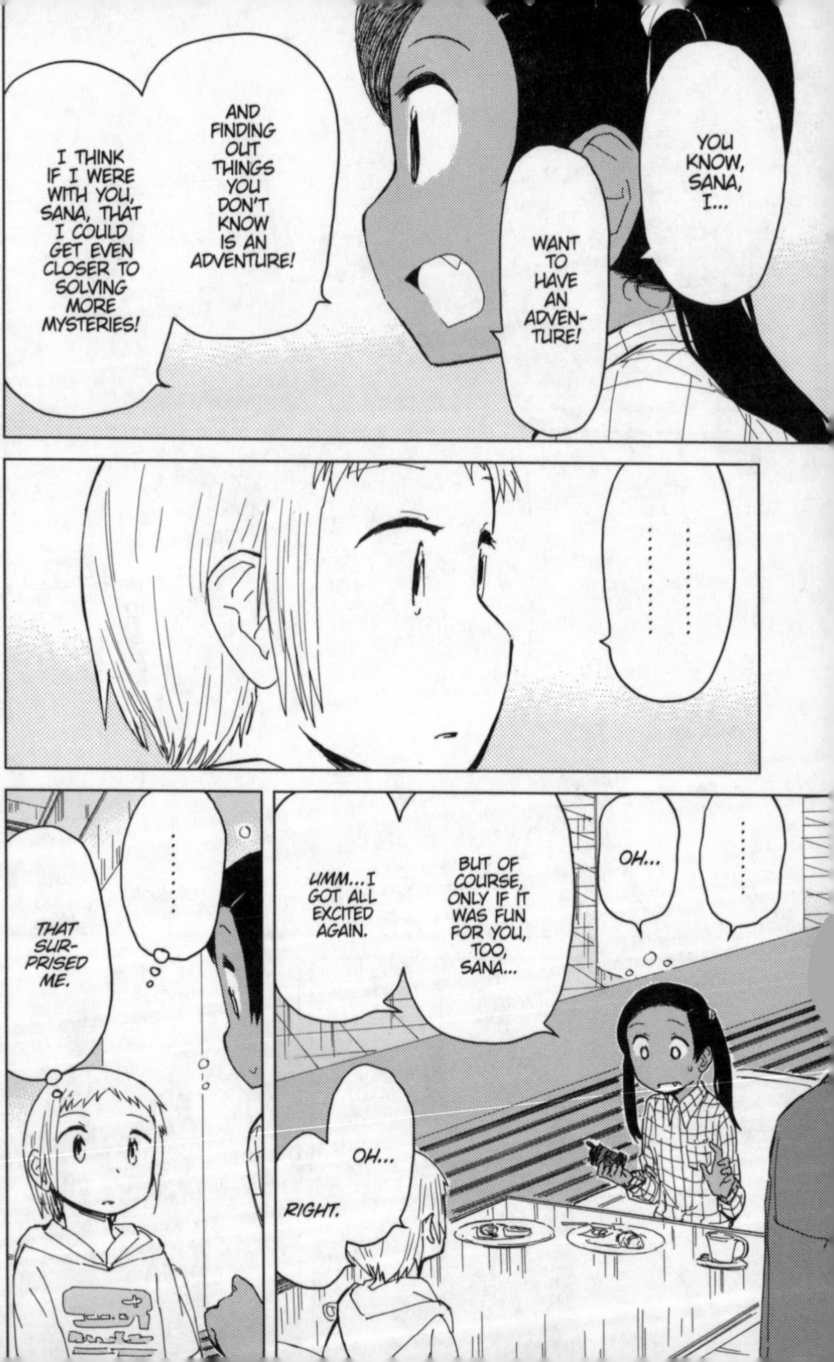
YOU KNOW, SANA, I...
WANT TO HAVE AN ADVENTURE!
AND FINDING OUT THINGS YOU DON'T KNOW IS AN ADVENTURE!
I THINK IF I WERE WITH YOU, SANA, THAT I COULD GET EVEN CLOSER TO SOLVING MORE MYSTERIES!
......
......
OH...
BUT OF COURSE, ONLY IF IT WAS FUN FOR YOU, TOO, SANA...
UMM...I GOT ALL EXCITED AGAIN.
OH...
RIGHT.
......
THAT SURPRISED ME.

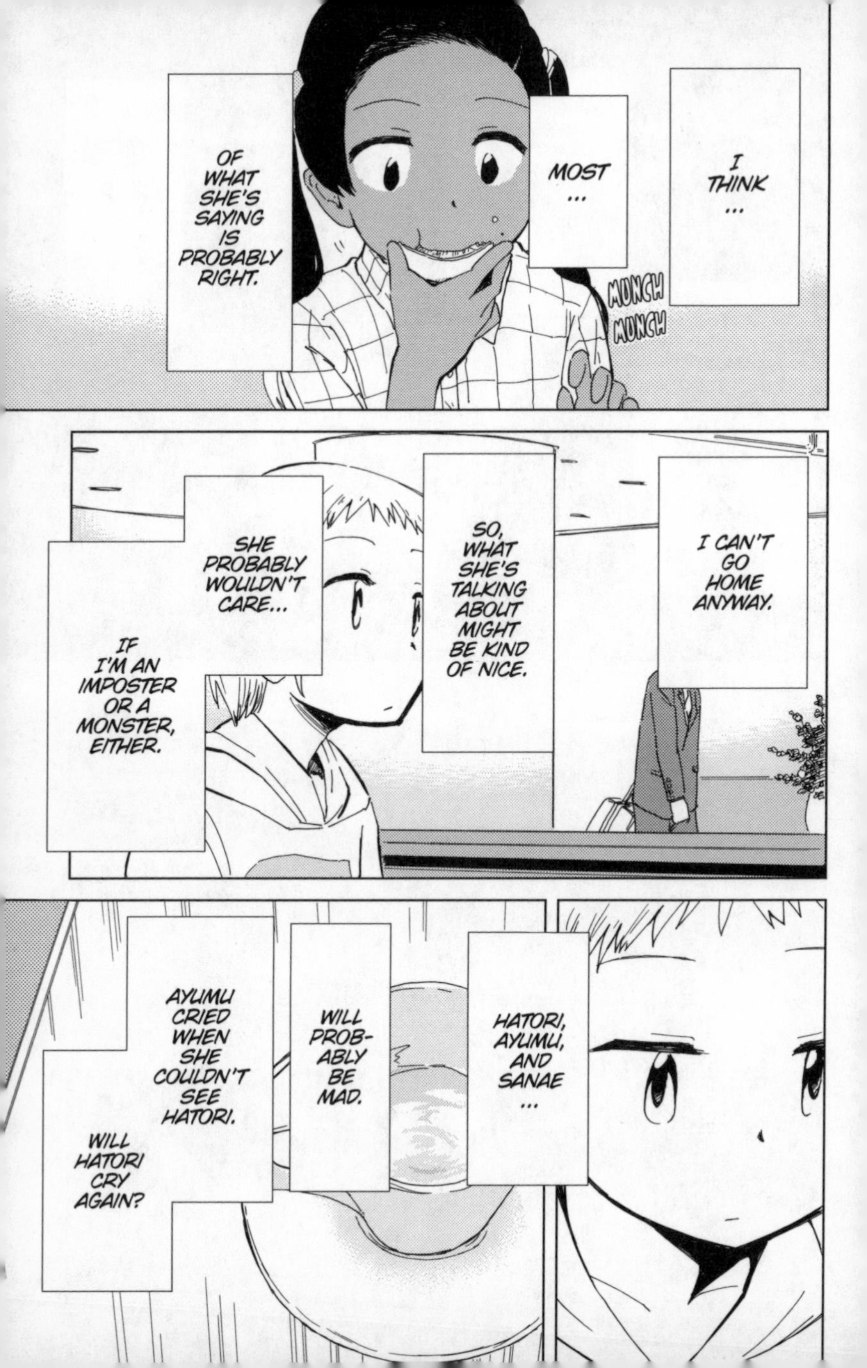
I THINK ...
MOST ...
OF WHAT SHE'S SAYING IS PROBABLY RIGHT.
MUNCH MUNCH
I CAN'T GO HOME ANYWAY.
SO, WHAT SHE'S TALKING ABOUT MIGHT BE KIND OF NICE.
SHE PROBABLY WOULDN'T CARE...
IF I'M AN IMPOSTER OR A MONSTER, EITHER.
HATORI, AYUMU, AND SANAE ...
WILL PROB-ABLY BE MAD.
AYUMU CRIED WHEN SHE COULDN'T SEE HATORI.
WILL HATORI CRY AGAIN?

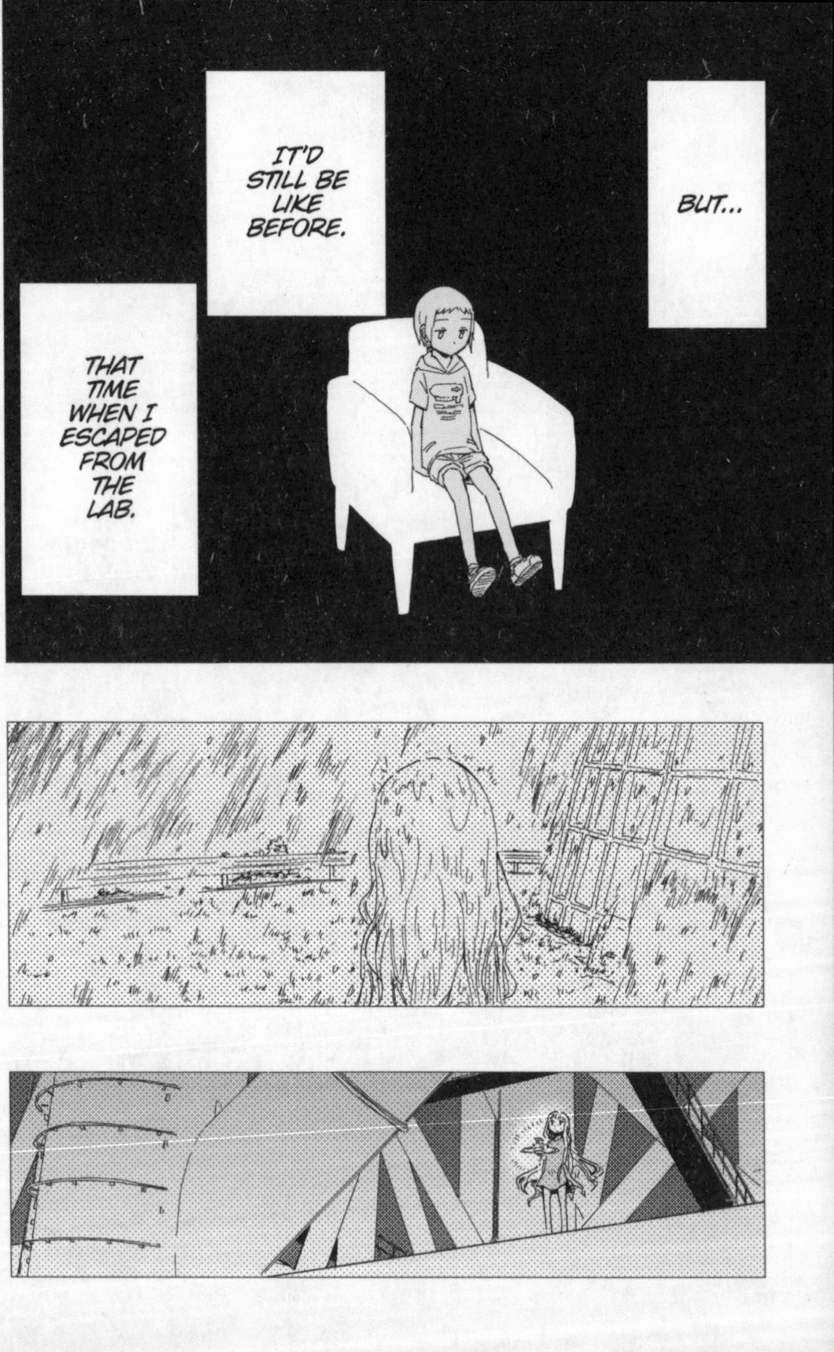
BUT...
IT'D STILL BE LIKE BEFORE.
THAT TIME WHEN I ESCAPED FROM THE LAB.

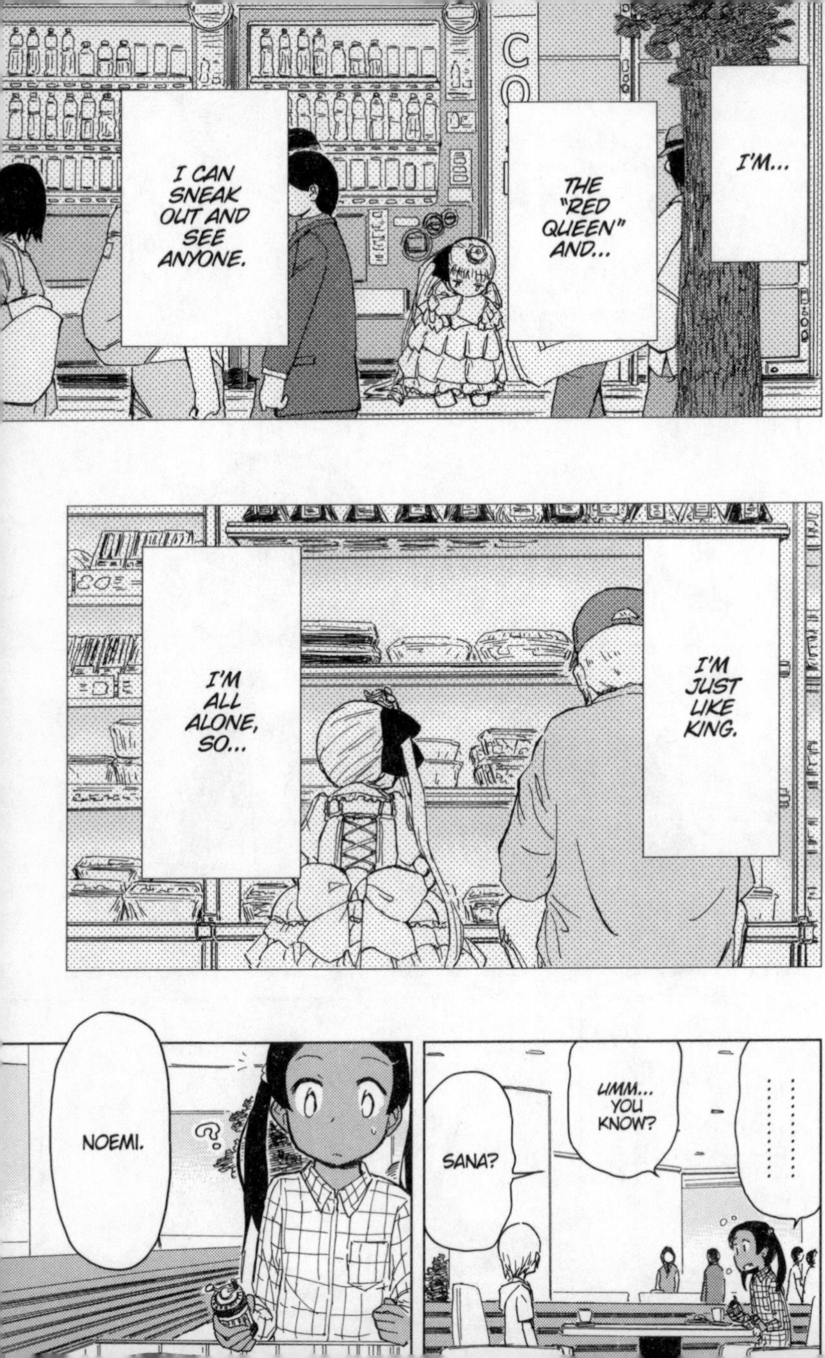
I'M...
THE "RED QUEEN" AND...
I CAN SNEAK OUT AND SEE ANYONE.
I'M JUST LIKE KING.
I'M ALL ALONE, SO...
......
UMM... YOU KNOW?
SANA?
NOEMI.

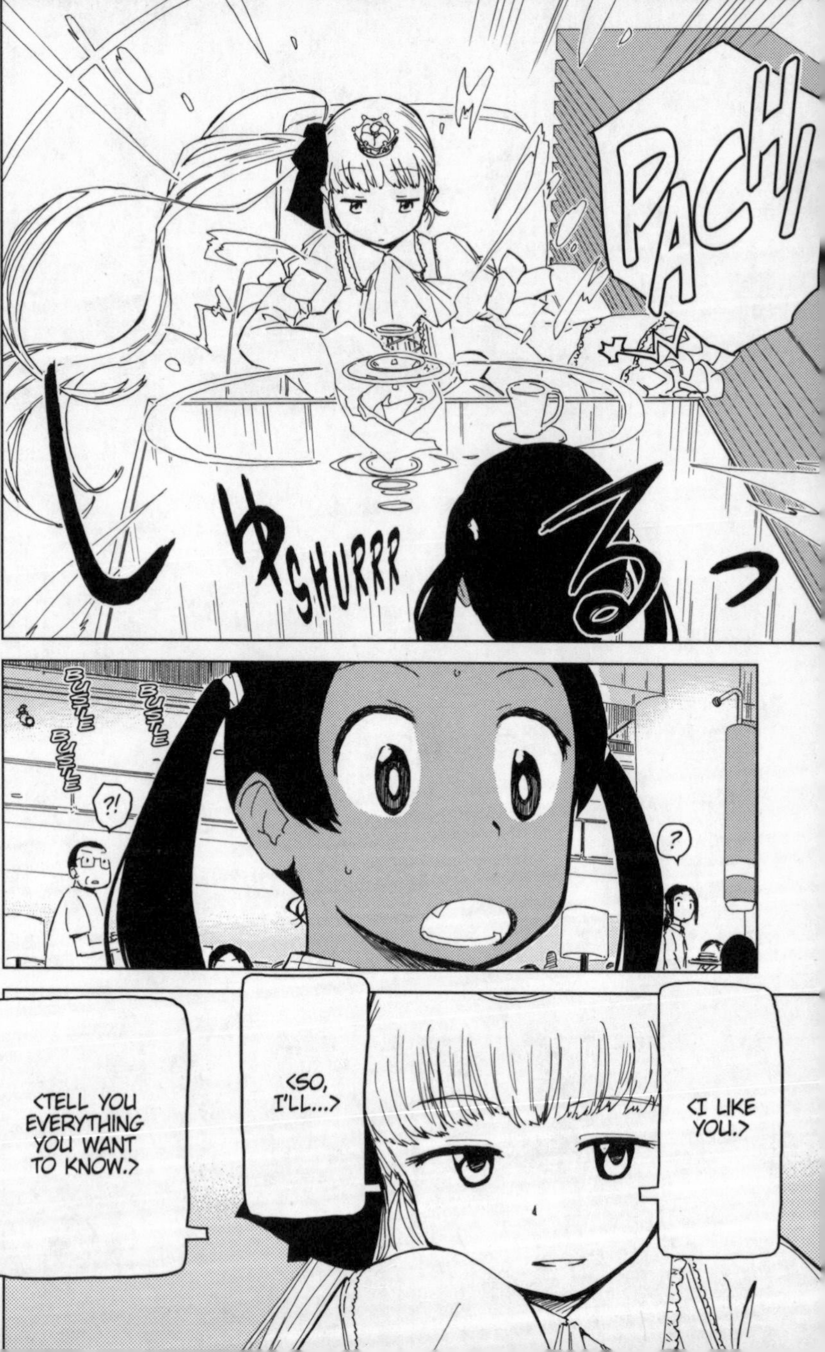
PACHI
しゅるっ
SHURRR
?
BUSTLE BUSTLE BUSTLE
?!
<I LIKE YOU.>
<SO, I'LL...>
<TELL YOU EVERYTHING YOU WANT TO KNOW.>

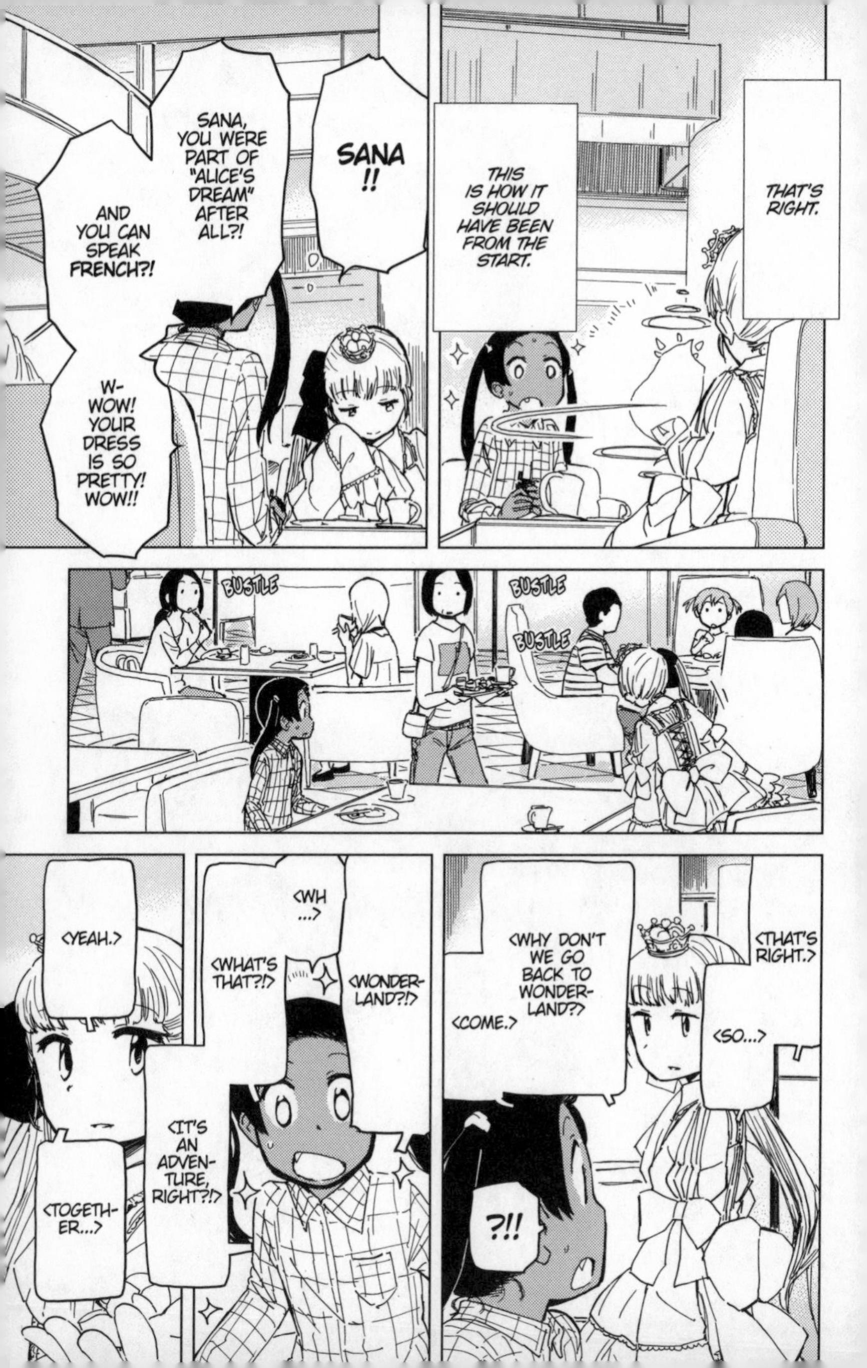
THAT'S RIGHT.
THIS IS HOW IT SHOULD HAVE BEEN FROM THE START.
SANA!!
SANA, YOU WERE PART OF "ALICE'S DREAM" AFTER ALL?!
AND YOU CAN SPEAK FRENCH?!
W-WOW! YOUR DRESS IS SO PRETTY! WOW!!
BUSTLE
BUSTLE
BUSTLE
<THAT'S RIGHT.>
<SO...>
<WHY DON'T WE GO BACK TO WONDERLAND?>
<COME.>
?!!
<WH...>
<WONDERLAND?!>
<WHAT'S THAT?!>
<IT'S AN ADVENTURE, RIGHT?!>
<YEAH.>
<TOGETHER...>

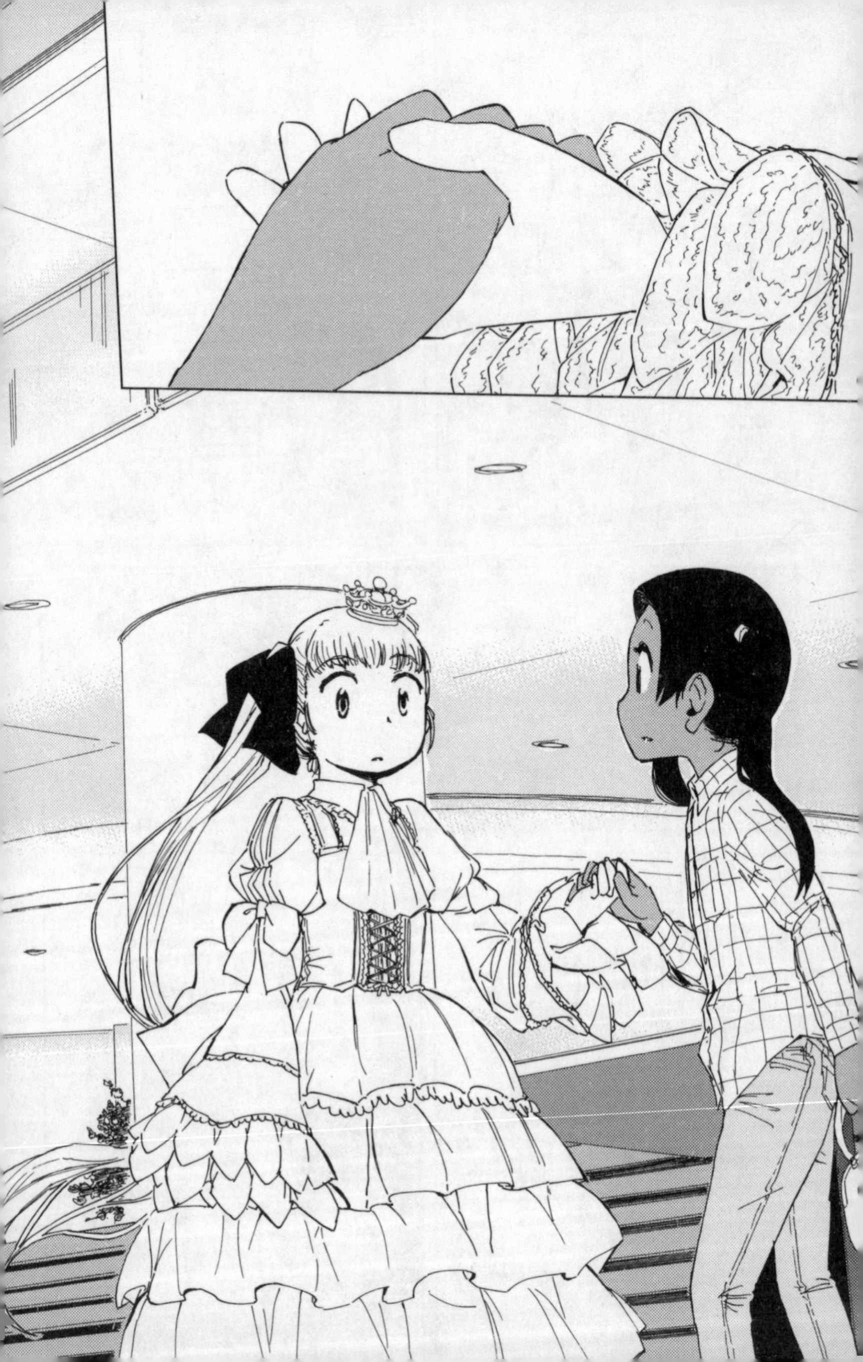

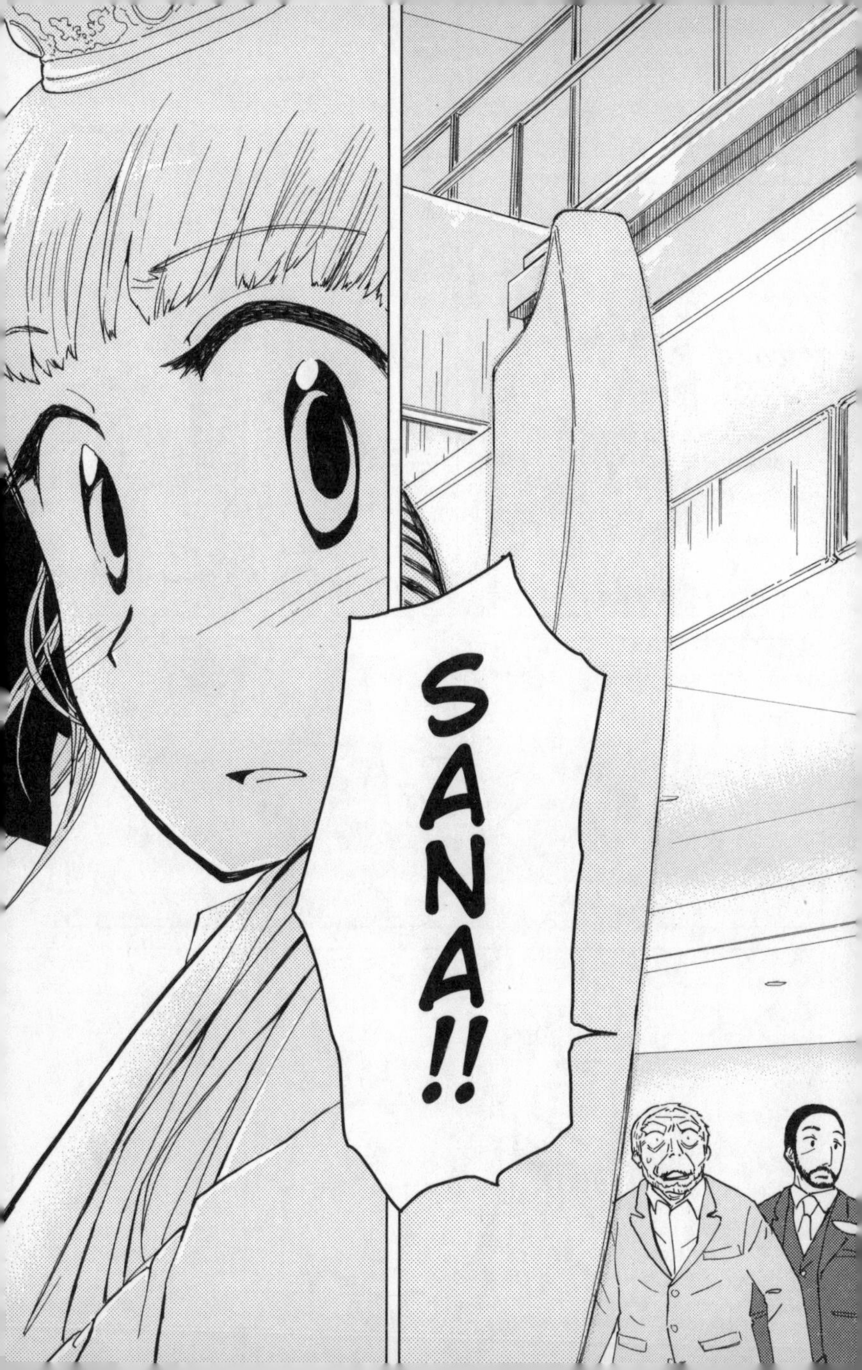
SANA!!

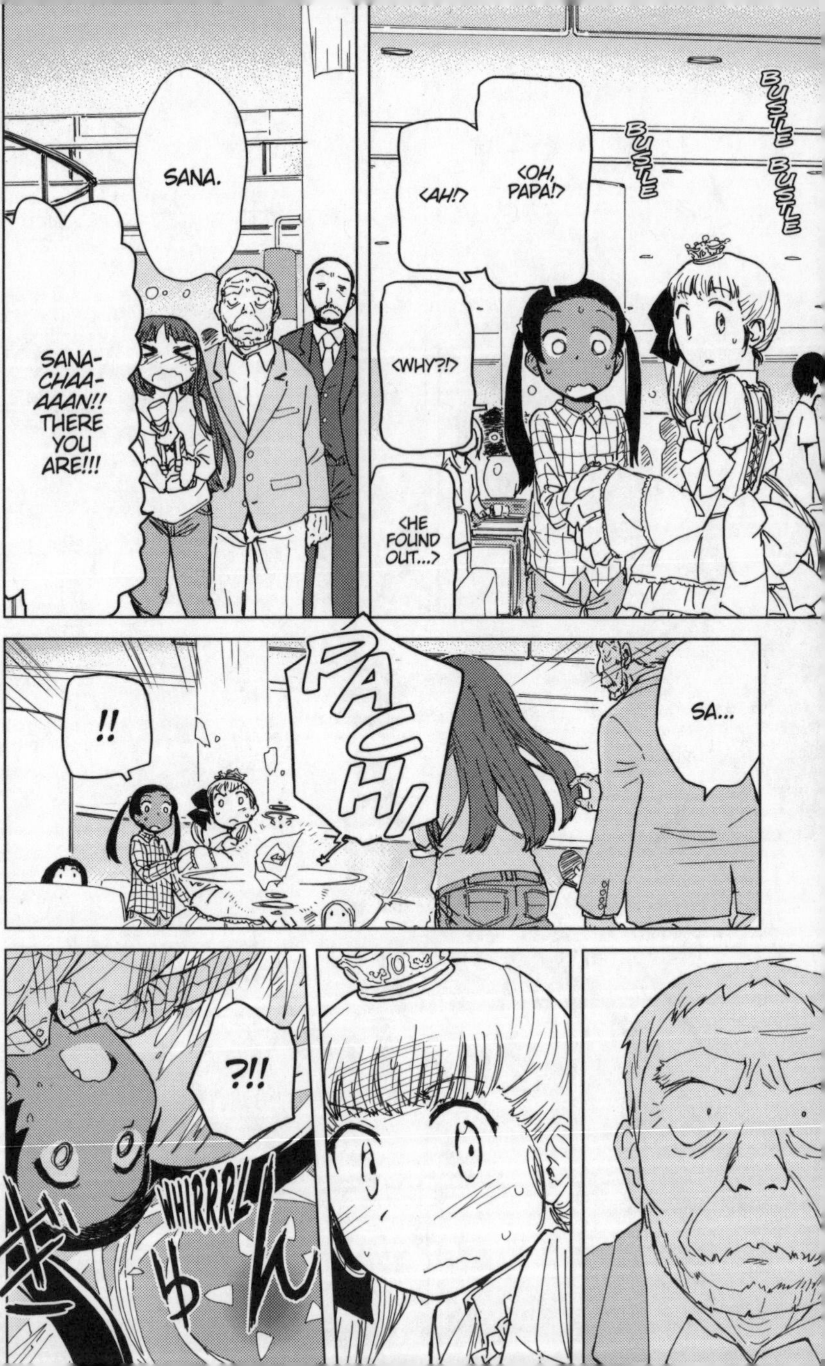
BUSTLE BUSTLE
BUSTLE
<OH, PAPA!>
<AH!?>
<WHY?!?>
<HE FOUND OUT...>
SANA.
SANA-CHAAAAAN!! THERE YOU ARE!!!
SA...
PACHI
!!
?!!
WHIRRRL

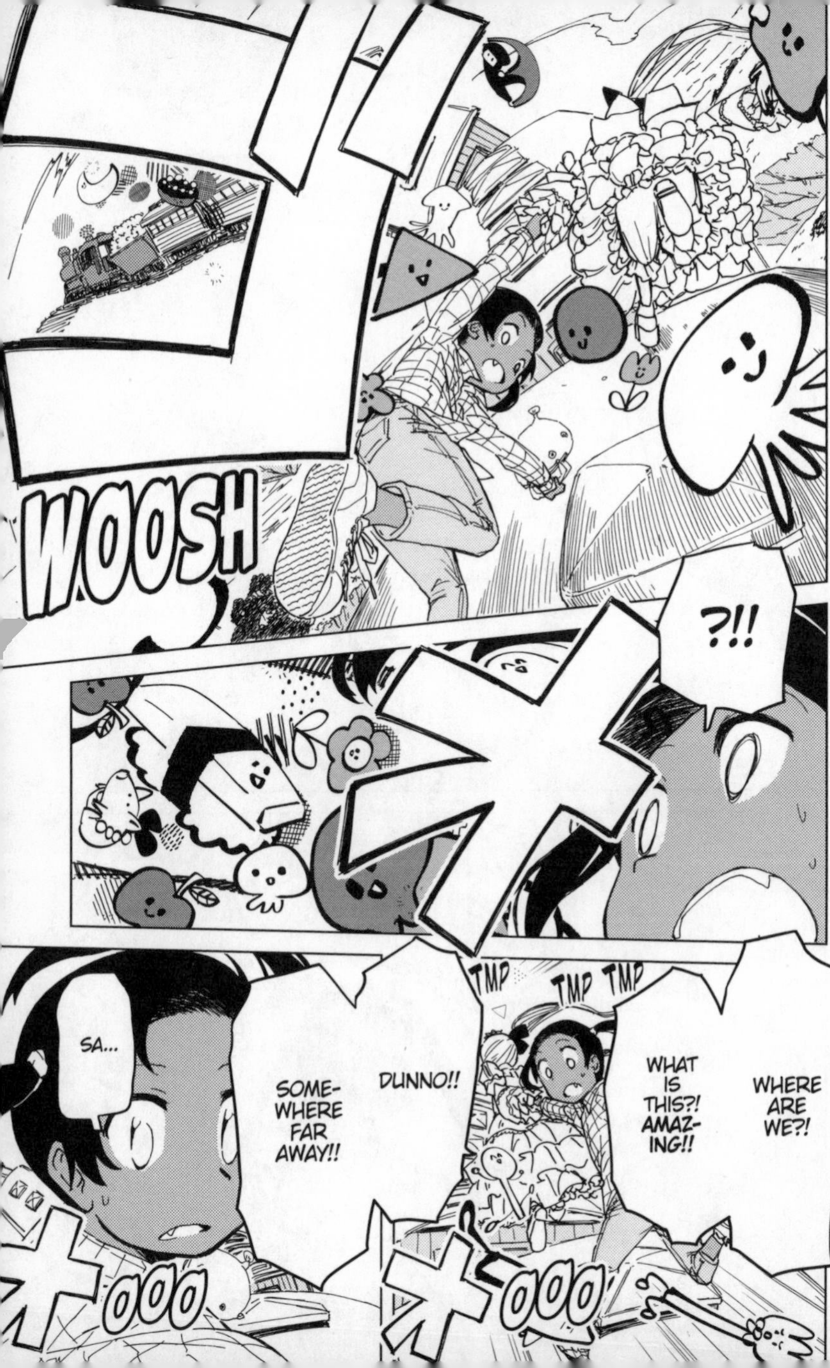
WOOSH
?!!
TMP TMP TMP
WHERE ARE WE?!
WHAT IS THIS?! AMAZING!!
OOO
DUNNO!!
SOMEWHERE FAR AWAY!!
SA...
OOO

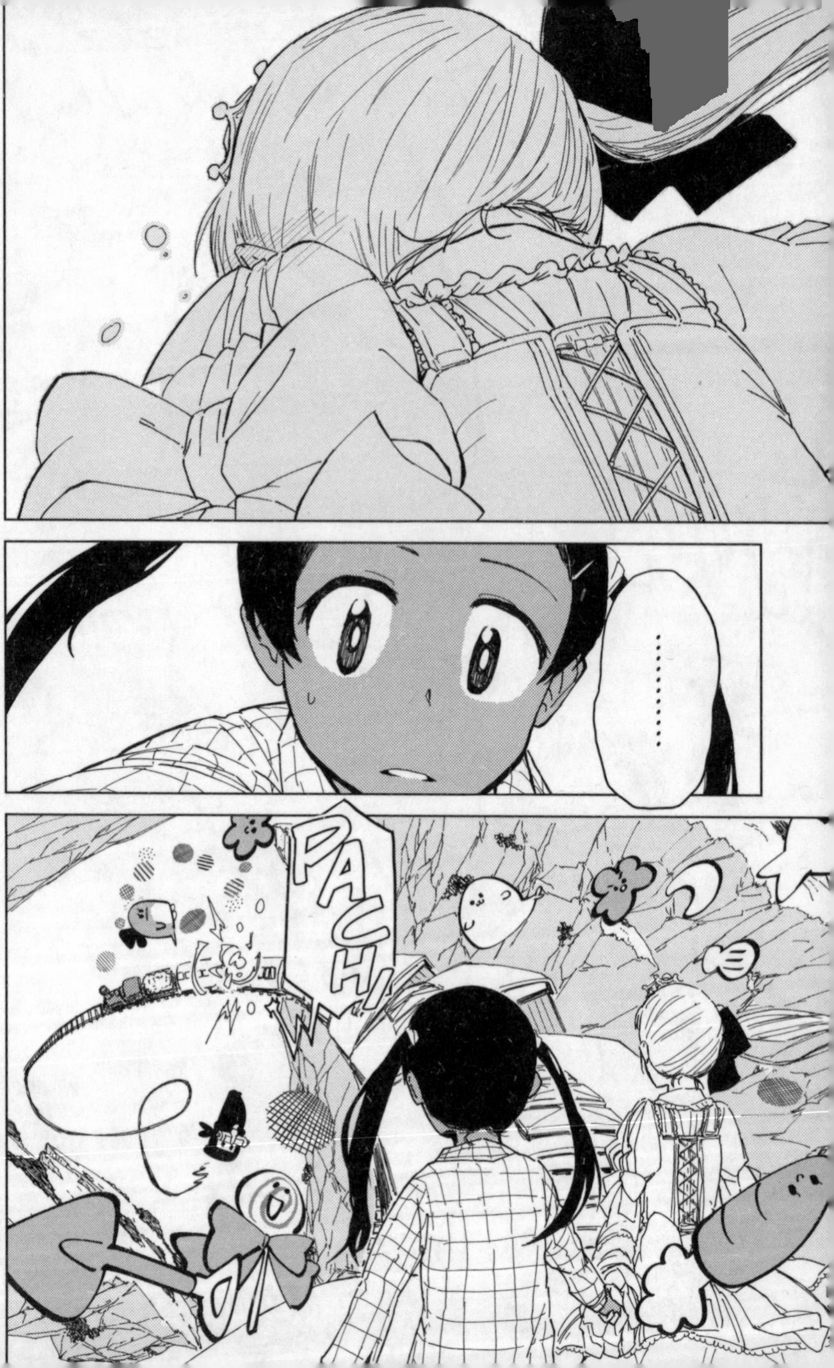
......
PACHI!

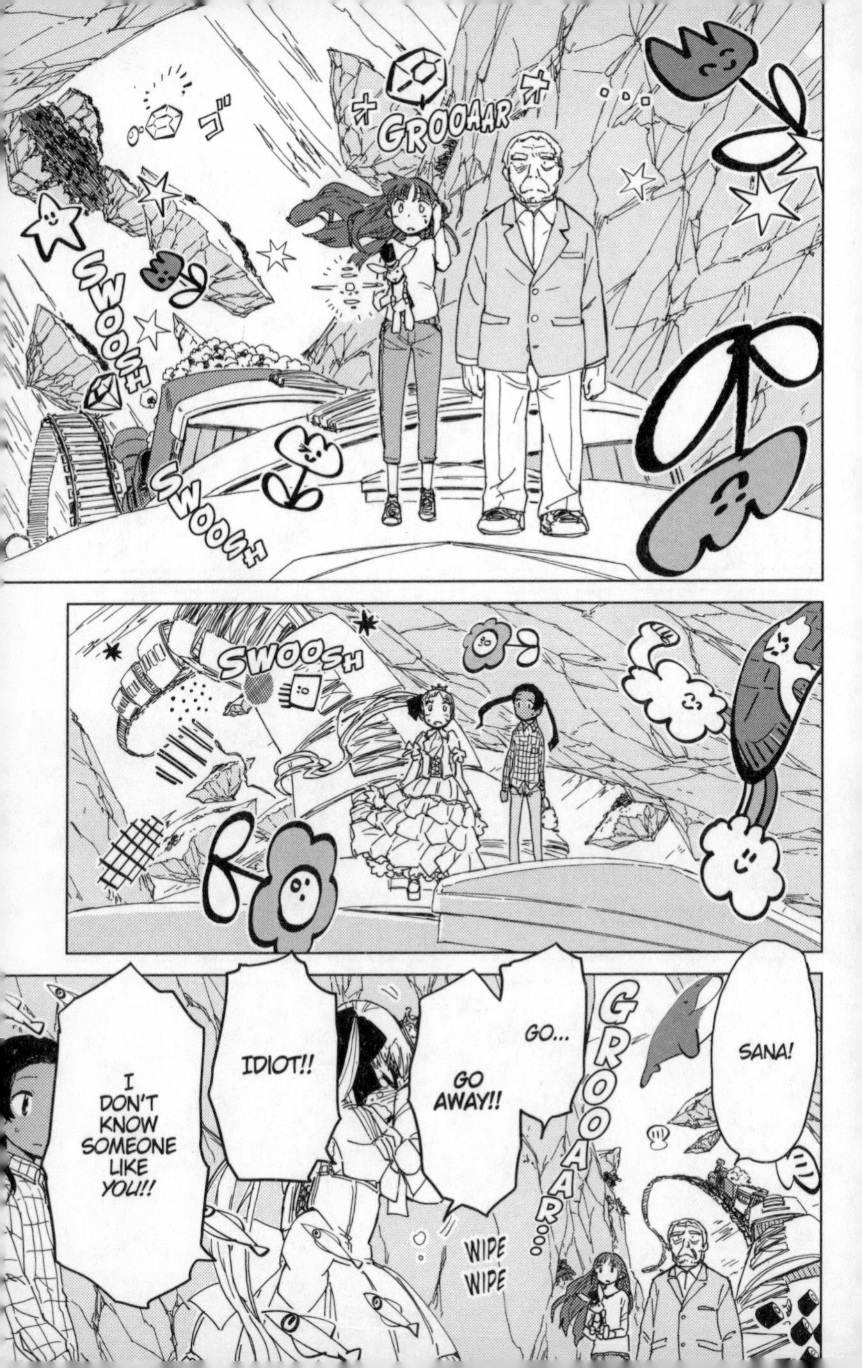
GROOAAR
SWOOSH
SWOOSH
SWOOSH
SANA!
GROOOAAR...
GO...
GO AWAY!!
IDIOT!!
I DON'T KNOW SOMEONE LIKE YOU!!
WIPE WIPE

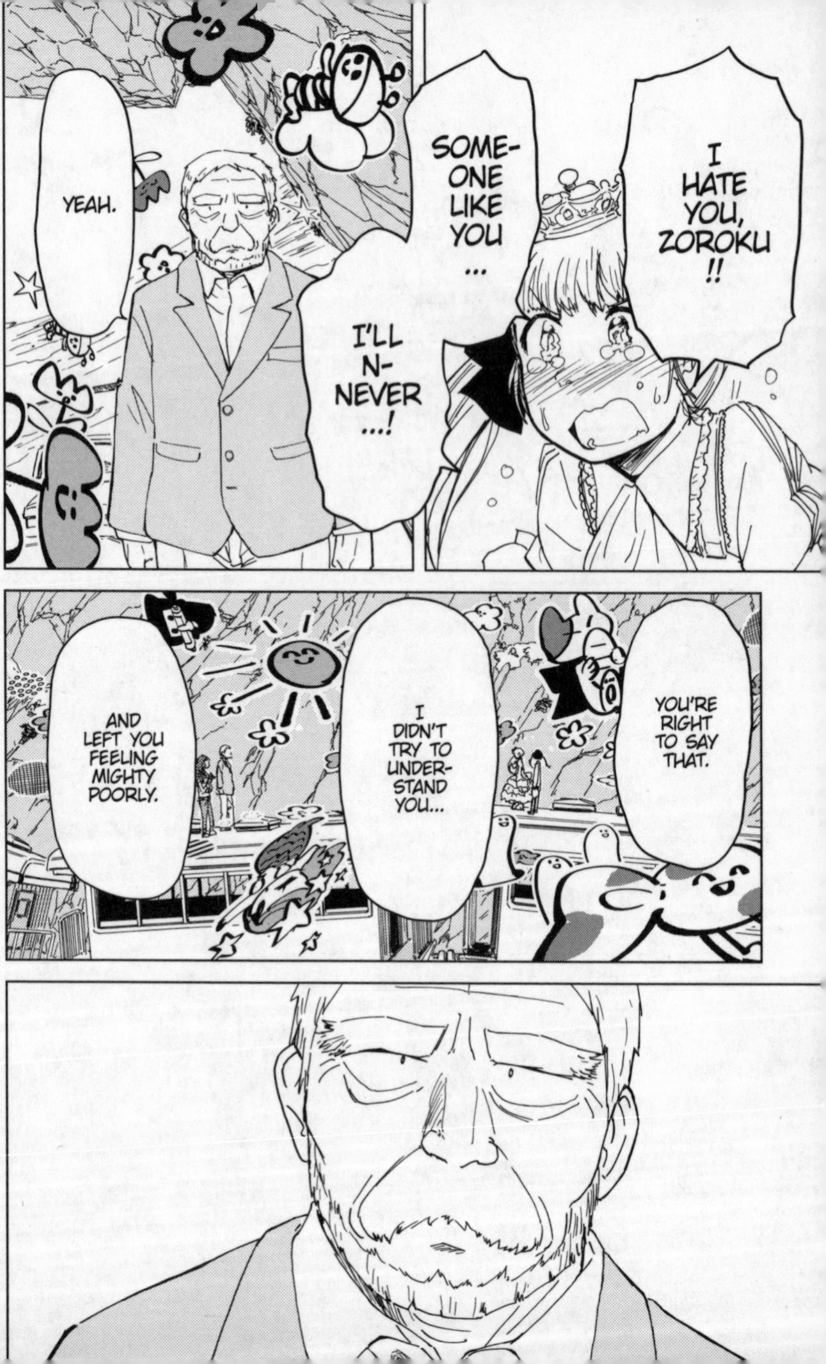
I HATE YOU, ZOROKU!!
SOME-ONE LIKE YOU ...
I'LL N-NEVER ...!
YEAH.
YOU'RE RIGHT TO SAY THAT.
I DIDN'T TRY TO UNDER-STAND YOU...
AND LEFT YOU FEELING MIGHTY POORLY.

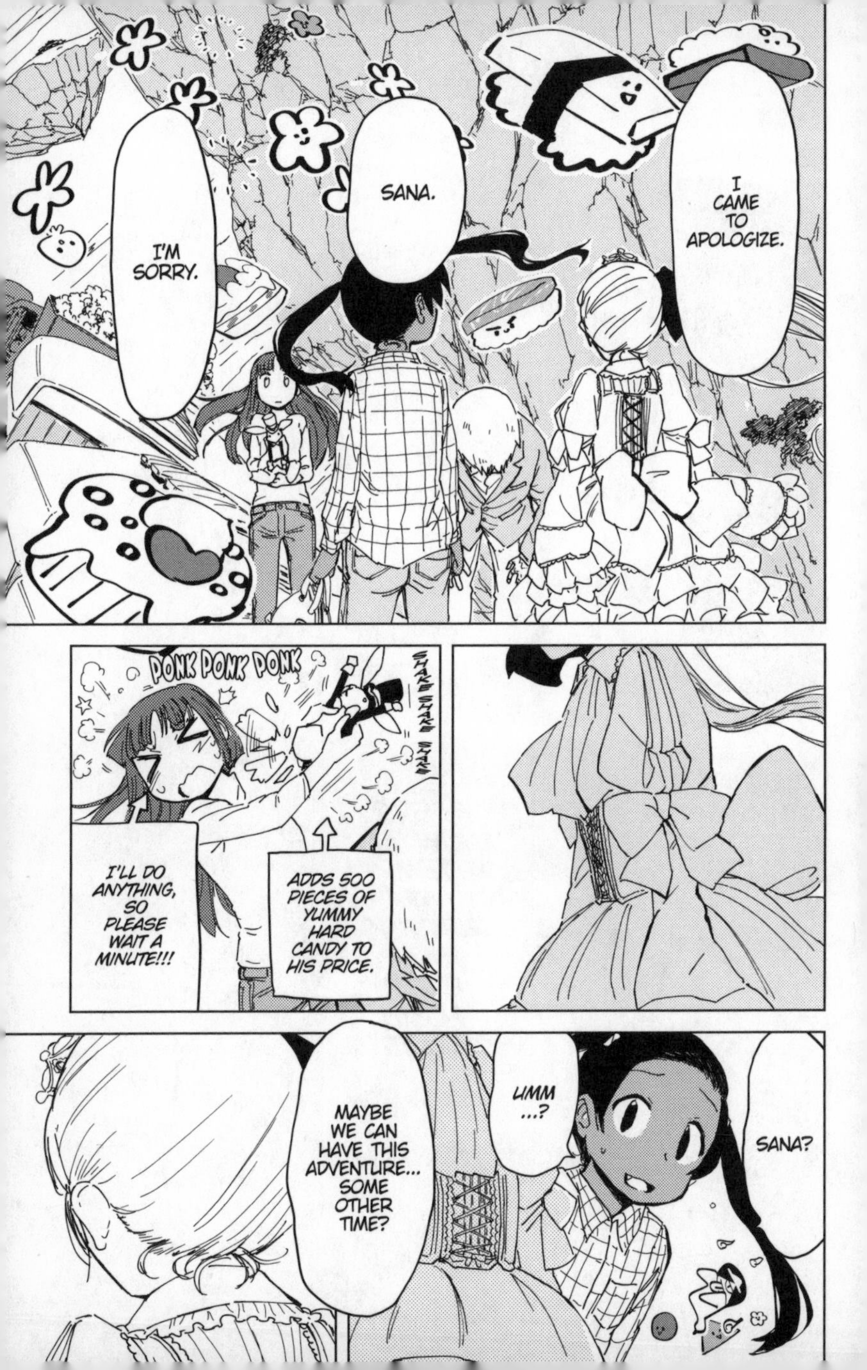
I CAME TO APOLOGIZE.
SANA.
I'M SORRY.
PONK PONK PONK
SHAKE SHAKE SHAKE
ADDS 500 PIECES OF YUMMY HARD CANDY TO HIS PRICE.
I'LL DO ANYTHING, SO PLEASE WAIT A MINUTE!!!
SANA?
UMM ...?
MAYBE WE CAN HAVE THIS ADVENTURE... SOME OTHER TIME?

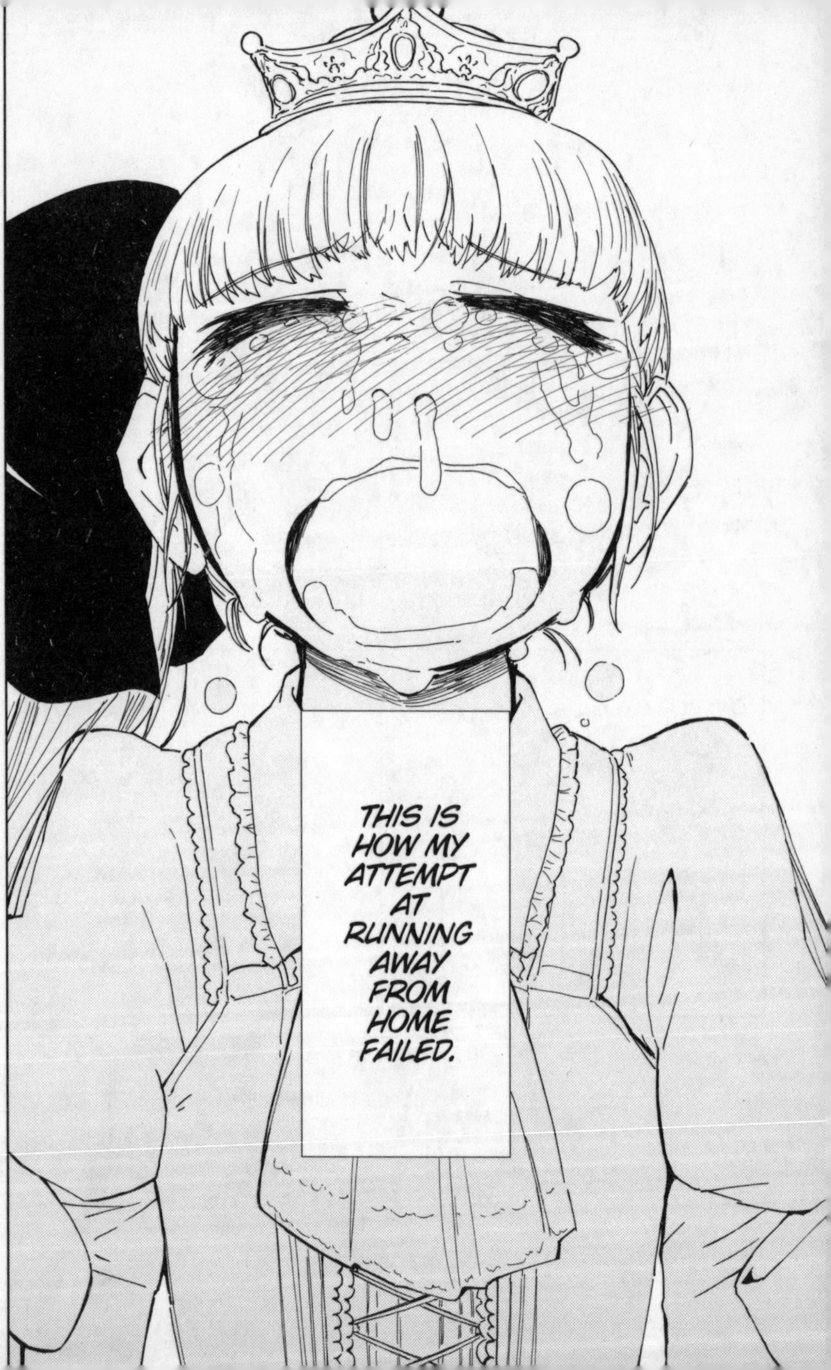
THIS IS HOW MY ATTEMPT AT RUNNING AWAY FROM HOME FAILED.

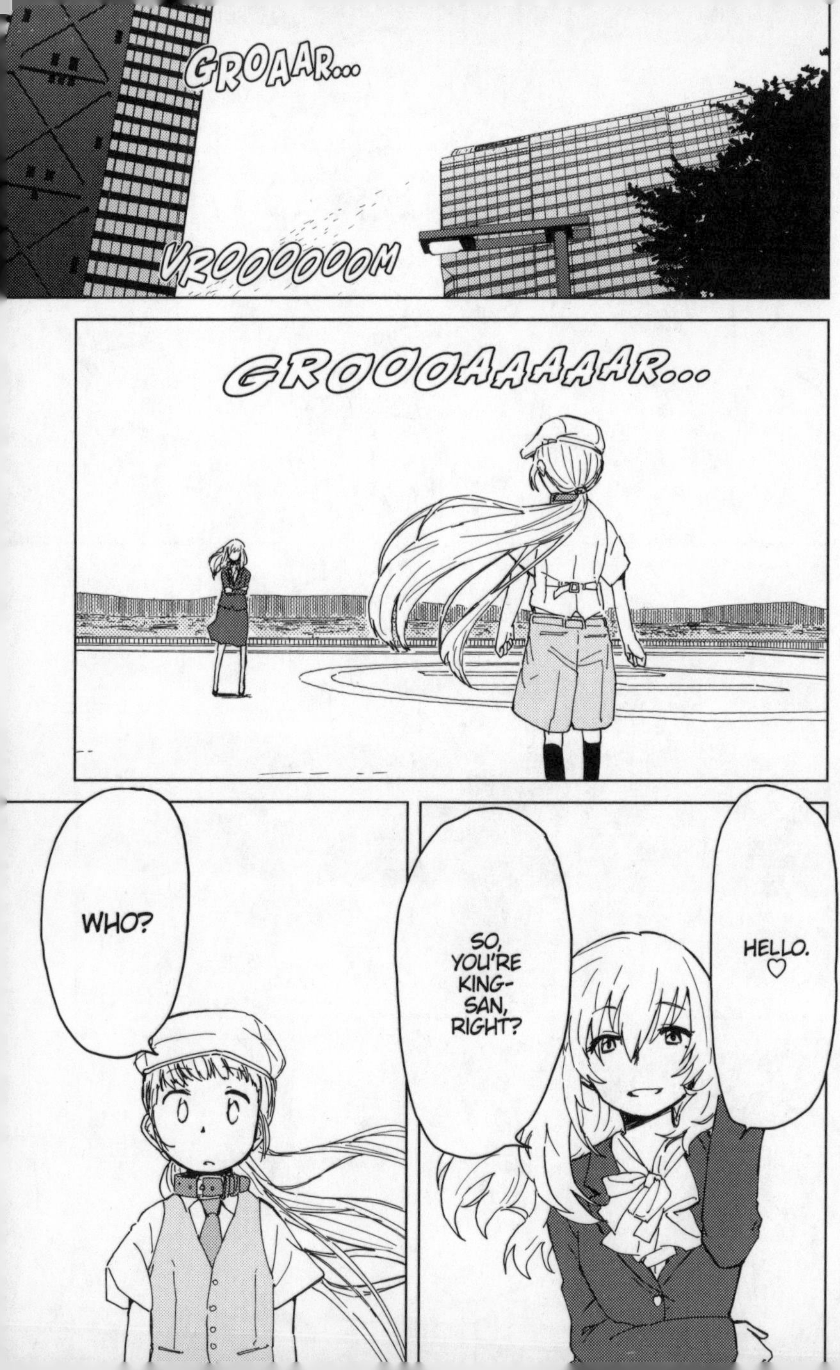
GROAAR...
VROOOOOOOM
GROOOAAAAAR...
HELLO. ♡
SO, YOU'RE KING-SAN, RIGHT?
WHO?

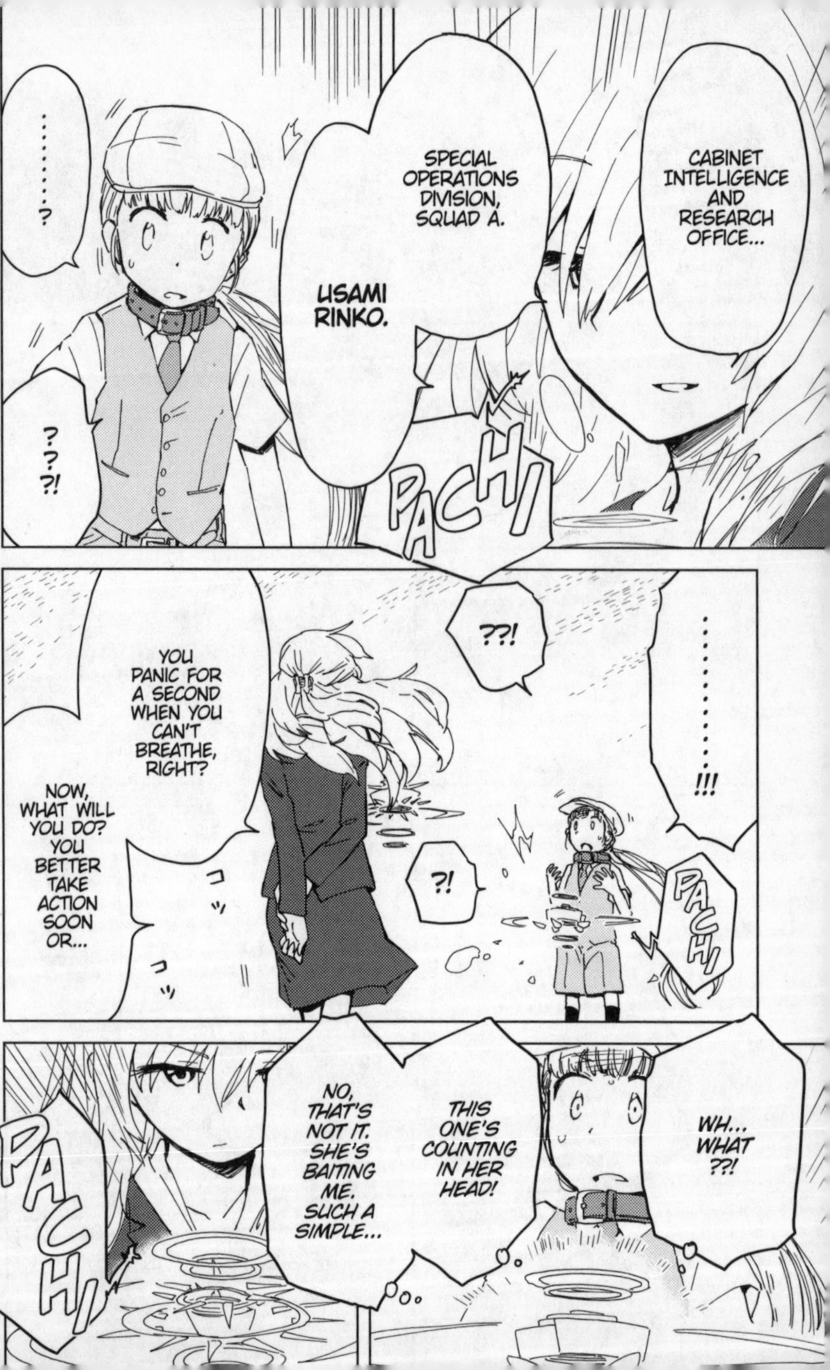
CABINET INTELLIGENCE AND RESEARCH OFFICE...
SPECIAL OPERATIONS DIVISION, SQUAD A.
USAMI RINKO.
PACHI
......?
? ? ?!
......!!!
PACHI
??!
?!
YOU PANIC FOR A SECOND WHEN YOU CAN'T BREATHE, RIGHT?
NOW, WHAT WILL YOU DO? YOU BETTER TAKE ACTION SOON OR...
コッ
コッ
WH... WHAT ?!
THIS ONE'S COUNTING IN HER HEAD!
NO, THAT'S NOT IT. SHE'S BAITING ME. SUCH A SIMPLE...
PACHI

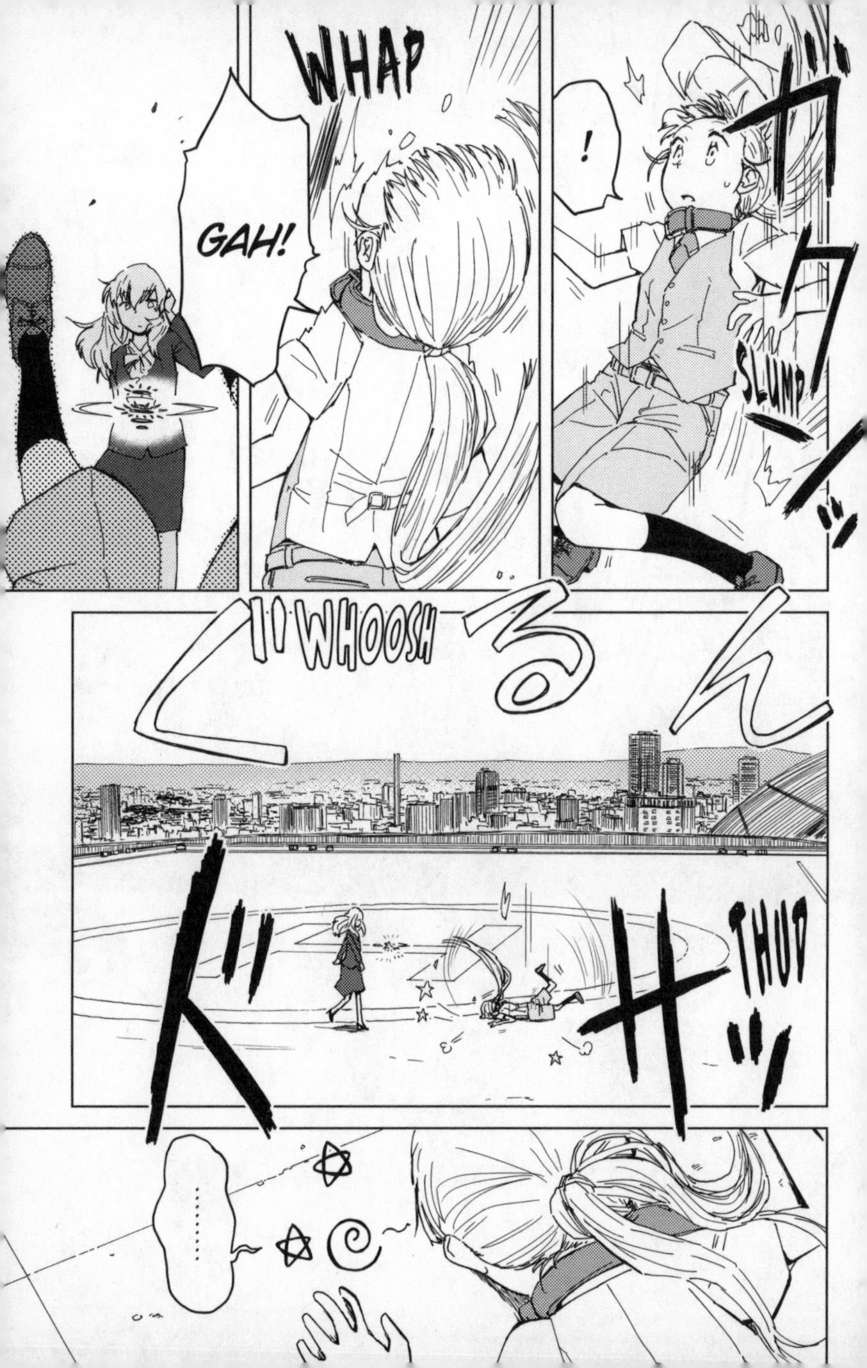
!
SLUMP
WHAP
GAH!
WHOOSH
くるん
THUD
ドサッ
……

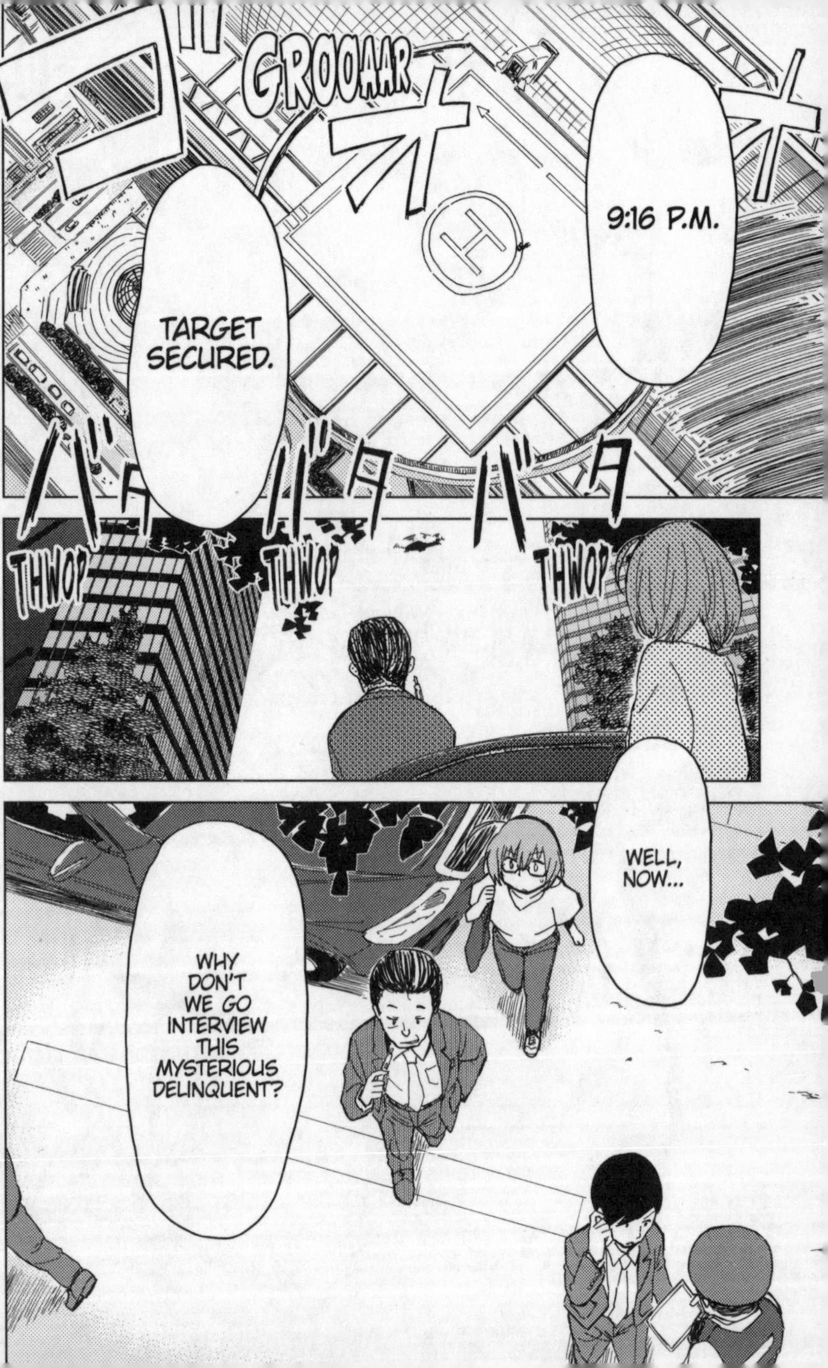
9:16 P.M.
GROOAAR
TARGET SECURED.
THWOP
THWOP
THWOP
WELL, NOW...
WHY DON'T WE GO INTERVIEW THIS MYSTERIOUS DELINQUENT?

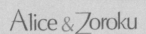

9

Editor
Inogai Kanta
(COMIC Ryu Editorial Department)

◆

Design and Formatting
AFTERGLOW

◆

Report Assistance
The People at Massa & Artists
Hanappa   Nozaki Isao-san

◆

3D Work
Subaru SUBARU
Tomohiko Suge
Reika Nakashima
Nanaka Shiga

◆

Design Assistance (Chapter: 37)
Fumiko Fumi

Alice & Zoroku

SEVEN SEAS ENTERTAINMENT PRESENTS

Alice & Zoroku

story and art by TETSUYA IMAI

VOLUME 9

TRANSLATION
Beni Axia Conrad

ADAPTATION
Asha Bardon

LETTERING
Ludwig Sacramento

COVER DESIGN
Hanase Qi

PROOFREADER
Dawn Davis
B. Lillian Martin

EDITOR
Shannon Fay

PREPRESS TECHNICIAN
Rhiannon Rasmussen-Silverstein

PRODUCTION MANAGER
Lissa Pattillo

MANAGING EDITOR
Julie Davis

ASSOCIATE PUBLISHER
Adam Arnold

PUBLISHER
Jason DeAngelis

ALICE TO ZOROKU VOLUME 9
© TETSUYA IMAI 2020
Originally published in Japan in 2020 by TOKUMA SHOTEN PUBLISHING
CO., LTD, Tokyo.
English translation rights arranged with TOKUMA SHOTEN PUBLISHING
CO., LTD, Tokyo, through TOHAN CORPORATION, Tokyo.

Seven Seas press and purchase enquiries can be sent to Marketing Manager
Lianne Sentar at press@gomanga.com. Information regarding the distribution
and purchase of digital editions is available from Digital Manager CK Russell
at digital@gomanga.com.

Seven Seas and the Seven Seas logo are trademarks of
Seven Seas Entertainment. All rights reserved.

ISBN: 978-1-64827-902-7
Printed in Canada
First Printing: November 2021
10 9 8 7 6 5 4 3 2 1

FOLLOW US ONLINE: *www.sevenseasentertainment.com*

READING DIRECTIONS

This book reads from *right to left*, Japanese style.
If this is your first time reading manga, you start
reading from the top right panel on each page and
take it from there. If you get lost, just follow the
numbered diagram here. It may seem backwards at
first, but you'll get the hang of it! Have fun!!

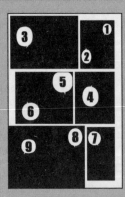